CHINESE AND INDIAN STRATEGIC BEHAVIOR

ational
in the
Asia
ent of
re; (2)
efense
nomic
utility
is also
estern

firm
tional
ly the
join-
earch
ngton
venty-
d has
d his

n and
enior
ished
, and
nono-
d as a
spent
e. He

Chinese and Indian Strategic Behavior

Growing Power and Alarm

GEORGE J. GILBOY

ERIC HEGINBOTHAM

CAMBRIDGE
UNIVERSITY PRESS

CAMBRIDGE UNIVERSITY PRESS
Cambridge, New York, Melbourne, Madrid, Cape Town,
Singapore, São Paulo, Delhi, Mexico City

Cambridge University Press
32 Avenue of the Americas, New York, NY 10013-2473, USA

www.cambridge.org
Information on this title: www.cambridge.org/9781107661691

First published 2012

Printed in the United States of America

A catalog record for this publication is available from the British Library.

Library of Congress Cataloging in Publication data
Gilboy, George J., 1964–
Chinese and Indian strategic behavior : growing power and alarm /
George J. Gilboy, Eric Heginbotham.
p.   cm.
Includes bibliographical references and index.
ISBN 978-1-107-02005-4 (hbk.) – ISBN 978-1-107-66169-1 (pbk.)
1. China – Foreign relations – 21st century.   2. Strategic culture – China.   3. China –
Military policy.   4. China – Foreign economic relations.   5. India – Foreign relations – 21st
century.   6. Strategic culture – India.   7. India – Military policy.   8. India – Foreign
economic relations.   I. Heginbotham, Eric.   II. Title.
JZ1734.G55   2011
355′.033551–dc23   2011046091

ISBN 978-1-107-02005-4 Hardback
ISBN 978-1-107-66169-1 Paperback

To our parents and our wives

Contents

Figures

Tables

Acknowledgments

Our learning, and this book, could not have been completed without the help and support of our families, teachers, friends, and colleagues.

We thank William Overholt, who first inspired us to compare Chinese and Indian strategic behavior. Evan Medeiros and Stephen Cohen read the entire manuscript and provided detailed comments that helped us improve the book immeasurably. Evan Medeiros's encouragement to develop further the policy implications of the work was invaluable. Stephen Cohen's wise counsel taught us much and helped us sharpen and refine our analysis of India and South Asia. Alice Miller provided constructive feedback that helped us clear some final hurdles. Alice also shared numerous insights on Indian and Chinese foreign policy, diplomatic history, and military modernization, all of which helped us improve our work. Two anonymous reviewers provided detailed critiques from a comparative, historical perspective and assisted us in improving our policy recommendations.

We thank Richard Samuels of MIT for his intellectual support throughout this project, as well as for his friendship and guidance over many years. Dick read an earlier version of this book in its entirety and provided useful comments and advice on what was needed to bring it to its final form. Chris Twomey, another friend and scholar with links to MIT, has been a source of advice and intellectual guidance. He contributed directly to our thinking on strategic forces and stability issues. Reinhardt Matisons, a friend and leader in the Australian energy industry, also read an earlier version of the entire manuscript and provided useful and constructive feedback, especially on economics, trade, and outward investment.

Michael Urena shared his expertise on U.S. South Asia policy, and the issues that the United States faces there. Christine Fair, Michael Glosny, Arthur Kroeber, Gavin Thompson, Adam Wang, Xu Yiqing, and Zhong Ninghua helped us through detailed conversations on foreign policy, military forces, energy markets, and government budgets. We thank Ashley Tellis for sharing observations on Indian military doctrine and joint operations issues. Dan Rosen shared many insights on Chinese and Indian economic development, trade, and foreign investment. Gavin Thompson, Arthur Kroeber, and Deborah Seligsohn read Chapter 7 and provided helpful critiques. We also thank Deng Yiting, Christine Wang Linjuan, Wang Yingyao, and Li Zi, who each assisted us in developing interview notes and gathering archival material. We also thank Bindu Vinod, the team at Newgen, and Ellie Heginbotham for essential editing and proofreading.

Scott Parris, our editor at Cambridge University Press, not only guided us through the process of bringing this book from a draft manuscript to a final product, but his editor's insight, advice, corrections, and friendly instruction improved our work in every way.

George Gilboy. Some thanks are individual in nature. Dick Samuels and colleagues at the MIT Center for International Studies have provided a stimulating and supportive environment for conducting research. Reinhardt Matisons has inspired me and guided me with his leadership, both in our workplace and outside of it. Thanks to the National Committee on U.S.-China Relations, especially to Steve Orlins and Jan Berris. The National Committee broadened my access to Chinese and Indian scholars and policy makers through the Public Intellectuals Program. The Boren Fellowship helped fund my PhD research. The research for this book was conducted as part of fulfilling my fellowship service commitment.

Sean Rodrigues encouraged me to return to my interests in India, where I worked briefly in the late 1980s. Sean has helped me meet many people in the Indian business, government, and diplomatic communities on recent visits to India. Bill McCahill has been a source of insight on numerous questions of diplomatic, business, and cultural history. K. F. Yan and Sherry Xu have provided me with invaluable advice and guidance on energy markets over many years. I offer my sincere thanks and gratitude to Joerg Wuttke. In addition to building success in industry, Joerg has also built bridges between business, government, and academic communities in Europe, the United States, and China – and has helped many people like me cross them. Christine Wang Linjuan joined me for a new career in an unfamiliar industry in 2005. Since then, she has set about improving the effectiveness of everyone around her and making work more cheerful every day. Many thanks, Chris. I thank my friends who have, through many conversations, encouraged me to write and to seek improvement wherever possible: James P. Andrews, Matt Farr, Mark Hanna, Michael Johnsen, Chris Magner, Scott Roberts, Mike Rowe, Christopher Twomey, and John Zogby.

I am truly a fortunate son in that my family, in particular George A. Gilboy, Jr., Dorothy and Joe Connors, and John Gilboy, have always encouraged me to pursue knowledge and to finish whatever I have started. Dorothy and Joe Tulimieri sustained me through high points and low, and taught me about faith and generosity. The most important support and help of all is my partner, my home, my wife, Coral Shan Gilboy. Her patience, advice, and encouragement were essential to me at every stage of writing this book and in everything else.

Eric Heginbotham. Evan Medeiros not only provided extremely useful feedback on this book, but has also been a terrific partner on a variety of China-related projects. I owe both Evan and Christopher Twomey, at the Naval Post Graduate School, thanks for including me in efforts to engage Chinese counterparts on strategic nuclear issues – a worthy, if sometimes frustrating, endeavor. Ely Ratner, whose many academic and organizational talents will surely bring him great success, has been an effective sounding board on this book, as well as a collaborator on Japan and Korea topics. Christine Fair contributed greatly to my understanding of South Asian dynamics, particularly the complex relationship between India and Pakistan.

Without being able to do justice to each, I have learned a tremendous amount from Adam Segal and Elizabeth Economy on Chinese technology and economy, Roger Cliff on the PLA Air Force, Alan Vick and David Shlapak on Asian basing and security issues, Michael Nixon and Paul DeLuca on naval subjects, Jeff Hagen and Forrest Morgan on air and space, and Andrew Scobell on a variety of China topics. Throughout my tenure at RAND, I have been blessed with managers who have also been friends and intellectual partners. Paula Thornhill brings a keen understanding of U.S. military practices and perspectives, as well as great patience for those of us with less knowledge of this topic. In addition to his friendship and support, Bill Overholt has enhanced my understanding of Asian business and politics. Thomas McNaugher has been instrumental in connecting people and resources to develop innovative research on Asia. Special thanks are due to Andrew Hoehn, who, apart from being an outstanding thinker on U.S. strategic issues and an exceptional leader, has encouraged me to pursue external academic interests, including this book.

My deepest debts of gratitude are to my family. My parents, Erland and Eleanor Heginbotham, sparked an early interest in Asia, tolerated a fascination with military affairs, and nurtured a love of academic pursuits. Thanks to my sister, Robin, for being an ally from the very beginning. My uncle, Stanley Heginbotham, has played a special role in my life. Stanley is a gentleman and scholar who has always taken an interest in my intellectual activities. Thanks also to Toshio Miki, my Japanese "blood brother," and to his wonderful family. Most of all, I owe more than I can say to my wife, Katsue Heginbotham, for her support and camaraderie throughout this and other endeavors, and to our three wonderful boys, Naoki, Hiroki, and Kazuki Heginbotham, for showing me every day what is really important.

Finally, we would add that our analysis and conclusions represent our own personal views, not the views of any of the people or institutions mentioned here. We alone are responsible for any faults that remain in this book.

Preface

China and India are large, rapidly developing countries with the potential to emerge as superpowers in the twenty-first century. The two states share key similarities including large populations, nuclear weapons, rising economic and military power, troubled borders, internal security challenges, domestic inequalities, incomplete economic reforms, and uncertain ambitions. Despite the uncertainties they themselves face, the rise of China and India – in particular the growing relative power of China – has inspired alarm in the United States. Some American political leaders and strategists advocate sharply divergent policies toward China and India. China is viewed as a potential competitor more than a potential partner, whereas the reverse is true of India. Washington "hedges" against Beijing while it seeks to increase Indian power and enlist New Delhi as a partner in that hedging. Yet American choices may not be as simple as defining enemies and allies. Both China and India will present the United States with sustained challenges as well as opportunities in the coming years, and Washington will need nuanced, if distinct, approaches to each.

The purpose of this book is to create a framework for objective assessment of the strategic behavior of the world's two most important rising powers. The book fills an important gap in the literature on rising Indian and Chinese power and American interests in Asia by presenting a side-by-side comparison of Chinese and Indian international strategic behavior in four areas: (1) strategic culture; (2) foreign policy and use of force; (3) military modernization (including developments in defense spending, doctrine, and force modernization); and (4) economic strategies (including international trade and energy competition). We do not examine the origins of U.S. policy toward India and China, nor do we evaluate the effectiveness of those policies. However, our analysis challenges key arguments that support a recent sharpening divergence in the U.S. approach toward the two countries.

These four issue areas have been selected for three reasons. First, they offer a wide cross-section of observable strategic behavior, providing comparative context across issue types. This framework permits a systematic and rigorous examination of some of the most prominent challenges America will face as China and India continue to develop in the twenty-first century.

Second, these issues have been singled out by many U.S. policy makers and scholars as areas where China is prone to unusually problematic or aggressive behavior. To some observers, China's strategic culture and tendency to use force make China more likely to challenge American interests in Asia. Movement toward a more offensive military doctrine and rapidly increasing and nontransparent defense budgets are said to differentiate China from other rising powers. China is also seen as willing to flaunt international political and economic norms in its pursuit of economic growth. In contrast, there is less discussion, and almost no prominent criticism, of Indian behavior in similar areas. Shared democratic values are seen to make India more likely to behave in ways commensurate with U.S. interests than nondemocratic China.

Third, this framework allows us to separate Taiwan-related issues from wider questions about general patterns in Chinese behavior. The challenge of Taiwan, which could potentially draw the United States into a war with China, places Sino-U.S. relations in a unique context. As a result, the essential question for many U.S. observers has become identifying and neutralizing the challenge posed by Beijing's military modernization. In the case of India, questions are posed across a greater range of issues, but most frequently revolve around strategic opportunities for collaboration with New Delhi in the context of rising Chinese power in Asia. This approach to India tends to leave both potential conflicts of interest and opportunities for non-security-related collaboration underexplored. As in all analytical endeavors, the questions asked often decisively shape the conclusions. While not claiming a monopoly on good questions related to China or India, this book does ask a uniform set of questions about each country and evaluates the behavior of both against a common standard.

To clarify and prioritize challenges and opportunities with both rising powers, the United States needs a more balanced framework for assessment. This study, then, aims to create a standardized framework for evaluating the international strategic behavior of Asia's two rising powers.

Findings

This study finds that the broad patterns of Indian and Chinese strategic behavior are not widely divergent – strong evidence that in the twenty-first century, the United States faces a complex, dual challenge from Asia's rising powers rather than a simple, singular challenge of balancing China's growing relative power. The two rising powers are equally wont to pursue and defend their interests. Their patterns of strategic behavior are similar to that of other great powers. In some respects, they pursue policies of greater integration with the international status quo compared to other rising powers in history. However, both are willing to use state power, including force, when they perceive key interests to be at stake. There are important differences between the two, but those differences do not reveal Beijing consistently more prone than New Delhi to pursue its own narrow self-interests, use force, or build military power to secure its objectives.

These findings do not imply that U.S. policy should treat China and India identically. Nor does evidence of similar strategic behaviors put to rest concerns about U.S.-China frictions or preclude a closer U.S.-India relationship. Instead, the comparisons provide a better understanding of Chinese and Indian interests and capabilities and the means Beijing and New Delhi use to achieve their objectives. This, in turn, will help clarify American interests relative to both emerging powers. Even though past behavior does not dictate future trajectories, it provides an empirical baseline for making policy judgments. The book concludes with suggestions on how the United States might adjust its current policies to avoid potential pitfalls in its bilateral relationships with China and India and advance broader U.S. interests in Asia. In the remainder of this preface, we summarize the analysis and implications for U.S. policy.

Strategic Culture

Strategic culture is an inherited body of political-military concepts based on shared historical and social experience and often embodied in classic military texts. Strategic culture may shape leaders' interpretation of international events and preferences for responses. Several U.S. analysts have argued that ideas codified in China's classic texts on strategy shape modern Chinese leadership thought in ways that may incline Beijing toward the frequent use of force, an emphasis on deception and duplicity, and a preference for offense. This analysis has gained influence in official circles and has found at least passing reference in official U.S. national security documents.

Comparison of the core texts in Chinese and Indian strategic thought provides no grounds for expecting markedly different behavior from China and India. Elements of a calculated realism, as well as idealism, are found in both traditions. Classic Indian texts, like the *Arthashastra* and *Mahabharata*, paint an even more vivid picture of a zero-sum world of conquest than Chinese texts such as *Sun Zi Bingfa* (*The Art of War*). Chinese classics are not clearly more influential in today's China than Indian classics are in today's India. The classical traditions of both countries must also share space in today's leadership curricula with many modern (including Western) works on strategy and politics. References to ancient Chinese texts are thus not sufficient grounds to differentiate American expectations about modern Chinese or Indian strategic preferences or behavior.

Foreign Policy: Use of Force and Border Disputes

Indian and Chinese foreign policy trends, propensity to use force, and border dispute behavior do not justify starkly differentiated views of the two nations. In recent years, both China and India have followed similar – and, from an American perspective, largely desirable – foreign policy trajectories. According to the University of Michigan's data on Militarized Interstate Disputes (MIDs), China has been involved in more militarized conflicts than India since 1949. But the behavior of both countries has changed over time, particularly China's since its reform and opening began in 1978. From 1980 to 2001 (the last year covered by the Michigan database), the frequency of Chinese and Indian use of force has been equal. Both Beijing and New Delhi have made concerted efforts to resolve border disputes over the last fifteen years. In some respects, China has moved further in negotiating territorial and border issues than India, notwithstanding Beijing's recent assertion that its "core interests" are at stake in territorial issues. An analysis of Indian and Chinese voting records in the UN General Assembly shows that on a number of key international issues, those two nations are often more closely aligned with each other than either is with the United States. Nevertheless, despite a number of similarities, on several issues, such as Taiwan, nuclear weapons proliferation, and stability in South and Central Asia, China and India present quite different challenges to U.S. policy.

Military Doctrines, Force Modernization, and Budgets

China's military policies have been singled out by U.S. officials: China's defense budgets are opaque and growing at an extraordinary pace; China's military doctrine has become more offense-oriented; and PLA acquisitions are extending China's reach and enhancing its power projection capabilities. These issues raise questions about China's intentions and ambitions. However, parallel comparisons to Indian military policy suggest that China is not unique in any of these areas.

India's defense spending is lower than China's in absolute terms, but higher as a percentage of GDP, even with off-budget items included. The extent of China's defense spending has been distorted in much Western reporting. Often this is a result of errors in calculating off-budget spending and conflating actual spending with notional equivalents based on the inappropriate use of purchasing power parity (PPP) multipliers. If applied to Indian defense spending, PPP adjustments would have a greater relative effect in magnifying India's "equivalent" military spending. However, India is seldom subject to such analyses – an inconsistency in methodology that skews comparisons of the two states.

In recent years, both countries have been moving toward operational military doctrines oriented more toward offensive action. Comparing the two, Indian operational doctrine is more offensive than China's and explicitly calls for preemptive attack under a range of circumstances. Currently, the United States appears to view Indian doctrinal developments as less threatening. Yet the United States has broad interests in Asia in addition to dealing with a rising China, including a critical interest in a stable Pakistan and the avoidance of intensified security competition in South and East Asia. In this context, more ambitious Indian strategies and more offense-oriented Indian doctrines, potentially enhanced by U.S. arms sales and support for India's rise to great-power status, may exacerbate region-level security dilemmas in Asia.

China has made significant strides in modernizing its military. China is developing a military with fewer but better units and weapons systems. China is also developing some capabilities to project power beyond its immediate periphery and the approaches to Taiwan. Some of these, such as conventional missile strike capabilities, are potentially more threatening than others because they could exacerbate general security competition with both the United States and other states in Asia. Like China, India is also rapidly modernizing its forces as its economy grows. In some areas of naval and air power, India already possesses greater power projection capabilities than China and has more experience using them. Although they are both producing new capabilities and considering some new roles for their militaries, Chinese and Indian force modernization programs continue to focus primarily on traditional security scenarios. For China, it is Taiwan (and thus the United States), and for India, it is Kashmir and Pakistan, although both New Delhi and Beijing also view each other as potential security concerns.

Economic Strategies: Development, Trade, and Energy

China began its economic reforms and integration with the global economy more than a decade earlier than India. China's economy is more open and integrated with the global trade and financial system. China's economy is about four times the size of India's at market exchange rates, and its trade with the United States is about ten times the size of U.S. trade with India. The scale of the Sino-American bilateral economic relationship tends to exacerbate the intensity of economic disputes with China. In contrast, the smaller size of the U.S.-India economic relationship means that trade and investment disputes have not yet become politically sensitive, although pundits often exaggerate India's relative economic importance. U.S. trade and investment disputes with India and China are similar, including barriers to trade and investment, state support for domestic firms, official corruption, and widespread intellectual property violations. These problems are also proportional to the size of the two economies, indicating that trade conflicts with India may intensify as economic ties grow. Both China and India have used mercantilist strategies to back their diplomacy.

Chinese and Indian international energy market behaviors are not markedly different. With government support, Indian as well as Chinese firms pursue energy investment opportunities in "rogue regimes" including Sudan, Myanmar, and Iran. Neither Indian nor Chinese investments threaten to disrupt world energy markets.

Regime Type and Strategic Behavior

Democracy forms a strong common attraction between the United States and India. The lack of common democratic values and institutions is seen to put U.S. relations with China on a path toward conflict. In both official and academic discourse, common democratic values are also seen to help ensure that U.S. and Indian foreign policy and security interests will converge and that democratic India will be a force for peace in Asia. These expectations are based on an extension of an international relations concept called democratic peace theory. However, tests of both the logic of democratic peace theory and the empirical evidence to support it reveal serious doubts about the application of the theory to general foreign policy behavior. There is, for example, no theoretical or empirical support for predicting that the foreign policy interests of individual democratic states will converge or that shared democratic values will tend to promote alignment on issues of international security.

Conclusions and Recommendations

Having assessed Chinese and Indian strategic behavior along these axes, we offer eight suggestions for observers and policy makers. First, the results of this study indicate that official U.S. political-military and techno-economic threat assessments and academic studies of rising Indian and Chinese power should make greater use of comparative context to improve analysis and policy recommendations.

Second, evidence from a side-by-side comparison of actual Chinese and Indian strategic behavior counters expectations of stark differences in international behavior based on regime type. A nuanced realism that accounts for historical, cultural, and moral differences – while recognizing the primacy of material interests in security – is a better guide to expectations and foreign policy.

Third, the analysis highlights the dangers of Asia's nested security dilemmas. The United States has prioritized global and system-level challenges such as terrorism and a rising China. However, Asian neighbors still see each other as primary security threats, and U.S. policies designed to address perceived global challenges can have unsettling or destabilizing effects at the regional or subregional level.

Fourth, although America's India policy should not be defined by India-Pakistan rivalry alone, the United States must take account of Pakistan in both its India and China policies. American arms and assistance to support a rising India as a balance to Chinese power could spur a regional response from Pakistan, which could further impoverish Pakistan and exacerbate instability there. India-Pakistan rivalry also plays out in Afghanistan.

Fifth, the findings indicate there may be potential for U.S. regrets in its engagement with India. India's domestic politics remain susceptible to persistent suspicions about U.S. intentions and threats to Indian sovereignty. These limit the prospects for Indian alignment with U.S. foreign policies regardless of U.S. provision of geostrategic support to India. Further, some Indian conceptions of India's own security interests and its global role could challenge American interests in the future. Indian leaders envision Indian primacy in the Indian Ocean and South Asia, seek to increase Indian influence in central Asia, support an offensively oriented conventional deterrence strategy vis-à-vis Pakistan, and retain doubts about India's interest in the U.S.-led international trade and financial system.

Despite its limitations, India's policy of strategic partnership with Iran offers one example of these different views. Motivated by shared interests, competition with Pakistan, and a strong desire to develop foreign policy autonomy and status, India actively develops trade and investment ties with Iran. The two countries have some limited defense cooperation. India upgraded Iran's Kilo-class submarines in 1993, signed the New Delhi Declaration with Iran in 2003 providing for further defense cooperation, conducted joint naval exercises with the Iranian navy in 2006, and allowed Iranian officers to participate in exchange programs in India in 2007. Like Beijing, New Delhi views Iran's nuclear program differently than Washington does.

Sixth, the United States should rebalance and deepen its engagement with New Delhi. Both India and the United States would benefit from increasing bilateral trade and investment, lowering trade barriers and encouraging market reforms, broadening exchanges on education and energy-environment technologies, and improving diplomatic alignment on multilateral approaches to security, global trade, finance, and climate change issues. Trade, investment, and support for market reforms will help reduce poverty and make India wealthier. Increased wealth will provide the strongest support to India's goal of becoming a great power. Stronger economic and political relations would give greater substance to the potentially powerful logic for closer U.S.-India security cooperation.

Seventh, the findings suggest that the United States should apply a consistent approach to international behavior it finds objectionable. For example, policy discourse in the United States frequently identifies the issue of energy investment in "rogue regimes" as a China problem. Indian firms, among others, are also major players in the same countries. A consistent approach will enhance U.S. credibility and the efficacy of American diplomacy.

Finally, with regard to China, the most important steps for meeting the long-term China challenge are domestic: revitalizing American manufacturing, technological innovation, and human capital advantages that underpin relative wealth and military power. The United States should respond appropriately to evolving Chinese military capabilities and ensure that it maintains American military superiority in Asia. American leaders should take steps to curb mutual suspicion and reestablish a minimum of trust in Sino-U.S. relations. At the same time, the United States must prioritize among issues that represent conflicts of interest, particularly Taiwan. The salience of other Sino-U.S. disputes and connections between them should be examined before they are considered part of a systemic Chinese challenge to American power. Managing the Taiwan issue – and, more broadly, China's rising power in Asia – will require not only U.S. deterrence, but also U.S. diplomacy. Those efforts will be most effective when U.S. assessments of China and India are based on cross-national, empirical comparison of international strategic behavior rather than comparison to an idealized norm.

Abbreviations

AEW	Airborne Early Warning
AIP	Air-Independent Propulsion
AMRAAM	Advanced Medium Range Air to Air Missile
ASAT	Anti-Satellite
ASBM	Anti-Ship Ballistic Missile
ASEAN	Association of South-East Asian Nations
ASM	Anti-Ship Missile
ASW	Anti-Submarine Warfare
AWACS	Airborne Early Warning and Control System
BOE	Barrel of Oil Equivalent
BRIC	Brazil, Russia, India, and China
C4ISR	Command, Control, Communications, Computers, Intelligence, Surveillance, and Reconnaissance
CAGR	Compound Annual Growth Rate
CCP	Chinese Communist Party
CIA	Central Intelligence Agency
CNSA	China National Space Administration
DRDO	Defence Research and Development Organisation
E&P	Exploration and Production (petroleum)
EEZ	Exclusive Economic Zone
EMP	Electro-Magnetic Pulse
FDI	Foreign Direct Investment
FMCT	Fissile Material Cutoff Treaty
FTA	Free Trade Agreement
G-20	Group of 20
GATT	General Agreement on Tariffs and Trade
GDP	Gross Domestic Product
HMS	Her/His Majesty's Ship

IAF	Indian Air Force
IBSA	India-Brazil-South Africa Forum
ICBM	Intercontinental Ballistic Missile
IIPA	International Intellectual Property Association
IISS	International Institute for Strategic Studies
IMF	International Monetary Fund
IN	Indian Navy
INS	Indian Navy Ship
IOC	International Oil Company
IPR	Intellectual Property Rights
IRBM	Intermediate Range Ballistic Missile
ISRO	Indian Space Research Organization
KMT	Kuomintang (or Guomindang)
LAC	Line of Actual Control
LACM	Land Attack Cruise Missile
LCAC	Landing Craft Air Cushion (amphibious assault hovercraft)
LCM	Landing Craft, Mechanized (amphibious assault landing craft)
LNG	Liquefied Natural Gas
LOC	Line of Control
LPD	Landing Platform Dock (amphibious assault transport dock)
LSM	Landing Ship, Mechanized (amphibious assault landing ship)
LST	Landing Ship Tank (amphibious assault tank landing ship)
M&A	Merger and Acquisition
MER	Market Exchange Rate
MFN	Most Favored Nation
MID	Militarized Interstate Dispute
MOU	Memorandum of Understanding
MTCR	Missile Technology Control Regime
NAM	Non-Aligned Movement
NATO	North Atlantic Treaty Organization
NOC	National Oil Company
OECD	Organization for Economic Cooperation and Development
OTH	Over the Horizon (surveillance system)
PACOM	Pacific Command
PAP	People's Armed Police
PLA	People's Liberation Army
PLAAF	People's Liberation Army Air Force
PLAN	People's Liberation Army Navy
PPP	Purchasing Power Parity

PRC	People's Republic of China
QDR	Quadrennial Defense Review
RBI	Reserve Bank of India
RMB	Renminbi
Rs.	Rupees
SAARC	South Asian Association for Regional Cooperation
SAM	Surface to Air Missile
SIPRI	Stockholm International Peace Research Institute
SLBM	Submarine-Launched Ballistic Missile
SRBM	Short Range Ballistic Missile
SS	Ship, Submersible
SSBN	Ship, Submersible, Ballistic, Nuclear
SSG	Ship, Submersible, Guided Missile
SSK	Ship, Submersible, Diesel-Electric
SSM	Surface to Surface Missile
SSN	Ship, Submersible, Nuclear
TIV	Trend-Indicator Value
TOW	Tube-launched Optical-tracked Wire-guided Missile
TT	Torpedo Tube(s)
UN	United Nations
UNCLOS	UN Convention on the Law of the Sea
USCC	U.S.-China Economic and Security Review Commission
USD	U.S. Dollar
USSR	Union of Soviet Socialist Republics
VLS	Vertical Launching System
WMD	Weapons of Mass Destruction
WTO	World Trade Organization

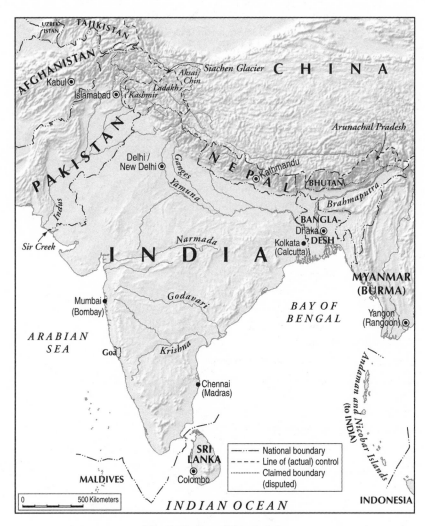

Map 1. India and South Asia

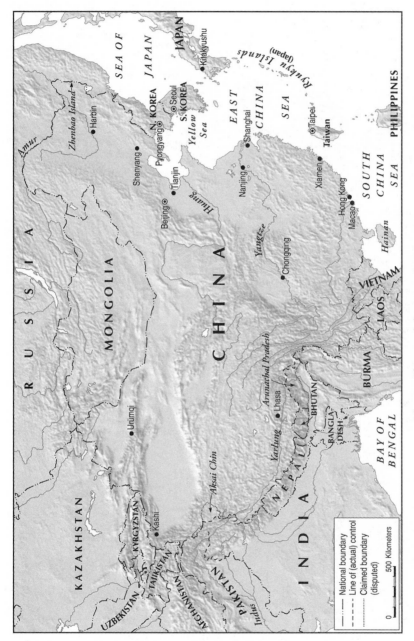

Map 2. China and the Asian Continent

xxix

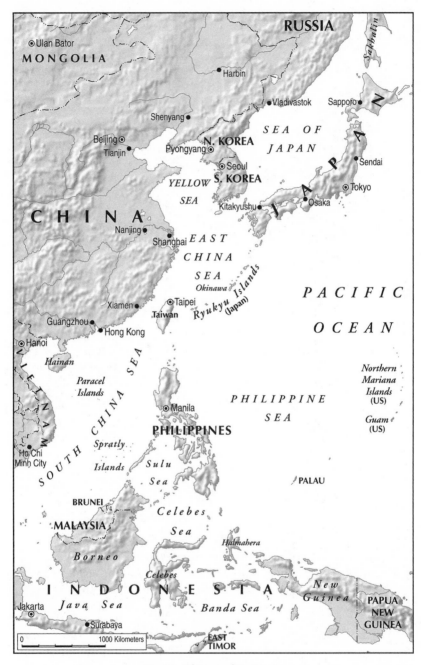

Map 3. China and East Asia

Introduction

Most recent studies of India and China put these quite different countries into a single category called "Asia's rising giants," followed by descriptions painted in broad-brush strokes. They have large populations – a source of some strength but also a source of terrible pressure on resources at home. Each is primarily a continental power, although each has long coastlines and substantial trade. Each has troubled borders, and each has one seemingly intractable territorial conflict that is bound up in its sense of national self-identify and its regime legitimacy – Taiwan for China and Kashmir for India. Each faces threats to domestic peace and internal stability, including poverty, inequality, and incomplete economic reforms, as well as ethnic, religious, and social conflict. Each has nuclear weapons and is modernizing its military capabilities. And, of course, each has launched a program of domestic reforms and integration with the global economy that has resulted in high rates of growth. This has put both on track to become economies that will – at least in absolute size – rival the U.S. economy within decades. Although they remain great power works-in-progress, Beijing and New Delhi may each harbor grand ambitions for what they will do with their growing power. Certainly, a shifting balance of power between states, such as the shift that appears to be occurring between the United States and the rising powers in Asia, has long been seen as an essential underlying cause of great power conflict.

The subtitle of this book, "Growing Power and Alarm," echoes a passage in Thucydides' *The Peloponnesian War*. Analyzing the causes of conflict between the great powers Athens and Sparta (Lacedaemon), Thucydides attributed the real cause of conflict to "the growth of the power of Athens, and the alarm that this inspired in Lacedaemon."[1] Yet Thucydides also

---

[1] Robert B. Strassler, ed., *The Landmark Thucydides: A Comprehensive Guide to The Peloponnesian War* (New York: Simon and Schuster, 1998), Book I, 23, and Book I, 88.

highlighted difficulties a dominant state faces in accurately evaluating any challenge from rising powers. How does a dominant state judge the relative power balance – itself a complex mix of material, political, and moral capabilities? How does the international behavior of a rising state affect this judgment? In a world with multiple interests and threats, should the dominant state focus on a single potential challenger, or must it also beware potential challenges from other rising states?[2]

Today, the United States faces a shifting balance of global power. For Washington, the analytical and policy difficulties reflected in Thucydides' classic account resonate more strongly than at any point since World War II. This book addresses the challenges faced by the United States in evaluating the rising power of China and India. As Thucydides might have posed the question, to what extent should the United States be alarmed by the reemergence of these Asian states as great powers, and how can Washington respond appropriately and effectively?

Despite their key similarities, China and India are viewed differently in Washington. The growth of Chinese power is viewed with alarm by many in the United States. China is seen as a potential competitor more than as a potential partner. The reverse is true of India. Washington hedges against Beijing. Meanwhile, it seeks to increase Indian power and enlist New Delhi as a partner in its hedging strategy against China. In part, this divergent treatment is the result of a key difference in the two bilateral relationships. The United States has a direct interest in Taiwan, which could potentially draw it into a war with China, whereas there is no similar flashpoint that could draw the United States into war with India. This creates an analytical focus on security competition with China that shapes (and may skew) U.S. views of China's strategic intentions. In contrast, the fortunate absence of such a stark and potentially catastrophic conflict of interest with India means less rigorous American scrutiny of India's strategic behavior in South Asia and beyond. Unfortunately, that lack of attention and understanding may also expose both Washington and New Delhi to unrealistic mutual expectations.

Rising Chinese and Indian power also strikes at another question for American foreign policy. Should American leaders *expect* divergent

---

[2]   In recounting speeches made by key participants in the conflict, Thucydides offers rich discussion of interstate relations and the "true" cause of the war: Sparta's fear of the growing "greatness" of Athens (including both material and political power), and how this alarm justly or unjustly "pressured" Sparta toward declaring war. See Thucydides, *History of the Peloponnesian War*, translated by C.F. Smith (Cambridge, MA: Loeb Classical Library, Harvard University Press, 2003), Book I, 23; 68–71; 73–78; 80–85; 86; and 88.

behavior from these two states, rooted in the differences between their domestic regime types and political values? American conservatives have criticized "realist" foreign policies that move away from assumptions based on political values toward a greater focus on material interests and balances of power.[3] Such criticism has been especially strident with regard to Washington's treatment of authoritarian regimes such as China.[4] Critics from the center and left of American politics have also disparaged a "realist" approach, and for similar reasons. They argue that political realism excessively compromises American values and ignores essential differences in behavior and interest between states with different political systems.[5] The question of how to handle rising Chinese and Indian power thus touches on perennial debates in American foreign and security policy.[6] No single

---

[3] Aaron Friedberg, "Should we fear Obama's 'realism'?" *Foreign Policy*, March 9, 2009, http://shadow.foreignpolicy.com/posts/2009/03/09/should_we_fear_obamas_realism; Howard LaFranchi, "Obama at One Year: New Realism in Foreign Policy," *Christian Science Monitor*, January 19, 2010.

[4] Michael J. Green, "Obama's self-defeating 'realism' in Asia," *Foreign Policy*, October 6, 2009, http://shadow.foreignpolicy.com/blog/12381; Robert Kagan "Foreign Policy Sequels," *Washington Post*, March 9, 2009. Daniel Blumenthal, "Obama's Asia trip: a series of unfortunate events," *Foreign Policy*, November 18, 2009, http://shadow.foreignpolicy.com/posts/2009/11/18/obamas_asia_trip_a_series_of_unfortunate_events

[5] Richard N. Haass, "Regime Change is the Only Way to Stop Iran," *Newsweek*, January 22, 2010. "During Visit, Obama Skirts Chinese Political Sensitivities," *New York Times*, November 17, 2009. Stephen Zunes, "Human Rights: C+," *Foreign Policy in Focus*, January 25, 2010, http://www.fpif.org/articles/human_rights_c

[6] The struggle to balance both a concern for relative power and material interest and the promotion of American political values is a recurring theme in the work of many of America's most influential strategic thinkers. Alexander Hamilton, "Federalist 6," "Federalist 7," and "Federalist 11," in Gary Wills, ed., *The Federalist Papers* (New York: Bantam Books, 1982, originally published 1787–1788), 21–32; 49–55; Hans J. Morgenthau, *Politics Among Nations: The Struggle for Power and Peace* (New York: Alfred A. Knopf, sixth edition 1985, first edition published 1948); George F. Kennan, *American Diplomacy* (Chicago: University of Chicago Press, expanded edition 1985, first edition 1951); Felix Gilbert, *To the Farewell Address: Ideas of Early American Foreign Policy* (Princeton, NJ: Princeton University Press, 1961); John Stoessinger, *Crusaders and Pragmatists: Movers of American Foreign Policy* (New York: W.W. Norton, 1979); Samuel P. Huntington, "American Ideals Versus American Institutions," *Political Science Quarterly*, 97:1 (Spring 1982): 1–37; Robert O. Keohane, ed., *Neorealism and Its Critics* (New York: Columbia University Press, 1986); Henry Kissinger, *Diplomacy* (New York: Simon and Shuster, 1995); Walter Russell Mead, *Special Providence: American Foreign Policy and How it Changed the World* (New York: Routledge, 2002); John Lewis Gaddis, *Surprise, Security, and the American Experience* (Cambridge, MA: Harvard University Press, 2004); Robert Jervis, *American Foreign Policy in a New Era* (New York: Routledge, 2005); Kenneth N. Waltz, *Realism and International Politics* (New York: Routledge, 2008); Paul Wolfowitz, "Think Again: Realism," *Foreign Policy*, September/October 2009, http://www.foreignpolicy.com/articles/2009/08/17/think_again_realism; Stephen M. Walt, "REAL Realism," *Foreign Policy*, August 27, 2009, http://walt.foreignpolicy.com/

volume can resolve all of these questions, but greater clarity and discipline can be brought to the debate.

The Purpose of this Study

This book sets out to put broad patterns of Indian and Chinese strategic behavior in comparative context. This will help clarify the challenges and opportunities the United States faces from both countries. We examine and evaluate the empirical track record of Chinese and Indian strategic behavior in four areas: (1) strategic culture; (2) foreign policy, use of force, and border dispute settlement; (3) military modernization, including defense spending, military doctrine, and force modernization; and (4) foreign economic policy and strategies, including international trade and energy resource competition. After concluding the empirical comparison, we also evaluate the utility of a prominent international relations theory, "the democratic peace," for predicting Chinese and Indian international behavior.

We do not examine the origins of U.S. policy toward India and China, or evaluate its effectiveness. American policy toward China and India may have multiple motivations. Certainly, policy can and has been justified in terms of concern for balances of power, economic interests, common values, or a combination of these. We do not attempt to determine which of these logics may be dominant, or which "explains" U.S. policy. However, our analysis does challenge some arguments that commonly appear in U.S. policy discourse about China and India: that China is an outlier in its behavior and that democratic India exhibits international behavior that is sharply different from authoritarian China and more "naturally" aligned with American interests. Such assessments have increasingly taken root as the conventional wisdom in Washington and appear to support a recent sharpening divergence in U.S. policies toward the two rising powers in Asia.

An empirical, comparative approach offers insight into what kind of great powers these two countries are becoming. Past behavior is no guarantee of future performance. However, side-by-side comparison provides context for evaluating which specific rising power interests, policies, and behaviors present the greatest challenges to the United States. Comparison can also help specify genuine differences between China and India as

posts/2009/08/23/real_realism; Zbigniew Brzezinski, "From Hope to Audacity: Appraising Obama's Foreign Policy," *Foreign Affairs*, 89:1, (January/February 2010).

international actors. This will assist U.S. policy makers seeking to maximize America's bilateral interests with both countries, while also securing America's broader interests in Asia.

The Significance of this Study

This book fills an important gap in the literature on security, power transition, and international relations in Asia. No major study follows the approach undertaken here: a structured, side-by-side comparison of a broad selection of Indian and Chinese international strategic behaviors. There is no shortage of studies of the two countries. China and India receive unprecedented attention from policy, scholarly, and media communities. Some proclaim a new world order on the basis of general descriptions of the rising relative power of China and India.[7] Others believe that the new global order will be shaped by Sino-Indian rivalry.[8] These studies focus on rising relative power and offer speculation on what China and India might do with that power, rather than providing analysis of their actual behavior.

Most comparative studies of India and China focus on their economic development, which is said to underpin their newfound global influence.[9] Some of these comparisons equate the two countries in a single category called "Chindia," a term that overstates the global economic importance of

[7] Daniel Drezner, "The New New World Order," *Foreign Affairs*, 86:2 (March/April 2007): 34–46. Other, more promotional accounts also argue that the next century will be dominated by either China or India, although these do not engage in any comparison that would permit a judgment of which of the two countries would lead, or how. See, for example, Martin Jacques, *When China Rules the World: The End of the Western World and the Birth of a New Global Order* (New York: The Penguin Press, 2009); Kamal Nath, *India's Century: The Age of Entrepreneurship in the World's Biggest Democracy* (New York: McGraw-Hill, 2007); Laurence J. Brahm, *China's Century: The Awakening of the Next Economic Powerhouse* (New York: Wiley Press, 2001).

[8] Robert D. Kaplan, "Center Stage for the 21st Century," *Foreign Affairs*, 88:2 (March/April 2009): 16–32.

[9] Tim Harcourt, "The Elephant and the Dragon: Can India's rise match China's?" Australian Trade Commission, Sydney, October 7, 2004. Pranab Bardhan "Crouching Tiger, Lumbering Elephant? The Rise of China and India in a Comparative Perspective," *Brown Journal of World Affairs*, 13:1 (Fall/Winter 2006): 49–62; Robyn Meredith, *The Elephant and the Dragon: The Rise of India and China and What It Means for All of Us* (New York: W.W. Norton & Co., 2008); David Smith, *The Dragon and the Elephant: China, India and the New World Order* (London: Profile Books, 2007); Ashok Gulati and Shenggen Fan, *The Dragon and the Elephant: Agricultural and Rural Reforms in China and India* (Washington, DC: International Food Policy Research Institute, 2007); Appa Rao Korukonda, Giovanna Carrillo, Chenchuramaiah Bathala, and Mainuddin Afza, "The Dragon and the Elephant: A Comparative Study of Financial Systems, Commerce, and Commonwealth in India and China," *The Icfai Journal of International Business*, 2:3 (August 2007): 7–20.

India relative to China and may mask more than it reveals.[10] There are many explicit, empirical comparisons of the two countries in the field of development economics.[11] One strain within comparative political economy focuses on the effect of different regime types – democratic versus authoritarian – on long-term modernization and development.[12] Another comparative approach studies Chinese and Indian domestic politics, including constitutions and other domestic institutions.[13] The literature on comparative political economy and development aims to identify the proper mix of policies for domestic Indian and Chinese development. These are critical issues, but they do not address the full spectrum of concerns for U.S. Asia policy, particularly with regard to security.

There are several excellent assessments of the China-India relationship.[14] Some of the studies of Sino-Indian relations specifically highlight implications of the Sino-Indian relationship for the United States.[15] These analyses come closest to side-by-side comparison of Chinese and Indian international behaviors. Their focus, however, is on assessing the prospects for bilateral Sino-Indian rivalry or cooperation, rather than on the regional (or global) strategic behavior of these two countries and the implications of those behaviors for U.S. Asia policy.

[10] See for example, Pete Engardio, ed., *Chindia: How China and India are Revolutionizing Global Business* (New York: McGraw Hill, 2007); Jairam Ramesh, *Making Sense of Chindia: Reflections on China and India* (New Delhi: India Research Press, 2005). Some business-oriented analyses do try to separate the two countries from the "Chindia" label, but still focus on broad generalizations about business culture and motivations; see Tarun Khanna, *Billions of Entrepreneurs: How China and India Are Reshaping Their Futures and Yours* (Cambridge, MA: Harvard Business School Press 2008).

[11] A recent example is L. Alan Winters and Shahid Yusuf, eds., *Dancing with Giants: China, India, and the Global Economy* (Washington, DC: World Bank, 2007). On the advantages of a comparative perspective, see Scott Kennedy, "Overcoming Our Middle Kingdom Complex: Finding China's Place in Comparative Politics," in Scott Kennedy, ed., *Beyond the Middle Kingdom: Comparative Perspectives on China's Capitalist Transformation* (Stanford: Stanford University Press, 2011), 3–21.

[12] Edward Friedman and Bruce Gilley, eds., *Asia's Giants: Comparing China and India* (New York: Palgrave Macmillan, 2005); Yasheng Huang and Tarun Khanna, "Can India Overtake China?" *Foreign Policy*, 82:4 (July/August 2003):74–81.

[13] See, for example, Sue Ellen M. Charlton, *Comparing Asian Politics: India, China, and Japan, Second Edition* (Boulder: Westview Press, 2004).

[14] For example, John W. Garver, *Protracted Contest: Sino-Indian Rivalry in the Twentieth Century* (Seattle: University of Washington Press, 2001); Jing Dong Yuan, "The Dragon and the Elephant: Chinese-Indian Relations in the 21st Century," *The Washington Quarterly*, 30:3 (Summer 2007): 131–144; Pang Zhongying, "The dragon and the elephant," *The National Interest*, May 1, 2007; Waheguru Pal Singh Sidhu and Jing-Dong Yuan, eds., *China and India: Cooperation or Conflict?* (Boulder: Lynne Rienner Press, 2003).

[15] Francine R. Frankel and Harry Harding, *The India-China Relationship: What the U.S. Needs to Know* (Washington, DC: Woodrow Wilson Center Press, 2004).

Other sources compare Chinese and Indian military developments with a focus on U.S. interests, usually in separate chapters of a single volume.[16] Many of these studies have a strong regional focus, dividing East and Northeast Asia from South Asia. A number of edited volumes indirectly compare Chinese and Indian foreign policy, with different authors penning separate chapters on each country or region.[17] Despite editorial efforts to maintain a common focus or framework, however, authors in these edited volumes often adopt distinctive approaches and standards. These efforts result in fewer direct comparisons between China (seen primarily as an East Asian or Northeast Asian power) and India (a South Asian power).

Notwithstanding these many studies of varying focus and depth, side-by-side comparisons of Chinese and Indian international behaviors and strategies are rare. The few that do take an explicitly comparative approach do not evaluate actual international behavior across the issue areas of most relevance to U.S. foreign and security policy in Asia.[18] A detailed empirical comparison of Chinese and Indian international strategic behavior would be useful in itself, but the trend toward increasingly divergent American expectations about the behavior of these states makes such a comparison all the more timely and meaningful.

In the next section of this chapter, we begin with an overview of America's post–World War II relations with each country, then turn to focus on U.S. policies since the late 1990s. This section highlights the issue of Taiwan as an important factor shaping a divergent American approach to India and

[16] A useful example of this approach is found in Ashley J. Tellis and Michael Wills, eds., *Strategic Asia 2005–2006: Military Modernization in an Era of Uncertainty* (Washington, DC: National Bureau of Asian Research, 2005).

[17] This approach is taken in David Shambaugh and Michael Yahuda, eds., *International Relations of Asia* (New York: Rowman and Littlefield, 2008), and Muthiah Alagappa, ed., *Asian Security Practice: Material and Ideational Influences* (Stanford: Stanford University Press, 1998). Another approach to a theoretical framework for understanding Asian international order focuses on cross-border issues such as international institutions, but necessarily dilutes explicit empirical comparisons of national strategies. See Muthiah Alagappa, ed., *Asian Security Order: Instrumental and Normative Features* (Stanford: Stanford University Press, 2002).

[18] Rollie Lal's *Understanding India and China: Security Implications for the United States and the World* (Westport, CT: Praeger Security International, 2006) is one of the few studies that do compare national interests, identity, and foreign policies side by side. However, Lal's data and analysis are based on interviews with elites in both countries, with a focus on the motivations for international behavior, not on the empirical track record of actual behavior. David B. H. Denoon's *The Economic and Strategic Rise of China and India: Asian Realignments after the 1997 Financial Crisis* (New York: Palgrave Macmillan 2007) examines broad prospects for political and economic alignment among all Asian countries in response to the 1997 financial crisis.

China. It also identifies several other propositions about India and China that shape U.S. strategic thought and policy. These ideas are evident in U.S. policy statements and actions, as well as in influential American policy analyses and academic studies. They inform U.S. leadership perceptions of China as an outlier in its strategic behavior and as a challenge that goes well beyond the Taiwan issue. They also fuel a perception that common values and common interests will support ever-greater alignment of U.S. and Indian interests and policies. Having reviewed the study's findings in the Preface, in the next section of this chapter, we outline the structure of the book. We conclude this chapter with a brief overview of some enduring questions and debates in international relations that this study engages.

China and India in U.S. Strategic Thought and Action

The United States has had an uneasy relationship with both India and China since Indian independence in 1947 and the founding of the People's Republic of China (PRC) in 1949. Both relationships have been character-ized by alternating conflict and cooperation. After the Communist victory in China, the United States denied the legitimacy of the Chinese Communist Party (CCP) government. It supported the Kuomintang (KMT) as China's legitimate government, defended the KMT on Taiwan, and found itself in frequent conflict with the Chinese regime over foreign policy issues and Beijing's treatment of its own people. American and Chinese forces fought each other in the Korean War, with terrible casualties on both sides. The United States and China have continued to confront each other across the Taiwan Strait. The Taiwan issue in particular remains an enduring con-flict of interest and is prone to periodic crises. Both China ("unofficially" in 1995) and the United States ("officially" in 1958) have raised the spec-ter of using nuclear weapons against one another over Taiwan. The United States and China have also come to loggerheads over other national inter-ests. In the 1960s and into the 1970s, China supported violent revolution-ary movements in developing countries, including a murderous regime in Cambodia. China was a key source of both nuclear weapons and missile technology proliferation, especially in the 1980s.[19] It also has asserted views

---

[19] Via Pakistan, Chinese nuclear technologies were proliferated to North Korea, Libya, and Iran. Some suspect that via North Korea, these originally Chinese nuclear technologies may have been spread to countries like Syria. For a brief but authoritative history of nuclear weapons development and proliferation, see Stephen M. Younger, *The Bomb: A New History* (New York: Harper Collins, 2009).

on maritime rights and maritime claims versus its Asian neighbors that differ sharply from American perspectives.

Still, Sino-American relations have also seen the development of significant common interests. China joined the United States in balancing against the Soviet Union from the 1970s through the 1980s. China and the United States also conducted limited intelligence sharing and military exchanges in the 1980s. During the same period, China also purchased some U.S. military equipment. This was suspended in the wake of the June 1989 Tiananmen incident in which Chinese troops attacked and killed Chinese civilians demanding political and economic reforms. Since that time, Sino-American military-to-military relations have been limited and punctuated by stops and starts.

Although China continues to maintain a cooperative relationship with North Korea, Beijing has also played a constructive role in the Six-Party Talks process to address the problem of North Korea's nuclear weapons program. Since the 1980s, the United States has encouraged China's reforms and integration with the global economy and supported China's decision to join the WTO. Like other powers, China has engaged in certain protectionist policies. But China supports a relatively liberal global trade and financial system, as well as institutions such as the WTO, World Bank, IMF, and G20. Despite remaining cautious about burden sharing, Beijing wishes to be seen as a "responsible" power. The Sino-U.S. trade and investment relationship, despite its frictions, has become a critical source of mutual benefit to both sides.

The United States and India have also had a history of mixed relations. The two countries share important political values, including a respect for rule of law and political systems based on separation of powers, electoral democracy, and universal suffrage. Indian and U.S. forces have never fought against each other. India assisted American attempts to support Tibetan forces against Chinese troops in the 1950s, and the United States provided significant intelligence and military support to India during and after its 1962 border war with China.

However, India frequently opposed U.S. diplomacy during the Cold War period on ideological grounds. India was aligned with the Soviet Union during key periods of the Cold War, developing close defense ties including large-scale purchases of Soviet military equipment. New Delhi refused to condemn the Soviet invasion of Afghanistan in the 1980s, and it contested U.S. policies in Afghanistan due in part to America's reliance on Pakistan in that effort. Like China, India continues to maintain close ties with the defense industry of a revitalized, authoritarian Russia. Unlike the Taiwan issue with China, the United States does not believe it has a core interest in India's claim on Kashmir or other territories. Yet the United States has frequently opposed Indian policies toward Pakistan and has engaged in coercive diplomacy against India during some of the latter's conflicts with Pakistan.

India's nuclear program has been a source of friction in U.S.-India relations. India has not directly transferred nuclear weapon technologies to dangerous third parties as China did with Pakistan. However, by the example of its own nuclear program, nuclear weapon tests, and its unwillingness to join international nonproliferation regimes, India has challenged U.S.-led international efforts to contain the proliferation of nuclear weapons. Many American officials saw both India's "peaceful nuclear explosion" in 1974 and its much more advanced 1998 nuclear weapons tests as significant challenges to core U.S. interests, because they accelerated nuclear development and weaponization in an unstable Pakistan and set a precedent that regimes in North Korea and Iran apparently intend to imitate.

Although the challenge of industrial espionage and illegal transfer of dual-use technology is less intense than with China, the United States has charged Indian firms and Indian government agencies with conspiracy to circumvent U.S. restrictions on the export of dual-use and weapons technology.[20] Washington has also placed sanctions on Indian as well as Chinese companies for proliferating weapons of mass destruction (WMD) and missile technologies to countries like Iran.[21]

Iran-related issues are likely to remain a potential source of conflict in relations between New Delhi and Washington.[22] Reflecting New Delhi's deeply held views, a November 2008 speech in Teheran by India's external affairs minister Pranab Mukherjee highlighted the potential for Iran to

---

[20] "U.S. Cites Indian Government Agencies in Weapons Conspiracy," *New York Times*, April 3, 2007. K. Alan Kronstadt and Kenneth Katzman, "India-Iran Relations and U.S. Interests," Congressional Research Service Report for Congress, Order Code RS22486, August 2, 2006.

[21] See Paul K. Kerr, "U.S. Nuclear Cooperation with India: Issues for Congress," Congressional Research Service Report for Congress, Order Code RL 33016, November 3, 2008, 9–10; Sharon Squassoni, "India and Iran: WMD Proliferation Activities," Congressional Research Service Report for Congress, Order Code RS2253, November 8, 2006; K. Alan Kronstadt, "U.S.-India Bilateral Agreements and Global Partnership," Congressional Research Service Report for Congress, Order Code RL 33072, March 10, 2006, 22.

[22] Bruce Stokes, "The U.S. and India: Friendship, Warily," *The National Journal*, February 13, 2010.

follow India's pathway toward nuclear capability. Speaking to an audience that included Iran's foreign minister, Mukherjee justified India's resistance to international efforts to restrict its nuclear program as part of a foreign policy of opposing "unequal treaties" and described India's choice to pursue its nuclear program as ultimately "vindicated."[23] In July 2010, the Indian Ministry of External Affairs proposed a variety of "creative mechanisms" by which Indian businesses could avoid United States and United Nations sanctions while continuing to do business with Iran. The suggested mechanisms included creating new entities that would not have financial exposure in the United States and forming consortia with Russian or Chinese companies to make it more difficult for the United States to assign responsibility.[24] Commercial gain is certainly one objective, but the Ministry of External Affairs made clear that New Delhi's enduring political objectives are at the heart of India's Iran policy.[25]

Despite such differences, the U.S. relationship with India has improved dramatically in recent years, and bilateral trade and investment, while much smaller than U.S.-China trade and investment, is growing. Defense cooperation with New Delhi is also growing, with joint military exercises, U.S. arms sales, and new defense and technology cooperation agreements in place since 2005. Geostrategic ties were reinforced by a U.S.-India nuclear technology cooperation agreement in 2008, and they have continued to improve despite some shift in U.S. attention toward Pakistan and China in the early years of the Obama administration.

Historical relationships and conflicts of interest weigh heavily on U.S. attitudes toward both countries, and the rise of both of these powers will undoubtedly present the United States with new challenges. Yet it is important to note that the United States shares common interest and mutual benefit on a wide range of critical issues with both India and China. Perhaps the most impressive feature of current relations between the single superpower

---

[23] Address by H. E. Mr. Pranab Mukherjee, Minister of External Affairs, at "Seminar on India and Iran: Ancient Civilizations and Modern Nations," Teheran, November 2, 2008, http://meaindia.nic.in/speech/2008/11/02ss01.htm

[24] "To Engage Iran, India Looks to Beat US, UN Sanctions by Being 'Creative,'" *Express India*, August 3, 2010, http://www.expressindia.com/latest-news/To-engage-Iran-India-looks-to-beat-US-UN-sanctions-by-being-creative/655365/

[25] Ministry of External Affairs, "International Sanctions on Iran and Way Forward for India-Iran Relations" (New Delhi: Ministry of External Affairs, July 2010). See also analysis of this report in N. V. Subramanian, "China Drives India-Iran Ties," *The Diplomat*, August 9, 2010, http://the-diplomat.com/indian-decade/2010/08/09/china-drives-indian-iran-policy/; and Anna Newby, "India-Iran-U.S. Relations," Center for Strategic and International Studies, August 11, 2010, http://csis.org/blog/india-iran-us-relations

and Asia's two rising powers is the breadth and depth of their common interests. Moreover, any short list of common interests between the United States and India has a great deal of overlap with a similar short list of common interests between the United States and China. All three countries oppose religious extremism and terrorism. All three support the continued deepening of global economic integration and trade liberalization. And all three are explicitly committed to a peaceful, stable, and prosperous environment in Asia, conducive to pursuing further economic and social development.

However, U.S. attitudes toward India and China have been shifting since the late 1990s, resulting in different approaches toward the two countries. This divergent treatment has sharpened in recent years. Key elements of U.S. policy vis-à-vis China are aimed at "hedging" against that state – in other words, aimed at developing diplomatic relationships and deploying military capabilities capable of confronting China if necessary – while new U.S. policies aim to promote the rise of Indian power as one part of that hedging effort.[26]

Sharpening Views: A Strategic Competitor and a Natural Ally

U.S. Asia policy has evolved significantly since the end of the Cold War and now includes policies to strengthen engagement with both China and India. With China, engagement has focused primarily on trade and investment. American China policy has also grown to include some military-to-military contacts and new initiatives in areas of common interest such as Korean peninsula nuclear issues and clean energy. This is part of an effort to encourage China to cooperate with the West as a "responsible

---

[26] U.S. policy makers and diplomats are usually careful not to declare openly that hedging against China is a principal motivation behind U.S. India policy. Some U.S. officials differentiate between "hedging" and "balancing" against China, with hedging seen as more benign and less aggressive than balancing. From the Indian and Chinese perspective, such distinctions may not fundamentally affect their own responses. Indian strategists recognize and openly discuss Washington's desire to gain Indian assistance in hedging against Chinese power as a key rationale for U.S. India policy. Most do not draw clear distinctions between hedging and balancing when considering India's response. It would be surprising if Chinese policy makers did not also consider the strengthening U.S.-India ties in this light. See, for example, Sumit Ganguly, "India's Alliances 2020," in Michael R. Chambers, ed., *South Asia in 2020: Future Strategic Balances and Alliances* (Carlisle: U.S. Army War College, 2002), 374; see also Harsh V. Pant, ed., *Indian Foreign Policy in a Unipolar World* (New York: Routledge, 2009).

stakeholder," an approach common to both Democratic and Republican administrations.[27]

Yet China and the United States have continued to eye each other warily. Beijing has grown anxious about precedents set by Washington's international military interventions, such as in the Gulf War (1991), Kosovo (1999), Iraq (2003), and Libya (2011). Mutual suspicion was also reflected in Chinese and American actions leading up to and during the Taiwan Straits Crisis of 1995–1996, in China's reaction to the U.S. bombing of the Chinese embassy in Belgrade in 1999, in an incident involving the collision of a U.S. spy plane and a Chinese fighter jet near China's borders in 2001, and in a similar confrontation with a U.S. surveillance ship off China in 2009.

In addition to Taiwan, Sino-U.S. relations also remain susceptible to recurring conflicts over China's relationships with authoritarian regimes such as Iran, Sudan, and Myanmar, as well as the Chinese government's abuses of human rights in China. Most recently, Beijing's increasingly assertive claims to military prerogatives in its exclusive economic zones (EEZs), its behavior during a 2010 flare-up in tensions with Japan over disputed islets in the East China Sea, and its new and somewhat ambiguous language on its "core interests" with regard to sovereignty claims in the South China Sea have, taken together, heightened concerns in Washington and in many Asian capitals.[28] It remains to be seen whether these developments signal a long-term shift in Chinese foreign policy. Regardless, China's assertions prompted an American restatement of its own "critical interest" in the South China Sea, as well as nascent balancing against China among Asian countries.[29]

---

[27] Thomas J. Christensen, "Shaping the Choices of a Rising China: Recent Lessons for the Obama Administration," *The Washington Quarterly*, 32:3 (July 2009): 89–104; Kenneth Lieberthal, "The U.S.-China Relationship Goes Global," *Current History*, 108:719 (September 2009): 243–249; Robert Zoellick, "Whither China: From Membership to Responsibility?" Speech at the National Committee on U.S.-China Relations, New York, September 21, 2005.

[28] "外交部举行例行记者会," [Foreign Ministry Holds Meeting with Reporters] 《人民日报》 [People's Daily], March 3, 2010. "China urges U.S. to respect its core interests," *People's Daily* (English), March 02, 2010. For Western media coverage of the outcome of March 2010 meetings between Chinese and American officials in Beijing, see "Chinese Military Seeks to Extend Its Naval Power," *New York Times*, April 23, 2010. For analysis of overstated media coverage, divergent interpretations of Chinese "assertiveness," and Beijing's use of the "core interests" language, see Michael Swaine, "China's Assertive Behavior, Part One: On 'Core Interests,'" *China Leadership Monitor*, 34 (Fall 2010).

[29] "Offering to Aid Talks, U.S. Challenges China on Disputed Islands," *New York Times*, July 23, 2010. On Asian states "bandwagoning" with the United States to balance what they view as a newly assertive China, see Malcolm Cook et al., *Power and Choice: Asian Security*

Meanwhile, American presidents of both parties have long contemplated better relations with India. The Clinton administration saw India's nuclear program and its implications for regional crisis stability and global WMD proliferation as a major challenge, something that India could not accept. Yet the Clinton administration also saw opportunities for closer relations with India, particularly in the wake of U.S. diplomatic intervention with Pakistan and India during the 1999 Kargil crisis. The trend toward better U.S.-India relations was also given impetus by growing trade, particularly the outsourcing of U.S. services business to India and the emergence of a successful and influential community of Indian scientists, engineers, and entrepreneurs in the United States. Building on these foundations, a major initiative to improve relations occurred under the George W. Bush administration, especially between 2001 and 2005. In an effort to buttress stability in Pakistan and promote U.S. interests in Afghanistan, the Obama administration urged India to reduce frictions with Pakistan, eliciting protests from New Delhi. However, from 2008 to 2010, the Obama administration also pushed forward key elements of geostrategic cooperation with India, including military equipment sales and American support for India's accession to the Nuclear Supplier's Group and to a permanent seat on the U.N. Security Council.[30]

From the 1990s through the first decade of the 2000s, U.S. policy underwent a clear geopolitical shift in its treatment of India and China. China came to be seen as a potential strategic competitor. The 2006 *National Security Strategy of the United States* argued that U.S. security policy must hedge against the potential for China to emerge as a threat to U.S. interests.[31] The 2006 *Quadrennial Defense Review* found that of the major and emerging powers, China has the greatest potential to compete militarily with the United States and field disruptive military technologies that over time could offset traditional U.S. military advantages.[32] The 2008 U.S.

Futures (Sydney: Lowy Institute for International Policy, 2010), 22–24; and "China's Fast Rise Leads Neighbors to Join Forces," *New York Times*, October 30, 2010.

30 "Obama Is Not Likely to Push India Hard on Pakistan," *New York Times*, November 5, 2010. "India welcomes US support for membership in Nuclear Suppliers Group," *Asian News International*, November 8, 2010, http://www.thaindian.com/newsportal/india-news/india-welcomes-us-support-for-membership-in-nuclear-suppliers-group_100456482. html; "Countering China, Obama Backs India for U.N. Council," *New York Times*, November 8, 2010.

31 *The National Security Strategy of the United States* (Washington, DC: The White House, 2006), 42.

32 *Quadrennial Defense Review* (Washington, DC: United States Department of Defense, February 2006), 29.

Department of Defense (DoD) report on Chinese military power warned that Chinese military modernization posed challenges to U.S. interests.[33] The 2010 Quadrennial Defense Review (QDR) Report contained a more nuanced assessment of China compared to preceding official documents but still raised questions about China's "future conduct and intentions."[34]

The emerging view of China as particularly threatening to U.S. interests is not limited to the executive branch or the Defense Department (and it is worth noting that some naval and military officers have resisted such views).[35] Although political assessments are not unanimous, the idea that China presents unique security challenges crosses party lines. For example, in March 2009, Democratic Senator James Webb expressed his concern that China's offense-oriented military doctrine and developing military capabilities may threaten U.S. interests.[36] Public attitudes have responded to China's rising relative power. A February 2010 poll found that more than 40 percent of Americans believed that the twenty-first century would be more of a Chinese century than an American century, and that the loss of American influence relative to China would have a negative impact on American interests.[37]

American policy has followed from its leaders' reservations about the potential direction of Chinese strategic behavior. The United States has used its influence to restrict arms sales to China from Israel and Europe. Washington has continued to sell arms to Taiwan and deployed new forces to Asia to better position them to counter China.[38] Many of these actions

---

[33] See U.S. Department of Defense, *Military Power of the People's Republic of China* (Washington, DC: Office of the Secretary of Defense, 2008); the 2009 and 2010 versions of this annual report continue a recent trend toward more balanced analysis and moderate language since the report was first published in 2002. See also, "China Plans Steep Increase in Military Spending," *New York Times*, March 5, 2008.

[34] *Quadrennial Defense Review Report* (Washington, DC: Office of the Secretary of Defense, February 2010), 31.

[35] Recent Pacific Command (PACOM) commanders Joseph Prueher, Dennis Blair, William J. Fallon, and Timothy Keating (among other officers) were prominent advocates of robust U.S. deterrent capability in Asia, but also of more careful assessments of China, as well as balanced engagement with Beijing and the PLA.

[36] Both Democratic and Republican senators take a keen interest in China-related security issues. See "Hearing to Receive Testimony on the Current and Future Worldwide Threats to the Security of the United States," U.S. Senate Armed Services Committee, March 10, 2009.

[37] "Poll shows concern about American influence waning as China's grows," *Washington Post*, February 25, 2010. See also Steven Mufson and John Pomfret, "There's a new Red Scare. But is China really so scary?" *Washington Post*, February 28, 2009.

[38] Megan Scully, "Pentagon begins military buildup on Guam," *Congress Daily*, November 17, 2005. After a shift completed in 2007, the U.S. Navy now deploys more than 50% of

can be traced directly to U.S. concerns about possible conflict over Taiwan and improvements in People's Liberation Army's (PLA) military capabilities. Yet others appear to be less directly relevant to Taiwan scenarios, reflecting a hedging policy that is broader in both geographic and political scope. For example, the strengthening of the alliances with Japan and Australia might provide assistance during Taiwan crisis, but these policies also reflect U.S. concern for China's growing diplomatic and economic clout in Asia. Stronger ties to Australia, Indonesia, and Singapore are at least partly motivated by concerns about China's ambitions in Southeast Asia. Washington has in recent years made greater efforts to expand relations with nontraditional partners in the region, such as Mongolia. Finally, the United States is developing closer security ties to India, which is far from Taiwan and unlikely to be of any assistance to the United States in a Taiwan crisis.

In contrast, India's rising relative power has come to be seen in a different light. Both Indian and American officials have characterized India and the United States as partners and "natural allies," singling out common democratic values and institutions as a foundation for this natural partnership.[39] That partnership extends to a U.S. policy of assisting India to become a major power, particularly through defense and security ties. Defense ties are becoming stronger despite some claims that the Obama administration has focused on other issues at the expense of its attention to U.S.-India relations.[40]

its ships in the Pacific Fleet, up from 45% in the mid-1990s. According to public sources, the U.S. Navy has also met a 2006 QDR mandate to homeport 60% of its submarines in the Pacific by the end of 2010. The United States also approved significant arms sales to Taiwan late in the George W. Bush administration.

[39] See "President, Prime Minister of India Discuss Freedom and Democracy" (Washington, DC: U.S. Department of Defense, July 18, 2005). "President Bush and Prime Minister Singh of India Discuss Growing Strategic Partnership" (Washington, DC: The White House, March 3, 2006). "U.S.-India Joint Statement" (Washington, DC: The White House, March 2, 2006). "U.S. – India Defense Relationship Fact Sheet" (Washington, DC: U.S. Department of Defense, March 2006). See also, Colin Powell, confirmation hearings, *Washington File*, January 17, 2001, cited in Amit Gupta, *The U.S. – India Relationship: Strategic Partnership or Complementary Interests?* (Carlisle: U.S. Army War College, 2005). For similar views from former Clinton administration officials, see Strobe Talbott, *Engaging India: Diplomacy, Democracy and the Bomb* (Washington, DC: Brookings Institution, 2004), 44–45. The notion of a "natural" tendency to United States-India alignment or even alliance is a recurring theme in recent American national security thinking. See Richard L. Armitage, Nicholas Burns, and Richard Fontaine, *Natural Allies: A Blueprint for the Future of U.S.-India Relations* (Washington, DC: Center for a New American Security, 2010).

[40] David C. Mumford, "US-India Relationship to Reach New Heights," *The Times of India*, March 31, 2005; B. M. Jain, *Global Power: India's Foreign Policy 1947–2006* (Lanham: Lexington Books, 2008), 92–101. "China Gains in U.S. Eyes, and India Feels Slights," *New York Times*, November 23, 2009.

In addition to extensive joint military exercises and training, the United States has recently sold major weapons systems to India, including an amphibious warfare ship (or LPD), helicopters, new maritime patrol aircraft, and military transport aircraft. Additional weapons and dual-use technology sales to India are possible. In October 2008, Washington and New Delhi finalized a nuclear cooperation agreement that will allow U.S. and international support for India's civilian nuclear programs. This agreement will permit India to focus more of its own scarce domestic resources on its nuclear weapons program. The nuclear cooperation agreement also has great symbolic significance as a shift in geostrategic alignment – it is a high-level political affirmation of close U.S.-India relations.[41] In contrast to its treatment of China, the *2010 Quadrennial Defense Review* views growing Indian military power as helping provide net security benefits in South Asia and beyond.[42] For their part, Indian officials also want to alter the balance of power in Asia and have come to believe that the United States no longer aims to contain India, a view that Indian elites held for many years.[43]

American officials acknowledge that this help is offered in the expectation that India will directly or indirectly balance the rise of Chinese power.[44] When U.S. Defense Secretary Robert Gates visited India in February 2008 to further strengthen defense ties, senior U.S. defense officials acknowledged that these moves were being taken with a view toward hedging against rising Chinese power.[45] Ashley Tellis, a respected adviser to the Bush administration on India policy, has described recent American policy toward India as motivated by the aim of consolidating U.S. primacy in the face of rising Chinese power.[46]

---

[41] For further analysis of the geopolitical implications of the U.S.-India nuclear cooperation agreement, see Stephen Blank, "India and Central Asia: Part of the New Great Game," in Pant, ed., *Indian Foreign Policy in a Unipolar World*, 277–304.

[42] *Quadrennial Defense Review Report*, February 2010, 31.

[43] For India, "natural" partnership with the United States also fits with a pattern of diplomacy developed since the early 1990s. India identifies special bilateral relationships and "strategic partnerships" with many countries while aiming to give offense to none. "Special" or "strategic" relationships include Japan, European nations, and China, as well as the United States.

[44] For example, a senior U.S. official accompanying U.S. Secretary of State Condoleezza Rice on a 2006 trip to Asia acknowledged that beyond developing ties to India, strengthening U.S. ties to Australia and Japan was part of a policy aimed at China. Steven Weisman, "Rice Seeks to Balance China's Power," *The New York Times*, March 19, 2006.

[45] "Gates in India to Expand Security Ties," *New York Times*, February 28, 2008.

[46] According to Tellis, "The effort to build a new partnership with a rising India was shaped clearly by Bush's determination to consolidate U.S. primacy in the face of prospective geopolitical flux caused by new rising powers in Asia, such as China." Ashley Tellis, "The

Outline of the Book

U.S. policies toward India and China reflect American concerns with core security interests, America's alliance with Japan, and the struggle to combat terrorism and stabilize Afghanistan and Pakistan. Certainly, the challenge of Taiwan is a factor that places Sino-U.S. relations in a unique context, encouraging strategic thought, reflection, and critical analysis of China that have little parallel in American assessments of Indian strategic aims or international behavior.[47]

However, several other influential arguments in U.S. policy discourse about China and India also appear to underpin a sharpening divergence in U.S. policies toward the two rising powers in Asia. These propositions fall into two broad categories. First, China is seen as an outlier in its international strategic behavior. In assessments performed by U.S. scholars and policy makers, China's traditional political-military strategic culture, foreign policy, use of force, border settlement behavior, defense spending, military doctrine, force modernization programs, trade strategies, and pursuit of international energy resources have been singled out as particularly threatening or divergent from the strategic behavior of other states. In contrast, India's behavior in these areas is either underexamined or assumed to be favorable to U.S. interests. A second proposition is that India's democratic values and institutions will reduce conflicts of interest with the United States in these areas, whereas the opposite is true of China's authoritarian regime. Although Washington's approach toward each country may in fact have multiple motivations, these assessments have come to form a common language and interpretive baseline for U.S. Asia policy. They are also increasingly used to justify American action, both in debates among foreign policy elites and to the American public.

In the remainder of this book, we review U.S. assessments of Chinese behavior in several of the most important issue areas and undertake side-by-side comparisons of empirically observed Chinese and Indian behavior. Specifically, we examine questions related to Chinese and Indian strategic culture, use of force, military policy (including doctrine, budgets, and force structure), and foreign economic policy and competition for energy resources. These issues provide a wide cross-section of observable strategic behavior and a broad survey of areas where the United States may

Merits of Dehyphenation: Explaining U.S. Success in Engaging India and Pakistan," *The Washington Quarterly*, 31:4 (Autumn 2008), 21–42; quote on 24.

47 See Richard C. Bush and Michael E. O'Hanlon, *A War Like No Other: The Truth about China's Challenge to America* (New York: Wiley Press, 2007).

face challenges as China and India continue to develop in the twenty-first century. We also examine the utility of a theory of international politics – democratic peace theory – in making predictions about Chinese and Indian behavior.

In Chapter 2, we examine claims that China has unique cultural and strategic traditions that differentiate Chinese strategic preferences from those of other powers. Some see Chinese culture, with its long history and strong traditions, as a deeply powerful influence on modern Chinese strategy.[48] Western scholars and policy makers believe that lessons embodied in China's strategic culture, particularly in its classic texts, lead Chinese policy makers to view international politics in zero-sum terms and to develop aggressive foreign policies while justifying these as self-defense. However, there is little comparative context provided for these judgments. Are China's classical texts more influential in that nation's strategic thought than similar Indian texts are in India? Do the ideas embedded in the Chinese classics suggest the kinds of troubling behaviors outlined previously any more than the ideas found in classical Indian texts on strategy and politics?

In Chapter 3, we examine key elements of Chinese and Indian foreign policy. Some Western observers view China's foreign policy as relatively assertive.[49] China, it is claimed, uses force more frequently than other states, particularly with respect to its many border and territorial conflicts.[50] These assessments invite comparison and context. We examine the recent evolution of Chinese and Indian foreign policy and grand strategy and the two countries' use of force since the late 1940s. We also compare the Chinese and Indian record on resolving border disputes.

The next three chapters address the development of Chinese and Indian military power, starting in Chapter 4 with an assessment of defense

---

[48] Alastair Iain Johnston, *Cultural Realism: Strategic Culture and Grand Strategy in Chinese History* (Princeton: Princeton University Press, 1995); Andrew Scobell, "'Cult of Defense' and 'Great Power Dreams': The Influence of Strategic Culture on China's Relationship with India," in Michael R. Chambers, ed., *South Asia in 2020: Future Strategic Balances and Alliances* (Carlisle: U.S. Army War College, 2002), 329–384; William H. Mott, IV and Jae Chang Kim, *The Philosophy of Chinese Military Culture: Shih vs. Li* (New York: Palgrave MacMillan, 2006).

[49] See Samuel P. Huntington, *The Clash of Civilizations and the Remaking of World Order* (New York: Touchstone, 1996); John Mearsheimer, *The Tragedy of Great Power Politics* (New York: W.W. Norton, 2001).

[50] Larry M. Wortzel, "China's Foreign Conflicts Since 1949," in David Graff and Robin Higham, eds., *A Military History of China* (Boulder: Westview Press, 2002), 267–284; Andrew Scobell, *China's Use of Military Force: Beyond The Great Wall and the Long March* (New York: Cambridge University Press, 2003).

spending issues. A number of U.S. political leaders, military officers, and civilian scholars have criticized China for its defense budgets, which are said to be particularly nontransparent and growing rapidly.[51] We compare Chinese and Indian defense spending, describe the core elements of their respective budgets, and assess the spending of both as a share of GDP and as a percentage of total government spending. We also critically examine methods for estimating Chinese and Indian defense spending, including the use of purchasing power parity methods for converting local currency spending.

In Chapter 5, we trace the evolution of modern Chinese and Indian military doctrine. Chinese military doctrine developments have been closely followed by Western analysts in recent years, with many now arguing that Chinese military doctrine is distinctive in its growing emphasis on offensive action.[52] Indian military doctrine has been less well studied in Western countries. Our comparison includes land, naval, and air force doctrine.

Chapter 6 presents a side-by-side comparison of Chinese and Indian military force modernization, including the development of power projection capabilities.[53] Both U.S. government officials and influential scholars argue that these attributes of China's military development are distinctive and raise questions about whether China intends to challenge U.S. interests in areas other than Taiwan. Yet most studies of Chinese military modernization are not explicitly comparative.[54] We examine that growing power in

---

[51] See "Beijing Accelerates Its Military Spending," *New York Times*, March 5, 2007. For non-Defense Department assessments, see Christopher Griffin "China's Defense White Paper: What It Does (and Doesn't) Tell Us," *China Brief*, 7:2 (May 9, 2007); and Congressman Duncan Hunter, "A Congressional Perspective," statement at the Hearing on "China's Military Modernization and Its Impact on the United States and the Asia-Pacific," United States China Economic Security Review Commission, March 29–30, 2007.

[52] See *Military Power of the People's Republic of China: Annual Report to Congress* (Washington, DC: Office of the Secretary of Defense, 2009); and Robert G. Sutter, *Chinese Foreign Relations: Power and Policy since the Cold War* (New York: Rowman & Littlefield, 2008).

[53] See Robert Kaplan, "How We Would Fight China," *Atlantic Monthly*, June 2005. The Chinese military has become a focus for U.S. conventional war scenario planning, budgets, and procurement since the 1990s. In addition to official U.S. documents such as the 2006 *Quadrennial Defense Review*, see, for example, Michael O'Hanlon, *Defense Planning for the Late 1990s: Beyond the Desert Storm Framework* (Washington, DC: Brookings Institution, 1995); and Michael O'Hanlon, *Defense Policy Choices for the Bush Administration 2001–2005* (Washington, DC: Brookings Institution, 2001).

[54] See Richard D. Fisher, *China's Military Modernization: Building for Regional and Global Reach* (London: Praeger Security Press, 2008); Anthony H. Cordesman and Martin Klieber, *Chinese Military Modernization: Force Development and Strategic Capabilities* (Washington, DC: Center for Strategic and International Studies, 2007); and Peter Howarth, *China's Rising Sea Power: The PLA Navy's Submarine Challenge* (New York: Routledge Press,

comparative context of India's force modernization and considerable power projection capabilities.

In Chapter 7, we assess Chinese and Indian economic strategies and behavior and their impact on international markets. Many Western observers and political leaders see China as pursuing mercantilist economic policies and flaunting accepted norms of international behavior.[55] We examine Indian and Chinese trade and direct investment policies, as well as competition for international energy resources. We also review the activities of state-owned firms from both countries that invest in states governed by "rogue" regimes.

After conducting side-by-side empirical comparison of modern Chinese and Indian strategic behavior, in Chapter 8 we investigate the second broad proposition, namely whether there is any basis in international relations theory or in broad historical trends for expecting sharply divergent international behavior from democratic India and authoritarian China based on their different regime types. In one influential and widely accepted view, the fact that India and the United States are both democracies ensures that the two countries will not go to war against one another. This is the core argument of the "democratic peace theory."[56] However, an extension of that view is also becoming more popular and influential in policy circles: Shared democratic values help ensure that India will be a force for peace in Asia, and U.S. and Indian foreign policy goals will tend to converge.[57] In contrast, U.S. official statements and academic discourse

2006). On China's defense industry see, for example, Tai-Ming Cheung, *Fortifying China: The Struggle to Build a Modern Defense Economy* (Ithaca: Cornell University Press, 2009).

[55] A view of China as an outlier in its trade behavior and a threat to U.S. economic interests is reflected in both broad American public opinion and views in the U.S. Congress. See, for example, *2010 Report to Congress of the U.S.-China Economic Security Review Commission, One Hundred Eleventh Congress, Second Session* (Washington, DC: U.S.-China Economic and Security Review Commission, November 2010), as well as hearings and testimony available at http://www.uscc.gov. On China's role in international energy markets, see Deputy Secretary of State Robert B. Zoellick, "Wither China? From Membership to Responsibility," Speech at the National Committee on US-China Relations, New York, September 21, 2005. Senator Joseph I. Lieberman, "China-U.S. Energy Policies: A Choice of Cooperation or Collision – Remarks at Council on Foreign Relations" (Washington, DC: Council on Foreign Relations, November 30, 2005).

[56] Bill Clinton, "1994 State Of The Union Address," January 25, 1994.

[57] For a view of democracy as one basis for common U.S.-India interests from a former Clinton administration official, see Strobe Talbott, *Engaging India: Diplomacy, Democracy and the Bomb* (Washington, DC: Brookings Institution, 2004), 44–45. For the George W. Bush administration views on U.S.-India interests and democracy, see *Remarks by President Bush and Prime Minister Manmohan Singh of India in Joint Press Availability* (Washington, DC: The White House, Office of the Press Secretary, July 18, 2005). For

often claim that a lack of common democratic values and institutions between the United States and China will tend to drive Sino-U.S. relations toward conflict. To examine these arguments, we review the logic and the empirical evidence supporting democratic peace theory, both as a general proposition and as it may or may not apply to predicting Indian and Chinese behavior.

Finally, in Chapter 9, we summarize the findings of the study. Based on our empirical analysis and the challenge to many Western assumptions about both China and India as great powers, we offer several specific suggestions for U.S. policies toward each country and in Asia as a whole.

Enduring Questions

This book primarily aims to conduct a systematic empirical comparison of Indian and Chinese strategic behavior from the time of their respective modern foundings in 1947 and 1949 to the present. Nevertheless, the study and its results touch on a number of enduring questions for international relations theory and foreign policy. The first set of these are questions about power transition in the international system. The title of the book refers to one aspect of this problem: the difficulty leaders in a dominant state have judging not only the material capabilities of a rising power, but also its behavior and intentions. Alarm and expectations may affect judgments about gaps and trends in relative power on both sides.

Beyond describing the importance of shifts in the balance of power, theories of power transition have been weak in addressing other recurring questions. States do not set out to compete for an abstract title called "global hegemon." In light of this, when and how do the specific interests of a dominant power and a rising power come into conflict? One potential answer is their involvement in subregional disputes. But how does competition between great powers such as the United States, China, and India affect subregional security dynamics? In the concluding chapter, we suggest a new analytical framework for the study of subregional and cross-regional

general arguments about regime type and common or converging foreign policy interests among democracies, see Condoleezza Rice, "Rethinking the National Interest: American Realism for a New World," *Foreign Affairs*, 87:4 (July/August 2008): 2–26; Condoleezza Rice "The Promise of Democratic Peace," *The Washington Post*, December 11, 2005; and John McCain, "An Enduring Peace Built on Freedom: Securing America's Future," *Foreign Affairs*, 86:6 (November/December 2007): 19–34. This view is also popular in the U.S. Congress; see *Advance Democratic Values, Address Nondemocratic Countries, and Enhance Democracy Act of 2005*, 109th Congress, 1st Session, S. 516, March 3, 2005.

security dynamics – what we label "nested security dilemmas." Applied to regional case studies in Northeast Asia and South Asia, this framework permits us to examine how security dilemmas at different levels of the international system (global and subregional) interact.

For American leaders facing rising powers, policy questions emerge from these theoretical debates about how power transition proceeds. How do American actions, including the provision of security assistance to partners and allies in Asia, affect regional balances of power and stability? As China and India modernize their militaries, how can the United States preserve its own advantages in military power without exacerbating regional security competition and undermining crisis stability? What is the appropriate balance between seeking greater relative gains from trade and investment with the rising Asian powers on the one hand and promoting the greatest possible absolute benefits on the other? In a modern, globalized economy, how should relative gains be measured? Given the domestic challenges both India and China face, how can Washington best manage the volatility in both economic and security relations that domestic change in those countries is bound to engender?

A second group of perennial questions revolve around the relationship between various state-level variables and international behavior. Prominent among these is the debate over the connection between regime type and interstate behavior. We do not conduct formal theory testing, but Chapters 2 through 7 all provide comparative empirical evidence that addresses this question. The theory and logic underpinning arguments about regime type and interstate behavior are examined in Chapter 8.

Similar debates concern the effects of ideas on strategy and foreign policy. Chapter 2 explores debates about the relationship between strategic culture, which is sometimes said to be reflected in classical texts on strategy, and contemporary strategic behavior. Chapter 5 touches on the relationship between military doctrine (a set of ideas about how a military should fight) and military budgets and force structures, as well as the relationship between doctrine and the perceptions of other states. The results of the study buttress the case for a nuanced political realism, one that recognizes that differences in domestic regime type may influence international behavior in a variety of ways, but does not provide a simple or fixed guide to state interests or alignment.

A third set of questions bear on what will become an enduring American foreign policy debate in the twenty-first century. With two large, rapidly rising powers in Asia, what is the proper balance to strike in crafting bilateral policies toward each of them? Also, to what extent should the United

States base these policies on calculations of relative material power alone, as opposed to a broader calculus of the national interest? Of the two powers considered in this book, China's material capabilities are the more substantial. However, an excessive focus on the challenge from China could cause the United States to overlook other important challenges and opportunities. China and India are both substantial states, and the behaviors of both present challenges to U.S. interests (as discussed in Chapters 3, 5, 7, and 9). Opportunities for common interest and cooperation differ, but they are present in both U.S.-China and U.S.-India relations. The complex mix of common and conflicting interests the United States has with both powers raises questions about the practicability of a simple strategic approach to either one.

Finally, a fourth set of questions concerns what methods of analysis may best contribute to knowledge and understanding in international relations. Single-country and single-issue studies are valuable for their depth of analysis, but they also have important disadvantages. They often lead to the conclusion that the country under examination is an outlier in one or more dimensions when in fact its behavior may be little different from that of others. Single-country studies may also overstate the significance of change in a given state or its capabilities when the state's own past is used as the only point of reference. But if comparison is useful to provide perspective, how should it be done? The comparative framework we have built in this study is only one potential method, and we hope it will spur others to build on this structure or offer alternatives and improvements.

The primary purpose of this volume is to build a systematic empirical baseline against which to compare the strategic behavior of China and India. This book does not attempt to provide complete answers to all of the enduring questions posed immediately above. However, by conducting a careful empirical comparison of Chinese and Indian international behavior, the book aims to provide greater discipline and perspective to contemporary public debates about the significance of rising Chinese and Indian power for American interests.

2

Strategic Culture

Unique Paths to a Veiled *Realpolitik*

Some scholars argue that nations possess distinctive strategic cultures. Strategic culture is an inherited body of political-military concepts based on shared historical and social experience. Strategic culture may shape leaders' interpretation of international events, thereby producing certain preference orders regarding how and under what circumstances military force should be used. Many policy makers also appear to hold a set of images or perceptions about the behavior patterns of other states. These images amount to an understanding of the strategic cultures that shape the choices of their counterparts in other countries. These images and perceptions are often unexamined, yet they appear to exert a powerful effect in shaping leadership expectations.

Strategic culture is often seen as a product of unique lessons that are internalized by successive generations of leaders. This occurs primarily through their education in classic texts that embody a national political-military literary tradition. In this view, having learned these consistent lessons, leaders then form a set of relatively stable ideas about "how the world works." They also form stable preferences for strategic and military action.[1] Despite important theoretical and methodological challenges, the strategic culture approach is a potentially valuable complement to realist perspectives.[2] It

---

[1] The strategic culture approach has a number of logical and methodological problems, the most important of which is the difficulty in proving that state actions were actually a product of any particular belief held by any particular leader in any particular case. Despite these problems, there is utility in trying to gain a deeper and subtler understanding of leadership values and preference orders in other countries. Yet these logical and methodological limitations do caution against relying on this approach to derive strong conclusions about likely future behavior.

[2] By realism, we mean a view of international politics as politics primarily among nation-states which are concerned about their own security and act in pursuit of their own interests. In this view, states exist in an anarchic system in which they must rely on their own

helps build a better overall understanding of state behavior and foreign policy by drawing attention to cultural factors that may influence the logic of policy makers in other societies.

Chinese strategic culture has been the subject of much discussion and debate.[3] Some Chinese scholars believe that Chinese strategic culture is unique, with an emphasis on ethical and human factors in security, in contrast to a Western tradition that emphasizes material interests and military power.[4] In this view, China's strategic culture imparts a preference for nonviolent means of conflict resolution. Some Western scholars agree that China's strategic culture is unique, but reject the argument that it favors nonviolence. Alastair Iain Johnston detects a form of *realpolitik* in Chinese strategic culture, influencing Chinese leaders to view war as a central feature of interstate relations.[5]

Other prominent students of Chinese strategic culture argue that its traditions incline China toward the use of force and that its contemporary record of actual behavior supports this claim. Andrew Scobell, notable for the influence of his ideas on the subject within the U.S. security community,

---

efforts, or "self-help," to achieve security. Political realism also recognizes the propensity of states to maximize power. The literature on realism is rich and varied, but these are the core concepts that set realism apart from values-based views of international politics such as idealism or moralism.

[3] Examples of prominent work on this subject include Allen S. Whiting, *The Chinese Calculus of Deterrence: India and Vietnam* (Ann Arbor: University of Michigan Press, 1975); Mark Burles and Abram N. Shulsky, *Patterns in China's Use of Force: Evidence from History and Doctrinal Writings* (Santa Monica: RAND, 2000); Alastair Iain Johnston, *Cultural Realism: Strategic Culture and Grand Strategy in Chinese History* (Princeton: Princeton University Press, 1995); Allen S. Whiting, "China's Use of Force 1950–1996, and Taiwan," *International Security*, 26:2 (Fall 2001): 103–131; Larry M. Wortzel, "China's Foreign Conflicts Since 1949," in David Graff and Robin Higham, eds., *A Military History of China* (Boulder: Westview Press, 2002), 267–284; Andrew Scobell, *China's Use of Military Force: Beyond the Great Wall and the Long March* (New York: Cambridge University Press, 2003); and Andrew Scobell, "'Cult of Defense' and 'Great Power Dreams': The Influence of Strategic Culture on China's Relationship with India," in Michael R. Chambers, ed., *South Asia in 2020: Future Strategic Balances and Alliances* (Carlisle: U.S. Army War College, 2002), 329–384.

[4] Zhang Junbo and Yao Yunzhu, "Traditional Chinese Military Thinking: A Comparative Perspective," in Zhao Suisheng, ed., *Chinese Foreign Policy: Pragmatism and Strategic Behavior* (Armonk: M.E. Sharpe, 2004), 128–139.

[5] Johnston, *Cultural Realism*, 30; 107–108; 249. Johnston defines *realpolitik* as a view of interstate relations that argues that the best way to deal with security threats is to eliminate them through the use of force. This view does recognize that a state's capabilities relative to other states constitute an important factor limiting the implementation of such a strategy. However, if a state's leaders subscribe to *realpolitik* views, then as the state's relative capabilities grow it may be expected to act more coercively toward other states. Johnston, *Cultural Realism*, ix–xi.

has argued that strategic culture should be a significant dimension for study of contemporary Chinese security policy for two reasons. First, he argues that it has been recognized that culture affects the tendency to use force, and contemporary Chinese policy is heavily influenced by China's ancient and enduring civilization. Second, China has a "unique traditional philosophy."[6] In Scobell's view, the interaction between a Confucian strand (represented by the writing of Sun Zi) and a *realpolitik* tradition (represented by a variety of other classics) has produced a "Chinese Cult of Defense." This cult is a paradox: Chinese assumptions about the perennial justness of China's position increase China's propensity to use force by providing a "defensive" moral rationale for using force, even offensive force.[7]

Another interpretation of Chinese strategic culture also contends that the Chinese perspective "extends into antiquity" and affects today's policy choices, but this view sees Chinese cultural precepts as emphasizing duplicity and deception in competition between states.[8] Many Western military professionals and scholars appear to hold a fascination for close study of Chinese preferences for deception in war.[9] U.S. Department of Defense analyses have adopted the view that China's strategic culture and traditions may exert a powerful effect on its contemporary strategic decision making.[10]

---

[6] Andrew Scobell, "'Cult of Defense,'" in Michael R. Chambers, ed., *South Asia in 2020*, 2002, 329–384. In later work, Scobell has acknowledged theoretical challenges to the strategic culture approach, particularly in proving the existence of causal links between "mindset" and specific policy decisions. Scobell also allows that Chinese strategic culture may not be monolithic. Civilian and military mindsets may compete with and balance one another, and Chinese strategic culture is not entirely unique, having some features in common with other countries. See Andrew Scobell, "Soldiers, Statesmen, Strategic Culture, and China's 1950 Intervention in Korea," in Zhao Suisheng, ed., *Chinese Foreign Policy: Pragmatism and Strategic Behavior* (Armonk: M.E. Sharpe, 2004), 107–127; 118–120.

[7] Andrew Scobell, *China's Use of Military Force: Beyond the Great Wall and the Long March* (New York: Cambridge University Press, 2003), 15.

[8] William H. Mott IV and Jae Chang Kim, *The Philosophy of Chinese Military Culture*: Shih vs. Li (New York: Palgrave MacMillan, 2006), 8–14; and Thomas G. Mahnken, "Secrecy & Stratagem: Understanding Chinese Strategic Culture," Lowy Institute for International Policy, February 2011.

[9] See for example the United States Department of Defense annual report, *Military Power of the People's Republic of China*, various years 2002–2010; and Jan Van Tol et al, "AirSea Battle: A Point-of-Departure Operational Concept" (presentation slides), Center for Strategic and Budgetary Assessments, May 18, 2010, http://www.csbaonline.org/4Publications/PubLibrary/R.20100518.Slides_AirSea_Batt/R.20100518.Slides_AirSea_Batt.pdf. For an academic study with greater context and interpretation, see Ralph Sawyer, *The Tao of Deception: Unorthodox Warfare in Historic and Modern China* (New York: Basic Books, 2007).

[10] *The Military Power of the People's Republic of China* (Washington, DC: Office of the Secretary of Defense, 2008), 8.

In this chapter, we do not evaluate arguments that the strategic culture approach adequately explains either Chinese or Indian foreign policy or military action. Similarly, we note but generally leave aside objections to the strategic culture approach that are based on methodological issues. We focus instead on a different set of questions. First, does a comparison of key texts that underpin respective strategic cultures reveal sharply divergent Chinese and Indian traditions favoring the use of force, either offensive or defensive? Second, do the teachings of the most important Chinese or Indian texts provide any *prima facie* reason to believe that one or the other will better fit into U.S. visions of peace and prosperity in the Asian region?

Some of the experiences that form the bases for Indian and Chinese strategic thought are intriguingly parallel. Leaders in both countries are aware that India and China are the world's only two modern states that encompass civilizations largely within state borders. They both firmly believe their civilizations have produced some of the world's greatest scientific, philosophical, and political contributions. As a result, leaders in both countries believe their states have a moral role to play in world affairs. This is an ideational element of foreign policy that has risen and fallen in importance over time but never entirely disappeared. The moralism that runs through the philosophical, religious, and political traditions in both civilizations veils the martial and strategic teaching in both cultures. Foreign observers are often surprised to discover the extent to which both Chinese and Indian thinkers have given thought to the use of deception and violence in pursuit of power. Both civilizations produced outstanding early treatises on the conduct of international relations that were, despite important differences, essentially realist in outlook. Both civilizations suffered prolonged defeat and humiliation at the hands of "foreign invaders." In modern times, this meant Western imperial powers. This may have heightened what were already strong realist tendencies to fear internal chaos and vulnerability, dependence on external powers, and foreign manipulation of internal weakness.

Indian Classic Texts

Indian philosophical traditions are remarkably eclectic. This diversity is a source of Indian civilizational strength.[11] Ancient Buddhist texts, as well

---

[11] Sarvepalli Radhakrishnan and Charles A. Moore, eds., *A Sourcebook in Indian Philosophy* (Princeton: Princeton University Press, 1957). This work is designed for Western students and contains substantial excerpts from most of the classic Indian works in philosophy,

as modern Buddhism and Jainism, strongly influenced Indian leaders including Gandhi and Nehru. The themes of idealism, restraint, and tolerance found in the Buddhist and Jainist traditions are part of a complex weave of influences on modern Indian politics.[12] Yet in security and foreign policy, the most influential strain of Indian political philosophy evokes realist principles.

Kautilya's *Arthashastra* (variously translated as "science of politics" or "treatise on polity") is acknowledged by Indian scholars as the most important ancient Indian text on strategy.[13] Kautilya is still an inspiration to modern Indian strategic and military thought.[14] The *Arthashastra*, like many of the classic Chinese texts, is a complex and subtle work, and as such is vulnerable to selective reading and interpretation. Moreover, the *Arthashastra* does not form the whole of Indian strategic tradition – there exists a more violent, less compromising tradition as well. Whereas the *Arthashastra* emphasizes both political flexibility and military mobility, an older tradition represented by another Indian classic text, the *Mahabharata*, emphasizes annihilation of the enemy through systematic attrition.[15] In the view of one former Indian military officer, the *Mahabharata* continues to have relevance for modern mechanized combat, and its focus on

including Vedic and epic texts, as well as Buddhist and Jainist works. For a modern history that brings together interconnections of Indian ideals and their impact on today's Indian society, see Ramachandra Guha, *India after Gandhi: The History of the World's Largest Democracy* (New York: Harper Collins, 2007).

[12] See Stephen P. Cohen, *Emerging Power: India* (Washington DC: Brookings Institute, 2001).

[13] Some scholars use the English spelling "Arthasastra." Kautilya, *Arthashastra*, translated by L. N. Rangarajan (New Delhi: Penguin Books, 1987). Kautilya, also referred to as Vishnugupta, is commonly said to have been an advisor to the Magaha king Chandragupta in the fourth century B.C. Some scholars challenge the date of Kautilya's work but none place it later than 150 A.D. See also I. W. Mabbett, "The Date of the Arthasastra," *Journal of the American Oriental Society*, 84:2 (April 1965): 162–169. All references to the *Arthashastra* in this book are from the 1987 Rangarajan translation.

[14] See for example, Subrata Mitra, "Engaging the World: the Ambiguity of India's Power," in Subrata Mitra and Bernd Rill, eds., *India's New Dynamics of Foreign Policy* (Munich: Hanns Seidel Foundation, 2006), 18–19; and Manjeet Singh Pardesi, "Deducing Indian's Grand Strategy of Regional Hegemony from Historical and Conceptual Perspectives," Institute of Strategic and Defense Studies, Singapore, April 2005, http://dr.ntu.edu.sg/handle/10220/4475. One of India's best-known strategic thinkers, Kanti Bajpai, refers to "good old Kautilya" as an essential tool for analyzing Indian foreign policy. Kanti Bajpai, "Nuclear Policy, Grand Strategy, and Political Values in India." Seventeenth P.C. Lal Memorial Lecture, New Delhi, February 18, 2000, http://www.ceri-sciences-po.org/archive/jan01/nuclear.pdf.

[15] Some Indian scholars trace the origins of the *Mahabharata* as far back as 1,500 years ago; authorship is usually attributed to "Vyasa," a possibly mythical or historically composite sage.

force-on-force attrition warfare still informs elements of modern Indian Army doctrine.[16]

Some of the classic Indian teachings on strategy might surprise those accustomed to images of a democratic, inclusive, peaceful modern India. These include teachings in the *Arthashastra* on pursuit of power through *realpolitik*, the recommended use of offensive force, deception, treachery, assassination, and deceit, and the view that conquest and the establishment of hegemony is the proper policy of the "good" leader. These teachings are the equal of any of the most worrisome lessons discovered in Sun Zi's *Art of War* or any other Chinese text on strategy.

Power, according to the *Arthashastra*, is the object of interstate relations, and "dissension and force" are the natural state of international relations.[17] Power is relative and must be maximized both in absolute and relative terms, for survival and success.[18] There is a clear *realpolitik* in Kautilya, as well as an "offensive doctrine."

In this sense, the *Arthashastra* is similar to realist interpretations of *The Art of War* and the texts that inform the Chinese strategic culture tradition.[19] Indeed, in the view of some Western scholars, Kautilya offered his treatise as a science of world conquest. According to this interpretation, one either conquers or suffers conquest. According to Roger Boesche, "[Kautilya] did not say to himself, 'Prepare for war, but hope for peace,' but instead, 'Prepare for war, and plan for conquest.'"[20] As far as the means to that end, Kautilya's advocacy of making treaties while planning to break them, as well as recommending the use of spies and secret agents to assassinate enemy leaders, led Max Weber to label the *Arthashastra* "Truly radical 'Machiavellianism,' in the popular sense of the word .... Compared to it, Machiavelli's *The Prince* is harmless."[21] On a first reading, there is little in the core text of Indian strategic thought that might clearly differentiate it from a *realpolitik* Chinese strategic culture.

With the observations of Boesche and Weber on Kautilya, however, another similarity in studies of Chinese and Indian strategic culture is evident. This is the tendency of many Western observers to engage in selective reading and citation of these works. This leads some to focus on the worst

---

[16] G. D. Bakshi, *The Indian Art of War: The Mahabharata Paradigm (Quest for an Indian Strategic Culture)* (New Delhi: Sharada Press, 2002).

[17] Roger Boesche, "Kautilya's *Arthasastra* on War and Diplomacy in Ancient India," *The Journal of Military History*, 67:1 (January 2003): 9–37.

[18] Rangarajan, *Arthashastra*, 543; also verses {6.2.30–34; 7.1.20–22; 7.1.2–19}.

[19] Rangarajan, *Arthashastra*, 15; 34; 546; 552–554; also verse {6.2.13}.

[20] Boesche, "Kautilya's *Arthasastra*," 19.

[21] Cited in Boesche, "Kautilya's *Arthasastra*," 9.

in the classic texts and to overlook their subtle and not-so-subtle warnings about the dangers of war and the need for prosperity, good governance, and legitimate rule to maintain power.[22]

Perhaps the most commonly cited idea from Kautilya is the concept of *mandalas*, or circles. Those closer in the circle, on the borders of the state, will be enemies. Those farther away will be allies. This discussion of natural enemies and natural allies has led some to interpret Kautilya's work as consistent with balance-of-power politics (or defensive realism). This interpretation is overly mechanistic, however. Kautilya's idea of concentric circles is not meant to be one of fixed geographic relationships. Rather, for Kautilya, *mandalas* apply to relationships of power, influence, and interest, not only geographic proximity.[23] Relationships are not so fixed that all border states must be enemies, although Kautilya believed that bordering states were more likely to be enemies or objects of conquest than not. In contrast to Sun Zi, Kautilya explicitly advocates conquest and holds the opinion that the best leader is a "conqueror" who actively seeks to maximize power at all times, and who also constantly prepares for war either actively or passively.[24]

However, Kautilya counsels on matters broader than war alone. He also notes that war is dangerous and uncertain, and that if there is no prospect of one's decline relative to an enemy, then peace (while continuing to maximize prosperity and the fruits of recent conquest) is preferable to war.[25] Furthermore, generating and sustaining wealth and political legitimacy are also critical.[26] Kautilya was deeply concerned with the moral quality of leaders, the welfare of the people, justice, and the legitimacy of the regime.[27] In his view, justice and legitimacy in foreign policy, as well as military prowess, were necessary for a leader's success.[28]

In the United States, only a handful of scholars have studied India's classic texts and the social factors that have contributed to modern Indian strategic

---

[22] Boesche's reading of Kautilya is in this case matched to popular misunderstanding of Machiavelli. On Kautilya, see "Introduction" in Rangarajan, 1987. On Machiavelli, see Leo Strauss, *Thoughts on Machiavelli* (Chicago: University of Chicago Press, 1958); and Leo Strauss, "Machiavelli," in Leo Strauss and Joseph Cropsey, eds., *History of Political Philosophy* (Chicago: University of Chicago Press, 3rd edition, 1987).

[23] Rangarajan, *Arthashastra*, 542.

[24] Rangarajan, *Arthashastra*, verses {6.2.13–14; 6.2.30–38; 7.1.2–37; 7.2.1–5}.

[25] Rangarajan, *Arthashastra*, 547; also verses {12.1.1–9; 7.2.1–2; 7.5.13–20}.

[26] Rangarajan, *Arthashastra*, 14; also verses {2.1.16; 7.5.27}.

[27] Rangarajan, *Arthashastra*, 36–38; also verses {1.17.30–37; 1.10.17–22; 3.18.5; 3.19.4; 4.8.11; 9.4.26}

[28] Rangarajan, *Arthashastra*, 37; also verses {7.3.12; 7.5.16–18; 7.13.11–12; 7.16.17–28; 11.1.56; 13.5.3–15}.

culture.[29] Western scholarship on Indian strategic culture has influenced security discourse in India, but it has had relatively little effect on policy debates in Washington. In contrast, the more voluminous Western studies of China's strategic culture have had much greater influence on policy debates in the United States and other Western countries.[30]

Chinese Classic Texts

In the United States, much of the strategic culture literature has focused on China. In the case of China, U.S. scholars point to the lessons of classic texts, as well as to China's historical experience, and argue that these have produced a unique Chinese preference for *realpolitik*, the use of offensive force or coercive diplomacy, and a dangerous tendency to justify the use of force as purely defensive.

Support for these views can be found in China's classic texts on strategy and in China's military historical record. However, as with studies of classic Indian texts, the discovery of supporting evidence in some passages does not necessarily provide a complete or balanced view of the work as a whole.

---

[29] One of the most influential views on modern Indian strategic culture is George Tanham's 1992 essay, "Indian Strategic Thought: An Interpretive Essay." This essay and a number of responses to it by Indian strategists are contained in Kanti P. Bajpai and Amitabh Mattoo, eds., *Securing India, Strategic Thought and Practice: Essays by George K. Tanham with Commentaries* (New Delhi: Manohar Publishers, 1996). See also Stephen P. Cohen, *Emerging Power: India* (Washington, DC: Brookings Institute, 2001), 146–155. In addition to covering philosophical and cultural influences, Cohen's book also tracks shifts in Indian strategic thought and orientation, both in response to changing international circumstances and changes in domestic politics. For an Indian view that notes some ways in which Indian strategic culture may pose challenges to closer U.S.-India strategic alignment, see Kanti Bajpai, "Indian Strategic Culture," in Michael R. Chambers, ed., *South Asia in 2020: Future Strategic Balances and Alliances* (Carlisle: U.S. Army War College, 2002), 245–303.

[30] Work by Tanham, Cohen, and other foreign scholars has influenced Indian thinking, triggering a wave of Indian writing on strategy and grand strategy in the 1990s. However, neither Tanham's work on Indian strategic culture nor the Indian responses to it have been as theoretically or methodologically rigorous as the Western scholarship on Chinese strategic culture. Moreover, in contrast to the excellent work of several students of Allen Whiting, who have improved both theory and methodology for assessing Chinese strategic culture, there has been relatively little influential scholarship and policy work that has built directly on Tanham's essay. Nor has Tanham's work or its legacy had as much influence among U.S. defense planners. Some introductory studies have been done for U.S. government agencies. See, for example, Rodney W. Jones, "Indian Strategic Culture," Science Applications International Corporation, October 31, 2006, http://www.fas.org/irp/agency/dod/dtra/india.pdf. Whereas the Pentagon now bases its analysis of Chinese power and intentions at least partly on an examination of China's strategic culture and traditions, similar analysis of India has not penetrated into public policy or official statements.

Although many studies of Chinese strategic culture have revealed valuable insights, there has been a tendency within the analytical literature to overlook elements in the same original texts that warn of the dangers of war and stress the need for legitimate governance and benevolent domestic policy.

Sun Zi's *The Art of War* is the first, as well as the most influential and widely read, of China's "Seven Military Classics." Written in the sixth century, *The Art of War*, like the *Arthashastra*, emphasizes the role of military force in international relations: "Warfare is the greatest affair of state," the treatise begins, "the basis of life and death, the Way (Tao) to survival or extinction."[31] Several points about *The Art of War* are frequently noted. First, the text appears to suggest ambivalence about employing violence. "One who excels at employing the military," Sun Zi says, "subjugates other people's armies without engaging in battle."[32] "No country," he adds, "has ever profited from protracted fighting."[33] Second, Sun Zi places emphasis on stratagem or deception. "Warfare is the Way (Tao) of deception," he writes.[34] Finally, Sun Zi offers hope for the materially inferior to defeat a superior enemy by, among other things, assuming a posture of strategic defense.

As Alastair Iain Johnston has noted, the relative importance of these aspects of Sun Zi's writing – and similar themes in the other texts of the "Seven Military Classics" – has been exaggerated by contemporary scholars. Sun Zi's text is about war. Its notions of stratagem appear designed to support other war operations. And passages clearly suggest that, all things being equal, victory in battle goes to the big battalions. Nevertheless, if Sun Zi is a realist, he is, to borrow Johnston's phrase, a "prudent realist." Most importantly, according to Johnston, Sun Zi's modern Chinese descendants have themselves focused on the *realpolitik* side of his teaching.[35]

However, as Ralph Sawyer has shown, no single text can be said to encompass all of Chinese military and strategic thought.[36] This same complexity

---

[31] Sun Tzu, *The Art of War*, translated by Ralph Sawyer (New York: Basic Books, 1994), 167. For students who wish to study the text in original Chinese with side-by-side English translation and commentary, see Sun Tzu, *The Art of War*, translated by Roger Ames (New York: Ballantine Books, 1993). Another side-by-side Chinese-English translation and commentary (first published in 1910) is Lionel Giles, *Sun Tzu on The Art of War: The Oldest Military Treatise in the World* (Toronto: Global Language Press, 2007). All references to *The Art of War* in this book are from the 1994 Sawyer translation.

[32] Sawyer, *The Art of War*, 177.

[33] Sawyer, *The Art of War*, 173.

[34] Sawyer, *The Art of War*, 168.

[35] Johnston, *Cultural Realism*, 248–266.

[36] Ralph D. Sawyer, "Military Writings," in David Graff and Robin Higham, eds., *A Military History of China* (Boulder: Westview Press, 2002), 97–114.

applies to India as well, with its interweave of idealist (Buddhism) and realist (Kautilya, Vyasa) traditions. For China, although *The Art of War* is the best known of Chinese texts on strategy, there are other highly influential texts and traditions as well, including *Wu Zi* (Teachings of Wu Qi), *Sima Fa* (The Minister of War's Methods), *Wei Liao Zi* (Teachings of Wei Liao), *Tai Gong Liu Tao* (Six Secret Teachings of Tai Gong, or Lu Shang), *Huangshi Gong Sanlue* (Three Strategies of the Duke of Yellow Rock), *Tang Taizong Li Weigong Wendui* (Dialogue of Tang Taizong and Li Weigong), and *Sun Bin Bing Fa* (Sun Bin's Art of War).

Even within Sun Zi's *The Art of War*, there are more than simply questions of how best to fight and win. As Johnston and others have noted, *The Art of War* focuses on fighting and *realpolitik* as they are popularly understood. Yet fundamental political questions about the risks and purposes of war are also important topics. Before Sun Zi offers his famous prescriptions for offensive operations and deception, he offers his first lesson: War is dangerous and risky for all, including for any leader who might initiate it. Therefore, war should not be undertaken lightly.[37] This lesson in caution is not frequently highlighted in Western reviews of Chinese strategic culture.

Other Chinese texts build on the political lessons that underpin sound military strategy and reveal the depth of Chinese strategic culture. The *Wu Zi* teaches that good government, including benevolent policies toward the people, is essential to maintaining power and building military strength.[38] In addition to emphasizing the importance of maintaining a prosperous and well-governed state, the *Wu Zi* teaches that military success requires institutional capabilities, such as systems for selecting qualified generals, sound organization, training, and a system of legitimate military discipline.

Matters of good governance and legitimacy are even more central in the *Sima Fa*. As in Western writings, the *Sima Fa* notes that power hierarchies and order are established through violence and killing, but it also notes that violence must only be applied in limited circumstances, and the use of force must be morally and politically legitimate.[39] Furthermore, the *Sima Fa* advises that the civil and military realms must be kept separate, and that the prosperity of the people is paramount. The *Wei Liao Zi* and the *Tang*

---

[37] This most basic, most conservative, and cautionary lesson is also taught by Kautilya. In the Western tradition, it is also taught by Clausewitz. See Carl Von Clausewitz, *On War*, translated and edited by Michael Howard and Peter Paret (Princeton: Princeton University Press, 1989), 86–87; 101; 104; 119–121; 259–260.

[38] Ralph Sawyer notes that the *Wu Zi* is considered an essential complement to the Sun Zi *Bing Fa*. See Sawyer, "Military Writings," 97–114.

[39] Sawyer, "Military Writings," 102.

Taizong Liu Tao also stress the need for benevolent policies toward the people and the notion that prosperity is the basis for military power, although these last two also teach that benevolent government must be backed by ruthless law enforcement.[40]

These examples are not intended as evidence that Chinese strategic traditions are morally superior, or that Chinese military thought is benign. Rather, they shed light on the larger literature that forms the core of Chinese strategic tradition beyond *The Art of War*. The Chinese political philosophy and strategic tradition – and the strategic culture to which it may give rise – is more subtle and balanced than is often claimed to be the case. In short, any Chinese political or military leader familiar with the operational utility of offensive action, psychological warfare, and deception from reading *The Art of War* is likely to also have read Sun Zi's cautionary points about the dangers of war. Likewise, a Chinese leader exposed to other classic texts on politics and strategy would also have absorbed lessons about the importance of prosperity and popular welfare, good government and benevolence, and the need for legitimacy in civil and military policy. Further, like their Indian counterparts, modern Chinese strategists and military officers have also been exposed to Western thought on strategy and war, including notions of balances of power, security dilemmas, deterrence, arms racing, and neoliberal views on the role of institutions and cooperation in international politics.

Conclusions: A Common, Veiled *Realpolitik*

Much can be learned from the study of strategic culture. However, caution is called for in predicting specific contemporary policy decisions based on a purported direct link with cultural traditions. It is difficult, if not impossible, to prove a causal link between a particular strategic culture, thought, or set of preferences and an actual action by state leaders.

All of this raises questions about arguments that emphasize direct links between culture and policy decisions (or patterns of decisions). There is, firstly, little reason to assume direct influence between a reading of a classic text and a contemporary leader's specific decision on any one particular issue. Any particular decision may be strongly influenced by material as well as moral concerns, and it is difficult to separate the relative causal influence of these considerations. This problem applies even when explaining history with the aid of leaders' own memoirs, to say nothing of attempts to predict future behavior. This is a basic difficulty in employing a strategic

---

[40] Sawyer, "Military Writings," 106–107.

culture approach in crafting any particular policy response to either China or India. Further, each reader brings to any text his or her own biases conditioned by other elements of educational background, experience, and daily pressures and interests. No good student takes away the lessons of a text in unvarnished, uninterpreted form.

The most popular and widely cited literature on strategic culture often seems to assume a lack of critical distance between Chinese and Indian readers and their indigenous classic core texts. Yet the vast and varied body of political philosophy literature in China and India belies such an assumption. Even more fundamentally, it is largely unknowable which texts a nation's leaders have read, which lessons from these texts they have absorbed and integrated into their thinking, and how and under what circumstances specific lessons would be applied. Furthermore, the penchant in Western analyses to prioritize certain texts deemed canonical to strategic culture (e.g., *The Art of War*) is misleading when read against the larger body of literature that informs the broader culture. Even if the area of study is limited to the culture of strategy alone, more than one text or teaching plays an important role in rich civilizations such as India and China.

The role of core texts as building blocks of strategic thinking should be put in perspective. Ideas contained in classic texts bear weight within each cultural context by virtue of their historical prestige and broad recognition. This may be particularly true in China and India, both countries with abundant literary traditions regularly cited by leaders as sources of national pride.

Leaving methodological questions about the link between cultural influence and modern policy decisions aside, our comparison of the classic Chinese and Indian teachings on the risks and rewards of using force offers scant support for the view that among nations, China's leaders will be uniquely committed to seizing the initiative and using offensive force. Nor does comparison of the classic Chinese and Indian texts on strategy reveal a Chinese traditional culture that is a stronger advocate of conquest, or offensive realism, than the Indian tradition. Indeed, the Chinese and Indian classic texts have much in common, including depth of thought on legitimacy, justice, and the risks of war that are often overlooked by Western analysts. Nothing in the ancient texts that supposedly underpin modern strategic culture justifies sharply divergent expectations about Chinese and Indian international behavior.

A more cautious analytical approach would be to grasp the range of ideas contained in core texts and to assess the ways in which these ideas are employed rhetorically and materially in present-day discussions of strategy. Because strategic culture is thought to be founded on lessons from classic texts, the selection and interpretation of the texts to be studied is a critical step. Even where classic texts are taught to prospective leaders, it is likely that in some curricula they are presented in abridged or interpretive versions. Across generations, interpretations of lessons learned from classic are revised. The classics themselves are embedded in complex literary traditions – no single text is the final authority on all questions.

Although beyond the scope of this study, further research on strategic culture should take an explicitly comparative approach rather than rely primarily on translation and assessment of one or a few texts within a single cultural tradition. Analysis and especially recommendations for U.S. policy should take into account the modern educational curricula and experiences that affect the "world view" of current Indian and Chinese political leaders. Scholars, military officers, and strategists in China and India may actually be imbibing and paying heed to modern Western literature on international relations and strategy – in some cases perhaps more so than their own respective classic texts. Some versions of Western thought on international relations such as offensive realism may be much more worrisome than the layered, more subtle views in classic texts of either Indian or Chinese origin.

Yet even a survey broadened to consider the popularity of foreign works is not sufficient to establish that these works themselves will have a decisive effect on actual policies and decisions. Consider the recent popularity in both India and in China of Alfred Thayer Mahan's ideas on maritime strategy, summarized in his 1890 book, *The Influence of Sea Power Upon History, 1660–1805*.[41] It is not clear that the "turn to Mahan" in scholarship in either country has been translated directly into decisions about how to actually employ naval forces. Moreover, although the Western focus has been on China, it is difficult to find references to Mahan in prominent Chinese official documents. References to Mahan appear in Indian official documents justifying budgets and missions with comparative frequency.[42]

---

[41] See James R. Holmes and Toshi Yoshihara, *Chinese Naval Strategy in the 21st Century: The Turn to Mahan* (New York: Routledge, 2009); and James R. Holmes and Toshi Yoshihara, *Asia Looks Seaward: Power and Maritime Strategy* (New York: Routledge, 2008).

[42] See *Freedom to Use the Seas: India's Maritime Military Strategy* (New Delhi: Integrated Headquarters, Ministry of Defence [Navy], May 2007). On India's official maritime doctrine, see Vijay Sakhuja, "Indian Navy: Keeping Pace with Emerging Challenges," in Lawrence W. Prabhakar, Joshua H. Ho, and W. S. G. Bateman, eds., *The Evolving Maritime Balance of Power in the Asia-Pacific: Maritime Doctrines and Nuclear Weapons at Sea* (Singapore: World Scientific Publishing Company, 2006), 95–116.

More importantly, Mahan must compete with other influential thought. For example, many strategists in China and in India may implicitly or explicitly understand the limits to Mahanian thinking, including the centrality of the "heartland" for continent-sized land powers. These lessons may be available from domestic writings, national experience, or from study of Halford Mackinder's 1904 paper to the Royal Geographical Society, "The Geographical Pivot of History." In other words, the citation of a classic text in scholarly work is not evidence that *leaders* are reading these writings, to say nothing of whether leaders are making decisions based on lessons from this text. Evidence of a discourse on one body of thought, such as Mahan's, does not rule out that both scholars and leaders have been influenced by other factors or other texts, such as Mackinder's.[43]

Thus, any American strategist that would base U.S. policy on assumptions about Chinese or Indian intentions derived from a reading of strategic culture faces difficult problems of judgment about the influence of particular ideas on strategy and action. To put this in perspective, we might consider what lessons a non-Western observer might glean about potential future U.S. patterns of use of force from reading a single Western text – or even a handful of sources as disparate as Thucydides, Machiavelli, Kant, Clausewitz, Mahan, and Mackinder.

The Chinese and Indian strategic traditions are unique in origin and detail. Yet comparison of the core texts does not indicate that either country has a strategic tradition or culture that would lead one to be significantly more prone to aggression, conquest, or peace than the other. Despite the veil cast by the moralist traditions in each culture that support peace and harmony, each also has strong cultural traditions that are in line with realist views. These include appreciation of interstate relations as anarchic systems based on self-help and the propensity of states to maximize power. Core texts in both traditions contain passages that recommend the use of overwhelming offensive force in the event that force must be used.

In each tradition, there is recognition of the utility of deception and a *realpolitik* approach to dealing with enemies.[44] In each tradition, this

---

[43] Although Mahan may perhaps be popular among scholars of maritime issues, strategists will do well to explore other potential influences on strategic thinking, including Mackinder. See Paul Kennedy, "Mahan vs. Mackinder," in *The Rise and Fall of British Naval Mastery* (Amherst: Humanity Books, 3rd edition, 2006), 177–202.

[44] Regard for deception is not limited to the Orient. Students of classical Western strategy and military history will be aware of the numerous deceptions Themistocles used to save the Greeks at the battle of Salamis. A modern Western example is found in the extraordinary deception effort undertaken by the United States and Britain against Germany in World War II. See Robert B. Strassler, ed., *The Landmark Herodotus: The Histories*

pragmatism toward the use of force and treachery is balanced by equally pragmatic warnings about the need for caution, including the inherent dangers of resorting to force, and the need for legitimate governance, benevolent rule, and general prosperity. These observations in themselves offer good grounds to doubt unambiguous conclusions about unique preferences for action derived from a review of strategic thought and culture. Yet what of the historical track record of foreign policy and the actual use of force?

(New York: Random House, 2007), {Verses 8–58 to 8–109}, 623–647. Barry Strauss, *The Battle of Salamis: The Naval Encounter That Saved Greece – and Western Civilization* (New York: Simon and Schuster, 2004), 109–123; Anthony Cave Brown, *Bodyguard of Lies: The Extraordinary True Story Behind D-Day* (New York: Harper and Row, 1975); William Stevenson, *A Man Called Intrepid: The Secret War* (New York: Harcourt Brace Jovanovich, 1976).

3

Foreign Policy, Use of Force,
and Border Settlements

Some assessments of Chinese foreign policy argue that China's strategic culture inculcates aggression, leading China toward assertive foreign policies, including the use of force. As the preceding chapter indicates, however, when compared to core texts that may shape Indian strategic thought, the Chinese classics on strategic thinking appear less unique. In this chapter, we examine the two countries' foreign policy trajectories, their use of force, and their record of border conflict and settlements. This will provide further comparative context for making judgments about Chinese and Indian international strategic behavior.

In many influential studies of Chinese foreign policy, judgments have already been made. Some scholars believe the People's Republic of China (PRC), like its imperial predecessor, uses force "frequently," with the implication that this means China uses force more frequently than other states.[1] In this view, using force is a primary – perhaps preferred – Chinese method for conducting international politics.[2] Another view argues that Chinese security policy is characterized by a "cult of defense," which causes Chinese leaders to rationalize the use of offensive force as being purely defensive and increases the chances that China will be involved in future war.[3]

These views are not limited to students of Chinese military history. One widely read textbook on Chinese foreign policy argues that the Chinese government has resorted to the use of force in international affairs more frequently than other governments in the modern period.[4] A seminal work

---

[1] Larry M. Wortzel, "China's Foreign Conflicts Since 1949," in David Graff and Robin Higham, eds., *A Military History of China* (Boulder: Westview Press, 2002), 270.

[2] Wortzel, "China's Foreign Conflicts Since 1949," 282.

[3] Andrew Scobell, *China's Use of Military Force: Beyond the Great Wall and the Long March* (New York: Cambridge University Press, 2003), 15.

[4] Robert G. Sutter, *Chinese Foreign Relations: Power and Policy since The Cold War* (Lanham: Rowman & Littlefield, 2008), 137.

on Chinese grand strategy found that China has used force "frequently" and that "the use of force is endemic in Chinese history" over the period between 618 A.D. and 1911.[5] Samuel Huntington saw Chinese foreign policy becoming more assertive over time, driven in part by a clash of interests with Western and other Asian powers and in part by a clash of cultures and values.[6] John Mearsheimer holds that China is becoming more assertive as its power grows. Given rising Chinese power and the anarchic structure of international politics, he argues, China and the United States are on an inevitable collision course for superpower conflict.[7]

Yet by their very strength and conviction, these conclusions invite comparison of the Chinese experience to that of other states. Most large modern states – for example, the United States, Russia, and Germany – are also the product of hundreds of years of armed conflict. Indeed, one theory of why the modern nation state, armed with modern technology, emerged in the West and not elsewhere highlights the incentives created by perennial interstate warfare in Europe.[8] One might simply respond to arguments that China has used force "frequently" with an argument that war is frequent and endemic to the history of all states, especially large states.[9] This would take things to the opposite extreme, arguing that China's patterns of foreign policy and use of force are indistinguishable from those of others.

Instead, comparison to the behavior of other states in similar circumstances will make analysis and judgments about China's foreign policy patterns more useful. Although in recent years India has fallen behind China in terms of its relative power, especially economic power, India remains a good point of "peer" comparison for China in regard to foreign policy and use of force.

---

[5] Michael Swaine and Ashley Tellis, *Interpreting China's Grand Strategy: Past, Present, and Future* (Santa Monica: RAND, 2000), 45–65. Swaine and Tellis believe that China's material and political interests, not cultural factors, determine its use of force. Swaine and Tellis are careful to note that China's use of force has been "pragmatic and limited" and primarily restricted to its immediate periphery. They also note that historically, China's use of force was concentrated in the early period of the consolidation of new regimes.

[6] Samuel P. Huntington, *The Clash of Civilizations and the Remaking of World Order* (New York: Touchstone, 1996), 168–174; 218–238; 312–315.

[7] John Mearsheimer, *The Tragedy of Great Power Politics* (New York: W.W. Norton, 2001), 375–376; 401–402.

[8] Charles Tilly, *Coercion, Capital, and European States: 990–1992* (Oxford: Blackwell Publishers, 1990).

[9] For an argument that reduces the origin and legitimacy of all modern states to war and the ability to conduct war, see Philip Bobbit, *The Shield of Achilles: War, Peace, and the Course of History* (New York: Random House, 2002).

India is a developing country with a large, diverse population and long borders with many states (six, compared to China's fourteen).[10] Like China, India underwent a violent period around the time of its modern founding in the late 1940s. As with the early years after the founding of the People's Republic of China (PRC), modern India's founding was followed by a period of consolidation of regime power and sometimes sharp adjustment of relations with traditional tributary states and neighbors. Like China, India has been largely a regional power, which differentiates both countries from the United States and the former Soviet Union, superpowers with global interests that drew them into a variety of conflicts. A comparison of Chinese and Indian foreign policies, frequency of using force, and track record of border dispute settlement helps put the strategic behavior of both countries in perspective.

We first present an overview of Chinese and Indian strategic and foreign policy trends since the late 1940s. We then relate these broad foreign policy trajectories to the specific case of Chinese and Indian strategic relationships with United States. In the third section, we compare the two countries' use of force, assessing both the frequency with which the two have used force and the terms on which they have done so. In the final section, we examine the efforts Beijing and New Delhi have made to resolve their respective boundary disputes.

Foreign Policy Trajectories: The Rise of the Preoccupied Powers

Grand strategies and the strategic thought that inform major foreign policy trends are "sticky" and do not change easily. The factors that could produce fundamental shifts in Indian and Chinese foreign policy are themselves relatively resistant to frequent change. These factors include the structure of the international system (currently characterized by a single superpower and a globally integrated economy) and essential political and economic conditions within China and India. Although the core of grand strategy and foreign policy is, like a nation's core interests, resistant to change, national direction is clearly not immune to evolution and adjustment. Even where basic tenets of strategic thought remain relatively stable, foreign policy

---

[10] India has a 14,103-km land border with six countries. See Central Intelligence Agency, *CIA World Factbook*, https://www.cia.gov/library/publications/the-world-factbook/geos/in.html. China has a 22,117-km land border with fourteen different countries: (ibid., https://www.cia.gov/library/publications/the-world-factbook/geos/ch.html).

application and emphasis evolve in step with changes in international circumstances. Thus, despite elements of long-term consistency, Chinese and Indian foreign policies have also undergone significant change over several periods since the late 1940s, reflecting shifting strategic thought and, more often, shifting international circumstances.[11]

In the next section, we briefly outline the development of Chinese and Indian foreign policy since the founding of their modern states in 1949 and 1947, respectively. We focus on describing observable external foreign policies and strategic behavior. We do not present a full review or interpretation of the sources of Chinese or Indian grand strategy and foreign policy. Neither China nor India publishes documents that codify their evolving grand strategies, but it is possible to detect important changes by observing foreign policy action and key official statements.

A summary of the two countries' foreign policy trajectories, organized by date and the major theme of foreign policy during that period, is presented in Figure 3.1.[12]

Both states have seen periods of assertive international behavior, including coercive diplomacy on their peripheries and attacks on neighboring countries. Neither country has an expansionist tradition beyond its dealings with bordering tribes and states. Both are gaining relative power through economic reform and growth, and both are "returning" to larger roles in global politics in the early twenty-first century. In both cases, the broad trend has been toward improved relations with neighbors and integration with the global economy. In both cases, the most dramatic foreign policy change followed from thoroughgoing economic reforms, beginning around 1978–1979 in China and 1991–1992 in India. These trajectories are consonant with U.S. interests. Indeed, U.S. policies helped bring about these trends.

---

[11] Grand strategy is not simply foreign policy; it is a state's theory about how it can cause security for itself – a means-ends chain that accounts for the external threat environment, the relative power and weakness of the state itself, and a theory about how certain means will work better than others to make the state secure. See Edward Mead Earle, "Introduction," in Edward Mead Earle, ed., *The Makers of Modern Strategy* (Princeton: Princeton University Press, 1943), 3–25; Barry Posen, *The Sources of Military Doctrine: France, Britain, and Germany Between the World Wars* (Ithaca: Cornell University Press, 1984), 13–15; 24–25; Barry Posen, "A Grand Strategy of Restraint," in Michèle Flournoy and Shawn Brimley, eds., *Finding Our Way: Debating America's Grand Strategy* (Washington, DC: Center for a New American Security, 2008), 83–102.

[12] Defining foreign policy periods is difficult because states typically go through transition periods before a clear new trend is identifiable. Sources for this table are listed in the following sections on Chinese and Indian foreign policy trends.

China		India	
Time Period	Major Theme	Time Period	Major Theme
1949-	**Consolidation** • Reassert control over borders and near abroad • Lean to Soviet Union • Balance against United States	1947-	**Consolidation / Classic Nehruvian** • Partition and consequences • Reassert control over borders, colonial legacies • Moralist, non-aligned; Indian realism "veiled"
1962-	**"Offensive" Maoist** • Frictions with Soviet Union • Oppose both U.S. and Soviet Union • Support global revolutionary movements • 1964 nuclear weapons test	~1962-	**1962 Shock** • Defeat in border war with China • Rebuild military • Continue to lead non-aligned movement (NAM)
1970-	**Transitional** • Balance Soviet Union • Détente with United States • Admitted to U.N. • Support for global revolutions wanes • Modest increase in international trade	~1965-	**Post-Nehru Pragmatism** • Global moralist, regional realist • 1965 Pakistan War • Friendship treaty with Soviet Union • 1971 East Pakistan attack/intervention, establish Bangladesh
		~Early 1970s-	**Exclusionary / Lean to Soviet Union** • Oppose "China-U.S.-Pakistan axis" • Indira Doctrine: oppose external influence in South Asia and Indian Ocean • 1974 test of nuclear "device" • Soviet arms purchases, tacit acceptance 1979 Soviet Afghan invasion undercut relations with NAM and West
~1979-	**Opening** • Omnidirectional, no single "enemy" • Join global economy, encourage inward FDI • Continue to balance Soviet Union through mid-1980s • Limited defense cooperation with U.S.	~1984-	**Regional Hegemon** • More assertive in South Asia compared to 1947–1983 • Military spending increases • Regional intervention, Sri Lanka
~1991-	**Limits of Opening** • Re-evaluate U.S. after Gulf War I and Balkans interventions • Accelerate military modernization • South China Sea islet seizures • 1995–1996 Taiwan missile tests / intimidation • Outward investments begin	~1991-	**Reassessment** • Domestic economic crisis and collapse of USSR • Support for NAM wanes • 1992 "Look East" policy, opening to East Asia • 1998 nuclear weapons test • Rapprochement with U.S. • Market reforms; inward FDI and international trade grow slowly
~2000-	**Regional Reassurance** • Pro-actively shape international environment • Rhetoric: "peaceful rise," "harmonious world" • Omnidirectional "strategic partnerships" • Taiwan: military build-up continues, post-2008 economic enticement, political initiatives • Outward investment accelerates, especially Central Asia, Africa, South America	~2001-	**Aspiring Great Power** • Consolidate "de-hyphenation" from Pakistan • Omnidirectional "strategic partnerships" • Without NAM, South-South identity experiments India Brazil, South Africa (IBSA) • Establish economic, diplomatic, military presence in Central Asia, Afghanistan • Inward FDI and exports grow, some outward FDI • Concern with China's rise intensifies
~2009-	**New Assertiveness?** • More assertive compared to 2000–2008 • EEZ rights, South China Sea, Diaoyu/Senkaku Islands, rare earths trade embargo • G20 / global economic agenda-setting • Greater trade frictions with developed economies, developing country frictions with Chinese investment	2005-	**Aspiring / Lean to United States?** • 2005–2006 defense cooperation, nuclear cooperation agreements with United States • Military modernization, new arms imports • Inward FDI, outward investments accelerate • Maintain formal autonomy: Iran, Myanmar, military deployments

Figure 3.1. **Continuity and change in foreign policy.**

Nevertheless, India and China are not simply rising powers. They also remain preoccupied powers. The leadership in each country is preoccupied with serious domestic challenges: ensuring domestic economic and social development, buttressing social stability, and fending off internal challenges to their respective political systems. These domestic challenges are long-term issues that will take decades to address, and they hold out prospects for constraining the role that either India or China will play in global politics.

Evolution of Post-1949 Chinese Foreign Policy

From a closed, outwardly hostile posture under Mao, Chinese foreign policy has shifted dramatically over the past sixty years in response to changes to the structure of the international political system as well as to politics within China.[13] Rather than isolation and violent ideological opposition to the international status quo, China's twenty-first-century foreign policy emphasizes integration with the global economy to assist China's domestic development and its rise to great-power status.[14]

Since the founding of the People's Republic of China in 1949, Beijing has placed highest priority on Chinese Communist Party (CCP) regime survival. To Chinese leaders, this domestic political priority underpins key foreign policy continuities, among them a need to promote national territorial

[13] There is little agreement among Western or Chinese scholars about precisely where the inflection points in PRC foreign policy lie. There is, however, more agreement about general trends over periods of decades. For a useful review of different efforts to periodize this history, see 李承红 [Li Chenghong], "当代中国外交的根本转型与分期问题——一个外交政策分析理论的视角" [The Question of the Fundamental Reorientation and Periodization of China's Contemporary Diplomacy: A Point of View on Foreign Policy Analysis Theory], 《外交评论》 [*Foreign Affairs Review*], 107, December 2008.

[14] Recent studies that trace the evolution of Chinese foreign policy include Thomas W. Robinson and David Shambaugh, eds., *Chinese Foreign Policy: Theory and Practice* (New York: Oxford University Press, 1994); Suisheng Zhao, ed., *Chinese Foreign Policy: Pragmatism and Strategic Behavior* (Armonk: M.E. Sharpe, 2004); David Shambaugh, ed., *Power Shift: China and Asia's New Dynamics* (Berkeley: University of California Press, 2005); Sutter, *Chinese Foreign Relations*; and Marc Lanteigne, *Chinese Foreign Policy: An Introduction* (New York: Routledge, 2009). The links between domestic politics and institutions and Chinese foreign policy have been examined in Lu Ning, *The Dynamics of Foreign-Policy Making in China* (Boulder: Westview Press, 1997); David M. Lampton, ed., *The Making of Chinese Foreign and Security Policy in the Era of Reform* (Stanford: Stanford University Press, 2001); and Susan L. Shirk, *China: Fragile Superpower* (New York, Oxford University Press, 2007). Several studies assess China's role in international institutions and its evolving international behavior, including Alastair Iain Johnston, *Social States: China and International Institutions, 1980–2000* (Princeton: Princeton University Press, 2008); and Evan S. Medeiros, *China's International Behavior: Activism, Opportunism, and Diversification* (Santa Monica: RAND Corporation, 2009). Studies of Chinese grand strategy and security policy include Avery Goldstein, *Rising to the Challenge: China's Grand Strategy and International Security* (Stanford: Stanford University Press, 2005); Swaine and Tellis, *Interpreting China's Grand Strategy*; Andrew Nathan and Robert S. Ross, *The Great Wall and the Empty Fortress: China's Search for Security* (New York: W.W. Norton & Co., 1997). For pre-reform periods of Chinese foreign policy, see A. Doak Barnett, *China and the Major Powers in East Asia* (Washington, DC: Brookings, 1977); John Garver, *Foreign Relations of the People's Republic of China* (Englewood Cliffs: Prentice Hall, 1993); and Chen Jian, *Mao's China and the Cold War* (Chapel Hill: University of North Carolina Press, 2001). For a review of continuity and change in imperial and post-imperial Chinese views of foreign relations, see John K. Fairbank, ed., *The Chinese World Order: Traditional China's Foreign Relations* (Cambridge: Harvard University Press, 1968).

unification (including Taiwan) as a key element of regime legitimacy. However, through the late 1990s and the early 2000s, China also developed new policies aiming to maximize the mutual benefits of its multilateral and bilateral relations, while minimizing the potential for anti-China balancing and conflict with other great powers.[15]

China's foreign and security policy was dominated by Mao Zedong from the founding of the PRC in 1949 to his death in 1976. One of Mao's guiding foreign policy principles was an extension of his strategy for domestic political struggle: For each period of development, identify a single "main enemy" against which the nation must struggle.

From 1949 to the late 1950s, China identified the United States as the main threat to its interests and was closely aligned with the Soviet Union, a policy described as "leaning to one side" (一边倒 [*yi bian dao*]).[16] The foreign policy emphasis during this early period lay in consolidating the Communist Party victory within mainland China and expanding control over China's periphery. The People's Liberation Army (PLA) occupied several historical tributary states and regions, including Xinjiang, Tibet, and Inner Mongolia.[17] Beijing also sought to minimize superpower influence in areas near China's borders. China intervened in the Korean War in November 1950, attacking U.S.-led UN forces that had defeated the North Korean army and were driving north toward the Chinese border. Although unable to defeat the Kuomintang (KMT) on Taiwan, mainland forces conducted artillery bombardments of Taiwan's offshore islands in 1954 and 1958.

Mao's growing suspicion of the Soviet Union, motivated by a combination of differences over ideology and foreign policy issues, led to Sino-Soviet

---

[15] Evan S. Medeiros and M. Taylor Fravel, "China's New Diplomacy," *Foreign Affairs*, 82:6 (November/December 2003): 22–35; David Shambaugh, "China Engages Asia," *International Security*, 29:3 (Winter 2004/2005): 64–99; Samuel S. Kim, "Chinese Foreign Policy Faces Globalization Challenges," in Alastair Iain Johnston and Robert S. Ross, eds., *New Directions in the Study of China's Foreign Policy* (Stanford: Stanford University Press, 2006), 276–306.

[16] 章百家 [Zhang Baijia], "从'一边倒'到'全方位':对50年来中国外交格局演进的思考" [From "Lean to One Side" to "All Directions": Reflections on The Evolving Pattern of Chinese Foreign Policy Over the Last 50 Years], 《中共党史研究》 [Research in Chinese Communist Party History], Issue No. 1, 2000, 21–28. Zhang has also authored a useful English-language overview of China's post-reform foreign policy, also reflecting official CCP views and characterizations of foreign policy periods and trends. Zhang Baijia, "The Evolution of China's Diplomacy and Foreign Relations in the Era of Reform, 1976–2005," in Yufan Hao, C. X. George Wei, and Lowell Dittmer, eds., *Challenges to Chinese Foreign Policy: Diplomacy, Globalization, and the Next World Power* (Lexington: University of Kentucky Press, 2009), 15–33.

[17] Sutter, *Chinese Foreign Relations*, 60–85.

friction by the late 1950s and a withdrawal of Soviet economic advisors in 1960.[18] Throughout the 1960s, Chinese strategists could not identify a "main enemy" or a single direction of strategic threat and adopted a strategy of "opposing two hegemons." This became known as opposing both the United States and the Soviet Union (or 反两霸 [*fan liang ba*]). Beijing became more committed to an offensive, "revolutionary" strategic stance and a foreign policy that sought the violent overthrow of regimes it deemed to be imperialist or reactionary. Aid to communist parties and guerrilla movements in Asia, Africa, and Latin America increased steadily after 1962.[19] Not least, Beijing sent both arms and military personnel to assist North Vietnam in fighting against the United States during the Vietnam War. At the same time, Beijing's rivalry with Moscow began to take on increasingly military tones, particularly after 1965. Soviet military strength along the border grew rapidly, rising from thirteen divisions in 1965 to forty-four divisions in 1971.[20] China responded in kind, reinforcing its border areas.

Under Mao, Chinese foreign policy was based on a view that war with great powers was inevitable, likely to be early, and would be total, to include the use of nuclear weapons.[21] Thus, China also vigorously pursued the

---

[18] Chinese observers date the shift toward "opposing two hegemons" anywhere from 1958 to the mid-1960s. We would date the change in Chinese policy direction to 1960 (when cooperation effectively ended between China and the Soviet Union) or to 1962 (when Zhou Enlai articulated and linked the concepts of "opposing imperialism" and "opposing revisionism"). Zhang Baijia, "从'一边倒到'到'全方位'" [From "Lean to One Side"]; Li Chenghong, "当代中国外交的根本转型" [The Question of the Fundamental Reorientation and Periodization of China's Contemporary Diplomacy]; 舒建国 [Shu Jianguo], "毛泽东'反帝反修'外交战略的内涵及其实践效应" [The Meaning and Practical Effects of Mao Zedong's "Anti-Imperialist and Anti-Revisionist" Diplomacy], 《南昌大学学报》, [Journal of Nanchang University], 39:3, May 2008.

[19] Overseas assistance rose from 0.7 percent of the PRC government budget in 1960 to 2.79 percent in 1962 and continued to rise as a percentage of spending until 1973. 杨奎松 [Yang Kuisong], "'反帝反修'的历史困惑——1960年代中国对外政策的历史考察"[The Historical Puzzle of "Anti-Imperialist and Anti-Revisionist": A Review of the History of 1960s Foreign Policy], 《领导者》 [Leaders], 26, February 2009; and Tang Shiping, "From Offensive to Defensive Realism: A Social Evolutionary Interpretation of China's Security Strategy," in Robert S. Ross and Zhu Feng, eds., *China's Ascent: Power, Security, and the Future of International Politics* (Ithaca: Cornell University Press, 2008), 152–156.

[20] For a U.S. government assessment of shifting military capabilities along the border from the 1950s through the 1970s, see Director of Central Intelligence, "Soviet Military Forces in the Far East," National Intelligence Estimate, Vol. I – Key Judgments, February 1982, http://www.foia.cia.gov/docs/DOC_0000261311/DOC_0000261311.pdf

[21] On Mao's view of nuclear weapons and war, see Christopher P. Twomey, *The Military Lens: Doctrinal Difference and Deterrence Failure in Sino-American Relations* (Ithaca: Cornell University Press, 2010), 64–66, 147–148; Tang Shiping, "From Offensive to Defensive Realism," 153–154; and John Wilson Lewis and Xue Litai, *China Builds the Bomb* (Stanford: Stanford University Press, 1988), 5–7; 35–42.

development of nuclear weapons, first with Soviet help and, after 1959, autonomously. It conducted its first nuclear weapon test in 1964. On the economic front, China found itself more isolated from world trade than it had been even during the 1950s.

By late 1969, after clashes with Soviet troops at several points along the border, Mao and other Chinese leaders were sufficiently alarmed about the threat from the Soviet Union that foreign policy shifted again. Ultimately, Mao settled on a "one line" (一条线 [*yi tiao xian*]) approach, or balancing against the USSR.[22] In response to the Soviet threat, Beijing sought to end its isolation and improve its position in the international community. Signs of this transitional period became evident in early 1970, when Mao reached out through intermediaries to improve Beijing's relations with the United States. U.S. national security adviser Henry Kissinger went to Beijing in July 1971, paving the way for President Richard Nixon's historic visit to China in February 1972.

Beijing also campaigned for and in 1971 gained admission to the United Nations, providing Beijing with many of the normal and customary diplomatic tools available to others – and denying these tools to Taiwan. Also as part of Beijing's efforts to rejoin the world, China reduced its support for revolutionary regimes after 1973, and its foreign trade increased substantially. These various changes culminated in 1978, when Beijing normalized ties with both the United States and Japan.

These developments, and Mao's death in 1976 (with its ensuing shift in domestic politics), set the stage for the period of "reform and opening" that began in 1978–1979. The grand strategic vision that emerged under Deng Xiaoping's leadership after 1979 contrasted starkly with Mao's policies. Deng believed that China must become prosperous and more integrated with the world economy if the Communist Party was to survive in power. He also asserted that international politics had "changed," and that great-power war could be postponed or even avoided. This represented an opportunity to concentrate on domestic development, which was necessary in part to prevent further relative decline in Chinese power.

However, if Deng believed that large-scale wars of survival were not likely, he nevertheless anticipated limited wars around China's periphery. Already

---

[22] Mao did not articulate the "one line" as such until 1973, but the reorientation in policy occurred earlier and most analysts date the change to 1969, after the March clash with Soviet forces. See, for example, Chen Jian, *Mao's China and the Cold War* (Chapel Hill: University of North Carolina Press, 2001), 238–276; and 颜永琦 [Yan Yongqi], "新中国外交 '一条线' 外交战略评析" [Evaluating the New China's "One Line" Diplomatic Strategy], 《党史研究与教学》 [Party History Research and Teaching] 1, 2004; and Zhang Baijia, "从 '一边倒到' 到 '全方位'" [From "Lean to One Side"], 26–27.

in 1974, the PLA Navy had seized the Paracel Islands from Vietnam.[23] China continued to oppose the expansion of Soviet influence in the late 1970s and the 1980s. Beijing saw the 1978 invasion of Cambodia by Vietnam, a Soviet ally, as a dangerous expansion of Moscow's superpower influence on China's periphery. China responded by attempting to "punish" Vietnam through a short but costly attack into northern Vietnam in early 1979. The PLA did not perform well.[24] Skirmishes continued along the Sino-Vietnamese border well into the 1980s, and in 1988, Chinese and Vietnamese forces fought naval engagements near the Spratly Islands in the South China Sea. China's continued fears of Soviet power also convinced Beijing to deepen its strategic relations with the United States during the 1980s, including limited U.S. arms purchases and some intelligence-gathering cooperation. Also during the 1980s, China engaged in several cases of deliberate nuclear weapons and missile technology proliferation.[25]

With U.S. power resurgent by the mid-1980s, Chinese foreign policy gradually abandoned the practice of defining itself relative to a main enemy and moved toward an "independent" or "omnidirectional" ("全方位" [*quan fang wei*]) posture.[26] That reassessment was reinforced and accelerated by a series of international and domestic shocks between 1989 and 1991. Beijing was caught off guard by the sudden collapse of communism in Eastern Europe and the demise of the Soviet Union. It was unprepared for the international reaction against China in the wake of Deng's decision to use deadly force against peaceful protesters in and around Tiananmen Square in June 1989. The 1990–1991 Gulf War also demonstrated how far China had fallen behind the West in both techno-economic and military power.

Despite these events, Chinese foreign policy continued to hew to the decision to open China to the world and to integrate the Chinese economy with the global economy. This decision reflected Beijing's continued assessment that the circumstances of international politics favored great-power

---

[23] On the Paracel Islands, see Wortzel, "China's Foreign Conflicts since 1949." Later, Deng developed close relations with the PLA Navy as part of his strategy for forming alliances within the PLA to counter conservative military opposition to domestic reform. Eric Heginbotham, "The Fall and Rise of Navies in East Asia: Military Organizations, Domestic Politics, and Grand Strategy," *International Security*, 27:2 (Fall 2002), 86–125.

[24] Wortzel, "China's Foreign Conflicts since 1949," 279–280.

[25] Bates Gill, "China's Changing Approach to Nonproliferation," in Nathan E. Busch and Daniel H. Joyner, eds., *Combating Weapons of Mass Destruction: The Future of International Nonproliferation Policy* (Athens: University of Georgia Press, 2009), 245–262.

[26] 孙艳玲[Sun Yanling], "中国外交政策的调整与中苏关系正常化" [The Adjustment of Chinese Foreign Policy and the Normalization of Sino-Soviet Relations], 《中共党史研究》2009第二期 [Research in Chinese Communist Party History], 2, 2009; Zhang Baijia, "从'一边倒'到'全方位'" [From "Lean to One Side"], 27, 37.

peace and that China urgently needed to modernize and develop its economy and society if the CCP was to remain in power.[27]

The 1990s did, however, bring new Chinese assertiveness in some aspects of its behavior, as well as a reaction from China's Asian neighbors.[28] In 1992, China passed a Territorial Law, declaring most of the South China Sea "historic Chinese waters" and reasserting China's claim to sovereignty over both the Paracel and Spratly islands. The PLA Navy built structures on several of the Spratly islands and occupied Mischief Reef, claimed by the Philippines and lying just 130 miles from Palawan. In mid-1995 and again in early 1996, the PLA conducted ballistic missile "tests" in waters off Taiwan to discourage "separatism" and, in the 1996 case, to influence Taiwan's electoral politics. Beijing's assertiveness heightened regional concerns about China's direction and resulted in a nascent balancing reaction. Indonesia and Australia signed an unprecedented Security Agreement in December 1995, and Japan and the United States strengthened their Defense Cooperation Guidelines in 1997.

In the late 1990s and, to an even greater extent, in the early 2000s, Beijing demonstrated that it could, under the right conditions, learn from external feedback. With the advent of the Hu Jintao–Wen Jiabao regime in 2002–2003 and in the wake of the nascent anti-China balancing that had emerged in the mid 1990s, China adjusted its foreign and security policy, aiming to reassure regional neighbors. This adjustment was in line with an important post-1978 continuity in Chinese foreign policy: the grand strategic design of seeking to maintain the peaceful international environment required for China's internal growth and development. Beijing expanded its foreign policy repertoire to include more active foreign economic diplomacy and greater participation in multilateral institutions and international peace-keeping. It also sought greater influence in Asia and other regions, particularly through trade and investment.[29]

Beijing also experimented with several rhetorical and theoretical frameworks for its foreign policy. In 1997, Chinese leaders outlined a "new security concept" (新安全观 [*xin anquan guan*]), which defined security as mutual, not zero-sum, and emphasized participation in multilateral institutions. China's "peaceful rise" (和平崛起 [*heping jueqi*]), associated with scholars

---

[27] Swaine and Tellis, *Interpreting China's Grand Strategy*, 98–100; 112–114; Goldstein, *Rising to the Challenge*, 22–48.

[28] On Chinese behavior during this period, as well as the regional reaction to it, see Goldstein, *Rising to the Challenge*.

[29] Medeiros and Fravel, "China's New Diplomacy"; Bates Gill, *Rising Star: China's New Security Diplomacy* (Washington, DC: Brookings Institution, 2007).

said to be close to Hu Jintao, laid out three core principles for Chinese foreign policy: China's rise to wealth and power depends on its own continued economic reform; China's rise will take a long time; and China's rise cannot be accomplished at the expense of other nations.[30]

Heading into the second decade of the twenty-first century, many Asian and Western observers question whether Beijing has again shifted course and is embarked on a more assertive foreign policy.[31] Seeking to enforce China's broad interpretation of its maritime and security rights in its Exclusive Economic Zones, Chinese ships harassed a U.S. ship gathering naval intelligence about seventy-five miles from Hainan Island in March 2009. Also in 2009, both China and India hardened their positions and rhetoric on their mutual territorial disputes, which had seen progress toward negotiation and settlement over the previous several years. In September 2010, China responded with unprecedented vigor during a flare-up in tensions with Japan. In response to Japan's arrest of a Chinese fishing boat captain who rammed two Japanese coast guard vessels around contested islets in the East China Sea, Beijing imposed an embargo on the export of rare earth minerals to Japan and arrested four Japanese citizens in China in apparent retaliation. Meanwhile, Beijing refused to sanction or even publicly criticize its North Korean ally, despite North Korean attacks on South Korea. China's growing investments in developing countries, its relations with "rogue regimes," and its new protectionist trade and industrial technology policies also came in for intense scrutiny.[32]

---

[30] Although the peaceful rise label fell from official use, it has been supplanted by similar concepts, include "peaceful development" (和平发展 [heping fazhan]) and creating a "harmonious world" (和谐世界 [hexie shijie]). On "peaceful rise," see Robert L. Suettinger, "The Rise and Descent of 'Peaceful Rise,'" *China Leadership Monitor*, No. 12 (Fall 2004), http://www.hoover.org/publications/china-leadership-monitor/article/7739; Zheng Bijian, "China's 'Peaceful Rise' to Great Power Status," *Foreign Affairs*, 84:5 (September/October 2005): 18–24; Bonnie S. Glaser and Evan S, Medeiros, "The Changing Ecology of Foreign Policy-Making in China: The Ascension and Demise of the Theory of 'Peaceful Rise,'" *The China Quarterly*, 190 (2007): 291–310.

[31] For Western views of the aspects of Chinese foreign policy that became more assertive in 2009 and 2010, as well as reaction to this assertiveness in the United States and in Asia, see Aaron Friedberg, "The New Era of U.S.-China Rivalry," *The Wall Street Journal*, January 17, 2011 and Minxin Pei, "Chance to Make Amends," *South China Morning Post*, January 1, 2011, http://www.carnegieendowment.org/publications/index.cfm?fa=view&id=42221

[32] There is already a large literature on China's relations with troublesome regimes such as Iran, and its role in developing countries. See for example, John W. Garver, *China & Iran: Ancient Partners in a Post-Imperial World* (Seattle: University of Washington Press, 2006); Joshua Eisenman, Eric Heginbotham, and Derek Mitchell, eds., *China and the Developing World: Beijing's Strategy for the Twenty-first Century* (Armonk: M.E. Sharpe, 2007); Robert I. Rotberg, ed., *China Into Africa: Trade, Aid, and Influence* (Washington, DC: Brookings Institution, 2008); R. Evan Ellis, *China in Latin America: The Whats and*

Less dramatic but of potentially greater long-term impact are questions about Beijing's employment of language and policies revolving around China's "core interests." Beijing's application of the term "core interest" to Chinese foreign policy priorities dates to 2003 but has been used with increasing frequency since the latter part of the 2000s.[33] With some variation, Chinese officials stipulate that core interests include: (1) the maintenance of China's "fundamental system" and state security; (2) state sovereignty and territorial integrity; and (3) the continued stable development of the economy and society.[34] Chinese strategists explain that the concept of "core interests" is modeled on U.S. statements about its "vital national interests."[35] As such, the language can be viewed as simply a diplomatic linguistic tool, similar to those employed by other states.

Nevertheless, questions about how general principles will be interpreted and applied remain unanswered. Thus far, official public statements limit the discussion of territorial integrity to Tibet, Xinjiang, and Taiwan. Less clear is whether these claims might come to be applied explicitly to disputed areas in the South China Sea, East China Sea, or along the Sino-Indian border.[36] Of particular concern, the language of "core interests" could come to be used by hardliners during periods of heightened tensions to constrain Chinese leaders and block their ability to compromise.

China's recent statements and behavior have refocused attention in Washington and in Asian capitals, drawing an American restatement of its own "critical interest" in the South China Sea, as well as nascent balancing

---

Wherefores (Boulder: Lynne Rienner Publishers, 2009). For an overview of frictions in the bilateral economic relationship as of early 2010, see Eswar S. Prasad, "The U.S.-China Economic Relationship: Shifts and Twists in the Balance of Power," Testimony to the U.S. China Economic and Security Review Commission, revised March 10, 2010.

[33] For an assessment of the use of this concept, see Michael D. Swaine, "China's Assertive Behavior, Part One: On 'Core Interests,'" *China Leadership Monitor*, No. 34 (Fall 2010).

[34] This definition was provided by State Councillor Dai Bingguo at the U.S.-China Strategic and Economic Dialogue in July 2009. See "首轮中美经济对话" [First Round of China-U.S. Economic Dialogue], 中国新闻网 *[China News Net]*, July 29, 2009, http://www.chinanews.com/gn/news/2009/07–29/1794984.shtml

[35] Discussions with PLA and Ministry of Foreign Affairs officials, as well as scholars at Chinese foreign policy think tanks, Beijing, November 2010.

[36] Reports that Chinese officials stipulated the South China Sea was a "core interest" during meetings with U.S. counterparts in March 2010 appear to have been exaggerated. The statement was apparently made, but only in a sidebar meeting, and it has not been followed by an official statement that would affirm inclusion. Nevertheless, even if the areas in question are not explicitly included as "core interests," Chinese officials are unlikely to explicitly exclude those areas. Swaine, "China's Assertive Behavior." For the original, somewhat misleading reporting on the meeting in question, see "Chinese Military Seeks to Extend Its Naval Power," *New York Times*, April 23, 2010.

against China throughout the Asian region.[37] There is evidence that some in China are aware that these events and the tone of China's diplomacy in 2010 harmed some Chinese interests and carried costs for Beijing.[38] An awareness of such costs will be essential for maintaining moderation in Chinese foreign policy. However, this awareness appears to be missing or wilfully ignored in the statements of some Chinese military officers. A number of Chinese military officers have become increasingly familiar faces and voices in Chinese media, sometimes going so far as to criticize implicitly China's own foreign policy.[39]

As Chinese power grows, international expectations about Chinese behavior and claims on its resources and cooperation are also growing.[40] A 2011 report for a U.S. Congressional commission found that China has come to play a more constructive role in many international institutions.[41]

[37] "Offering to Aid Talks, U.S. Challenges China on Disputed Islands," *New York Times*, July 23, 2010. On Asian states "bandwagoning" with the United States to balance what they view as a newly assertive China, see Malcolm Cook, et al, *Power and Choice: Asian Security Futures* (Sydney: Lowy Institute for International Policy, 2010), especially 22–24, and "China's Fast Rise Leads Neighbors to Join Forces," *New York Times*.

[38] 达巍 [Da Wei],中国为什么要宣示核心利益？ [Why Does China Want to Proclaim Core Interests?],《环球时报》 [Global Times] July 27, 2010; 韩旭东 [Han Xudong], "慎用' 国家核心利益'"[Use "National Core Interests" Carefully],《瞭望 新闻周刊》 [Outlook Weekly], July 25, 2010; 庞中英 [Pang Zhongying], "南海问题, 不妨换个思路" [South China Sea Problem: Might As Well Change Thinking] 《环球时报》 [Global Times], August 6, 2010.

[39] See for example, comments by retired PLA General 徐光宇 [Xu Guangyu], in "Chinese admiral says U.S. drill courts confrontation," *Reuters*, August 13, 2010; China Military Science Academy Assistant Secretary-General, General 罗援 [Luo Yuan], "武力炫耀的背后是霸道——评美国航母拟赴黄海参加军演," [Tyranny is Behind the Show of Force: Comment on the American Aircraft Carrier Preparing to Participate in Yellow Sea Exercises], 《解放军报》 [People's Liberation Army Daily], August 12, 2010; and People's Liberation Army Navy Admiral 杨毅 [Yang Yi], "是中国反应过度, 还是美国无端指责？——再评美国航母拟赴黄海参加军演" [Chinese Overreaction, Or Unprovoked American Criticism? – Further Considerations on the American Aircraft Carrier Preparing to Participate in Yellow Sea Exercises], 《解放军报》 [People's Liberation Army Daily], August 12, 2010. Senior Chinese diplomats such as Wu Jianmin have criticized militaristic statements in the Chinese press about China's interests in the South China Sea and its relations with the United States; see "吴建民：中国不怕西方张牙舞爪" [Wu Jianmin: China Does Not Fear Western Saber Rattling], 《发展论坛》 [Development Forum], July 27, 2010.

[40] For one argument about how Chinese cooperation is needed to accomplish America's global goals, see Kenneth Lieberthal, "The U.S.-China Agenda Goes Global," *Current History*, 108:719 (September 2009): 243–249.

[41] The report for the United States-China Economic and Security Review Commission also found that China has become more adept at wielding influence within these institutions. See Stephen Olson and Clyde Prestowitz, "The Evolving Role of China in International Institutions," The Economic Strategy Institute, January 2011.

However, China has responded cautiously in taking on a larger global role. In part, China's relative caution may be a function of China's geographical circumstances, situated amid a number of great powers that can balance against it, including Japan, India, and Russia.[42] Its caution may also be reinforced by persistent material and moral limitations to Chinese power and influence in world politics, which cannot be easily or quickly overcome.[43] Like India, China faces daunting domestic challenges of poverty alleviation and the need to correct economic and social imbalances that threaten its internal stability. China has a regime-threatening official corruption problem. Unlike India, China faces a severe domestic socioeconomic challenge in its aging population.[44] Notwithstanding important foreign policy interests, it is these and other domestic issues that preoccupy China's leaders and will likely continue to do so for years to come.

Evolution of Post-1947 Indian Foreign Policy

Like Chinese foreign and security policy, India's external posture since independence has seen some core continuities, such as New Delhi's opposition to external influence in South Asia, but also major shifts. Oscillations in Indian foreign policy have perhaps been somewhat more frequent and more pronounced than shifts in Chinese foreign policy. India's geographical circumstances and regional security environment (with relatively weak but volatile neighbors), its lack of direct conflict with either superpower, and the nature of India's democratic domestic politics have, at different times, fed change.[45] India's founding in 1947 was marked by tragic ethnic and religious conflict, mass killings, and mass migration of both Hindus

---

[42] Avery Goldstein, "Parsing China's Rise: International Circumstances and National Attributes," in Ross and Zhu, eds., *China's Ascent*, 55–86; Robert S. Ross, "The Geography of the Peace: East Asia in the Twenty-first Century," *International Security*, 23:4 (Spring 1999): 81–118.

[43] Many observers note the potential for domestic issues to derail China's current growth path and limit its influence as a global power for some time. See Bates Gill and Yanzhong Huang, "Sources and Limits of Chinese Soft Power," *Survival*, 48:2 (Summer 2006): 17–36; Shirk, *China: Fragile Superpower*; David M. Lampton, *The Three Faces of Chinese Power: Might, Money, and Minds* (Berkeley: University of California Press, 2008); Evan S. Medeiros, "Beijing, the Ambivalent Power," *Current History*, 108:719 (September 2009): 250–256.

[44] Barry Friedman, Estelle James, Cheikh Kane, and Monika Queisser, "How Can China Provide Income Security for Its Rapidly Aging Population?" *Policy Research Working Paper No. WPS 1674*, World Bank, October 10, 1996; Jim O'Neill et al., *BRICs and Beyond* (New York: Goldman Sachs, 2007), especially 45–58.

[45] B.M. Jain, *Global Power: India's Foreign Policy 1947–2006* (Lanham, MD: Lexington Books, 2008), 20; see also Ashok Kapur, *India – From Regional to World Power* (New York: Routledge Press, 2006), especially 17–83.

and Muslims. Fighting included organized combat in Punjab and Kashmir between the forces of what became the state of Pakistan and India. Ever since that time, much of India's foreign and security policy has been centered on its relationship with Pakistan – or India's views of the relations of other states with Pakistan.

The issue of disputed territory in Jammu and Kashmir goes to the heart of the political foundation and governmental legitimacy of modern India. India's position on Jammu and Kashmir is no more compromising than China's position on Taiwan. Both governments see these issues as "internal matters" that involve core interests in security, national identity, and government legitimacy and survival.[46] Beijing asserts its right to rule in Taiwan, by force if necessary, yet cannot exercise that rule. The Indian government uses force to maintain rule in parts of Jammu and Kashmir, where a substantial portion of the local population does not wish to be ruled from New Delhi.[47]

From independence to the early 1960s, Jawaharlal Nehru dominated Indian security policy making. In foreign policy, Nehru emphasized moral values and sought a leading global role for India in world affairs, particularly via the Non-Aligned Movement (NAM). At the same time, Nehru downplayed external threats, especially from the communist world, and sought "global influence without military power."[48] Defense spending averaged a relatively modest 2 percent of GDP from 1949 to 1962.[49] Throughout this period, India's foreign policy, like China's postfounding foreign policy, focused on regime and border consolidation, including reassertion of control over territories deemed to be traditionally a part of "India." Armed forces were used to absorb the princely state of Hyderabad in 1948 and the Portuguese colonial enclave of Goa in 1961. India also obliged weak neighboring states to sign treaties of friendship that gave India the right to restrict their foreign and defense policies. Such treaties were signed with Bhutan in 1949, Sikkim in 1950, and Nepal in 1950.[50]

---

[46] The dispute over territory and self-rule in Jammu and Kashmir is central to Indo-Pakistan relations, but a resolution to those problems would not by itself fully resolve the security and diplomatic conflicts between them. For an Indian view, see Jain, *Global Power: India's Foreign Policy 1947–2006*, 184–186.

[47] For a balanced account of the Kashmir dispute and its complex history, see Sumantra Bose, *Kashmir: Roots of Conflict, Paths to Peace* (Cambridge, MA: Harvard University Press, 2003).

[48] A. Z. Hilali, "India's Strategic Thinking and Its National Security Policy," *Asian Survey*, 41:5 (October 2001): 737–764; quote on 739.

[49] Raju G. C. Thomas, "The Armed Services and the Indian Defense Budget," *Asian Survey*, 20:3 (March 1980): 281.

[50] Stephen P. Cohen, *India: Emerging Power* (Washington, DC: Brookings, 2001), 130–131.

Indian foreign policy also had a strong ideological or value-laden element. Nehru's ideology, focusing on peaceful opposition to imperialism and colonialism, was quite different from Mao's. But as was the case with Mao's approach, Nehru's moralism and his ideology of anti-imperialism did not cause foreign policy realism in India to disappear. Rather, a relatively consistent strain of realism was veiled by pronouncements that India would maintain a foreign policy of "independence" and "equidistance" between the West and the Communist Bloc.[51]

Nehru maintained a more traditional Indian realism with regard to contested territory on India's borders. These included disputes with the newly established PRC around Aksai Chin in the west (between Kashmir and Tibet) and the area around Tawang in the east (east of Bhutan and north of Assam). Nehru also saw the Indian claim as a moral and political stand that could not be compromised. Though he sanctioned discussions, he ruled out negotiated compromise with China over the border line.[52] Beginning in November 1961, Nehru instructed the Indian army to assume a forward-leaning stance to advance India's territorial claims. The refusal to compromise, combined with the decision to push Indian troops forward (in some cases behind existing Chinese army positions), made armed conflict highly likely, if not inevitable. In October 1962, the two sides clashed in a border war that saw Indian arms defeated and Nehru humiliated.[53]

Sino-Indian conflicts of interest over Tibet served as a backdrop to the 1962 border war.[54] At its founding, India had a claim, which it later

---

[51] Baldev Raj Nayar and T.V. Paul argue that Indian foreign policy has a realist tradition, and that this was evident even under Nehru, who sought to combine it with moralism and anti-imperialism. They argue that Nehru's integration of realism and idealism in his foreign policy was not fully effective. See Baldev Raj Nayar and T.V. Paul, *India in the World Order: Search for Major Power Status* (Cambridge: Cambridge University Press, 2003), 141–144.

[52] The Indians were willing to talk but not to countenance actual compromise of ceding territory. It appears the Chinese side was willing to exchange its claim in the eastern sector for territory in the western sector. This has been a long-standing Chinese position on the border dispute with India. For a variety of reasons, India has not accepted the idea of a negotiated outcome involving concessions and exchanges. See John W. Garver, *Protracted Contest: Sino-Indian Rivalry in the Twentieth Century* (Seattle: University of Washington Press, 2001), 79–109.

[53] See Srinath Raghavan, "A Bad Knock: The War with China, 1962," in Daniel P. Marston and Chandar S. Sundaram, eds., *A Military History of India and South Asia: From the East India Company to the Nuclear Era* (Westport: Praeger Security International, 2007), 157–174. A more critical view of Nehru's judgment is taken in Neville Maxwell, *India's China War* (New York: Random House, 1970). Analysis of the Indian advances and several instances of Chinese restraint leading up to the war can be found in Wortzel, "China's Foreign Conflicts Since 1949," 275–277.

[54] Raghavan, "A Bad Knock: The War with China, 1962"; Maxwell, *India's China War*, 89–90; 257–288.

abandoned, on territory in Tibet itself.[55] By the 1950s, in the wake of the PLA's entry into Tibet and suppression of Tibetan resistance there, India was home to a large Tibetan exile community, which the United States subsequently engaged to assist large-scale covert operations aimed at weakening Beijing's control over Tibet in the 1950s and 1960s.[56] To reinforce its control over these areas, China sought to strengthen road and other infrastructure links between Tibet and Xinjiang and the rest of China. From Beijing's perspective, this required (and still requires) control over territories that cross parts of Indian-claimed Kashmir and Aksai Chin.[57]

The 1962 defeat was a shock and sparked significant change in Indian strategic thinking and priorities.[58] Military spending rose to an average of 3.6 percent of GDP between 1963 and 1973, and the military turned from Britain to the United States and, especially, the Soviet Union for organizational models and equipment.[59] The commitment to nonviolence and moralism, as well as civilian disregard for the Indian military, also changed.

India came into conflict with Pakistan again in 1965. Pakistani infiltration into Indian-controlled Jammu and Kashmir and in the sparsely populated Rann of Kutch area led to clashes and then to a division-sized Pakistani offensive in April 1965. India sought to "raise the stakes" for Pakistan and launched an offensive in another border region, threatening the Pakistani city of Lahore.[60] The 1965 war ultimately ended in a stalemate, with neither side able to decisively defeat the other or force major territorial concessions.

By the 1970s, Prime Minister Indira Gandhi[61] completed a shift away from Nehru's early moralism toward an Indian *realpolitik*. The "Indira doctrine,"

---

[55] Garver, *Protracted Contest*, 51.

[56] Garver, *Protracted Contest*, 55.

[57] With Sino-Indian border issues still unresolved in the twenty-first century, it is possible that the Tibet issue in Sino-Indian relations could flare up again. India still hosts a large Tibetan exile population (including the Dalai Lama, age seventy-six in 2011), which has significant political support within India. Further, as a result of the various territorial claims and ethnic interests, China will remain a stakeholder in any future resolution of the Kashmir conflict, and India will remain a stakeholder in any political settlement to conflicts between the dominant Han Chinese/CCP regime and ethnic Tibetans in China.

[58] Jain, *Global Power: India's Foreign Policy 1947–2006*, 22–24; Nayar and Paul, *India in the World Order*, 149–151. For an account of the 1962 war with China from a military history perspective, see Raghavan, "A Bad Knock: The War with China 1962." On the incompleteness of some strategic and military reforms, see Stephen P. Cohen and Sunil Dasgupta, *Arming without Aiming: India's Military Modernization* (Washington, DC: Brookings Institution Press, 2010).

[59] Thomas, "The Armed Services and the Indian Defense Budget," 282.

[60] Bhashyam Kasturi, "The State of War with Pakistan," in Marston and Sundaram, eds., *A Military History of India and South Asia*, 139–156, especially 143–146.

[61] Nehru's daughter, and prime minister between January 1966 and March 1977 and again between January 1980 and October 1984.

developed in the early 1970s, laid down two principles: no foreign power would be allowed to cross the crest of the Himalayas, and India would consider the presence or influence of any foreign power in the region as inimical to Indian interests unless that power recognized Indian preeminence.[62] The Indira Doctrine was motivated by a fear, bordering on paranoia, of outside intervention in Indian affairs.[63] Stephen Cohen has argued that, "for about twenty years, no major strategic community in the world could match India's in terms of the number and variety of perceived threats."[64]

In 1971, with the frustrating stalemate of the 1965 war in mind, the Indian leadership determined that East Pakistan (today's Bangladesh, then a part of the Pakistani state) was both unstable and a threat to India's flank should India again fight Pakistan. Indian leaders also saw an opportunity to weaken Pakistan both militarily and ideologically by capitalizing on discontent in East Pakistan and working to split it away from the rest of Pakistan.[65] With more adept planning than it has sometimes mustered in strategic policy, New Delhi orchestrated a series of events in and around East Pakistan, including arming and supporting rebels inside that province and conducting an eight-month Indian army buildup on its eastern border.[66] Fearing potential Chinese and American intervention, India sought diplomatic cover in advance by signing a twenty-year treaty of friendship and cooperation with the Soviet Union in August 1971. In December 1971, Indian military forces invaded East Pakistan and defeated a smaller Pakistani army force there, ultimately leading to the establishment of an independent Bangladesh.

In addition to exhibiting India's capacity (like most other powers) for setting aside ideals in pursuit of interest, the 1971 war was significant in other ways.[67] Washington put considerable diplomatic pressure on New Delhi to

---

[62] Cohen, *India: Emerging Power*, 138.

[63] For an insider account of Indian intelligence activities that explores Indian suspicions of the United States, see B. Raman, *The Kaoboys of R&AW: Down Memory Lane* (New Delhi, Lancer Press, 2007), especially 39–48. "Kaoboys" is a pun on the name of Rameshwar Nath Kao, former head of India's intelligence service, the Research and Analysis Wing (R&AW).

[64] Cohen, *India: Emerging Power*, 42. For an Indian view of threats from the "Pakistan-America-China coalition," see Ashok Kapur, *India – From Regional to World Power* (New York: Routledge Press, 2006), 77.

[65] Sumit Ganguly, *Conflict Unending: India-Pakistan Tensions Since 1947* (New York: Oxford University Press, 2001), 51–52.

[66] Cohen, *India: Emerging Power*, 135.

[67] George Tanham found that although India has no expansionist tradition beyond the subcontinent, the ideological commitment to nonaggression and pacifism among Indian elites does not apply to matters within South Asia. See George Tanham, "Indian Strategic

halt its attack. As the war wound down, Washington dispatched the aircraft carrier *Enterprise* to the region. *Enterprise* remained far from the fighting in East Pakistan, staying in waters south of Sri Lanka. The ship's movements were probably seen by the United States as a symbolic gesture to mollify its defeated partner, Pakistan, not as a serious threat to India.[68]

Nevertheless, the Indian response to the *"Enterprise* affair" was intense, and its legacy long-lasting. It fueled Indian suspicions of U.S. motives for decades, and among many Indian strategists, it is still seen as a seminal event. Further, because the *Enterprise* likely carried nuclear weapons, Indian leaders interpreted its movements as a veiled nuclear threat. This interpretation of events, whether justified or not, intensified India's commitment to develop nuclear technology and helped ensure that India would view future U.S. nuclear nonproliferation efforts as a threat to Indian interests. The *Enterprise* incident influenced India's decision to conduct a "peaceful nuclear explosion" in 1974.[69]

India's motivation for seeking nuclear weapons was also heavily influenced by a belief among Indian elites that possessing nuclear weapons would confer status on India that had long been unfairly denied. Moral political factors, including a desire for status and respect, may have had as much to do with Indian decisions to test weapons and develop its nuclear arsenal as did calculations of the military balance of power and the potential security consequences of arms races with both Pakistan and China. India's conventional military superiority over Pakistan has actually been devalued by the acquisition of nuclear weapons by both sides.[70] Once in possession of nuclear technology, India has not engaged in deliberate nuclear weapons proliferation, although the United States has in the past accused individual Indian citizens of weapons of mass destruction (WMD) proliferation activities.

Thought: An Interpretive Essay," in Kanti P. Bajpai and Amitabh Mattoo, eds., *Securing India, Strategic Thought and Practice: Essays by George K. Tanham with Commentaries* (New Delhi: Manohar Publishers, 1996), especially 77–79.

[68] Cohen, *India: Emerging Power*, 136.

[69] T. V. Paul places Indira Gandhi's decision to test a nuclear explosive device in 1974 in the context of a search for deterrent power in the wake of the 1971 movements of *Enterprise* in South Asian waters. See T. V. Paul, "India, the International System, and Nuclear Weapons," in D. R. SarDesai and Raju G. C. Thomas, eds., *Nuclear India in the Twenty-First Century* (New York: Palgrave-MacMillan, 2002), 85–104, especially 90–91. Similar views have also been attributed to the former Indian Army chief of staff, Krishnaswamy Sundarji; see Rajesh Kadian, "Nuclear Weapons and the Indian Armed Forces," in SarDesai and Thomas, eds., *Nuclear India in the Twenty-First Century*, 211–227, especially 219.

[70] Raju G. C. Thomas, "Wither Nuclear India?" in SarDesai and Thomas, eds., *Nuclear India in the Twenty-First Century*, 3–24, especially 18–19; on the same point, see George Perkovich, "What Makes the Indian Bomb Tick?" in SarDesai and Thomas, eds., *Nuclear India in the Twenty-First Century*, 25–60, especially 54–55.

India's foreign policy and security posture thus changed significantly with changing international and domestic circumstances. [71] Prior to 1962, India focused primarily on a global moral and anti-imperialist message and on a single threat, Pakistan. From 1962 until the development of the Indira Doctrine in the early 1970s, New Delhi focused on two threats: Pakistan and China. Beginning around 1971, in response to America's developing anti-Soviet Cold War partnership with Pakistan and a perception that the United States was willing to intervene in the region in opposition to Indian interests, India sought to develop a capability to engage and deter any outside power that might enter the South Asian region.[72] Also beginning in the early 1970s, India concluded another series of trade and security treaties with its smaller neighboring states (notably Bangladesh), ensuring Indian regional dominance.[73] Sikkim was absorbed into the Indian Union in 1974.

From about 1984, Indian foreign policy saw yet another shift that was to last until the early 1990s. In this phase, India undertook more assertive and activist policies throughout the South Asian region.[74] This new activism followed from a resurgent belief in what some Indian observers have described as India's perception of itself as the "rightful regional hegemon in South Asia."[75] Defense budgets doubled in real terms between 1980 and 1989. Indian intelligence operatives intervened to support Tamil rebels in Sri Lanka in 1983, and India attacked and captured Pakistani positions at the Siachen Glacier leading to heavy fighting in 1984.

Two years later, New Delhi followed with a large-scale military exercise, called *Brasstacks*, on the Pakistani border. Some observers believe the exercise may have been intended to draw Pakistan into a conventional war showdown before both sides fully developed and deployed nuclear weapons.[76] By bringing on a militarized diplomatic crisis, *Brasstacks* also

---

[71] See Sumit Ganguly, "The Genesis of Nonalignment," in Sumit Ganguly ed., *India's Foreign Policy: Retrospect and Prospect* (New Delhi: Oxford University Press, 2010), 1–10.

[72] Cohen, *India: Emerging Power*, 145.

[73] Cohen, *India: Emerging Power*, 130; 137–138.

[74] Sunil Dasgupta and Stephen P. Cohen, "Is India Ending Its Strategic Restraint Doctrine?" *Washington Quarterly*, 34:2 (Spring 2011): 163–177.

[75] Sankaran Krishna, *Postcolonial Insecurities: India, Sri Lanka, and the Question of Nationhood* (New Delhi: Oxford University Press, 2000), 154, quoted in Ramachandra Guha, *India after Gandhi: The History of the World's Largest Democracy* (New York: Harper Collins, 2007), 588.

[76] For various views of India's intentions, see Kanti Bajpai, P. R. Chari, Pervaiz Iqbal Cheema, Stephen P. Cohen, and Sumit Ganguly, *Brasstacks and Beyond: Perception and the Management of Crisis in South Asia* (New Delhi: Manohar Press, 1995). Even a more benign interpretation of New Delhi's intentions sees the Indian maneuvers as having an

revealed weak coordination between strategic policy as conceived by the civilian leadership, and the implementation of that strategy as undertaken by Indian military leaders.

The period of relatively assertive Indian regional policy culminated in a large-scale military intervention in Sri Lanka in 1987. This foray into Sri Lanka was motivated in part by domestic Indian political interests and in part by New Delhi's desire to prevent the Sri Lankan government from seeking help from any foreign power in its battles against the Tamil rebels.[77] However, the Tamil rebels turned on Indian forces, and the intervention ended in heavy Indian casualties and eventual withdrawal in 1990. The Sri Lanka experience is also seen by Indian elites as another case of failed communication and coordination among ministries and the military, in this case causing misidentification of threats and an inadvisable military operation.[78]

The failure in Sri Lanka, the demise of India's Soviet partner, and China's surpassing economic growth all combined to convince New Delhi to reassess Indian strategy and foreign policy in the early 1990s. Sluggish domestic economic development was also a major consideration.[79] Indian strategists recognized that India lacked the economic and technological wherewithal to carry out its vision of Indian preeminence in South Asia, to say nothing of becoming a major global power. Indian leaders refocused attention on domestic development and began a new program of economic reform and restructuring in 1991. India also began to expand its diplomatic and trade contacts, initiating a "Look East" policy that sought greater integration with Southeast and East Asia in 1992.[80] By the early 2000s, India had become a major platform for global corporations looking to outsource services. It also began to attract new foreign direct investment, linked to sources of technological innovation and financial and managerial expertise

---

element of coercive diplomacy or "compellence." See Sumit Ganguly and Devin T. Hagerty, *Fearful Symmetry: India-Pakistan Relations in the Shadow of Nuclear Weapons* (Seattle: University of Washington Press, 2005), 71–73.

[77] Ramachandra Guha, *India after Gandhi: The History of the World's Largest Democracy* (New York: Harper Collins, 2007), 586–588; Cohen, *India: Emerging Power,* 148–150; Neil Devotta, "When Individuals, States, and Systems Collide: India's Foreign Policy towards Sri Lanka," in Sumit Ganguly ed., *India's Foreign Policy: Retrospect and Prospect,* 32–61.

[78] Jain, *Global Power: India's Foreign Policy 1947–2006,* 29.

[79] For comprehensive analyses of Indian economic development, see Francine Frankel, *India's Political Economy 1947–2004,* 2nd Edition (New York: Oxford University Press, 2005); and Arvind Panagariya, *India: The Emerging Giant* (New York: Oxford University Press, 2008).

[80] See Ranjit Gupta, "India's Look East Policy," in Atish Sinha and Madhup Mohta, eds., *Indian Foreign Policy: Challenges and Opportunities* (New Delhi: Foreign Service Institute, 2007), 351–382.

via a highly educated, English-speaking Indian diaspora in the United States and Europe.

The fall of the Soviet Union also strongly influenced New Delhi's decision to re-evaluate relations with the United States, which began to improve significantly by the late 1990s. India also became more sophisticated in its responses to Pakistani provocations in the Kashmir region. In the 1999 Kargil war, India responded to Pakistani incursions with military force but also employed skillful diplomacy to isolate and pressure Pakistan and improve its relationship with Washington.[81] Since 2001, Indian foreign policy has also sought to expand Indian interests in Central Asia.[82] It has established a military base in Tajikistan and undertaken robust diplomatic and economic activity to secure its interests in Afghanistan.[83]

Like China, India's post-reform foreign policy also seeks "strategic partnerships" with many countries, without much specific alignment or content. New Delhi also appears to go to great pains in its diplomacy to avoid "giving offense" to major powers, particularly in the Middle East and Asia.[84] Unlike China, India is not a permanent member of the UN Security Council, but India has a longer history of active participation in the United Nations and other international institutions. India has also been, and continues to be, an active participant in UN peacekeeping.[85]

Indian foreign policy has thus left behind some of its previous ideological baggage, while it has gained maturity and complexity.[86] Yet even though New Delhi seeks a global role – and particularly global status – Indian foreign policy remains committed to autonomy and nonalignment as an end in itself. Despite greater recent pragmatism, India remains influenced by a legacy of idealism.[87] This contributes to a lingering tension between

---

[81] P.R. Chari, Pervaiz Iqbal Cheema, and Stephen P. Cohen, Four Crises and a Peace Process: *American Engagement in South Asia* (Washington, D.C.: Brookings Institution, 2007), 185–186.

[82] David M. Malone, *Does the Elephant Dance? Contemporary Indian Foreign Policy* (New York: Oxford University Press, 2011), 214, 241.

[83] Jain, *Global Power: India's Foreign Policy 1947–2006*, 210–215; "India and Afghanistan sign security and trade pact," *The Washington Post*, October 5, 2011.

[84] See K. Shankar Bajpai, "Engaging with the World," in Atish Sinha and Madhup Mohta, eds., *Indian Foreign Policy: Challenges and Opportunities* (New Delhi: Foreign Service Institute, 2007), 75–90.

[85] See Chinmaya R. Gharekhan, "India and the United Nations," in Sinha and Mohta, eds., *Indian Foreign Policy: Challenges and Opportunities*, 193–215, especially 201–203.

[86] Sumit Ganguly, "India's Foreign Policy Grows Up," *World Policy Journal* 20:4 (Winter 2003/2004): 41–47.

[87] See Chandrashekar Dasgupta, "India and the Changing Balance of Power," in Atish Sinha and Madhup Mohta, eds., *Indian Foreign Policy: Challenges and Opportunities* (New

New Delhi's desire to work more closely with the United States and U.S.-supported global economic institutions on the one hand and its desire to continue to enhance its status as an alternative to Western powers on the other. The latter impulse is on display in New Delhi's close bilateral relations with Iran and in its support for exclusive regional institutions, such as the India-Brazil-South Africa forum (IBSA).[88] The contradictions between idealist and realist thought are also apparent in India's pursuit of "resource diplomacy" and its investment in most of the same states in which China also has investments, including Iran, Sudan, and Myanmar.

Despite recent institutional reforms, security policy remains plagued by poor coordination between civilian and military leaders and by frequent oscillations in Indian foreign policy.[89] The high priority Indian leaders place on status-related issues, along with the volatility of Indian domestic politics, also sometimes leads to gaps between Indian foreign policy aspirations and India's material capability to achieve them.[90]

India appears more eager than China to define a global role for itself as a player with major power status. Geographic circumstances and the absence of direct security conflicts with the United States may reinforce India's confidence and its ambitions. Like China, however, a rising India remains a preoccupied power, perennially limited by its own domestic challenges. For India, these include endemic poverty, large disparities of wealth, poor transportation infrastructure, massive new employment and social services requirements, persistent official corruption and bureaucratic inefficiency, ethnic and religious strife that occasionally flares into large-scale communal violence, and violent domestic insurgencies that have rendered large regions in central and northeast India ungovernable.[91]

Delhi: Foreign Service Institute, 2007), 91–112; and A. K. Damodaran, "Non-Aligned Movement and Its Future," in the same volume, 125–138.

[88] Jain, *Global Power: India's Foreign Policy 1947–2006*, 62–65. The IBSA dialogue is cast as pitting the less developed "south" against the developed "northern" states, including the advanced industrial democracies.

[89] Harsh V. Pant, "India's Search for a Foreign Policy," *Yale Global*, 26 June 2008. See also Harsh V. Pant, *Contemporary Debates in Indian Foreign and Security Policy: India Negotiates Its Rise in the International System* (New York: Palgrave-MacMillan, 2008), 65–90; Jain, *Global Power: India's Foreign Policy 1947–2006*, 20.

[90] Kapur, *India – From Regional to World Power*, 17–83; Nayar and Paul, *India in the World Order*, 1–3; 9–13; 42–64; Jain, *Global Power: India's Foreign Policy 1947–2006*, 35–36; 41–43; 93; George Perkovich, *India's Nuclear Bomb: The Impact on Global Proliferation*, 2nd ed. (Berkeley: University of California Press, 2001), 480–483.

[91] Brief introductions to some of these complex issues can be found in the following sources: Shubham Chaudhuri and Martin Ravallian, "Partially Awakened Giants: Uneven Growth in China and India," in L. Alan Winters and Shahid Yusuf, eds., *Dancing with Giants: China, India, and the Global Economy* (Washington, DC: World Bank, 2007), 175–210; "Maoist

As with China, domestic burdens may provide a powerful logic for caution in Indian foreign policy even as New Delhi enlarges its global and regional role. As is also the case with China, some of these factors, including nationalism and domestic instabilities, could provide the fuel for greater international conflict, especially in India's immediate neighborhood. Many of India's most controversial foreign policies – including the attack on East Pakistan, the intervention in Sri Lanka in the 1980s, the development of nuclear weapons and ever-larger missiles, and arms racing with Pakistan – have had strong political support across various groups and factions in India's vibrant democracy. This phenomenon is occasionally exacerbated by weakness in the leading Indian political parties, which obliges them to retain coalition partners, sometimes among smaller, relatively extreme parties.

Key Issues in U.S. Relations with China and India

Since initiating domestic reforms, and with the demise of the USSR, both China and India see their relations with the United States as critical to their continued economic development and rise to major power status in Asia. Each in its own way may be uncomfortable with U.S. global dominance. Yet each also recognizes the importance of access to U.S. markets, technology, and investment, as well as the influence Washington has in international politics and within international institutions. Hence, both Beijing and New Delhi aim, at a minimum, to avoid conflict with America. At the same time, China and India each also have critical interests that potentially conflict with those of the United States.

Challenges in U.S.-China Relations
Chinese leaders have determined that China should maintain good relations with Washington to avoid confrontation that could derail China's development and modernization (including military modernization). China's evolving foreign policy includes elements that are consonant with both near-term and long-term U.S. interests.[92] China also has a number of

---

Rebels Widen Deadly Reach Across India," *New York Times*, October 31, 2009; "India's Medical Emergency," *Time*, May 1, 2008; Louise Tillin "History of Indian Communal Violence," *BBC News*, March 2, 2002, http://news.bbc.co.uk/2/hi/south_asia/1850759.stm; Kalyani Menon-Sen and A.K. Shiva Kumar, *Women in India: How Free? How Equal?* (New Delhi: United Nations Office of the Resident Coordinator, 2001); Navdip Dhariwal, "Child Labour – India's 'Cheap Commodity,'" *BBC News*, June 13, 2006, http://news.bbc.co.uk/2/hi/5059106.stm

[92] The literature on Sino-U.S. relations is rich and varied; a noncomprehensive list of notable work includes John King Fairbank, *The United States and China* (Cambridge, MA: Harvard

conflicts of interest with the United States, which vary in terms of intensity and manageability.

Many shared Sino-U.S. interests parallel shared interests between the United States and India. These include support for a globalized, relatively open global trade and financial system with an important role for multi-lateral institutions such as the WTO and the G20. China shares an interest in a politically stable and prosperous Asia. Despite different priorities and approaches, both Washington and Beijing have an interest in a nuclear-free North Korea. Similarly (and connected to the North Korean issue), neither would benefit from a South Korea or Japan with nuclear weapons. China and the United States have a mix of conflicting approaches and common interests in combating terrorism.[93] Both have an interest in maintaining a number of arms control regimes (for example, the Non-Proliferation Treaty, the Missile Technology Control Regime and the activities of the Nuclear Suppliers Group).

Beijing's post-reform-era foreign policy also highlights differences of interest with Washington. Chinese leaders oppose U.S. intervention in other areas of the globe, in part because they fear potential U.S. intervention in issues they define as "domestic," including Tibet and Taiwan.

As with Kashmir for India, Taiwan is an economic, political, military, and territorial issue that has its roots in the founding of the current Chinese

University Press, 4th ed., 1983); David Shambaugh, *Beautiful Imperialist: China Perceives America 1972–1990* (Princeton: Princeton University Press, 1991); David Shambaugh, "Patterns of Interaction in Sino-American Relations," in Thomas W. Robinson and David Shambaugh, eds., *Chinese Foreign Policy: Theory and Practice* (Oxford: Oxford University Press, 1994), 197–223; Thomas J. Christensen, *Useful Adversaries: Grand Strategy, Domestic Mobilization, and Sino-American Conflict, 1947–1958* (Princeton: Princeton University Press, 1996); David M. Lampton, *Same Bed, Different Dreams: Managing U.S.-China Relations, 1989–2000* (Berkeley: University of California Press, 2001); Robert G. Sutter, "China's Regional Strategy and Why It May Not be Good For America," in David Shambaugh, ed., *Power Shift: China and Asia's New Dynamics*, 289–305; Wang Jisi, "China's Search for Stability with America," *Foreign Affairs* 395 (September/October 2005): 39–48; Shirk, *China: Fragile Superpower*, 212–254; Lampton, *The Three Faces of Chinese Power: Might, Money, and Minds*, 252–274; Robert J. Art, "The United States and the Rise of China: Implications for the Long Haul," in Ross and Zhu, eds., *China's Ascent*, 260–290. On elements of Sino-U.S. common interest see David Shambaugh, "China Engages Asia: Reshaping The Regional Order," *International Security*, 29:3 (Winter 2004/2005): 64–99; David M. Lampton, "China's Rise in Asia Need Not Be at America's Expense," in Shambaugh, ed., *Power Shift: China and Asia's New Dynamics*, 306–326; Richard Rosecrance and Gu Guoliang, eds., *Power and Restraint: A Shared Vision for The U.S.-China Relationship* (New York: Public Affairs Press, 2009).

93 Shirley A. Kan, *U.S.-China Counterterrorism Cooperation: Issues for U.S. Policy*, Congressional Research Service Report to Congress, Order Code RL33001, October 2007; Robert Zoellick, "Whither China: From Membership to Responsibility?" Speech at the National Committee on U.S.–China Relations, New York, September 21, 2005.

state and is now bound up in both elite politics and in the broader politics of national identity. Beijing claims sovereignty over Taiwan and maintains that it has the right to use force to prevent Taiwan from declaring de jure independence. Most analysts agree that the Chinese leadership sees the Taiwan issue as central to regime legitimacy and survival. For these reasons, China's pattern of behavior on Taiwan – like India's on Kashmir – is not necessarily a good guide to its overall international strategic behavior.

The Taiwan issue has prompted Sino-U.S. crises in 1954, 1958, and 1995–1996. Since the 1995 crisis, both the Chinese and U.S. militaries have spent considerable resources on preparing for potential conflict with one another. China has developed greater military potential to threaten Taiwan. It has actively pursued "anti-access" capabilities aimed at impairing U.S. intervention in the event of conflict with Taiwan. These capabilities include modern submarines and an array of short- and medium-range ballistic missiles capable of striking U.S. forward bases in Asia. Some Chinese systems, such as China's nuclear submarines and advanced cruise missiles, could be used to project power well beyond Taiwan. Other capabilities, which have not yet been fully developed and deployed, such as antiship ballistic missiles (ASBMs), electromagnetic pulse (EMP) weapons, and antisatellite (ASAT) weapons, could threaten U.S. regional interests in Asia and spark dangerous regional arms racing that could leave both sides less secure. Further development of Chinese "anti-access" capabilities could exacerbate another challenge in U.S.-China relations: the need to manage China's maritime disputes with U.S. allies and partners in the East and South China seas.

Despite the military competition surrounding Taiwan, both Washington and Beijing have for decades found ways to manage Taiwan-related disagreements and crises. Maintaining a balance of cross-Strait power has been and will continue to be important. Diplomatically, the immediate prospects for managing the issue are improved by the flexibility and restraint shown by both Beijing and Taipei since the return of KMT government in Taiwan in 2008.[94] A number of proposals have been floated for longer-term improvements in the cross-Strait relationship.[95] The United States should be prepared to react to possible discontinuities in the Taiwan-mainland relationship – positive as well as negative. In the meantime, however, Taiwan

---

[94] Steven M. Goldstein, "China and Taiwan: Signs of Change in Cross-Strait Relations," *China Security*, 5:1 (Winter 2009): 65–70; Alan D. Romberg, "Cross-Strait Relations: In Search of Peace," *China Leadership Monitor*, 23 (Winter 2008); Bates Gill, *Rising Star: China's New Security Diplomacy*, 139–143.

[95] See for example, Richard C. Bush, *Untying the Knot: Making Peace in the Taiwan Strait* (Washington, DC: Brookings Institution, 2005).

issues clearly rank as the most dangerous problem for U.S.-China relations and will require the careful attention and management of all parties.

Chinese policies toward North Korea and Iran also challenge U.S. interests. China fears the potential effects of a North Korean regime collapse on the security of its borders, as well as on its own internal security.[96] China sees potential threats emerging from North's nuclear weapons program and has cooperated with regional powers on that issue by hosting the Six-Party Talks process.[97] Nevertheless, Beijing will not support measures it believes will destabilize the regime in Pyongyang and rejects Washington's calls for tougher sanctions (including the withdrawal of Chinese energy supplies and aid to North Korea).

Like India, China has a complex set of interests with Iran that include cooperating on energy issues, developing Beijing's own diplomatic presence in the Middle East, and opposing what it sees as excessive U.S. influence in that region.[98] China halted its nuclear cooperation with Iran in 1997.[99] Since 2006, Beijing has joined the United States in voting for UN Security Council resolutions calling on Iran to halt processing of nuclear fuel and submit to International Atomic Energy Agency inspections. China has voted for UN sanctions on Iran for failing to comply with these Security Council resolutions. However, Beijing has moved more slowly on Iran sanctions than Washington would like, and it has also lobbied to dilute the strength of these sanctions.[100] China has become a large direct investor in Iran, and Chinese investment appears to be growing faster than that of other significant economic partners of Iran, such as India.[101]

---

[96] Shen Dingli, "North Korea's Strategic Significance to China," *China Security* (Autumn 2006): 19–34.

[97] Charles Wolf, Jr., "The Multilateral Path to Disarming North Korea," *Asian Wall Street Journal*, February 16, 2005; Joel S. Wit, Jon Wolfsthal, and Choong-suk Oh, "The Six Party Talks and Beyond: Cooperative Threat Reduction and North Korea," Center for Strategic and International Studies, December 2005; Zhu Feng, "Shifting Tides: China and North Korea," *China Security* (Autumn 2006): 35–51. China may see utility in the talks (as a Northeast Asia security dialogue) even if they do not result in disarming North Korea; see Chu Shulong and Lin Xinzhu, "The Six Party Talks: A Chinese Perspective," *Asian Perspective*, 32:4 (2008): 29–43.

[98] John W. Garver, "Is China Playing a Dual Game in Iran?" *The Washington Quarterly*, 34:1 (Winter 2011): 75–88. On India, see C. Christine Fair, "India and Iran: New Delhi's Balancing Act," *The Washington Quarterly*, 30:3 (Summer 2007): 145–159.

[99] Evan S. Medeiros, *Reluctant Restraint: The Evolution of China's Nonproliferation Policies and Practices, 1980–2004* (Palo Alto: Stanford University Press, 2007), 80–82; 244–245.

[100] Garver, "Is China Playing a Dual Game in Iran?" 76.

[101] China is Iran's largest trade partner, with nearly $27 billion in total trade in 2009. India was Iran's fourth-largest trade partner in 2009 after China, Japan, and the United Arab Emirates, with about $14 billion in total trade in 2009. Collectively, the European Union

China's foreign economic policies, although generally aligned with U.S. goals, also present some challenges to U.S. interests. China currently has serious imbalances in its own domestic development, in the valuation of its currency, and in trade. These conflicts are the subject of high-level U.S.-China bilateral dialogue as well as multilateral engagement.[102]

Challenges in U.S.-India Relations

Many of America's conflicts of interest with India appear to have been set aside since 2001, but they have not disappeared entirely. Moreover, virtually all have the potential to return with greater force as India gains relative power.

New Delhi's fear of U.S. interference in South Asian politics contributed to the decision to develop nuclear technology and detonate a nuclear explosive device in 1974.[103] India formally tested and acquired nuclear weapons in 1998. Motivated in part by domestic political considerations, India's 1998 nuclear weapons tests initially caused a souring of relations with Washington. The Indian nuclear tests did result in intense bilateral diplomacy in 1998 and 1999. This diplomatic activity, although sometimes tense, helped leaders in both New Delhi and Washington focus more attention on their relationship. Soon after, New Delhi accepted U.S. diplomatic intervention in the 1999 Kargil War with Pakistan.

The terror attacks on the United States in September 2001 and a subsequent attack by Islamic extremists on the Indian Parliament in December 2001 marked a watershed for U.S.-India relations. In addition to cooperation

---

had about $38 billion in total trade with Iran in 2009. Shayerah Ilias, "Iran's Economic Conditions: U.S. Policy Issues," Congressional Research Service Report to Congress, Order Code RL34525, April 22, 2010. European Commission, "Trade: Iran," April 15, 2011, http://ec.europa.eu/trade/creating-opportunities/bilateral-relations/countries/iran/

[102] See U.S. Department of State, "U.S.-China Strategic and Economic Dialogue 2010 Outcomes of the Strategic Track," May 25, 2010. Dennis Wilder, "The U.S.-China Strategic and Economic Dialogue: Continuity and Change in Obama's China Policy," *China Brief*, 9:10 (May 15, 2009). On multilateral dialogue, see "China Policy Main Topic for the G-20," *New York Times*, April 13, 2011.

[103] India's decision to develop nuclear weapons technology in the 1970s emerged in part from its earlier, less cooperative relationship with the United States, including the 1971 *Enterprise* affair. See T. V. Paul, "India, the International System, and Nuclear Weapons," in SarDesai and Thomas, eds., *Nuclear India in the Twenty-First Century*, 90–91; K. Subrahmanyam, "India and the International Nuclear Order," in the same volume, 63. Contrary to the way the incident is portrayed by many in India, U.S. Navy histories show that the *Enterprise* skirted the southern edge of the Bay of Bengal and did not sail north into it. The ship kept south of Sri Lanka, more than 1,000 nautical miles away from fighting in East Pakistan. See www.history.navy.mil/danfs/e4/enterprise-viiic.htm. See also C. Raja Mohan, "India, U.S. Bury the Ghosts of 1971," *The Hindu*, December 7, 2001.

on antiterrorism, a common concern about rising Chinese power was an important element in the calculations of both sides. A combination of Indian diplomacy and shifting U.S. interests prompted Washington to set aside traditional U.S. concerns over nuclear weapons proliferation and Indo-Pakistan arms racing. These developments culminated in a June 2005 defense cooperation agreement and the ratification of a U.S.-India nuclear agreement in October 2008. The new relationship emphasized security and geostrategic cooperation.[104]

However, India and the United States still face potential conflicts of interest, many of which concern core security interests on both sides. Indian leaders and the Indian strategic community remain suspicious of U.S. motives, and wary of U.S. influence on Indian decision making and foreign policy. This makes collaboration with the United States on many regional and global issues difficult. These issues include cooperation on the specifics of balancing Chinese power, dealing with Iran, and engaging on global trade and environmental regimes.

Depending on how it is implemented – and how implementation is interpreted by other states – the U.S.-India nuclear cooperation agreement could pose a challenge to WMD nonproliferation efforts. U.S. assistance to India's civilian nuclear programs could permit India to concentrate domestic resources on its nuclear weapons program. Despite the agreement, India still often declines to align with the United States on nonproliferation policies toward other states, including Iran.[105]

The nuclear deal with India has also fed directly into pressures on the nonproliferation regime elsewhere in Asia. For example, faced with a nuclear-armed North Korea that has recently launched attacks on the South, a 2011 survey found more than 68 percent of South Koreans favored the acquisition of nuclear weapons. At the same time, the South Korean government has sought to amend a 1974 agreement on civilian nuclear use with the United States to permit reprocessing (or "pyroreprocessing"). Despite safeguards, any such change would likely raise concerns in Asia about the development of a latent South Korean nuclear weapons capability. A study published by the Center for U.S.-Korea Policy notes that the Republic of Korea (ROK)

---

[104] For one analysis of common interests as well as challenges to closer ties, see Sumit Ganguly and Andrew Scobell, "India and the United States: Forging a Security Partnership?" *World Policy Journal*, 22:2 (Summer 2005): 37–43. See also Jain, *Global Power*, 92–93; and Michael A. Levi and Charles D. Ferguson, "U.S.-India Nuclear Cooperation: A Strategy for Moving Forward," Council on Foreign Relations, CSR No. 16, June 2006, http://www.cfr.org/india/us-india-nuclear-cooperation/p10795

[105] Malone, *Does the Elephant Dance? Contemporary Indian Foreign Policy*, 193–195.

government "finds it discriminatory that the United States has given India, Japan and EURATOM advance, long-term consent to reprocessing and to the use of plutonium while refusing the ROK the same treatment."[106] In particular, it chafes at the "preferential treatment to India, a non-NPT party."[107]

Perhaps the greatest challenge to U.S.-India relations is in South and Central Asia. The United States has no historical or legal commitments related to Jammu and Kashmir that parallel those associated with Taiwan. Further, the United States has no core interests in India's Central and South Asia neighbors, unlike its interests in Japan, South Korea, Australasia, and Southeast Asia. From this perspective, the prospect of Indian regional hegemony appears to be much less worrisome than the prospect of Chinese regional hegemony.

However, the United States has urgent interests in stability in Afghanistan and in a nuclear-armed Pakistan. This puts rising Indian power in the context of Asia's nested security dilemmas. Mitigating India-Pakistan arms racing and security competition is essential to improving internal stability in Pakistan, and via Pakistan, internal stability in Afghanistan. U.S.-India security policies and arms transfers may affect these relationships. New Delhi's increasing lead in conventional forces and new Indian nuclear weapons and missile capabilities exacerbate arms racing responses from Pakistan. This could cause Pakistan to divert scarce resources away from the grave internal threats to its stability.

India also pursues some diplomatic and foreign economic policies that conflict with U.S. interests in more direct ways. These include India's relations with "rogue regimes" such as Sudan and Myanmar. Although India is broadening and deepening its Middle East relations with Arab states and Israel, New Delhi also actively seeks greater trade, energy, and security cooperation with Teheran.[108] India still occasionally seeks

---

[106] The survey was conducted by the Asan Institute of Public Policy. Cited in "Majority of S. Koreans Want Atomic Bomb: Survey," *Straits Times*, March 23, 2011.

[107] Fred McGoldrick, "New U.S.-ROK Peaceful Nuclear Cooperation Agreement: A Precedent for a New Global Nuclear Architecture," Center for U.S.-Korea Policy, November 2009. See also Stephen M. Walt, "What's Behind the U.S.-South Korean Nuclear Flap," *Foreign Policy*, July 14, 2010, http://walt.foreignpolicy.com/posts/2010/07/14/what_s_behind_the_us_south_korea_nuclear_flap

[108] Some observers acknowledge that India seeks closer cooperation with Iran in energy, diplomatic alignment regarding international agreements on WMD, and on Afghan politics and security, but deny the strategic significance of the India-Iran relationship. See Harsh V. Pant, "India's Relations with Iran: Much Ado about Nothing," *The Washington Quarterly*, 34:1 (Summer 2007): 61–74. A more persuasive argument does not attempt to dismiss Indian ties to Iran. Instead, it views them as part of a complex mix of competing interests that New Delhi intends to continue to balance. See Fair, "India and Iran: New Delhi's Balancing Act."

to gain trade and diplomatic advantages by defining itself in opposition to Western nations and other industrial democracies. Examples of this include New Delhi aligning itself with a "pro-southern hemisphere" movement and blocking progress on trade liberalization and efforts to mitigate climate change.

India is not alone in these efforts, frequently finding assistance from China. However, the intensity and persistence of these diplomatic and economic misalignments, despite India's having secured major objectives with the United States in the security realm, is cause for concern.

Common Challenges: Evidence From United Nations Voting Records

The degree of alignment between New Delhi and Beijing on some foreign policy issues – and their common differences with the United States – comes into sharp focus when one considers their UN voting records. In this section, we present a comparison of voting on UN General Assembly resolutions regarding "rogue regimes" and the proliferation of weapons of mass destruction.

The data presented in this section cover only General Assembly resolutions that were adopted with a vote. Thus, the examples presented can only provide a partial snapshot of each country's policy and diplomatic behavior at the UN. The data cannot capture subtleties such as diplomatic efforts that prevent a resolution from coming to a vote, cooperation or conflict beyond the formal vote itself, or bilateral trade-offs on related issues. However, the data do illustrate the similarities and differences between the Chinese and Indian positions on four issues of interest to the United States: resolutions related to Iran, Sudan, Myanmar, and to WMD proliferation. We present the data in terms of how each country stands in relation to the other two on these votes: agreed (meaning an identical yes or no vote), or opposed (meaning one country has voted yes and one has voted no). The total number of UN resolutions on each issue is shown at the top of each column in the vote data tables. Each resolution offered each country one opportunity to cast a vote. Of these votes, we show the percentage of votes in which the United States, China, and India voted in agreement with each of the others (Table 3.1). We also show the percentage of votes in which each country has voted in opposition to the others (Table 3.2). The percentages for agreement and opposition do not add to 100 percent in all cases because in some cases one or more countries voted to abstain, or did not cast a vote.

Both China and India maintain close diplomatic, trade, and investment links with Iran and oppose the American approach to dealing with Iran. This is reflected in their bilateral policies and in their UN voting behavior.

Table 3.1. *Agreement in UN General Assembly resolutions adopted with recorded votes (Percent of total votes)*

	Iran (22 resolutions)	Sudan (12 resolutions)	Myanmar (4 resolutions)	WMD Proliferation (62 resolutions)
China-India Agreed	73	92	100	31
U.S.-China Agreed	5	0	0	19
U.S.-India Agreed	0	8	0	6

Source: UN Bibliographic Information System, accessed April 15, 2010, at http://unbisnet.un.org/. This table records only the percentage of total votes where two countries voted identically (i.e., both voted yes or both voted no).

Table 3.2. *Opposition in UN General Assembly resolutions adopted with recorded votes (Percent of total votes)*

	Iran (22 resolutions)	Sudan (12 resolutions)	Myanmar (4 resolutions)	WMD Proliferation (62 resolutions)
China-India Opposed	0	8	0	3
U.S.-China Opposed	77	75	100	52
U.S.-India Opposed	73	67	100	40

Source: UN Bibliographic Information System, accessed April 15, 2010, at http://unbisnet.un.org/. This table records only the percentage of total votes where two countries voted in opposition to each other (i.e., one voted yes and the other voted no).

China and India have voted in alignment with one another in 73 percent of adopted UN resolutions on Iran. (These votes were primarily on the situation of human rights in Iran. WMD-related votes are captured in the vote data on WMD.)

On Myanmar, India and China have aligned with each other in opposition to the United States on all UN resolutions where a vote was recorded.[109]

---

[109] United Nations Bibliographic Information System, accessed April 15, 2010, at http://unbisnet.un.org/

In twelve UN resolutions related to human rights in Sudan adopted by the UN General Assembly with a recorded vote since 1992, India and China were aligned in their vote on the resolution 92 percent of the time.[110]

The record of UN voting on resolutions adopted regarding the proliferation of WMD also reflects similar Chinese and Indian differences with Washington. China and India are rarely opposed to each other's position on these resolutions (they were opposed on only 3 percent of 62 total votes). However, they are both frequently opposed to the United States. China opposed the U.S. in 52 percent of votes, and India opposed the U.S. in 40 percent of votes. China has agreed with the U.S. position in adopted UN anti-proliferation resolutions more frequently than India. Beijing voted with Washington on 19 percent of votes, while New Delhi voted with Washington on 6 percent of WMD related votes. Both China and India have voted to abstain on numerous WMD-related General Assembly resolutions. India has abstained or remained unopposed to the U.S. position more frequently than China.

Voting at the United Nations illustrates the complex challenge the United States faces in rising Chinese and Indian power. India is not simply an alternative rising power to China. India does not always balance China on important matters of international politics. On issues such as dealing with "rogue regimes" and WMD proliferation, China and India appear more closely aligned with each other than either is aligned with the United States. Sometimes their common ground is rooted in opposition to the specific policies preferred by Washington. The voting records also show that China has in some cases been somewhat more positively aligned with U.S. policies than India. Finally, the UN voting records also indicate that both India and China can cooperate with the United States on issues including anti-proliferation, even if only by voting to abstain.[111] However, the process of securing alignment on global security issues with both India and China is likely to remain difficult. From a U.S. perspective, this record in UN General Assembly votes bears on the question of a potential permanent UN Security Council seat for India. There may be benefits from having India as a permanent member of the Security Council. However, Washington would also have to expect more difficult and complex Security Council negotiations on many issues, potentially including significant China-India alignment on

---

[110] United Nations Bibliographic Information System, accessed November 19, 2010, at http://unbisnet.un.org/

[111] Both China and India have joined the United States in voting to censure Iran for its nuclear program in resolutions passed by the International Atomic Energy Agency, which is an organization within the United Nations.

some issues within the Security Council. We now turn to examine Chinese and Indian behavior in cases where deliberation and negotiation have failed, and each has resorted to using force.

Chinese and Indian Use of Force

Examining historical patterns in the use of force may help identify the conditions under which China and India could use force in the future. Some observers believe China uses force "frequently" and as a preferred tool of foreign policy.[112] Students of China's military history have also argued that some aspects of Chinese political culture may make China more likely to use force than other states. Andrew Scobell sees a Chinese "cult of defense" in which Chinese elites justify the use of offensive force in terms of self-defense.[113] Scobell acknowledges that most countries justify the use of force as a defensive measure, but he believes such a cluster of beliefs is "particularly inviolable" in China, increasing the likelihood that China will be involved in future war.[114] The U.S. government shares similar concerns about "the potential for China to engage in military preemption, perhaps far from its borders, if the use of force protects or advances core interests, including territorial claims (e.g., Taiwan and unresolved border or maritime claims)."[115]

However, establishing a unique pattern of worrisome Chinese behavior requires comparative context that is not usually provided in analyses of China's use of force.[116] We use data from the University of Michigan's Militarized Interstate Disputes (MIDs) database to compare the track record of use of force and war for both China and India.[117] We select the

---

[112] Wortzel, "China's Foreign Conflicts Since 1949," 270, 282; Sutter, *Chinese Foreign Relations*, 137. Huntington, *The Clash of Civilizations*, 168–174; 218–238; 312–315; Mearsheimer, *The Tragedy of Great Power Politics*, 375–376; 401–402.

[113] Andrew Scobell, *China's Use of Military Force: Beyond the Great Wall and the Long March* (New York: Cambridge University Press, 2003), 27–28.

[114] Scobell, *China's Use of Military Force*, 15; Andrew Scobell, "'Cult of Defense' and 'Great Power Dreams': The Influence of Strategic Culture on China's Relationship with India," in Michael R. Chambers, ed., *South Asia in 2020: Future Strategic Balances and Alliances* (Carlisle: U.S. Army War College, 2002), 329–384, especially 333 and 341.

[115] *The Military Power of the People's Republic of China* (Washington, DC: Office of the Secretary of Defense, 2007), 12.

[116] A rare exception is Alastair Iain Johnston, "Is China a Status Quo Power?" *International Security* 27:4 (Spring 2003): 5–56.

[117] University of Michigan Militarized Interstate Disputes (MIDs) database v3.1, http://www.correlatesofwar.org/. See also Faten Ghosn, Glenn Palmer, and Stuart Bremer, "The MID3 Data Set, 1993–2001: Procedures, Coding Rules, and Description," *Conflict Management and Peace Science*, 21 (2004): 133–154.

period from 1949 to 2001, that is, from China's founding two years after the founding of the Indian Republic to the most recent year for which MIDs data are available.

To examine trends in behavior, we break the 1949–2001 period into two parts: 1949–1979 and 1980–2001. This allows us to compare the two countries over the period prior to China's "reform and opening" and the period after those reforms began to take hold. Specific results for average incidents per year and trends over any given time are sensitive to the choice of which years are selected for parsing and analyzing the data. However, this periodization is reasonable for capturing comparable history, as well as time periods relevant to U.S. interests.[118]

According to the MIDs data set, China was involved in the use of force (including war) more often than India between 1949 and 2001: eighty times for China, compared with forty-nine times for India (see Table 3.3).

The data show that the two countries have fought an equal number of wars (four), as defined by the MIDs methodology.[119] India has fought three wars with post-1949 Pakistan and one with China. In addition to the 1962 war with India, China fought in the Korean war (1950–1953) and wars with Vietnam (a short but intense 1979 border war, and an extended series of probes and attacks in a 1986–1987 border war).

The use of force is not distributed evenly across time. China used force slightly more than twice as often as India prior to 1979. However, between 1980 and 2001, China's frequency in using force was the same as India's. Each was involved in twenty cases of the use of force during this latter period. In other words, whereas China was more prone to the use of force than India during the first decades after the Chinese revolution, it has not been more prone to use force than India over the most recent two decades for which data are available. This finding also contradicts any claim that China's frequency and intensity of the use of force has not declined since the reform and opening process began in 1978–1979.

---

[118] This periodization also allows us to discount India's 1947–1948 war with Pakistan, which was born of partition and civil war at the country's founding. (China's state of war with the KMT on Taiwan is not coded as an "interstate war" in the data set.) Also, this allows us to compare the two countries over the same years, rather than choosing two different starting points such as 1947–2001 and 1949–2001.

[119] According to the Correlates of War methodology, a conflict is classified as an interstate war if at least two participants in sustained combat qualify as members of the interstate system, and there were at least 1,000 battle-related fatalities among all of the system members involved. A state involved is regarded as a participant if it incurs a minimum of 100 fatalities or has 1,000 armed personnel engaged in fighting. See http://www.correlatesofwar.org/cow2%20data/WarData/InterState/Inter-State%20War%20Format%20(V%203-0).htm

Table 3.3. *China and India (1949–2001): Use of force and war*

	Number of cases		Cases per year	
	China	India	China	India
Use of Force				
1949–1979	57	26	1.84	0.84
1980–2001	19	19	0.86	0.86
Total 1949–2001	76	45	1.43	0.85
War				
1949–1979	3	3	0.10	0.10
1980–2001	1	1	0.05	0.05
Total 1949–2001	4	4	0.08	0.08
Total Force and War				
1949–1979	60	29	1.94	0.94
1980–2001	20	20	0.91	0.91
Total 1949–2001	80	49	1.51	0.92

Source: Correlates of War (CoW) Militarized International Disputes (MIDs) 3.1 dataset, 1816–2001, available at http://www.correlatesofwar.org/. Data in this table include "use of force" (coded as "4") and "war" (coded as a "5" in the MIDs data set). Displays of military capability and threats of force (coded 1–3) are not included in this table.

India's Use of Force

Since independence in 1947, India has fought four wars with Pakistan (1947–1948, 1965, 1971, and 1999) and one with China (1962). It has had many armed skirmishes along its borders with both Pakistan and China, and in recent years, similar small-scale clashes along its border with Bangladesh. India has also engaged in military interventions among its smaller neighboring countries. Prior to its 1962 war with China, India's military operations were primarily focused on consolidating Indian territory. In addition to the war with Pakistan in 1947–1948, the Indian army seized the principality of Hyderabad in 1948, and its armed forces participated in absorbing the Portuguese colony of Goa in 1961. India's record of use of force is presented in Figure 3.2.

India attacked and captured Pakistani positions at the Siachen Glacier in 1984. It followed this in the late 1980s with assertive military exercises on its border with Pakistan that brought the two countries to the brink of war.[120] India intervened in the Sri Lankan civil war in 1987,

[120] Cohen, India: Emerging Power, 147. Chari et al., *Four Crises and a Peace Process*, 184.

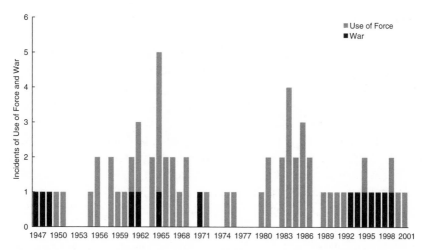

Figure 3.2. India: Use of force and war, 1947–2001.
Source: Correlates of War (CoW) Militarized International Disputes (MIDs) 3.1 dataset, 1816–2001, available at http://www.correlatesofwar.org/. Data in this figure include "use of force" (coded as "4") and "war" (coded as a "5" in the MIDs data set). Displays of military capability and threats of force (coded 1–3) are not included in this figure. The MIDs data set codes each use of force as a single event regardless of duration. However, in this figure, events that began in one calendar year but lasted into subsequent years are displayed as one event in each calendar year.

ultimately withdrawing in 1990 after sustaining heavy losses. India dispatched forces to suppress a Tamil Tiger–backed coup in the Maldives in November 1988.

In drawing a comparison with China, it is important to note that India's assertiveness and interventionism in the 1980s included elements of civilian militarism, with the lead taken by Indian diplomats and intelligence services in some cases. Advocates of a more assertive foreign and military policy enjoyed support from top civilian leaders, including Indira Gandhi and Rajiv Gandhi.[121]

This experience tends to undermine some assumptions about how democratic India might use its power in Asia. At the least, it is evident that despite political traditions of tolerance, inclusiveness, and democracy, India can behave as an interventionist regional hegemon. India's pluralist politics have played a role in foreign policy choices, with some civilian

---

[121] Dasgupta and Cohen, "Is India Ending Its Strategic Restraint Doctrine?" 166; Chari et al., *Four Crises and a Peace Process*, 22, 42, 46–47; See also Surjit Mansingh, *In Search of Power: Indira Gandhi's Foreign Policy 1966–1982* (New Delhi: Sage Publications, 1984).

leaders supporting greater assertiveness because they seek domestic political advantages.[122]

India has backed away from regional interventions since its experience in Sri Lanka. Further, India does not have a record of expansionism or of using force outside South Asia. Most of India's wars and incidents of use of force involve Pakistan, and India is becoming more skillful in its response to Pakistani provocations. In Kargil in 1999, India responded with force, but also leveraged American diplomatic pressure on Pakistan to help bring the conflict to a close on its terms. India also responded with restraint in response to the terrorist attack on the Indian Parliament in December 2001, which, like the deadly terrorist attack in Mumbai in 2008, was launched by militants with support from inside Pakistani territory.

China's Use of Force

China has a significant track record of using force since 1949 (see Figure 3.3). Between 1949 and 2001, China used force more frequently than India, especially in the first two decades of the PRC regime. According to the MIDs data, China has also fought four wars since 1949: Korea (1950–1953), India (1962), and Vietnam (1979 and 1986–1987). In 1950, the PLA forcibly entered and crushed resistance in Tibet, which had enjoyed a period of relative autonomy in the late Imperial and Republican eras.[123]

China has also engaged in multiple confrontations and military skirmishes with neighbors on its borders, including clashes with Taiwan (1954 and 1958), Burma (1960 and 1961), the Soviet Union (1969), and Vietnam (throughout most of the 1980s). It seized the Paracel Islands from Vietnam in 1974 and some of the Spratly Islands in 1988. China dispatched forces and military equipment to North Vietnam to support North Vietnam's war against the United States during the 1960s and 1970s.[124] It seized Mischief Reef (claimed by the Philippines) in 1995 and engaged in coercive diplomacy by firing missiles into the Taiwan Strait in 1995 and 1996.

The MIDs data show that in the period between 1980 and 2001, China's use of force declined in comparison to the early decades after the founding of the PRC. Many of China's cases of use of force since reforms began in

---

[122] Cohen, *India: Emerging Power*, 151; P. R. Chari et al., *Four Crises and a Peace Process*, 203–204.

[123] Western analysts differ on whether this was an invasion and occupation of an independent nation or an extension of the Chinese civil war. Certainly, Tibet was relatively autonomous prior to the PLA incursion (in relation to the relatively weak late-nineteenth and early-twentieth-century Chinese state). Yet during its history, Tibet had also been a traditional Chinese tributary.

[124] Chen Jian, *Mao's China & the Cold War*, 225–227.

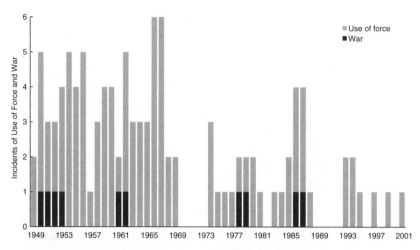

Figure 3.3. China: Use of force and war, 1949–2001.
Source: Correlates of War (CoW) Militarized International Disputes (MIDs) 3.1 dataset, 1816–2001, available at http://www.correlatesofwar.org/. Data in this figure include "use of force" (coded as "4") and "war" (coded as a "5" in the MIDs data set). Displays of military capability and threats of force (coded 1–3) are not included in this figure. The MIDs data set codes each use of force as a single event regardless of duration. However, in this figure, events that began in one calendar year but lasted into subsequent years are displayed as one event in each calendar year.

1978–1979 have involved Taiwan, or U.S. forces operating in international airspace and international waters near China's borders. Notable incidents involved a U.S. EP-3 surveillance aircraft in 2001 and the U.S. intelligence-gathering vessel *Impeccable* in 2009. Post-reform China has also been involved in multiple cases of use of force around disputed islands and islets that it claims in the South China Sea.

Use of Force in Comparative Context
Post-1947 India and post-1949 China have broadly similar characteristics in terms of economic and military power and geographical circumstances (Figure 3.4). Each has a significant track record of using force to achieve its objectives. China has been involved in more incidents of use of force since 1949, but the identification of supposedly unique patterns in China's use of force is problematic once comparisons are made.

The finding that India has used force as often as China over the twenty-one-year period between 1980 and 2001 puts China's post-reform record in some context. It serves as a reminder that strengthened U.S. political and military ties with India will not necessarily come on U.S. terms – India can and

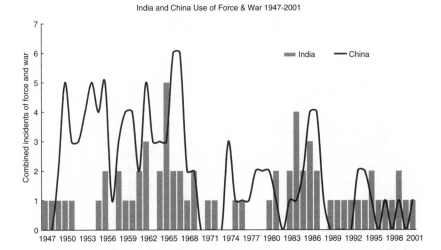

Figure 3.4. Indian and Chinese use of force and war, 1947–2001.
Source: Correlates of War (CoW) Militarized International Disputes (MIDs) 3.1 dataset, 1816–2001, available at http://www.correlatesofwar.org/. Data in this figure include "use of force" (coded as "4") and "war" (coded as a "5" in the MIDs data set). Displays of military capability and threats of force (coded 1–3) are not included in this figure. The MIDs data set codes each use of force as a single event regardless of duration. However, in this figure, events that began in one calendar year but lasted into subsequent years are displayed as one event in each calendar year.

will pursue its own interests according to its own views and will not shy from the use of force.[125] Further, like China, India has taken offensive action that it justified as defensively motivated. Examples include East Pakistan in 1971, the attack on the Siachen Glacier in 1984, and the forward advance of Indian troops to unoccupied disputed territory behind Chinese positions in 1962. Some students of Indian strategic affairs argue that India has a deep cultural predilection for justifying the use of offensive force on moral and defensive grounds, in much the way others have described Chinese use of force.[126]

It is possible to identify broad historical patterns of the use of force, but these patterns may not be entirely unique for either state. Michael Swaine and Ashley Tellis identify a historical pattern in China's use of force, with five core features: (1) an effort to protect a central heartland while maintaining

---

[125] For an in-depth examination of Indian use of force in four South Asian crises involving India between 1986 and 2002, see Chari et al., *Four Crises and a Peace Process*.

[126] Manjeet Singh Pardesi, "Deducing India's Grand Strategy of Regional Hegemony from Historical and Conceptual Perspectives," IDSS Working Paper No. 76 (Singapore: Institute of Defense and Strategic Studies, April 2005), 26, 47.

control over China's "strategic periphery"; (2) expansion or contraction of peripheral control dependent on the strength of the regime and its capacity; (3) the frequent yet limited use of force against external entities, primarily for heartland defense and peripheral control, and often on the basis of pragmatic calculations of relative power and effect; (4) a reliance on less-than-coercive strategies when the state is weak; and (5) a strong relationship between the power and influence of domestic leadership and the use of force.[127] Compared to the historical experience of large land powers such as France, Germany, and Russia, this is a description of China as a relatively conservative (and often weak or constrained) power.

Furthermore, a similar description appears to apply to Indian patterns of the use of force. In some cases (1965, 1986), India has shown that it prioritizes threats to its heartland, including the Punjab. India has certainly shown a track record of using force as well as diplomacy to control its periphery. New Delhi has also placed limits on its use of force, restraining or limiting its attacks on Pakistan in some cases, for example. In other cases, such as in terrorist attacks launched from Pakistani soil in 2001 and 2008, India refrained from using force entirely. India has employed less coercive strategies when it is relatively weak, most notably leveraging diplomacy with the Soviet Union to balance China and the United States. India appears more prone to the use of force under particularly strong governments, such as the Indira Gandhi–Rajiv Gandhi Congress governments, although weaker Indian coalition governments may also be tempted toward assertive external policies.

This analysis does not imply a moral valuation, positive or negative, of the actions of either state. Yet from the perspective of these countries' roughly sixty years of modern history, their patterns of the use of force do not appear to be sharply divergent. First, both India and China have shown they are willing to use force to defend or secure territories deemed essential to the political legitimacy of their respective regimes, with Jammu and Kashmir and Taiwan being the primary examples. Second, like China, India has also used force to claim or recover territory on its periphery. Third, most Chinese and Indian uses of force have been in response to perceived border or regional threats. Both countries have seen periods of assertive or forward-leaning behavior, including a willingness to strike at smaller states along their border. This is especially the case where they perceive those smaller states to be part of encirclement strategies by outside powers directed against themselves. However, neither country has a track record

---

[127] Swaine and Tellis, *Interpreting China's Grand Strategy*, 21.

of using force in areas far from its own borders. Fourth, both countries exhibited a decreasing frequency of use of force after their modern regimes were consolidated.

Each power has used force for similar reasons – to ensure territorial unification or the security and delimitation of borders. These common features can themselves be traced, at least in part, to a similar historical situation for both modern China and modern India. Each is a relatively new nation state in historical terms. Both of these states have emerged from earlier empires in a weakened condition, and their modern leaders have pursued similar territorial agendas, specifically converting frontier areas into modern borders.[128]

The specific circumstances for India and China have varied, of course. One important difference in the record of the use of force between the two is that in some of China's cases, the PLA fought directly against the Cold War superpowers in actions close to China's borders. These included attacking U.S.-led forces in the Korean War in 1950 and the use of force in multiple clashes against the Soviets on the Chinese border in the late 1960s. China's attack on Vietnam in 1979 and subsequent border clashes with Vietnam were also linked to Beijing's view of the Soviet-Vietnam security relationship.

From the perspective of realist international relations theory, China's frequent of use of force in the years after 1949 is not surprising – particularly given the relatively undefined state of China's pre-1949 borders, early Cold War events, continued superpower support for the CCP's enemies on Taiwan, and China's geographic position in Northeast Asia between Soviet and U.S. power. In contrast, neither of the superpowers deployed significant forces near India's borders during the Cold War. India did not engage in any use of force involving either of the superpowers. The different experience of the Cold War may account for a substantial portion of the difference in the early track record of the use of force between the two countries.

Geography has also been a significant factor shaping specific patterns of the use of force. India has been relatively more "hegemonic" in South Asia than China has been in East and Northeast Asia, in part because India is surrounded by relatively weaker states. Ironically, the geographic position of the "middle kingdom" is not an enviable one for contemporary China. China is literally in the middle, bordered on all sides by powerful states,

---

[128] We thank Alice Miller for helping us develop this point. See also M. Taylor Fravel, *Strong Borders, Secure Nation: Cooperation and Conflict in China's Territorial Disputes* (Princeton: Princeton University Press, 2008), and John Keay, *India: A History* (New York: Grove Press, 2000), especially 289–447 and 514–517.

including India, Russia, Japan, and South Korea. Via trade, alliances, and security relationships, the United States also has interests that abut China's territorial and maritime borders. These geographical circumstances contribute to different security dilemma dynamics for China and India. This involves not only their relations with great powers such as the United States, but also subregional security dynamics with weaker rivals.

China's use of force to enforce its territorial and maritime claims in the disputed areas of the East and South China Sea area is another difference. India has fewer maritime disputes. The geography of the East and South China Seas, hemmed in on all sides by continental and island states, contributes to overlapping claims. By comparison, the Indian Ocean and Arabian Sea are relatively open, at least to the south and west. Despite this, India's existing maritime disputes with Bangladesh and Pakistan share a characteristic with China's maritime disputes: They are not only issues of boundaries, but are also tied up with claims to purported natural resources, including oil and natural gas.

It is unlikely that the 1980–2001 pattern of an identical number of cases of Indian and Chinese use of force will be maintained indefinitely. The significant finding is that their records of using force are roughly comparable, both in frequency and intensity. While not identical, over time, the proximate causes and motivations for their respective use of force have been similar.

Chinese and Indian Boundary Dispute Behavior

Another way of examining Chinese and Indian foreign policy behavior is to assess their respective records in settling boundary issues. Here too, Beijing is seen in some quarters as an outlier in its behavior. For example, in a U.S. Army War College study, Beijing is described by one American analyst as tenaciously pursuing irredentist territorial claims ranging from border regions with India, to Taiwan, to the Spratly Islands.[129] Long-standing border issues have contributed significantly to the wars that both China and India have been involved in since the mid-1940s. To what extent are these states moving to resolve their respective border issues?

The assessment that follows shows that both Beijing and New Delhi have been moving to settle border disputes and reach agreements with neighbors.

---

[129] Sumit Ganguly, "India's Alliances 2020," in Michael R. Chambers, ed., *South Asia in 2020: Future Strategic Balances and Alliances* (Carlisle: U.S. Army War College, 2002), 329–384, especially 376–377.

China has moved relatively farther on the settlement of its land boundaries. India is relatively closer to resolution of its outstanding maritime disputes. As in the case of the use of force, it would be difficult to argue on the basis of border dispute resolution that China's behavior is in any broad sense more problematic than India's. Neither state has shown itself willing to depart from using both diplomacy and the threat of force in pursuit of its interests. But rather than holding strictly to irredentist claims, each appears to have at least partly redefined those interests over time.

Chinese Boundary Dispute Behavior

Since the start of its reform and opening period, China has moved to resolve most of its border disputes.[130] Borders with six states had been resolved during the 1960s, including those with Burma (1961), Nepal (1963), North Korea (1964), Mongolia (1964), Pakistan (1965), and Afghanistan (1965). More recently, Beijing has resolved boundary issues with six others, including Laos (1993), Vietnam (1999), Russia (2004), Kazakhstan (2002), Tajikistan (2002), and Kyrgyzstan (2004).[131] In many of these cases, confidence-building measures, including mutual force reductions along respective borders and agreements to provide notification of military exercises, helped both sides reach final settlements.[132] Taylor Fravel has shown that China also accepted substantial compromises in most of these settlements, usually accepting less than half of the disputed land.[133]

By 2008, China had settled border disputes with twelve of its fourteen neighboring states. Along its land borders, outstanding territorial disputes remain with only India and Bhutan. Prior to 2009, China and India had made significant if intermittent progress toward resolution of their border disputes with one another. In 1994, they agreed to respect the Line of Actual Control (LAC) along their disputed border areas (albeit not as a final settlement). In 2003, China recognized Sikkim as a part of the Indian Union in exchange for India's acknowledgment of China's sovereignty over Tibet. In

---

[130] Fravel, *Strong Borders, Secure Nation.* See also M. Taylor Fravel, "Regime Insecurity and International Cooperation: Explaining China's Compromises in Territorial Disputes," *International Security*, 30:2 (Fall 2005): 46–83; and M. Taylor Fravel, "Power Shifts and Escalation: Explaining China's Use of Force in Territorial Disputes," *International Security*, 32:3 (Winter 2007/2008): 44–83.

[131] Countries and dates are from M. Taylor Fravel, "Regime Insecurity and International Cooperation." See also Fravel, *Strong Borders, Secure Nation.*

[132] The Shanghai Five (China, Russia, Kazakhstan, Kyrgyz, and Tajikistan) agreed to reduce forces along their mutual borders in 1997. China and Vietnam conducted two large-scale mine-clearing operations along their border in 1992 and 1997.

[133] Fravel, "Regime Insecurity and International Cooperation."

July 2006, further progress was marked by the reopening of the Nathu La pass, linking Tibet and Sikkim.[134] Nevertheless, significant disputes remain on both eastern and western portions of their borders. And the negotiation process has led both sides to more vigorously assert their positions over the remaining disputed territory since late 2006, blocking further progress toward resolution.[135]

Beijing's unsettled boundary issues with Bhutan are closely linked to those it has with India. Bhutan's 1949 peace treaty with India stipulated that Bhutan would be "guided by the advice of the Government of India in regard to its external relations."[136] During Bhutan's 2005 negotiations with China, the Indian military exerted pressure on Bhutan not to make concessions at India's expense.[137] China and Bhutan have, nevertheless, been able to finalize strip maps, specifying intended border demarcation, on all areas of the disputed border that do not overlap with India.[138]

China's efforts to resolve its maritime boundaries have generally been less concerted than those related to its land borders. China, the Philippines, Vietnam, Malaysia, Brunei, and Taiwan have all claimed part or all of the Spratly Islands and parts or all of the surrounding waters. Progress has been made in minimizing the impact of outstanding differences on Beijing's relations with its neighbors. However, these issues remain subject to recurring tensions.

In 2000, Beijing dropped objections to multilateral negotiations over a code of conduct for the South China Sea. In 2002, China signed a Declaration on the Conduct of Parties in the South China Sea with all parties except Taiwan. The Declaration is not a binding agreement. Nevertheless, it indicates the potential for China to accept a multilateral approach to South China Sea disputes. In March 2005, Chinese, Vietnamese, and Philippine companies signed an agreement for joint oil and gas exploration

[134] "Historic India-China link opens," *BBC News*, July 6, 2006, http://news.bbc.co.uk/2/hi/south_asia/5150682.stm

[135] "India and China row over border," *BBC News*, November 14, 2006, http://news.bbc.co.uk/2/hi/south_asia/6145866.stm; "China denies visa to IAS officer from Arunachal," *Financial Express*, May 26, 2007, http://www.financialexpress.com/news/China-denies-visa-to-IAS-officer-from-Arunachal/200132/; "India cancels China defence exchanges after visa row," *BBC News*, August 27, 2010, http://www.bbc.co.uk/news/world-asia-pacific-11106235

[136] The treaty was amended in February 2007, but still suggests that the two "shall cooperate closely with each other on issues relating to their national interests."

[137] "Thimphu-Beijing Border Talks has [sic.] Delhi Worried," *Indian Express Online Media*, July 29, 2005, http://www.indianexpress.com/oldStory/75264/

[138] "Bhutan, India Reach 'Historic' Agreement Mapping Border," *Bhutan Broadcasting Service* [BBC Monitoring International Reports], December 14, 2006.

surveys.[139] This agreement expired in 2008, and many negotiations on this and other related issues since then have returned to a bilateral format. Separately, between 2000 and 2004, China and Vietnam delimited their maritime boundary in the Gulf of Tonkin (Beibu Gulf). China and Vietnam have conducted some joint patrols of fisheries zones in that area.[140] The two sides have discussed joint oil and gas projects in the Tonkin Gulf, although progress remains slow.[141] Moreover, underlying conflicts of interest between China and Vietnam in the South China Sea region have not been resolved and could lead to more serious clashes in the future.

Although no formal border settlement was included, China's twenty-five-year agreement to purchase liquefied natural gas (LNG) from Malaysia in 2006 effectively acknowledged Malaysian sovereignty over South China Sea gas fields up to 200 kilometers from the Sarawak coast. These are waters to which China has previously laid claim.[142] In contrast, China's dispute with Japan over the Diaoyu (Senkaku) Islands and the exclusive economic zone (EEZ) boundary line in the East China Sea remains active and a long way from resolution. Although the two sides have been in a stop-start dialogue and negotiation process for many years, tensions flared again in September 2010.[143]

Despite continuing disputes over island ownership and maritime boundaries, China has thus resolved land border differences with the majority of its neighbors and made some progress toward resolving maritime disputes. As important as the number of disputes resolved has been the flexibility

---

[139] Michael A. Glosny, "Southeast Asia," in Joshua Eisenman, Eric Heginbotham, and Derek Mitchell, eds., *China and the Developing World* (Armonk: M.E. Sharpe, 2007), 164–166. The March 2005 joint exploration agreement lapsed in 2008, largely because of objections from the Philippines. Ian Storey and Carlyle A. Thayer, "The South China Sea Dispute: A Review of Developments and Their Implications since the 2002 Declaration on the Conduct of Parties," in K. V. Kesavan and Daljit Singh, eds., *South and Southeast Asia: Responding to Changing Geo-Political and Security Challenges* (Singapore: Institute of Southeast Asian Studies 2010).

[140] Ian Storey, "Trouble and Strife in the South China Sea: Vietnam and China," *China Brief*, 8:8, April 16, 2008; "China, Vietnam hold joint patrol in Beibu Gulf," *China Daily*, August 21, 2009.

[141] "China's CNOOC Signs Tonkin Gulf Upstream Deal with Vietnam," *Platts Oilgram News*, November 21, 2006; "China Warns Some Oil Companies on Work With Vietnam, U.S. Says," *Bloomberg News*, July 16, 2009; Storey, "Trouble and Strife in the South China Sea: Vietnam and China"; see also Ian Storey, "Trouble and Strife in the South China Sea Part II: Vietnam and China," *China Brief*, 8:9 (April 28, 2008).

[142] "Malaysian LNG deal tests China's maritime borders," *Canberra Times*, March 31, 2010, 15.

[143] For a comprehensive discussion of the issues involved, see Selig S. Harrison, ed., *Seabed Petroleum in Northeast Asia: Conflict or Cooperation*, Woodrow Wilson International Center for Scholars Working Paper, 2005.

of the terms. These include a record of conceding territory and seeking negotiated exchanges, as well as confidence-building measures and troop reductions.

China's motives for flexibility and concessions are rooted in Beijing's judgment of its interests, including its aim to secure border stability, reduce external threats from other states, and engage regional states on issues of cross-border movements of people and material that might threaten China's internal security. When those threats could be better dealt with by compromising on borders and territory, China appears to have done so.[144] This picture does not match a description of a tenacious irredentist power. Rather it appears Chinese behavior is more responsive to assessments of how best to achieve China's broader interests.

India's Boundary Dispute Settlement

India's pursuit of regional stability while implementing its post-1991 program of economic reforms echoes China's behavior. This has led New Delhi to redouble efforts to resolve outstanding land and maritime disputes. India resolved its boundary disagreements with Bhutan in December 2006, and it has resolved most border-related issues with Burma. Progress has also been seen with China and Pakistan, although in those cases, significant disagreements remain. These differences are primarily in the Jammu and Kashmir region in the west (including Aksai Chin) and in the eastern region around Arunachal Pradesh. India and China have resolved some of their disputes, but progress on full normalization of the border has been at least temporarily halted as both sides have hardened positions on remaining areas beginning in late 2006.[145]

Likewise, India and Pakistan initiated talks in 2003 and a high-level "composite dialogue" in 2004, and the two sides held a series of meetings on all disputed boundaries. (The composite dialogue process itself has been periodically suspended.) Indian territorial conflicts with Pakistan include disputes in three areas – Siachen Glacier, Jammu and Kashmir, and Sir Creek. A ceasefire has held in the Siachen Glacier area since November 2003. India has offered to make the current Line of Control (LOC) in Jammu and

---

[144] Fravel, *Strong Borders, Secure Nation*, 6–9.

[145] Despite hardening rhetoric on claims in the Arunachal Pradesh area and tit-for-tat visa disputes, China-India border talks continue. The fourteenth round of official border discussions was completed in 2010. See "India, China making 'steady progress' on border dispute: Shivshankar Menon," *Press Trust of India*, November 30, 2010, http://www.dnaindia.com/india/report_india-china-making-steady-progress-on-border-dispute-shivshankar-menon_1474673

Kashmir permanent. While Pakistan has not accepted this proposal, it has signaled unofficially that it may no longer insist on a UN-sponsored plebiscite or control over the entire area.[146] The two sides are closest to resolution on the Sir Creek boundary, but final agreement remains outstanding.[147] The negotiation process is frequently interrupted by periodic clashes, such as the 2008 terrorist attacks on Mumbai by militants based in Pakistan.

Disputes with China and Pakistan are perhaps the most significant and difficult, but India's borders with Nepal, Bangladesh, and Burma also remain problematic. In December 2007, a team of Nepalese legislators asserted that India had taken over 14,000 hectares of Nepalese land, and in January 2008, Nepal's foreign minister said that the police and army should be mobilized along the border with India to combat Indian encroachment.[148] Nevertheless, unlike Pakistan, Nepal does not have the wherewithal to challenge India. Progress on the border dispute with Nepal remains stalled, although talks have continued.

Having failed to ratify a boundary agreement with Bangladesh in 1974, India agreed to form an Indian-Bangladesh Joint Boundary Working Group in 2003, and most of the border has since been delineated.[149] However, the disposition of enclaves (i.e., Bangladeshi communities on the western side of the border and Indian communities on the eastern side) continues to bedevil a final border settlement. In 2006, India deployed additional troops along the border, doubling the number present several years earlier.[150] More worryingly, Indian forces occasionally exchange fire with Bangladeshi units along the border, as occurred in January 2008.[151] In October 2009, Bangladesh announced that it would seek UN arbitration over the disputed maritime border. Even as India and Bangladesh worked to resolve the

[146] See, for example, "Musharraf Seeks 'Change of Status' for Kashmir: We Must Take Risks for Peace, Says Pakistani Leader," *The Daily Telegraph* (London), October 27, 2004; "India cool on Kashmir proposals," *BBC News*, October 26, 2004, http://news.bbc.co.uk/2/hi/south_asia/3953417.stm

[147] "Sir Creek Maps Exchanged," *The Statesman* (India), May 18, 2007.

[148] "Nepal Team Inspects Land Grabbed by India," *Radio Nepal* [BBC Monitoring South Asia], December 25, 2007; "Nepal Foreign Minister Urges Troop Deployment at Border with India," Rajhani (Kathmandu) [in BBC Monitoring South Asia], January 9, 2008.

[149] "India, Bangladesh to Form Working Group for Resolution of Border Issues," *PTI News Agency* (New Delhi), May 1, 2003. "Dhaka Puts Conditions for Allowing India-Myanmar Gas Pipeline," *Press Trust of India*, June 23, 2005.

[150] "India-Bangladesh Border Security 'Rejigged'; More Battalions Deployed," *The Telegraph* (Kolkata), July 26, 2006.

[151] "Bangladesh Border Crossfire Due to 'Illegal Fencing' by India – Official," *New Age Website* [in BBC Monitoring South Asia] January 30, 2008.

difficult enclave problem in early 2011, Bangladesh accused Indian border forces of encroaching into its territory.

Still, India has made substantial progress in some areas. In 2007, Nepal's Foreign Ministry claimed that the work of delineating the border areas with India was "98 percent complete."[152] On its maritime frontiers, India has resolved most of its boundary issues, many of these during the 1970s. These settlements include those with Sri Lanka (agreements in 1974 and 1976), Maldives (1976), Indonesia (1974, 1977, and 1978), Thailand (1978 and 1993), and Myanmar (1986 and 1993).[153] India has outstanding maritime disputes with Pakistan, around the Sir Creek boundary, and with Bangladesh. The areas at stake in both of these disputes are thought to be rich in natural gas resources.

Exclusive Economic Zones

The definition of rights in offshore exclusive economic zones (EEZs)[154] is not strictly an issue of national territorial boundaries. However, the question of strategic behavior within EEZs gained renewed prominence when Chinese vessels confronted a U.S. Navy ocean surveillance ship, the *Impeccable*, in March 2009.[155] The *Impeccable* was conducting surveillance activities outside of Chinese territorial waters, but within China's EEZ, about seventy-five miles south of China's Hainan Island. Hainan is home to a Chinese naval base that hosts some of China's newest submarines,

---

[152] "Nepal Ready to Resolve Border Disputes with India," *Annapurna Post* (Kathmandu) [in BBC Monitoring South Asia], December 29, 2007.

[153] "Q. 4551 Fixing of Maritime Boundaries," May 5, 2005. Written response by Indian Minister of State in the Ministry of External Affairs, Shri E. Ahamed, in response to parliamentary inquiry on maritime boundary issues, http://mea.gov.in/parliament/rs/2005/05/05 rs24.htm

[154] Articles 56, 58, and 59 of the UN Convention on the Law of the Sea (UNCLOS) define the exclusive economic zone and its uses. The EEZ is defined as that portion of the seas and oceans extending up to 200 nautical miles in which coastal states have the right to explore and exploit natural resources as well as to exercise jurisdiction over marine science research and environmental protection. Freedom of navigation and over flight, as well as other uses consented on the high seas, is allowed under UNCLOS. See "United Nations Convention on the Law of the Sea," http://www.un.org/Depts/los/convention_agreements/texts/unclos/closindx.htm. China is among 156 nations to have ratified UNCLOS. The United States has not ratified the treaty but recognizes most of it as customary law. There are numerous disputes over rights in EEZs, not only in the South China Sea, but also in Europe and in North America. Some of these, most famously the UK-Iceland "Cod Wars" of the 1970s, have involved confrontations between civilian and naval vessels.

[155] "China Draws U.S. Protest Over Shadowing of Ships," *The Washington Post*, Tuesday, March 10, 2009.

including ballistic missile submarines.[156] Five Chinese trawlers surrounded and sailed dangerously close to the American ship.[157]

The U.S. view is that under international law, foreign states and their military forces can conduct surveillance activities in the EEZs of other countries.[158] While the United States has a long history of conducting such operations close to China and other countries such as the former Soviet Union, China has long sought to limit such activities in its EEZ. Under its interpretation of the UN Convention on the Law of the Sea (UNCLOS), Beijing claims the right to refuse other nations access to its EEZ for the purpose of conducting marine scientific research activities, including naval and military activities such as those conducted by *Impeccable*. China has, however, conducted such research in Japanese EEZs. China argues that intelligence-gathering activities in its EEZ constitute "preparation of the battlefield." In Beijing's view, this amounts to a threat to use force, which it sees as a violation both of the UN Charter and of UNCLOS.[159] China claims to have recorded at least 200 incidents of American vessels conducting intelligence activities in its EEZ without its permission.[160] Chinese vessels and aircraft have shadowed and confronted other U.S. ships, such as the hydrographic survey ship *Bowditch*.

China is not the only state that asserts a right to refuse access to its EEZ for the purpose of conducting marine scientific research or intelligence-gathering activities. Other nations that take this view include Vietnam, Brazil, Malaysia, and India. India's position on its rights in its EEZ is in

---

[156] *Impeccable*'s capabilities allow it to conduct intelligence gathering related to such submarines. *Impeccable* is capable of tracking submarines and mapping ocean floors and channels, information that would assist the U.S. Navy in targeting or immobilizing Chinese subs in the event of conflict. This would be particularly sensitive if it involved Chinese ballistic missile submarines, which many analysts (including in the United States) believe to be the most survivable (and therefore most crisis-stable) element of China's nuclear deterrent forces. Hainan was the scene of another Sino-U.S. confrontation in 2001, when a Chinese fighter plane intercepted an American EP-3 intelligence-gathering aircraft in nearby international airspace, flew dangerously close to it, and collided with the American plane. The Chinese pilot was killed, and the American plane was forced to make an emergency landing in Hainan.

[157] Using ostensibly civilian vessels to threaten collision or to actually collide with the ships of other nations could emerge as a pattern of Chinese behavior in confrontations over disputed waters. The September 2010 flaring of tensions between Japan and China involved the apparently intentional collision of a Chinese fishing trawler with a Japanese coast guard vessel.

[158] "China Draws U.S. Protest Over Shadowing of Ships." *The Washington Post*.

[159] Mark Valencia, "The Impeccable Incident: Truth and Consequences," *China Security*, 14 (2009).

[160] Valencia, "The Impeccable Incident."

principle similar to China's, although the two countries may differ in the degree to which they seek to enforce these rights. The Indian declaration upon ratification of UNCLOS in 1995 states: "The Government of the Republic of India understands that the provisions of the Convention do not authorize other States to carry out in the exclusive economic zone and on the continental shelf military exercises or manoeuvres [sic], in particular those involving the use of weapons or explosives without the consent of the coastal State."[161]

Like China, India has also protested U.S. survey and intelligence-gathering activities in its EEZ, including the activities of *Bowditch* in 2001 and 2004.[162] However, India has not been as confrontational as China in its assertion of those rights. U.S.-India relations are not marked by the military sensitivity of the interactions between the United States and China around the submarine base at Hainan. However, this could change as India develops weapons such as nuclear ballistic missile submarines, especially if these are eventually deployed with missiles that could reach the United States. The U.S. Navy would likely seek to observe and understand the operations of such vessels. Based on its earlier statements and behavior, New Delhi could well object to such activity if it were performed within India's EEZ.

Comparison: Chinese and Indian Boundary Dispute Behavior

It is difficult to judge whether China or India has done better or gone farther in resolving territorial disputes with neighbors. India moved earlier and farther in resolving maritime boundary disputes. New Delhi has settled its maritime disputes with all but two countries. China has yet to reach final settlement with six parties (including Taiwan) in its maritime boundary disputes, although it has moved toward putting disputes in abeyance and

---

[161] Government of India, "Declaration made upon ratification (29 June 1995)," http://www.un.org/Depts/los/convention_agreements/convention_declarations.htm#India

[162] Questions about U.S. naval activities in India's EEZ were also raised in India's parliament in 2004. See Question 2245, Rajya Sabha, August 25, 2004/Bhadrapada 3, 1926 (Saka), http://www.rajyasabha.gov.in/dailyques/202/uq25082004.PDF, originally cited in Commander B. K. Verma (Indian Navy), "Cooperative Maritime Engagement – Exercise Aman 2009: Facilitating US Chinese Interaction," National Maritime Foundation (India), May 1, 2009, 6–7; fn 15, http://www.maritimeindia.org/pdfs/Commentry01May09.pdf. See also K. K. Agnihotri and Sunil Kumar Agarwala, "Legal Aspects of Marine Scientific Research in Exclusive Economic Zones: Implications of the Impeccable Incident," *Maritime Affairs: Journal of the National Maritime Foundation of India*, 5:2 (December 2009): 135–150; and Jon M. Van Dyke, "Military Ships and Planes Operating in the Exclusive Economic Zone of Another Country," *Marine Policy*, 28:1 (January 2004): 29–39.

exploring cooperative development with several of them. In 2009, Chinese statements and behavior regarding maritime disputes and its rights in its EEZ became more assertive than in the recent past. India's views of its rights in its EEZ are similar in principle to China's. It has protested similar activities to those China opposes, and there are those in India who also take an expansive view of India's maritime interests and the significance of its EEZs.[163]

On land boundary dispute settlement, China has made greater progress. China has settled its borders with twelve of the fourteen countries on its borders. India, for its part, has settled two of six land boundary disputes (with Bhutan and Burma), with substantial, albeit uneven, progress toward resolving two others (Nepal and Bangladesh) and some progress on the final two (China and Pakistan).[164] However, India has moved to fence its borders with virtually all neighbors and, in several cases, has reinforced its military presence in the lead-up to negotiations or expected agreements. This differs from the Chinese approach, which has generally relied on a combination of negotiated settlements, demilitarization, confidence-building measures, and border opening, particularly for trade.

Neither country can be described as dramatically more or less benign in its treatment of border and territory disputes. Both China and India have engaged in recalculation of their respective national interests over time. This has led both to entrench positions on some boundary disputes and to seek negotiated resolution to others. There are strong similarities in the two countries' approaches to border dispute resolution (with China appearing at times to be somewhat more pragmatic).

Conclusions: Foreign Policy

Although specific patterns vary across time and issue area, neither Chinese or Indian foreign policy trends, nor their respective propensity to use force, nor their respective border dispute behavior justify starkly differentiated views of the two countries' strategic behavior. In recent years, both states have followed similar foreign policy trajectories. Both countries have moved from periods characterized by ideology-driven foreign policy,

---

[163] See *Freedom to Use the Seas: India's Maritime Military Strategy* (New Delhi: Integrated Headquarters, Ministry of Defence [Navy], May 2007); and Admiral Madhvendra Singh (Ret.), "The Indian Navy in 2020," *Security Research Review*, June 21, 2006, http://www.bharat-rakshak.com/SRR/2006/02/56.html

[164] Some of these cases are ambiguous. Differences with Nepal are largely resolved, whereas those with Burma might still be regarded as not yet fully settled.

assertiveness, and even attacks on neighbors, to integrating with the global economy and with global institutions. Paradoxically, even as the two integrate with global markets and play a growing role in global politics, both remain preoccupied powers. Each is primarily inward-focused, seeking to maintain a peaceful external environment conducive to carrying out difficult and painful domestic development tasks, including economic and social reforms.

China has been involved in more incidents of the use of force than India since 1949, but not since China's period of reform and opening began in 1978. Both Beijing and New Delhi have made a more concerted effort to resolve border disputes over the last fifteen years. In some respects, China has moved farther in negotiating and resolving these territorial and border issues than India has.

However, on the issues of Taiwan, nuclear weapons proliferation, and stability in South and Central Asia, China and India present quite different challenges to U.S. policy. Taiwan in particular is exceptional. The United States has direct interests related to Taiwan and Northeast Asia, which have no parallel in South Asia. Although there is potential to continue to manage the Taiwan issue, it is also exceptionally dangerous. Taiwan holds the greatest potential to lead to direct conflict between the United States and one of Asia's two rising powers.

The United States must also remain mindful that even though India and the United States share many common interests, Indian and U.S. interests are not necessarily identical, nor are they permanently aligned. In particular, the United States has broad interests in global efforts to prevent proliferation of WMD, the prevention of arms races in South and East Asia, and a critical interest in the internal stability of Pakistan and Afghanistan. New Delhi may continue to prioritize these and other interests differently than Washington for decades to come.

4

Military Modernization

Defense Spending

What resources are being dedicated to support Indian and Chinese military modernization programs? Official defense budgets do not provide a complete answer in either case. Neither China nor India is unique in that regard. The official defense budgets published by most states fail to capture the full range of spending on national defense. Yet in China and India, varying degrees of nontransparency persist at the same time that the economies and defense budgets of both countries are growing rapidly.

In the Chinese case, the combination of significant defense spending increases and persistent nontransparency in accounting and reporting has drawn intense scrutiny.[1] According to the 2009 Pentagon report, *The Military Power of the People's Republic of China*, "China continues to promulgate incomplete defense expenditure figures and engage in actions that appear inconsistent with its declaratory policies. The limited transparency in China's military and security affairs poses risks to stability by creating uncertainty and increasing the potential for misunderstanding and miscalculation."[2]

Opacity in China's military affairs, and particularly in its defense spending, is often linked to questions about Beijing's long-term intentions.[3] The wide range of Western estimates for China's defense spending contributes

---

[1] *Military Power of the People's Republic of China* (Washington, DC: Office of the Secretary of Defense, 2009), 32. Since 2002, versions of the same report have made similar statements. Since mid-2007, criticism of Chinese military modernization became more focused, and U.S. statements more balanced. However, concern about opacity in budgets remains an issue for U.S. policymakers. See, for example, "Gates, in Fresh Tone for U.S., Offers to Work with China's Military to 'Build Trust Over Time,'" *New York Times*, June 2, 2007.

[2] *Military Power of the People's Republic of China, 2009*, II.

[3] See *The Military Power of the People's Republic of China* (Washington, DC: Office of the Secretary of Defense, 2006), I. Subsequent annual reports in this series make similar points.

to this uncertainty and unease. Some American officials appear to share a view that rising Chinese military spending is an indicator of potentially threatening Chinese strategic intentions, in part because many Americans do not believe that China faces legitimate security threats. In 2005, Defense Secretary Donald Rumsfeld summarized that view: "China's defense expenditures are much higher than Chinese officials have published. It is estimated that China's is the third largest military budget in the world, and clearly the largest in Asia.... Since no nation threatens China, one must wonder: Why this growing investment? Why these continuing large and expanding arms purchases? Why these continuing robust deployments?"[4]

The U.S. Congress has also expressed bipartisan concern about Chinese defense-spending trends and opacity in Chinese budget reporting. For example, both Democratic and Republican leaders of the United States China Economic and Security Review Commission wrote in 2007: "[China] has raised its defense budget 10 percent or more each year over the last 11 years. This March, Beijing announced that its 2007 defense budget [was] $44.94 billion. The Pentagon believes this figure is significantly understated and that China's actual defense budget is closer to two or three times this amount .... Because of the opacity of Beijing's expenditures, particularly those that are military-related, it is difficult for analysts to agree on precise amounts."[5]

Yet many published Western estimates of Chinese defense spending are themselves nontransparent, seldom spelling out methods for estimation and the precise spending items included in the estimate.[6] Thus, while it is now common for both specialists and the Western media to report that official defense budgets do not account for China's total defense-related spending, it is also quite common to find statements that China's spending is "two or three times" higher than official budgets without any detail on

4 "Secretary Rumsfeld's Remarks to the International Institute for Strategic Studies," June 4, 2005," http://singapore.usembassy.gov/060405.html

5 Carolyn Bartholomew and Daniel Blumenthal, "Letter to The Honorable Robert Byrd, President Pro Tempore of the Senate, and The Honorable Nancy Pelosi, Speaker of the House of Representatives," in *China's Military Modernization And Its Impact On the United States And The Asia-Pacific, Hearing Before the U.S.-China Economic and Security Review Commission*, One Hundred Tenth Congress, First Session, March 29–30, 2007 (Washington, DC: United States-China Economic and Security Review Commission, May 2007), 3.

6 An exception to this is Keith Crane et al., *Modernizing China's Military: Opportunities and Constraints* (Santa Monica: RAND Corporation, 2005), which in comparison to previous public estimates of Chinese defense spending provides significantly improved clarity about methods.

how such an estimate is determined.[7] The wide range of estimates is frequently repeated without critical examination, not only by popular media, but also by professionals in the international relations, security, and intelligence analysis fields.[8]

Many Western estimates of Chinese defense spending do not clearly differentiate between the effect of adding off-budget items to official budgets and the effect of adjusting all (or part) of that new budget figure for purchasing power parity (PPP). "Off-budget" refers to spending on defense-related items that are not included in the official defense budget number, such as military pensions and paramilitary forces. PPP is a methodology for adjusting currency exchange rates to reflect differences in domestic price levels between countries. PPP has nothing to do with hidden or off-budget spending. Rarely are the additions from either the off-budget or the PPP effects specified in a way that would permit examination or correction.

Media coverage of international defense spending rarely questions whether PPP adjustments reflect meaningful additions to relative military capabilities. In fact, the effect of price differentials is greatest in the areas of least lethal defense capability, such as military pensions, salaries, housing, clothing, and food. PPP methods are not typically suited to measuring the most lethal military capabilities, including advanced weapons systems. As we argue in more detail later in this chapter, in most cases, it is best to use market exchange rates rather than PPP-adjusted figures to compare defense spending across countries.

Adding to the confusion, most recent Western estimates of Chinese defense spending make comparison with other states difficult because the same standards of measurement are not usually applied to peer countries in the same way they are applied to China. Many estimates do not include the same off-budget spending items for all the countries under comparison.

---

[7] See, for example, "China Plans Steep Increase in Military Spending," *New York Times*, March 5, 2008; "Chinese Premier Pledges Help for the Rural Poor, Playing Down Growth of Military Spending," *New York Times*, March 5, 2006; and Mark Helprin, "We ignore China's growing military and economic power at our peril," *Wall Street Journal*, Monday, December 13, 2004, text available at http://conservapundit.blogspot.com/2004/12/we-ignore-chinas-growing-military-and.html

[8] See for example, "China plans to slow expansion of defense spending in 2010," *Washington Post*, March 5, 2010; Trefor Moss, "White paper reveals insight into Chinese Defence Rationale," *Jane's Defence Weekly*, January 28, 2009; Council on Foreign Relations, "The Scope of China's Military Threat," http://www.cfr.org/publication/10824/scope_of_chinas_military_threat.html; National Intelligence Council, *Mapping the Global Future: Report of the National Intelligence Council's 2020 Project* (Washington, DC: U.S. Government Printing Office, December 2004).

Western media typically fail to question whether published comparisons of Chinese defense spending to that of other countries are made on an equivalent basis.

Muddled methods for estimating and comparing defense spending can cause a number of problems. First, poor methods make accurate assessment of spending trends and international challenges more difficult. China is more frequently the object of these mismeasurements. Inaccurate estimates of Chinese military spending may distract American attention and resources from other security challenges elsewhere in the world. This is especially true if faulty analysis of defense spending becomes the basis for assertions about China's general strategic intentions. Second, imprecise (often exaggerated) estimates of general trends in overall defense spending distract attention from specific military capability developments that require more focused American attention. Third, faulty or exaggerated analysis undermines the credibility and effectiveness of American diplomacy with China and with America's allies in Asia.

In this chapter, we take a three-part approach to developing improved estimates of Indian and Chinese defense spending. The first section looks at the composition and trends in the official defense budgets provided by each country. It traces official defense spending over the last three decades and assesses spending as a percent of GDP and as a share of government expenditure. The second section of the chapter provides a fuller picture of defense spending by examining off-budget spending items. We detail these and, combining them with official defense budgets, build up a side-by-side comparison of similar defense-related spending programs in both countries. This analysis also sheds light on relative transparency of defense spending in the two countries. The third section examines the use and misuse of PPP methods to adjust defense-spending figures. We argue that unless certain conditions for precision in methods and calculations are met, employing PPP yields more misleading estimates of defense spending than not. We illustrate these methods by providing an example of appropriately adjusted defense spending in PPP terms for both India and China.

Each section successively builds up a detailed picture of the two countries' defense spending in two years, 2005 and 2010, based on the best available public information.[9] Many data sources for estimating China's total

---

[9] The year 2005 was selected because this year coincides with detailed World Bank data collection for PPP estimates, enhancing the accuracy of PPP adjustments for this year. As this manuscript was being finalized in late 2011, 2010 is the most recent year for which official data was available.

Table 4.1. *Indian and Chinese defense spending, 2005 and 2010*
(in billions except as noted)

	2005		2010	
	India	China	India	China
Official Defense Budget (Current USD market exchange rate)	18.5	30.2	30.6	78.5
Baseline Full Defense Spending [Including off-budget items] (Current USD, market exchange rate)	23.9	44.6	43.2	113.3
Baseline Full Spending Percent of GDP (%)	2.96	1.98	3.02	1.97
PPP-Adjusted Baseline Full Defense Spending (Appropriate USD PPP)	45.4	69.3	88.4	138.2

Note: Detailed explanations of terms and calculations are provided in subsequent sections. This table presents official defense budgets in U.S. dollars at market exchange rates of that year. It also shows our "baseline" estimate for full defense spending in U.S. dollars at market exchange rates of that year. (This includes off-budget items such as paramilitaries, arms imports, defense R&D, and subsidies to defense industries.) The table also shows the baseline estimate adjusted by an appropriate PPP method, in PPP equivalent U.S. dollars of that year. Nuclear weapons, space, and intelligence programs not included.

defense spending were identified in a 2005 RAND report, *Modernizing China's Military: Opportunities and Constraints*.[10] That report raised the bar for transparency, methodology, and accuracy in estimating Chinese defense spending. This chapter employs some of the same methods as the 2005 RAND report but builds on that foundation by offering several improvements.[11]

Table 4.1 presents a summary of our estimates for Indian and Chinese defense spending in 2005 and 2010. The baseline estimate for China's 2005 full defense spending (official budget plus off-budget items) at market exchange rates, $44.6 billion, was slightly less than double the size of India's estimated full defense spending of $23.9 billion. At that time, China's economy was three times the size of India's at market exchange rates. In 2010,

[10] Crane et al., *Modernizing China's Military*, 133.
[11] We use Indian data to generate an estimate for Indian defense spending comparable to the estimate for China. We use a more accurate upper boundary on spending for defense-relevant R&D and subsidies to industry for China. We provide comparable upper boundaries of defense-relevant R&D and subsidies to industry for India. Using Chinese sources, we add an estimate of Chinese military pensions and benefits to military families. We also improve on the use of PPP in the estimate by employing the latest available data on sector-level price differentials to develop a transparent and more accurate PPP methodology for estimating defense spending.

China's estimated full defense spending at market exchange rates of $113.3 billion was about 2.6 times India's estimated full defense spending of $43.2 billion. By 2010, China's economy was four times the size of India's. In 2005 and 2010, China spent about 2 percent of GDP on defense, and India spent about 3 percent of GDP on defense. (For reasons explained later in the chapter, the calculations for both Indian and Chinese full defense spending exclude nuclear weapons, space, and intelligence programs.)

Some comparison with the United States puts these estimates in greater context. The U.S. official defense budget excludes veterans benefits, nuclear weapons programs, space programs, intelligence programs, the costs of wars in Iraq and Afghanistan, and other special military programs that are not made public.[12] In 2005, the U.S. official defense budget was $474 billion, and in 2010, it was nearly $694 billion. The official U.S. defense budget accounted for 4.7 percent of GDP in 2010, and it was about nine times larger than China's official defense budget in 2010.[13] Ignoring other off-budget U.S. defense spending and adding only the costs of U.S. veterans' benefits to the official U.S. defense budget would bring 2010 U.S. spending to $802 billion (5.5 percent of GDP). This figure is more than seven times China's estimated 2010 full defense spending of $113.3 billion at market exchange rates. America's 2010 GDP of $14.6 trillion was about 2.5 times the size of China's 2010 GDP of $5.7 trillion at market exchange rates.

Official Defense Budgets

Significant elements of defense spending are not contained in Chinese and Indian official budgets. But official budgets in both countries do cover the bulk of defense spending exclusive of nuclear weapons, space, and intelligence programs. Official budgets also provide a relatively consistent data set that allows a first cut at trends across time. As the comparison of Indian and Chinese off-budget items later in this chapter show, China is not an outlier in leaving some defense-related programs out of its official defense budget.

---

[12] For a side-by-side comparison of spending items included (and not included) in Chinese and U.S. defense budgets, see Dennis J. Blasko, Chas W. Freeman, Jr., Stanley A. Horowitz, Evan S. Medeiros, and James C. Mulvenon, "Defense-Related Spending in China: A Preliminary Analysis and Comparison with American Equivalents," United States-China Policy Foundation, 2007, http://www.uscpf.org/v2/pdf/defensereport.pdf

[13] "Table 3.1 – Outlays by Superfunction and Function, 1940–2015," Office of Management and Budget, The White House, accessed March 4, 2010 at http://www.whitehouse.gov/omb/budget/fy2011/assets/hist03z1.xls; "Inside the Black Budget," *New York Times*, April 3, 2008 (corrected version), http://www.nytimes.com/2008/04/01/science/01patc.html?8dpc

Table 4.2. *India: Official defense budget, 2005 and 2010* (in billions)

	2005 Rupees	2005 USD	2010 Rupees	2010 USD
Army	307	7	605	12.2
Navy	63	1	98	2.0
Air Force	91	2	150	3.0
Defense ordnance factories	−3	−0.1	2	0.03
Capital outlay on defense	331	7	608	12.3
Defense R&D	28	1	52	1.1
Total	**817**	**18.5**	**1,516**	**30.6**
GDP	**35,709**		**70,842**	
Official defense-spending share of GDP (%)	**2.29**		**2.14**	

Source: Union Budget Speech 2005–2006, Union Budget Speech 2006–2007; Union Budget Volume II Expenditure Budget 2006–2007, available at http://indiabudget.nic.in. Union Budget Speech 2010–2011; Union Budget Speech 2011–2012; Union Budget Volume II Expenditure Budget 2011–2012, available at http://indiabudget.nic.in. GDP figures are from IMF, World Economic Outlook Database (October 2010). Note that some columns may not add precisely due to rounding. Nuclear weapons, space, and intelligence programs not included.

Official Defense Budgets: Components and Recent Trends (2005 and 2010)

Before moving on to consider budgetary trends over a longer period of time, we begin with a look at the component parts of Chinese and Indian defense budgets. We present these data for the years 2005 and 2010 (Tables 4.2 and 4.3).

India's official defense budget is made public each year in the Finance Minister's budget speech, and details are published in the annual Union Budget.[14] India's official defense budget includes figures for the Indian Army, Navy, and Air Force (each of which includes personnel costs and operations and maintenance), as well as separate military-wide figures for weapons and equipment (including arms imports), official defense research and development (R&D), and the cost of subsidies to defense ordnance factories. (When ordnance factories are profitable, this last number is subtracted from the official Indian defense budget.) China's official defense budget includes figures for the costs for military personnel, operations and training, and equipment. China's official budget includes both central and local government spending on defense. The official budget also includes

---

[14] Indian Union budget data are available at http://indiabudget.nic.in

Table 4.3. *China: Official defense budget, 2005 and 2010* (in billions)

	2005 Yuan	2005 USD	2010 Yuan	2010 USD
PLA all services personnel	83	10.2	181	26.7
PLA all services operations and training	81	9.9	179	26.5
PLA all services equipment	84	10.2	172	25.3
Total Official Defense Budget	**247**	**30.2**	**532**	**78.5**
GDP	**18,494**		**38,946**	
Official defense-spending share of GDP (%)		**1.34**		**1.37**

Sources: For 2005 and 2010, the total official defense budget number and the respective share for personnel, operations, and equipment are found in China's defense white papers, *China's National Defense in 2006* and *China's National Defense in 2010*. GDP for 2010 is an IMF estimate from World Economic Outlook Database (October 2010). Note that some columns may not add precisely due to rounding. Nuclear weapons, space, and intelligence programs not included.

(but does not specify amounts for) official defense R&D, militia forces, and a portion of military retirement costs. China's official defense budgets are reported in its Defense White Papers, as well as in annual statistical yearbooks published by the State Statistical Bureau and the Finance Ministry.

At 2005 market exchange rates, India's 2005 official defense budget was equivalent to $18.5 billion, and China's equivalent to $30.2 billion. India's official defense budget of 817 billion rupees amounted to 2.29 percent of India's GDP in 2005. At 247 billion yuan, China's official defense budget was equal to 1.34 percent of China's 2005 GDP. Five years later, in 2010, official defense budgets in both countries had changed only slightly as a percentage of GDP. India's official budget of 1.5 trillion rupees equaled 2.14 percent of GDP, or $30.6 billion at market exchange rates. China's official 2010 defense budget of 532 billion yuan accounted for 1.37 percent of GDP. At contemporary market exchange rates, China's official defense budget in 2010 was equal to $78.5 billion.

Defense spending has increased rapidly in both countries over the last decade. China's official defense spending tripled in real (i.e., inflation-adjusted) terms between 2000 and 2010. This equaled a compound annual growth rate (CAGR) of 11.8 percent over that period.[15] India's official defense budget did not grow as fast as China's but still nearly doubled in real

[15] A compound annual growth rate adjusts for volatility in annual growth over a period of years. It is a more accurate measure than an arithmetic mean of annual growth rates.

terms from 2000 to 2010 (a CAGR of 5.6 percent). Notably, China's economy also grew faster than India's over the 2000 to 2010 period, at a CAGR of 10.5 percent compared to India's 7.4 percent.

Official Defense Budgets: Longer-Term Patterns

The rising defense budgets of the last decade should be put in a broader context, one that considers longer-term trends and the growth of national economies. Mapped out over the last three decades, Chinese and Indian official defense-spending trajectories exhibit some similarities (Table 4.4). Both countries have seen significant real defense-spending growth over the long term. In real terms, Indian official defense spending increased by five times between 1980 and 2010. Over the same period, India's GDP increased six times in real terms. Chinese official defense spending increased by four times in real terms between 1980 and 2010. During this period, China's economy expanded nearly eighteen times in real terms.

Over the period of thirty years between 1980 and 2010 then, India and China saw roughly comparable levels of real compound annual growth in defense budgets, at 5.4 percent for India and 4.6 percent for China. However, China's economy grew much faster than India's in real terms, at a CAGR of 10.1 percent from 1980 to 2010, compared to India's 6.2 percent. Future economic growth trends will affect the sustainability of defense-spending levels and defense budget growth rates.

Each country also had an extended period when official defense spending was relatively flat in real terms (see Table 4.4). In each case, this was followed by a period of relatively high real growth. For China, the period of flat real defense spending was longer than India's, extending over the eighteen years between 1980 and 1998. India's official defense spending was flat in real terms over a period of about ten years, between 1986 and 1996. The data also show that in both countries, real growth in official defense spending has sometimes been higher and sometimes lower than real economic growth rates. Both countries have also seen periods of near-term volatility in defense-spending growth rates (Figures 4.1 and 4.2).

In both countries, defense spending actually shrank in real terms in some years (in China as recently as 1993 and in India as recently as 2002). In the thirty years between 1980 and 2010, real defense-spending growth was negative in about the same number of years – seven for India and eight for China. In both countries, real growth in defense spending was often lower than real GDP growth. China's annual real defense-spending growth was lower than annual real GDP growth in nineteen out of thirty years. India's

Table 4.4. *GDP and official defense budgets, 1980–2010* (in billions)

	India				China			
	GDP Current Rupees	GDP Real 2005 Rupees	Official Defense Budget Current Rupees	Official Defense Budget Real 2005 Rupees	GDP Current Yuan	GDP Real 2005 Yuan	Official Defense Budget Current Yuan	Official Defense Budget Real 2005 Yuan
1980	1,435	8,811	38	233	303	1,771	19	113
1981	1,708	9,356	46	252	287	1,863	17	109
1982	1,932	9,737	54	270	532	2,033	18	67
1983	2,230	10,356	64	295	596	2,255	18	67
1984	2,520	10,838	72	309	721	2,597	18	65
1985	2,839	11,368	79	315	902	2,948	19	63
1986	3,184	11,922	102	382	1,028	3,207	20	63
1987	3,606	12,418	125	431	1,206	3,579	21	62
1988	4,237	13,443	132	419	1,504	3,984	22	58
1989	4,902	14,359	145	425	1,699	4,147	25	61
1990	5,705	15,167	158	419	1,867	4,304	29	67
1991	6,581	15,491	164	385	2,178	4,701	33	71
1992	7,564	16,170	175	374	2,692	5,368	38	75
1993	8,701	16,969	215	419	3,533	6,120	43	74
1994	10,163	18,020	230	408	4,820	6,921	55	79
1995	11,924	19,345	269	436	6,079	7,676	64	80
1996	13,429	20,808	278	431	7,118	8,443	72	85
1997	15,402	22,957	361	538	7,897	9,229	81	95
1998	17,640	24,171	412	565	8,440	9,949	93	110
1999	19,678	24,962	485	615	8,968	10,705	108	128
2000	21,566	26,070	545	658	9,921	11,604	121	141
2001	23,189	27,083	570	666	10,966	12,566	144	165
2002	24,998	28,317	560	634	12,033	13,710	171	195
2003	27,733	30,257	603	658	13,582	15,094	191	212
2004	31,272	32,710	770	805	15,988	16,618	220	229
2005	35,709	35,709	817	817	18,494	18,494	247	247
2006	41,140	39,157	890	847	21,631	20,841	298	287
2007	47,633	43,029	960	867	26,581	23,799	355	318
2008	54,873	45,780	1,146	956	31,405	26,082	418	347
2009	59,520	48,380	1,363	1108	34,051	28,454	495	414
2010	(e)70,842	(e)53,057	1,516	1135	(e)38,946	(e)31,430	532	430

Source: Current year GDP data are from International Monetary Fund, World Economic Outlook Database (October 2010), http://www.imf.org/external/data.htm. GDP Data for 2010 are IMF estimates as of October 2010. GDP data in real terms 2005 local currency are estimated based on GDP deflators from IMF World Economic Outlook Database (October 2010). Indian defense budget data are from Indian Union Budget speeches, 1981–2011, available at http://indiabudget.nic.in. China defense budget data are from State Statistics Bureau, *China Statistical Yearbook*, various years; State Statistics Bureau, *50 Years of New China 1949–1999*.

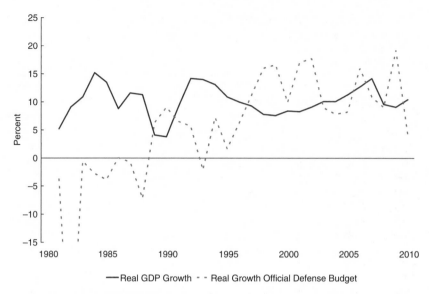

Figure 4.1. China: Real GDP growth and real official defense budget growth.

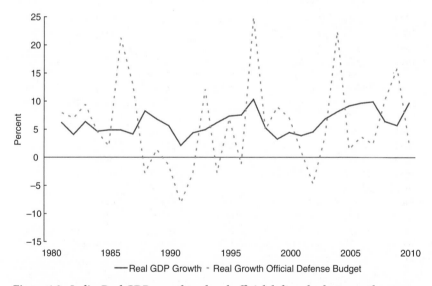

Figure 4.2. India: Real GDP growth and real official defense budget growth.

real defense-spending growth was lower than real GDP growth in eighteen out of thirty years.

In many ways, the relative effort spent on defense is a more meaningful measure of the state's security posture and its views of its security

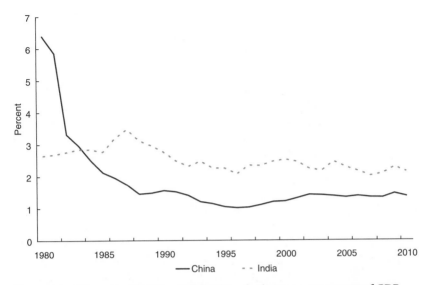

Figure 4.3. **Chinese and Indian official defense budgets as a percentage of GDP.**

environment than absolute spending levels. Examining defense spending as a percentage of GDP provides some insights on this issue. Over the three decades between 1980 and 2010, India's official defense budget averaged 2.5 percent of GDP each year. Over the same period, China's official defense budget averaged 1.8 percent of GDP each year (Figure 4.3). In 2010, India's official defense budget accounted for 2.14 percent of GDP, and China's official defense budget accounted for 1.37 percent of GDP.

Many observers recognize economic growth as a critical enabler of rising defense budgets in Asia and elsewhere. However, the growth of government extractive capacity and overall growth of government spending also helps explain rising defense spending in a number of rapidly developing countries. At very low levels of per capita income, the government's extractive capacity is generally low, but as economies grow from a low base, government revenues as a percentage of GDP often follow suit. In the Indian case, central government revenues rose from 16 percent of GDP in 1990 to 17 percent of GDP in 2010.[16] In China, the increased role of the central government in collecting revenues has been greater, especially since a major fiscal system reform in 1994. Chinese central government revenues rose from 5.3

---

[16] Data on revenues are available from Indian Union Budgets, see http://www.indiabudget. nic.in/ub1999-2000/rb/annex9.pdf and http://www.indiabudget.nic.in/ub2011-12/rec/ annex1.pdf

percent of GDP in 1990 to 11 percent of GDP in 2010.[17] Since the mid-1990s, increased central government revenues have helped China expand official defense spending slightly as a percentage of GDP and have helped India stabilize its levels of defense spending as a percentage of GDP.

Nevertheless, all of the factors that have supported increased defense spending have limits. Both India and China may face challenges in sustaining current high levels of GDP growth over the long term. Government revenue growth cannot indefinitely outstrip economic growth without costs to the economy. Competition over spending priorities may be even more important in determining whether recent defense-spending trends are sustainable. India and China face urgent domestic economic and social problems related to urbanization, education, health care, rural development, energy supply, environmental degradation, and the creation of social safety nets. All of these compete with defense for government resources and spending. Many of these claims on government attention and resources are linked to internal social stability in both countries. In that sense, they are not luxuries.

Increased attention to nondefense issues is reflected in figures for defense spending as a share of official central government budgets. Official defense spending has declined as a share of total central government expenditure in both countries (Figure 4.4). Official defense spending as a percentage of central government spending has seen a somewhat greater decline in China than in India. In China, official defense spending fell from nearly 17 percent of central government expenditure in 1995 to 11 percent of central government expenditure in 2010.[18] In India, the official defense budget fell from about 15 percent of central government expenditure to 12.5 percent of central government spending over the same period.[19]

Defense Spending and Domestic Budget Politics

With these long-term trends as background, it is easier to see how the politics of defense set the stage for the current era of defense-spending increases in both countries. The periods of zero or even negative real growth in

---

[17] State Statistical Bureau, *China Statistical Yearbook 2010*, Table 8-3, 288. See also "Full Text: Report on China's central, local budgets," *Xinhua News*, March 17, 2011.

[18] In our calculations, China's total official defense spending includes both central government and local government spending on defense. For China, central government expenditure includes both central government expenditure plus central government fiscal transfers to local governments.

[19] For India, official defense spending does not include any local government spending on defense. Central government expenditure for India includes both central government expenditure and fiscal transfers from the center to the states.

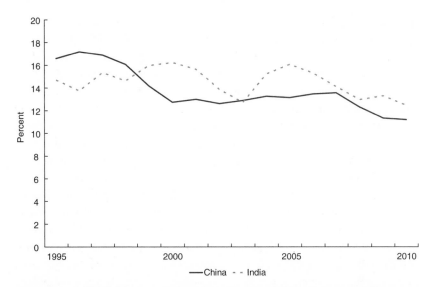

Figure 4.4. Official defense spending share in central government expenditure.
Note: In our calculations for both countries, "central government expenditure" includes central government direct expenditure and central government transfers to state governments.

defense spending during the 1980s were seen by the military in both countries as years of temporary sacrifice while the government pursued other critical economic and social goals. Both the PLA and the Indian military have subsequently demanded greater defense spending, aiming to make up for the gaps in capability relative to other nations that purportedly emerged during these years. This pattern of civil-military political and economic compact making is important when considering the potential for future defense-spending levels. The civil-military agreement regarding spending and modernization priorities changes in response to domestic and external circumstances. This casts doubt on the validity of any linear projections about long-term defense spending based on recent developments in either country.

In Indian defense circles, the period from the mid-1980s to the mid-1990s is referred to as the "lost decade." Although official defense budgets never accounted for less than 2.2 percent of GDP, official defense spending declined slightly in real terms between 1987 and 1996 as India saw low levels of economic growth, inflationary pressures, and large government budget deficits. However, economic reforms and increased economic growth beginning in the early 1990s subsequently enabled greater resources to be devoted to defense. By the late 1990s, the Indian military was arguing that it needed upgrades to its aging weapons systems and equipment, including tanks and armored vehicles, artillery, surface ships, submarines, and aircraft.[20] The Indian military's ability to persuade the government of its need for modernization and greater resources was supported by the domestic political effects of ongoing crises in Indo-Pakistan relations, including strategic competition in the wake of the 1998 nuclear weapons tests and the Kargil War in 1999. By the early 2000s, Indian military leaders were also citing the need to compete with China's developing military capabilities.

China's official defense spending suffered a similar "lost decade" (which actually stretched over almost two decades). In the interests of economic reform and revival, Deng Xiaoping forced the PLA to accept several years of absolute decline in defense spending during the 1980s. Chinese defense spending as a percentage of GDP declined from 6.4 percent in 1980 to 1.1 percent by 1998. The actual pattern of defense spending during the 1980s and early 1990s belied some Western forecasts, which, like earlier forecasts for Soviet defense spending, failed to accurately assess the sustainability of short-term trends in defense spending.[21]

In China, two factors have spurred increases in central government defense budgets since the early 1990s. First, China's perception of the security environment began to change with events in 1989 (both domestically and in Eastern Europe) and with the 1991 collapse of the Soviet Union. Beijing's sense of insecurity intensified with Western interventions in the Gulf War and Kosovo, and its sense of urgency was heightened with the worsening of cross-Strait tensions in 1995 and 1996. Second, domestic defense politics also played a major role, a factor less widely appreciated in most Western accounts of recent Chinese military developments. In the wake of years of real-term spending declines, by the early 1990s, the PLA pushed hard for commitments that it would no longer be forced to accept budget sacrifices for the sake of socioeconomic modernization.

[20] Stephen P. Cohen and Sunil Dasgupta, *Arming without Aiming: India's Military Modernization* (Washington, DC: Brookings Institution Press, 2010), 25–28; 54–63; 83–96.

[21] For an assessment that notes the absolute decline in Chinese defense spending in the 1980s, see Paul H. B. Godwin, "Force Projection and China's National Military Strategy," in C. Dennison Lane, Mark Weisenbloom, and Dimon Liu, eds., *Chinese Military Modernization* (New York: Kegan Paul International, 1996), 69–99. For an assessment that examines exaggerations of Chinese defense spending and the failure of some analyses to account for the effect of high inflation on real defense spending in the 1980s and early 1990s, see Joseph E. Kelly et al., *National Security: Impact of China's Military Modernization in the Pacific Region* (Washington, DC: United States General Accounting Office, GAO/NSIAD-95-84, June 1995). An overview of exaggerated American assessments of Chinese power from the late 1940s to the early 1990s can be found in Avery Goldstein, "Great Expectations: Interpreting China's Arrival," *International Security*, 22:3 (Winter 1997/1998): 36–73.

In 1997, PLA General Chi Haotian, then concurrently Vice Chairman of the Central Military Commission and Minister of National Defense, reported to the National People's Congress on the drafting of the 1997 National Defense Law. Drafting of that law began in 1993. In his report, Chi states that in 1994, 104 members of the National People's Congress (almost certainly members of the PLA delegation) submitted proposals to "ensure military expenditures as a proportion of GDP." According to Chi, "some departments and some comrades" also urged the CCP leadership to include binding provisions in the 1997 National Defense Law that would effectively link defense-spending growth rates to GDP growth. [22] According to another member of the National People's Congress' military delegation, military delegates pushed to peg defense spending to 3% of GDP.[23] Ultimately, the drafting committee rejected such binding provisions on the grounds that few other states guaranteed defense spending through legal or constitutional means.

Nevertheless, PLA leaders did succeed in inserting a clause (Article 35) into the 1997 National Defense Law that states: "The nation shall ensure necessary funding for national defense. The growth in national defense funding should be based on national defense needs and the *level of the civilian economy*" (emphasis added).[24] At roughly the same time, the PLA was also obliged to begin divesting itself of its factories and other businesses, partly to ensure discipline and professionalism and partly to ensure greater budgetary control over the army.[25]

Increased defense spending clearly imposes opportunity costs on both China and India. New Delhi and Beijing already face numerous and increasingly robust domestic constituencies, from the rural poor to a growing middle class, and these new constituencies will place new demands on spending. Data on official defense spending as a share of GDP and as a share of total central government budgets show that India has in some ways maintained a higher level of relative effort on defense than China. For a more

[22] 迟浩田[Chi Haotian], "关于中华人民共和国国防法 (草案) 的说明" [An Explanation of the PRC National Defense Law (Draft)], in 中华人民共和国第八届全国人民代表大会第五次会议文件汇编[Documents on the PRC Fifth Session of the Eighth National People's Congress] (Beijing: Zhejiang People's Press, 1997).

[23] Author interview, June 2011.

[24] 中华人民共和国国防法 (1997年3月14日) 第八届全国人民代表大会第五次会议通过[Law of the People's Republic of China on National Defense, Fifth Session of the Eighth National People's Congress, March 14, 1997], Chapter VI, Article 35, http://www.people.com.cn/zgrdxw/faguiku/jsh/P1010.html

[25] Divestiture did take place, but was never fully completed. See Crane et al., *Modernizing China's Military*, 111–124.

complete and accurate picture of effort, it is necessary to assess both official defense spending and "off budget" defense spending. Full defense spending includes both official defense spending and defense-related spending items not included in the official defense budget.

Full Defense Spending

Neither China nor India records all defense-related spending in official defense budgets. Further, Beijing and New Delhi each exhibit varying degrees of nontransparency in budget reporting. India's published budget reporting practices are more accessible overall, but only marginally so, particularly when language differences are taken into account.[26] This gap is also closing, as China's Ministry of Finance has gained in domestic power and authority in recent years and has begun publishing more detailed information on government finances.[27]

Official Defense Budgets: What Is Not Included
Neither country includes the substantial costs of nuclear weapons programs, military-related space programs, or intelligence activities in official defense budget numbers. This is not unusual. Most countries have similar practices.[28] Both China and India also exclude the cost of paramilitary internal security forces from their official defense budgets. China does not include the cost of weapons imports in its official defense budget. According to the State Statistical Bureau, China's official defense budget does include official defense R&D. This is not broken out from the total official budget figure and does not cover the full range of defense-related R&D.

---

[26] China publishes a wide range of statistical reports in English, many available online at http://www.stats.gov.cn/english/. Those with Chinese-language skills will find even more detailed Chinese-language information both online at http://www.stats.gov.cn and in the published reports of China's Ministry of Finance, http://www.mof.gov.cn; http://www.mof.gov.cn/mof/zhengwuxinxi/bulinggonggao/; and also http://www.mof.gov.cn/mof/zhengwuxinxi/caizhengshuju/. Detailed data and reports on India's economy are available in both English and Hindi from both the Reserve Bank of India at http://www.rbi.org.in/home.aspx, and the Indian Union Budget Web site, http://www.indiabudget.nic.in/

[27] China's Finance Ministry has an interest in somewhat greater transparency not only for the purpose of imposing fiscal discipline, but also because more transparent data help it and the CCP leadership arbitrate among various interests groups engaged in political struggles for more resources.

[28] In the United States, the costs of Department of Energy nuclear weapons programs, the Department of Veterans' Affairs, and special budgets for the ongoing wars in Iraq and Afghanistan are not included in the official defense budget.

Indian official budgets do include the cost of weapons imports. However, in many years, the Indian military requests supplemental budget support for imports, making weapons import spending difficult to track and highly volatile from year to year.[29] India's official defense budget figure does not include defense pensions, paramilitary forces, border security (coast guard, accommodations for paramilitary, and border defense works such as fences and fortifications), expenses for the Ministry of Defense secretariat, debt servicing on weapons import purchases, or subsidies to defense related industry. Defense pension costs were removed from India's official headline defense budget number in 1985.[30] One Indian expert suggests that these various exclusions were designed to make defense spending appear smaller.[31] Another Indian expert, Pavan Nair, estimates that India's actual defense budget in 2005–2006 was 31 percent higher than the official budget.[32]

In both countries, some of these off-budget items are easily found in other (i.e., nondefense) sections of published government budgets. For example, both countries report budget data for paramilitary units. In India, budget for paramilitary forces such as the Assam Rifles can be found under the Ministry of Home Affairs budget. In China, both the State Statistical Bureau and the Ministry of Finance report budget for the People's Armed Police in a separate section of the same sources that record official defense budgets. India reports the costs of military pensions separately from the official defense budget, but India's military pensions can be easily found in the detailed expenditure volume of the Indian government budget under

---

[29] Weapons import costs are accounted for in "Capital Outlays for Defence Services," which is part of the official budget. See Ministry of Defence, Controller General of Defence Accounts, *Classification Hand Book of Defence Services*, updated to CS No. 17 of 2009, http://cgda.nic.in/accounts/code_heads/, accessed on April 3, 2009. These accounts may or may not capture the full costs of all Indian weapons import programs. In many years, the Indian military does not spend its entire capital outlay budget because of delays in weapons procurement, resulting in requests for supplemental budget. See Bappa Majumdar, "India's defence budget rises, but problems remain," *Reuters India*, February 29, 2008.

[30] Pavan Nair, "Defence Budget Leaves out Rs 26,000 Crores," *India Together*, May 18, 2005.

[31] Laxman Kumar Behera, "The Indian Defence Budget 2007–2008," Institute for Defence Studies and Analyses (IDSA) Strategic Comments, March 9, 2007.

[32] Pavan Nair, "Defence Budget Leaves out Rs 26,000 Crores." Nair includes the cost of nuclear weapons programs, paramilitaries, and debt on arms imports, but does not include an estimate for subsidies to defense-related industry. Nair's estimate is broadly consistent with other estimates of actual Indian defense spending. See Sandy Gordon, "Indian Defense Spending: Treading Water in the Fiscal Deep," *Asian Survey*, 32:10 (October 1992): 934–950; and Praful Bidwai, "Military overdrive," *Frontline*, 25:07 (March 29–April 11, 2008).

"Defence Pensions," or "Defence (civil estimates)." China includes a portion of retirement costs for military officers in its official defense budget, but it is unclear how much of total pension expenditures are included in that budget.[33] China's Ministry of Civil Affairs publishes separate, and somewhat more detailed, figures for military retirement costs and other post-service benefits in its annual reports.[34]

In other cases, budget numbers are combined or presented in ways that make assessment more difficult. In both countries, spending on space and nuclear programs remains opaque (as does the division between civilian and military aspects of these programs).[35] Similarly, both China and India blur the line between overall government R&D and strictly defined defense R&D. Although both countries publish data on subsidies to industries, no breakdown is provided for subsidies to military-related industry other than data for ordnance factories in India. Both countries provide significant indirect subsidies to all manufacturing industry through energy pricing, low-cost access to land, and other policies.

Even in some analytically difficult or ambiguous areas, however, it is often possible to estimate the scope of spending or at least bound the problem. Despite relative opacity in defense-related R&D and subsidies in both countries, data can be found in official published sources. In both India and China, spending on subsidies to industry can be found in official published

---

[33] State Council Information Office, People's Republic of China, "China's National Defense in 2010," March 31, 2011.

[34] Relatively detailed reports can also be found on individual aspects of China's post-service benefits programs, allowances due to individuals under specific programs, total numbers of individuals that fall within different retirement or demobilization categories, and total spending by province (with most of the money provided by transfers from the central government). Historically, post-separation assistance to most military personnel largely takes the form of a modest one-time payment and important nonmonetary benefits, especially post-separation job placement. These job placement programs impeded the efficiency of receiving organizations, but were relatively inexpensive in financial terms. More recently, there has been an effort to persuade Chinese officers to accept regular payments – in other words, a pension. On the program and the number of officers who have accepted pensions and the number who have accepted job placement (by year) since the program began in 2001, see 盛大泉, 罗贞裁, 周燕红, 罗晶晶, 杨学娟, 胡琳 [Sheng Daquan, Luo Zhencai, Zhou Yanhong, Luo Jingjing, Yang Xuejuan, and Hu Lin], "2001–2010 自主择业十年报告, 转业军官编辑部" [Report on Self-job selection system 2001–2011: the demobilized army cadres editorial department," 《中国人才》 2011年02期 [China Talent], Volume 2, 2011. Overall, funding for payments to retired officers and noncommissioned officers tripled between the tenth five-year economic plan (2001–2005) and the eleventh five-year economic plan (2006–2010). See "全国军队离退休人员审定安置工作会在太原召开" [Conference on approval and resettlement of People's Liberation Army retirees held in Taiyuan], 黄河新闻网 [Yellow River News Service], March 30, 2011.

[35] India provides greater transparency on civilian space program budgets, although the military spillovers from these programs remain nontransparent.

statistics. Although China's military weapons imports are not listed as part of its official defense budget, the value of its arms imports can be estimated.[36] Defense R&D in China is not fully specified in any public source. However, detailed breakdowns of national R&D spending programs by industry and type are listed in China's *Science and Technology Statistical Yearbooks*, so reasonable bounding of defense-related R&D is possible.[37]

Beyond Official Budgets: Estimating Full Defense Spending

Based on data from sources such as those discussed earlier, we develop notional full defense budgets for both countries for 2005 and 2010. These notional full defense-spending estimates are not strictly comparable to estimates for full Chinese defense budgets published in the annual U.S. Department of Defense reports on Chinese military power. The DoD reports do not explain what is included in their estimates for Chinese defense spending, but since at least 2007 they appear to take a "bottom-up" approach that includes official budgets plus defense-related off-budget items such as military pensions, arms imports, nuclear weapons, space, and intelligence programs, as well as some form of PPP adjustment.

We exclude Chinese and Indian nuclear weapons, space, and intelligence programs from our estimates. We do this for two reasons. First, excluding these items is consistent with a standard practice for comparing defense spending across countries. For example, some NATO countries, including the United States, exclude most portions of the nuclear weapons and intelligence budgets (as well as other items identified earlier) from defense budget reporting. Second, there is no complete, publicly available budget information about nuclear weapons programs, military space activities, or intelligence programs in either India or China.[38] We base our

---

[36] The Stockholm International Peace Research Institute (SIPRI) maintains an excellent database of international arms transfers, with consistency in measurement and full transparency on methods, at http://www.sipri.org. Developing country arms imports are also the subject of regular, detailed reports from the Congressional Research Service. See for example, Richard F. Grimmett, *Conventional Arms Transfers to Developing Nations 2001–2008*, Congressional Research Service Report for Congress, Order Number R40796, September 4, 2009.

[37] In the case of Chinese R&D, programs for high-technology development with dual-use potential, such as the State High-Tech Development Plan (also called the 863 Program for the March 1986 policy decision that established it), can be identified and used to create reasonable boundaries on estimates of defense-related R&D programs. Other Chinese national R&D programs include the National Basic Research Program and (or 973 Program).

[38] Nuclear weapons, space, and intelligence programs are considered national strategic programs, and the full costs of these programs are classified in most countries, including in the United States.

estimates on publicly available data, so we have excluded these programs from this analysis.

We provide three different figures: a lower bound, a best estimate, and an upper bound. The lower and upper bounds should not be understood as "low" and "high" estimates, but as true boundaries. In the case of the former, we simply take the official defense budget as the lower bound for each country. Because we know that official figures do not include a variety of defense-related costs, full spending for both India and China must be higher than these figures.

We then build our "best estimate" by adding other categories of spending. In some cases, these figures are published in other official government sources. For India, this includes defense pensions, the costs of operating the Ministry of Defence, and the costs of paramilitary forces.[39] For China, other published data include spending on the paramilitary People's Armed Police and provincial government support to paramilitary forces.

Some potential resources for defense spending are either not published in detail or are not clearly parsed and must therefore be estimated. In our estimate for the Chinese case only, published Western estimates of arms sales profits and the value of arms imports are also added.[40] Profits are estimated to represent 30 percent of delivered arms sales revenues, a conservative (i.e., likely high) assumption for the profitability of Chinese arms profits compared to other international arms producers.[41]

We estimate Chinese military pensions (and benefits) based on data provided by the Ministry of Civil Affairs.[42] The figures provided are highly aggregated and include some nonpension categories of benefits that are not

---

[39] Costs for the Ministry of Defence include not only administrative costs, but also costs for the Indian coast guard and a paramilitary unit called the Jammu and Kashmir Rifles. Our estimate of spending on Indian paramilitary forces includes the cost of militias under the Home Ministry and half the cost of the central reserve police force, which performs some internal security as well as normal police duties.

[40] We add these items for China only because India is not a large arms exporter, and Indian arms imports are included in its published defense budget.

[41] Unlike some sources such as Crane et al. *Modernizing China's Military*, we use an estimate of profits on Chinese arms exports instead of total arms export revenues. Arms production has costs. A 30 percent margin estimate on Chinese arms sales is a conservative (or high) assumption given China's reputation for competing in the lower end of arms markets. For comparison, in 2007, one French armored vehicle manufacturer had profits of 151 million Euros on sales of 587 million Euros, and in 2008, the same manufacturer had profits of 99 million Euros on sales of 579 million Euros (25 percent and 17 percent profit margins, respectively).

[42] 中华人民共和国民政部 [Ministry of Civil Affairs of the People's Republic of China], 《2009年民政事业发展统计报告》 [2009 Civil Administration Affairs Development Statistical Report], June 10, 2010. Note that these figures may also include some monies

included in the Indian pension figures (e.g., disability benefits).[43] Hence, the military benefits figures for China are somewhat more inclusive than those for India. Even including all categories of benefits, China spends proportionately less on demobilized and retired soldiers than India – chiefly because of the differences between China's conscript force and India's volunteer army. Trends in Chinese spending on military benefits indicate that this pattern is changing as the force is professionalized and as nonmonetary benefits (e.g., job placement in state firms for officers) are phased out in favor of monetary ones. This shift is representative of the larger phenomenon of rising social spending requirements.

For China's spending on imported weapons, we use an estimate of the value of China's delivered arms imports as a proxy for its arms import spending that year.[44] For both countries, defense-relevant R&D and industrial subsidies are included. Defense-relevant R&D in each country is limited to energy, manufacturing equipment, information technology, biotechnology, nanotechnology, and "frontier science."[45] The baseline estimate

that are already counted within the official PLA budget (although we judge that this is not likely). According to China's 2010 white paper on national defense, some retirement costs, said to be limited to pensions for senior officers, are included in personnel figures for the defense budget. However, figures provided by the Ministry of Civil Affairs are unlikely to include outlays by the Ministry of Defense.

[43] For a variety of historical reasons, the Chinese system for handling ex-soldiers and officers is exceedingly complex and is handled under a wide variety of different compensation programs (depending, for example, on when and where the soldier demobilized). These are grouped by the Ministry of Civil Affairs Report under three headings: compensation (抚恤事业费), medical allowances (医疗补助), and separation arrangements (军休安置). The third category (RMB 16 billion in 2009) is closest to a standard pension system (with the bulk of funds allocated to officers who have met a certain service criterion). The first category (RMB 31 billion in 2009) includes a variety of disability allowances and monies for the families of "martyred" soldiers, but it also appears to include funding for older programs that provide allowances to larger groups of demobilized and retired soldiers and might also be considered pension money. It is therefore conservative to include both, but not unreasonably so.

[44] For Chinese delivered arms sales revenues and value of delivered arms imports, see Grimmett, *Conventional Arms Transfers to Developing Nations 2001–2008*, and Grimmett, *Conventional Arms Transfers to Developing Nations 2002–2009*.

[45] To estimate the baseline for Indian R&D with potential dual-use applications, we included government R&D spending in information technology, energy, engineering, manufacturing, biotechnology, nanotechnology, the national mapping research project, "frontier technology" R&D, and the national laboratories program. For some Indian R&D programs, we estimate only a portion of spending could have dual-use applications. This includes 50 percent of government R&D for vehicle manufacturing, 50 percent of government spending on energy research, 25 percent of government spending for the national internet backbone and e-governance project, and 25 percent of government biotech research. We take an even more inclusive approach in our accounting of Chinese R&D. Our baseline estimate includes all national R&D program spending for all potentially defense-related

also includes a subset of industrial subsidies, limited to state owned industrial firms in engineering and industrial sectors most closely linked to dual civilian and military uses.

Including similar spending programs for both countries allows us to develop a baseline estimate for comparable full defense spending. When in doubt, we have erred on the side of conservatism (i.e., higher estimates). A portion of domestic police forces is included in cases where those organizations also have internal security functions beyond policing duties. More significantly (from a funding perspective), entire categories of R&D are included when those categories could have military or dual-use functions, despite the fact that these areas also include projects with more purely civilian applications.

Our baseline estimates are therefore conservative in themselves. However, we also provide an estimate of an upper limit, representing a theoretical boundary that caps full notional defense spending in the categories included in this chapter.[46] To define this upper boundary, for each country we replace the estimate for dual-use R&D with the total R&D budget of the central government, a much larger figure. We also replace the estimate for subsidies to dual-use industry with total central direct government subsidies to state firms, again a much larger figure.[47] Thus, for the upper boundary, total government R&D and total direct subsidies to state firms are added to official defense budgets, other published defense-related spending such as paramilitaries, and estimates for items such as arms imports.[48] Details of the

sectors in the Key Technologies R&D Program, State High-Tech Development Plan (or 863 Program), and the National Basic Research Program (or 973 Program). These include industrial, energy, space, and defense sectors. The industry category is the largest component. This is a conservative estimate as not all of that R&D spending is defense-related.

[46] In principle, this means that higher defense spending estimates could only be generated by defining defense spending differently than we have done here – for example, by including additional categories of spending such as nuclear weapons programs.

[47] In 2005, India's total R&D spending was equal to about 0.85% of GDP, and the public sector accounted for more than 60% of total R&D spending. See Y. P. Kumar, "India's International Cooperation in Science and Technology," Speech to Federation of Indian Chambers of Commerce and Industry, IC Department, Science & Technology Ministry, December 4, 2006. For 2010, our estimate for total Indian R&D spending is equal to approximately 1 percent of GDP, with government spending accounting for about 80% of total R&D. See speech of Indian Science and Technology Minister Kapil Sibal to the Rajya Sabha, quoted in "India Lags China in R&D Spending: Sibal," *The Financial Express*, March 12, 2008.

[48] Official data for some 2010 detailed spending items had not been released as this manuscript was being completed. For these items we use official 2009 data plus an estimated growth rate based on officially announced budget targets. Detailed data on Chinese R&D is from the *2010 Science and Technology Statistical Yearbook*. For India, similar 2010 items are listed in multiple "Demands" in Volume II (Expenditure) of the 2011–2012 Union

Table 4.5. *Full defense-spending estimate and boundaries, 2005*
(in billions, except as noted)

	Lower boundary	Baseline Estimate	Upper boundary
		Full Defense Spending	
India			
Rupees	817.0	**1,057.8**	1,233.7
USD	18.5	**23.9**	27.9
Share of GDP (%)	2.29	**2.90**	3.45
China			
Yuan	247.4	**364.8**	383.7
USD	30.2	**44.6**	46.9
Share of GDP (%)	1.34	**1.98**	2.07

Note: Nuclear weapons, space, and intelligence programs not included.

upper boundary calculation are provided in the Appendix. A reasonable, conservative estimate for these categories of spending cannot be higher or lower than the two boundaries we have developed.

The results of our analysis are summarized in Tables 4.5 and 4.6, in both local currency and in U.S. dollars of the day at market exchange rates. By any reasonable estimate, off-budget items represent significant spending in both countries. For 2005, the baseline full defense-spending estimate for India is Rs. 1,057.8 billion ($23.9 billion), 29 percent higher than India's 2005 official budget. In China, the baseline estimate for 2005 is RMB 364.8 billion ($44.6 billion), 47 percent higher than the official 2005 defense budget of RMB 247 billion.

For India in 2010, the baseline estimate for notional full defense spending is Rs. 2,139.6 billion ($43.2 billion), 41 percent higher than India's official 2010 defense budget. For China in 2010, the baseline estimate for notional full defense spending is RMB 768.2 billion ($113.3 billion), 44 percent higher than China's official 2010 defense budget.

Tables 4.7 and 4.8 provide additional details on the components of our estimate for full defense spending for each country.

Several conclusions emerge from these estimates for full defense spending in each country. First, China is not unique in failing to report

Budget (which reports revised figures for 2010). Subsidies to state owned firms in India can be found in Demand 50, series Item 15 in the 2011–2012 Union budget. For total Indian R&D spending in 2010, see Indian Union Budget 2011–2012; and "India Lags China in R&D Spending: Sibal," *The Financial Express* March 12, 2008.

Table 4.6. *Full defense-spending estimate and boundaries, 2010*
(in billions, except as noted)

	Lower Boundary	Baseline Estimate	Upper Boundary
		Full Defense Spending	
India			
Rupees	1,515.8	**2,139.6**	2,550.3
USD	30.6	**43.2**	51.5
Share of GDP (%)	2.14	**3.02**	3.60
China			
Yuan	532.1	**768.2**	859.2
USD	78.5	**113.3**	126.7
Share of GDP (%)	1.37	**1.97**	2.21

Note: Nuclear weapons, space, and intelligence programs not included.

Table 4.7. *India: Estimated full defense spending, 2005 and 2010* (in billions)

	2005		2010	
	Rupees	USD	Rupees	USD
A. PUBLISHED DEFENSE SPENDING				
1. Official defense budget	817	18.5	1,516	30.6
2. Published defense-related spending (not in official budget)				
Defense pensions	127.2	3	340.0	6.9
Ministry of Defence Administration	15.4	0.3	41.6	0.8
Paramilitaries and Internal Security				
50% of Central Reserve Police budget	*15*		*38*	
National Security Guard	*1*		*4*	
Border Security Force	*33*		*71*	
Indo-Tibetan Border Police	*6*		*17*	
Assam Rifles	*11*		*24*	
Special Service Bureau	*5*		*15*	
Special Police	*4*		*25*	
Paramilitaries total	76.1	1.7	192.6	3.9
Subtotal A. Published Defense Spending	**1,036**	**23.4**	**2,090**	**42.2**
B. ADDITIONAL OFF-BUDGET ITEMS				
Government R&D with potential dual-use applications	19.3	0.4	45.3	0.9
Subsidies to potential dual-use industries	2.8	0.1	4.2	0.1
Subtotal B. Additional Off-Budget Items	**22**	**0.5**	**50**	**1**
Baseline Estimate Full Defense Spending	**1,058**	**23.9**	**2,140**	**43.2**

Note: Nuclear weapons, space, and intelligence programs not included.

Table 4.8. *China: Estimated full defense spending, 2005 and 2010* (in billions)

	2005		2010	
	Yuan	USD	Yuan	USD
A. PUBLISHED DEFENSE SPENDING				
1. Official defense budget	247	30.2	532	78.5
2. Published defense-related spending (not in official budget)				
Additional military family compensation and pensions	21.7	2.6	56.4	8.3
Paramilitaries and Internal Security	32.7	4.0	93.5	13.8
People's Armed Police (PAP)	*29*		*73*	*10.8*
Local Support to PAP	*4*		*20*	*3.0*
Subtotal A. Published Defense Spending	**301**	**36.8**	**682**	**100.6**
B. ADDITIONAL OFF-BUDGET ITEMS				
Government R&D with potential dual-use applications	49	6.0	72	10.6
Subsidies to potential dual-use industries	1.3	0.2	–	–
Arms imports	11.5	1.4	10.2	1.5
Arms sales profits	2	0.2	4.0	0.6
Subtotal B. Additional Off-Budget Items	**63.8**	**7.8**	**86**	**12.7**
Baseline Estimate Full Defense Spending	**365**	**44.6**	**768**	**113.3**

Note: Nuclear weapons, space, and intelligence programs not included.

all components of its full defense spending. Despite its more liberal and open political regime, India also "manages" reporting of its defense spending. Second, although some categories of defense-related spending are not included in the official defense budgets of both countries, some of these, such as spending on paramilitaries and internal security forces, are clearly reported in other parts of the budget. These spending categories represent similar additions to defense spending in each country. Third, items such as defense-relevant R&D and assistance to the broadly defined defense industrial base may also be estimated, though with somewhat less certainty.

This analysis shows that any useful study of defense spending in any one state requires comparison with that of other states. Most other countries also spend money on defense-related activities that are not included in official defense budgets. The key question is, how much relative to others? The answer in the Chinese and Indian cases: Excluding national strategic programs, notional full defense spending appears to be about 1.3 to 1.5 times officially reported defense budgets in both countries.

A final step in the comparative analysis of defense budgets is to make a balanced and consistent effort to estimate the difference in relative defense-spending power that might be accounted for by exchange rate differentials. This will also help translate both Indian and Chinese spending into currency units that can be compared across both developed and developing nations, in Asia and beyond.

The (Mis)use of Purchasing Power Parity (PPP) Adjustments

What is the most appropriate way to compare the economic dimensions of international power, such as defense spending? This spending is conducted in a local currency that must be converted to a common currency to make comparisons. In most cases, using market exchange rates is best, not least because the improper use of adjustments for PPP often results in significant distortion of defense-spending estimates.

According to the World Bank, "PPP estimates are useful to compare real living standards in different countries .... (T)ranslated through official exchange rates, the prices of many non-traded services are low in China (as in other developing countries) .... Prices of traded manufactured products, on the other hand, tend to be similar ... because international trade brings prices of traded goods to about the same level in all economies."[49]

In other words, PPP methods adjust for purchasing power for locally produced and priced goods. PPP methods are not appropriate for measuring relative international wealth and power that is based on internationally traded goods and services. PPPs are not designed to measure relative market share or relative capabilities in international finance and trade. Nor are PPPs designed to measure advanced industrial, technological, or military power, because substantial elements of these are comprised of manufactured goods and components sourced from international markets at international market prices.[50] Finally, PPP adjustments are designed to capture relative spending power or production value in certain areas but cannot be interpreted to mean that a country is hiding spending or spending more than an announced figure.

Nevertheless, analysts frequently misapply PPP methods to measure and compare relative international financial, trade, industrial, technological, and military power and influence. For example, in early 2010, economic historian Robert Fogel warned of a coming Chinese global "economic

---

[49] World Bank, *China Quarterly Update* (Beijing: World Bank, February 2008), 19–20.
[50] On these issues, see "Introduction to the International Comparison Program," in *ICP 2003-2006 Handbook* (Washington, DC: World Bank, April 2006); and *2005 International Comparison Program: Preliminary Results* (Washington, DC: World Bank, December 2007), Appendix Data Tables, 2.

hegemony" in an essay for the journal *Foreign Policy*.[51] He estimated that by 2040, China will account for 40 percent of world GDP, the United States will account for only 14 percent, and Europe only 5 percent. The estimate is based in part on a linear projection of 8 percent annual GDP growth in China over the period from 2000 to 2040. This growth assumption is questionable given the many social, political, and economic risks China faces over the next three decades.

The estimate in *Foreign Policy* also employs a PPP-adjusted price series published in 2000 (based on Chinese price data collected in the 1980s). In fact, by the time the projection was published in 2010, the year 2000 PPP estimates had already been superseded by a new World Bank PPP report published in late 2007 (based on much newer price data collected in 2005). The new data revealed that China's economy in PPP terms was roughly 40 percent smaller than was implied by earlier PPP estimates. The outdated PPP prices thus overinflated the starting point in the projection, producing a knock-on effect throughout the estimate up to 2040. This highlights one problem with using PPP-adjusted prices: As China (or any other developing country) becomes more integrated with the global economy, its domestic prices tend to converge with global prices. As this happens, the PPP differential for Chinese prices will decrease. This means that PPP exchange rate estimates are not simply permanent "rules of thumb." They must be periodically updated to remain relevant.

More fundamentally, PPP-adjusted figures are inappropriate for assessing China's global political-economic influence, or a coming Chinese international economic "hegemony." International economic influence is manifested largely via trade and international finance. Therefore it is usually more appropriate to compare relative international economic power using market exchange rates.[52]

[51] Robert Fogel, "$123,000,000,000,000: China's estimated economy by the year 2040. Be warned," *Foreign Policy*, 177 (January/February 2010).

[52] For another example of the assumption that PPP-adjusted economic data translate directly into international power and influence, see Ian Castles, "Measuring China's Size and Power," East Asia Forum, May 10, 2009. Other analysts improperly use PPP exchange rates to inflate Chinese and Indian production levels in individual industrial sectors. These PPP-inflated figures are then compared to a non-PPP-inflated total global production "pie," and the erroneous conclusion follows: China and India have gained outsized shares of global production in that sector. Ernest H. Preeg, *India and China: An Advanced Technology Race and How the United States Should Respond* (Arlington: Manufacturer's Alliance/MAPI, 2008); John Tkacik, "China's Superpower Economy," Heritage Foundation Webmemo No. 1762, December 28, 2007; and Organization for Economic Cooperation and Development, "China will become world's second highest investor in R&D by end of 2006, finds OECD," announcement of *OECD Science, Technology and Industry Outlook 2006* (Paris: OECD,

The application of PPP-adjusted exchange rates to defense spending can also be misleading, and for the same reasons.[53] PPPs are designed to measure relative living standards by equalizing prices for local goods of comparable quality to those found in other markets. Yet many of the most important components of military power, particularly the most lethal high-tech systems, are built from machinery, subsystems, and critical components sourced from international markets at market prices. A developing country may seek to substitute domestic technology for advanced manufactured goods. However, as data presented later in this chapter show, a developing country's purchasing power in such technology subsectors may actually be less than that implied by broad PPP measures of the entire economy. Despite these important limitations, some sources apply broad PPP measures to an entire defense budget.[54] The effect of applying PPPs in this way produces large variations to estimates of Chinese and Indian defense spending, often yielding dollar values of two to three times budgets calculated at market exchange rates.

Other sources apply PPP selectively and unevenly. For example, *The Military Balance 2011*, a standard reference work in the security studies field, presents defense-spending analysis for thirty-two Central Asian and East Asian countries. Of these, only China's defense spending is presented in PPP-adjusted terms, even though PPP adjustments would have a greater effect on the spending of other countries (including India).[55] Some U.S.

2006). For sources that take a critical view, see Bruce Einhorn, "Is OECD hyping China's R&D spending?" *Business Week Online*, December 2007, accessed at http://www.business-week.com/globalbiz/blog/eyeonasia/archives/2006/12/is_oecd_hyping.html; and Hawk Jia, "China's R&D budget overrated, warns official," *Science and Development Network*, 6 December 2006, http://www.scidev.net/en/news/chinas-rd-budget-overrated-warns-official.html

53 Richard A. Bitzinger has analyzed a number of difficulties in applying PPP to the Chinese defense budget, as well as the other methodological challenges in producing accurate assessments. See Richard A. Bitzinger, "Analyzing Chinese Military Expenditures," in Stephen J. Flanagan and Michael E. Marti, eds., *The People's Liberation Army And China In Transition* (Honolulu: University Press of the Pacific, 2004), 177–193; and Richard A. Bitzinger, "Just the Facts, Ma'am: The Challenge of Analysing and Assessing Chinese Military Expenditures," *The China Quarterly* 173 (2003): 164–175.

54 See for example, P. Stålenheim, C. Perdomo, and E. Sköns, "Military expenditure," in Stockholm International Peace Research Institute, *SIPRI Yearbook 2008* (New York: Oxford University Press, 2008): 175–206; "China's increasing defense spending threatens international stability: report," *Kyodo News*, May 24, 2006. See also C. Fred Bergsten, Charles Freeman, Nicholas R. Lardy, and Derek J. Mitchell, *China's Rise: Challenges and Opportunities*, 1st ed. (Washington, DC: Peterson Institute, 2008).

55 IISS, *The Military Balance 2011*, 195–292. In a separate chapter, the same source does present Chinese data more consistently in comparison to other nations (using market exchange rates). See IISS, *The Military Balance 2011*, 33.

government sources display defense budget estimates for China that have been adjusted for inclusion of off-budget items (and apparently also PPP) side by side with defense budget numbers for other countries, which have not been similarly adjusted.[56]

Perhaps the biggest problem with the presentation of U.S. government assessments of Chinese military spending is that they typically lack even rudimentary explanation of methodology. The CIA *World Factbook* estimate for 2006 Chinese military spending as a percentage of GDP is more than twice the percentage that we derive from our approach. The CIA may include nuclear, space, and intelligence programs, but without elaboration by the CIA, it is still difficult to understand how additional off-budget items alone could account for the difference.[57]

We do know that in some of its past estimates, the CIA has used an "equivalent cost" method that assesses what Chinese forces would cost if the West built and maintained those forces. Effectively, this methodology introduces a homebuilt version of PPP.[58] If this is an important part of the CIA method, then such a defense-spending estimate should not be compared to standard international financial statistics such as GDP figures or government budgets, because the defense-spending estimate may be derived through a nonstandard PPP method. In other words, such a defense-spending estimate and normal financial statistics would not constitute a compatible "apples to apples" comparison. These considerations highlight the main problem with most such publicly available U.S. government military spending estimates: The credibility and utility of the estimate are undermined by a lack of transparency about what is included and how it is measured.

Yet U.S. government estimates of Chinese defense spending are treated as authoritative and are circulated by institutions that shape both elite and broad public opinion in the United States.[59] These estimates are picked up by

[56] See *The Military Power of the People's Republic of China*, various years. The use of PPP in the Pentagon report *The Military Power of the People's Republic of China* appears to have shifted over time. The budget calculations in the 2008, 2009, and 2010 reports appear to rely less on the application of a broad PPP adjustment.

[57] According to one estimate, China spent $5.7 billion on its nuclear weapons program in 2010, while India spent $3.4 billion. Bruce G. Blair and Matthew A. Brown, "World Spending on Nuclear Weapons Surpasses $1 Trillion Per Decade," Global Zero Technical Report, June 2011.

[58] See, for example, Alan B. Smith, "Costing Nuclear Programs," Central Intelligence Agency, September 18, 1995, https://www.cia.gov/library/center-for-the-study-of-intelligence/kent-csi/vol10no1/html/v10i1a02p_0001.htm

[59] See National Intelligence Council, *Mapping the Global Future: Report of the National Intelligence Council's 2020 Project* (Pittsburgh: U.S. Government Printing Office, 2004). Other independent nonpartisan institutions repeat these figures. See Jayshree Bajoria,

sources elsewhere, including in India, where they are used to justify Indian defense budget increases.[60] The lack of clarity on methodology impedes the evaluation of those methods and can potentially lead to substantial errors in how the figures derived are used. For example, if the figures do in fact include some kind of PPP multiplier (whether from the World Bank or homegrown), then their publication without notation of that fact may invite scholars or other users to apply a PPP multiplier a second time, effectively compounding PPP.[61]

A final common problem is the assumption that relative purchasing power for locally priced goods can be translated into greater absolute spending power, or "bang for the buck," across all parts of the defense budget.[62] This assumption ignores actual sector-level PPP prices (Table 4.9) and their relationship to specific parts of the defense budget. Even if final systems are domestically assembled, most modern military equipment is based on technology or components sourced from international markets – usually best measured in market exchange rates.[63] But in developing countries (including

"China's Military Power," Council on Foreign Relations, February 4, 2009, http://www.cfr. org/publication/18459/chinas_military_power.html?breadcrumb=%2Fpublication%2Fp ublication_list%3Ftype%3Dbackgrounder%26page%3D2; and Esther Pan, "The Scope of China's Military Threat," Council on Foreign Relations, June 2, 2006, http://www.cfr.org/ publication/10824/scope_of_chinas_military_threat.html

[60] See Behera, "India's Defence Budget 2008–09"; and Bhartendu Kumar Singh, "Estimating China's defence expenditure" (New Delhi: Institute For Peace and Conflict Studies, Article no. 1775, June 24, 2005).

[61] The questionable application of PPP at least partly accounts for several particularly egregious estimates of Chinese defense spending. In 2007, Ed Feulner concluded that China's defense spending in 2006–2007 was $450 billion, or "about what the U.S. spends." Feulner used a CIA estimate of Chinese military spending as a percent of GDP. As noted earlier, the CIA does not provide clarity on what is included in its military spending estimate, nor does it clarify whether this estimate already employs some adjustment for PPP. Feulner then applied PPP to the entire budget (thus possibly compounding PPP adjustments). He did not distinguish different parts of the budget to which PPP adjustments may or may not apply. Further, the PPP price series he used had not been updated in two decades (and therefore gave a greatly inflated PPP effect). Feulner's estimate defies common sense. There is no evidence of China procuring the material that such a high budget figure implies. See Ed Feulner, "A New Arms Race America Must Win," *Chicago Sun-Times*, April 18, 2007, 47.

[62] See "Does China Pose a Military Threat?" Council on Foreign Relations Online Debate, March 26, 2007, http://www.cfr.org/publication/12901/does_china_pose_a_military_ threat.html

[63] Even domestically produced advanced manufactured goods embody a large proportion of value from imported or internationally traded goods. These include but are not limited to manufacturing equipment, software embedded in equipment or components, propulsion systems, electronic components, and specialty commodities that go into advanced steel and other materials.

Table 4.9. *Local PPP currency units per U.S. dollar* (2005 prices)

	China Yuan/USD	India Rupees/USD
Machinery and equipment	8.79	36.84
Market exchange rate (MER)	**8.19**	**44.26**
Clothing and footwear	6.86	16.72
Restaurants and hotels	6.78	26.93
Transport	5.98	32.46
Alcoholic beverages and tobacco	5.75	31.53
Food and nonalcoholic beverages	5.52	21.13
Furnishings, household equipment, and household maintenance	5.27	22.73
Miscellaneous goods and services	4.13	16.07
Recreation and culture	3.47	18.41
GDP at PPP (total size of economy for comparing relative living standards)	**3.45**	**14.67**
Housing, water, electricity, gas, and other fuels	3.37	12.33
Communication	3.14	17.46
Construction	1.93	10.21
Education	1.02	2.90
Health	0.69	3.00

Source: *2005 International Comparison Program: Preliminary Results* (Washington, DC: World Bank, December 2007).

China), local purchasing power for key military-industrial inputs such as high-technology goods and manufacturing equipment is sometimes *less* – not more – than what is implied by market exchange rate price levels. This is the reverse of the typical relationship analysts see between market exchange rates and purchasing power for low-tech, local goods such as clothing, food, and housing. Lesser purchasing power for high-tech goods is due in part to their relative scarcity in developing markets, smaller market scale, and a relative shortage of appropriate complementary supporting technologies and workforce skills.

According to the most recent World Bank PPP data released in December 2007, the overall implied PPP exchange rate for China in 2005 was 3.45 yuan to the dollar, compared to the official exchange rate of 8.19 yuan to the dollar. Thus a person in China would only have to spend 3.45 yuan to consume one U.S. dollar's worth of comparable domestic Chinese goods, not the 8.19 yuan that implied by the exchange rate of the time.[64] However, according to

---

[64] This represented overall purchasing power for domestic goods about 2.4 times greater than what was implied in the 2005 exchange rate (or approximately 40% less than the

the same study, the PPP exchange rate for "machinery and equipment" was 8.79 yuan to the dollar. In other words, in purchasing-power terms, a person in China would have had to spend *more* local currency units than the official exchange rate of 8.19 yuan to the dollar to consume a comparable international machinery and equipment item. Rather than a "bigger bang for the buck," this data indicates that Chinese purchasing power for some modern military equipment (and the capital goods to produce it) may be *less* than that implied by the market exchange rate.

Moreover, "bang for the buck" implies something about military effectiveness and spending trade-offs. It is true that countries like India and China may have lower relative prices for items like food and health care. However, those advantages do not apply to the purchase of high-tech weaponry. To the contrary, by reducing the number of personnel in their militaries in the interests of modernization, countries like China and India implicitly acknowledge that the advantages they achieve on personnel costs are not, after a certain point, worth the burden on military effectiveness.

Further, the validity of the PPP approach depends in part on the functional equivalence of products being compared across countries. PPP methods are designed to capture consumption power for "the same precisely-defined product."[65] Yet it is not at all clear that there is functional equivalence between a fighter plane manufactured in a developing country and a fighter plane manufactured in a developed country. Indeed, the difference in performance between them (determined by advanced supporting technologies as well as the technologies embodied in the planes themselves) may be quite large.

To summarize, PPP methodology applied selectively to any one country can exaggerate the relative international power and capability of a given state. At the same time, PPP adjustments can make a weakness – inferior technology, or manpower-intensive military establishments – appear to be an advantage instead of a disadvantage. Finally, in some cases, the net effect of improperly calculated PPP adjustments to defense spending is itself larger than the effect of including entire categories of off-budget spending in total defense expenditure. In such a case, PPP "theory" threatens to obscure the relative importance of actual spending items.

purchasing power of 3.9 times the exchange rate in pre-December 2007 World Bank PPP estimates for China).

[65] See "What are PPPs?" World Bank, International Comparison Program, http://web. worldbank.org/WBSITE/EXTERNAL/DATASTATISTICS/ICPEXT/0,,contentMDK:223 90971~pagePK:60002244~piPK:62002388~theSitePK:270065,00.html

Estimating PPP-Adjusted Indian and Chinese Defense Spending
The most lethal and important components of modern military power are based on advanced industrial products and technologies. Comparable advanced goods such as these are built using manufacturing technologies and components sourced from international markets. Thus, using market exchange rates to compare defense-spending levels across countries is the preferred method in most cases. However, a case can be made that using market exchange rates alone could result in some underestimation of the total purchasing power of developing nation defense spending. Any underestimation from using market exchange rates will be greatest where manpower and low-technology assets are most important. If PPP-adjusted estimates are to be done properly, each major category of defense spending must be adjusted by a sector-level PPP exchange rate appropriate for that category. For example, capital outlays should be adjusted by equipment-sector PPPs, and pensions adjusted by the PPP exchange rate for consumption (which reflects items such as clothing and food).

One such method is presented below, with fair warning to readers that this process requires attention to a number of minor details. In the end, many analysts may conclude that the limited additional insight to be obtained from an appropriate PPP-adjusted estimate is not worth the effort required to delve into sector-level pricing and to continuously update PPP price series each year. Getting PPP right requires considerable time and effort. Most importantly, even when done right, the figures yielded can take on a life of their own, and contribute further to confusion in the public discussion. Even the best journalists often misinterpret PPP-derived figures, and the limitations of a reporter's time and print space virtually ensure that the effects of PPP adjustments will be reported in ways that may mislead readers.

Consider the following statement by a *New York Times* reporter: "Foreign security experts ... say Beijing's real military spending is two or three times the announced figure."[66] The impression conveyed is that China may somehow be "hiding" up to two-thirds of its military spending. In fact the difference in estimates may be accounted for by including categories of spending (such as nuclear weapons) that the United States also does not count in its official military budget. The difference may also be attributable to adjustments for PPP. PPP adjustments may indicate a relative amount

---

[66] David Lague, "Chinese Military Spending Rises Sharply," *New York Times*, March 5, 2008.

of locally produced lower technology goods that China can afford to buy with its budget (like bullets, food, and uniforms), but PPP adjustments do not indicate that "real" spending is hidden, nor do they imply extra actual expenditure.

Nevertheless, the PPP methodology can be useful within the specialist community. In our estimates, we use the latest detailed sector-specific World Bank PPP price series for India and China. The data set is used to build up sector-level PPP prices to more accurately measure spending items in particular parts of the defense budget, such as personnel costs and equipment costs (see Appendix).

To convert spending on items such as military pensions to PPP terms, we use the World Bank PPP for overall consumption. Defense capital expenditure is converted to PPP terms using the World Bank price series for machinery and equipment. We also create a "military PPP" price level estimate, to convert spending on items such as military operations, training, and some establishment costs. This military PPP price level is a composite that we have developed for this study, based on the consumption PPP price level and the PPP price levels for machinery, equipment, and fuels. (This composite captures the varied components of military operations and training, which require things like equipment maintenance, services, food, fuel, and other consumables.) Weapon imports and the most competitive elements of manufacturing and R&D are based on internationally traded manufactured goods. Therefore, market exchange rates are applied to R&D, industrial subsidies, arms imports, and profits from arms sales.

The appropriate sector-level PPP prices are used to convert local currency defense spending in each category outlined earlier. This bottom-up approach produces more accurate results than applying an overall PPP at GDP prices adjustment to a single aggregate defense-spending estimate. Estimates for Indian and Chinese full defense spending in 2005 in both market exchange rates and PPP-adjusted terms are presented in Table 4.10. (All data and calculations are provided in the Appendix.)

The baseline estimate for PPP-adjusted Chinese defense spending in 2005 is $69.3 billion. The baseline estimate for PPP-adjusted Indian defense spending in 2005 is $45.4 billion. The baseline estimate for PPP-adjusted Chinese defense spending in 2010 is $138.2 billion. The baseline estimate for PPP-adjusted Indian defense spending in 2010 is $88.4 billion.

Using this more precise method, the PPP-adjusted baseline estimate ranges between 1.9 (2005) and 2.1 (2010) times the estimate based on market exchange rates for India. Similarly, PPP-adjusted baseline estimate

Table 4.10. *Full defense-spending market exchange rate and PPP-adjusted* (in billions)

	2005		2010	
	MER USD	PPP USD	MER USD	PPP USD
China	44.6	69.3	113.3	138.2
India	23.9	45.4	43.2	88.4

ranges between 1.6 (2005) and 1.2 (2010) times the market exchange rate-based estimate for China. Our detailed sector-specific PPP method yields differentials that are much lower than the purchasing power differential implied by using a single overall PPP at GDP price, which is 2.4 for China and 3.0 for India (based on the World Bank data for 2005). As expected, the differential is greatest for personnel-related costs, such as salaries, housing, and pensions.

The effect of using PPP on Indian spending is greater than the effect of using PPP on Chinese spending. This is because India is less developed and less integrated with the global economy than China, so its price levels are even lower compared to international price levels. Again, the greater purchasing power for local, noninternationally traded goods such as salaries, housing, and pensions does not mean that either country is hiding defense spending, or spending more than announced figures. Further, it is unclear how much the greater purchasing power for local goods adds to the relative lethality or effectiveness of either country's forces. The relative purchasing power advantage for nonlethal items may be offset by weaker purchasing power in important categories such as advanced technology and equipment.

The PPP differential in defense purchasing power relative to market exchange rates for China declined in 2010 compared to 2005, whereas the differential for India increased slightly.[67] In both countries, the difference between aggregate GDP at PPP prices and GDP at market exchange rates declined between 2005 and 2010. This reflects growing wealth and greater integration with global markets. Over time, as the two economies develop and become even more integrated with global markets, the effect of PPP price differentials could continue to decline.

---

[67] In India's case, this was due in part to the composition of Indian defense spending. Pension spending is adjusted at consumption PPP prices, and spending on paramilitary forces is adjusted at our estimated "military PPP" price series.

Conclusions: Defense Spending

Based on this analysis, a few conclusions are possible. First, the results of detailed comparisons for 2005 and 2010 show roughly similar levels of full defense spending as a share of GDP in each country across the two different years, with India devoting somewhat more effort to defense than China (measured as either a percentage of either GDP or of total national budget). Even when similar off-budget items are included, India spends a greater percentage of its national wealth on defense than China does. Moreover, because India is significantly poorer than China in per capita terms, the burden on India (relative to China) is even greater.

Second, both countries exhibit a certain degree of nontransparency in defense spending and reporting. Off-budget items constitute a significant portion of both Indian and Chinese defense. In our comparable baseline estimates for total defense spending, adding off-budget items to the official defense budget would bring total Chinese defense spending to 1.5 times the official budget in 2005 and 1.4 times the official defense budget in 2010 (not including nuclear weapons, space, and intelligence programs). For India, adding in the comparable off-budget items would bring total Indian defense spending to 1.3 times the official budget in 2005 and 1.4 times the official budget in 2010 (not including nuclear weapons, space, and intelligence programs).

The largest spending categories not included in the official budget are the same in both countries: spending on military pensions, paramilitary forces, and defense-related R&D. The Indian case – like many others – demonstrates that off-budget spending is not unusual. These general patterns show that the two countries share some similarities in defense spending and in budget reporting, and this finding again highlights the need for comparisons between countries if sensible conclusions are to be made about spending trends in any one country.

Third, in both cases, many discrepancies between official and actual defense spending often have more to do with bureaucratic budgetary divisions than a concerted effort to hide spending. Both Indian and Chinese paramilitary spending is listed in officially published budgets, but given the different agencies involved, they are not listed under a consolidated defense budget (in much the same way that spending by the U.S. Departments of Homeland Security and Veterans Affairs is not listed in U.S. defense budgets).

Fourth, Indian defense budgets are more detailed and somewhat more transparent than Chinese budgets. However, this difference is one of degree. For both countries, the level of transparency is broadly consistent with (and sometimes better than) that of many other states in the developing world.[68]

Fifth, the transparency of both Indian and Chinese national security spending is improving, although both have far to go. Indian spending is nontransparent in nuclear weapons programs, military-related space programs, intelligence programs, the full extent of defense-related R&D, state assistance to the defense industrial base, and, to a lesser extent, arms import costs. China is nontransparent in the same areas, and even less transparent than India in defense-related R&D and military pensions. Given the large size of both countries and their growing defense budgets, both will have to make further strides in transparency (and diplomacy) to dispel worries among their neighbors about the nature and significance of defense spending.

Defense-spending analysis can help identify trends and intensity of effort, and may indicate levels of sustainability when compared with other data, such as GDP, government revenue and expenditure, and domestic development indicators. However, as the 1980–2010 data show, linear projections from recent trends are not a good indicator of future spending. Future defense spending will be affected by change in both domestic and international circumstances. Further, our analysis of PPP adjustments provides reason to be cautious about extrapolating spending effectiveness or weapons system performance quality when converting local spending into a common currency such as the U.S. dollar.

Finally, while defense budget analysis can shed light on spending and modernization priorities, it also has limits. A number of analysts have shown that, when measured in isolation from other factors, tracking defense spending by itself does not lead to clear conclusions about a state's intentions.[69] One study in the late 1950s found that even U.S. federal

---

[68] In contrast to China, for example, which has published a defense white paper every two years since 1998, Thailand has published just one such document and it appeared more than a decade ago. The authors have tried to parse service spending, as well as other parts of the military budgets, for the Philippines, Indonesia, Taiwan, and Thailand, and in a number of areas are more opaque than the Chinese budget.

[69] See for example, Anthony H. Cordesman and Martin Klieber, *Chinese Military Modernization: Force Development and Strategic Capabilities* (Washington, DC: Center for Strategic and International Studies, 2007). During the Cold War, American defense and intelligence agencies frequently exaggerated Soviet defense spending and relative capabilities and failed to firmly link that analysis to Soviet intentions. See Raymond Garthoff, "CIA Estimates of Soviet Defense Spending: A Review," *Post-Soviet Geography and Economics*, 39:9 (1998); John Prados, *The Soviet Estimate: US Intelligence and Russian Military Strength* (New York: Dial Press, 1982); Donald P. Steury, ed., *Intentions and Capabilities: Estimates*

government budgets – generally transparent by international standards – were poor indicators of government intentions without significant additional institutional context and analysis of actual activities.[70] Conclusions about intentions require greater context than defense-spending analysis alone. The analysis of key features of foreign policy presented in the previous chapter is one part of that context. The modernization of both operational military doctrines and military forces also provides perspective. We turn to these topics in the next two chapters.

on Soviet Strategic Forces, 1950–1983 (Washington, DC: Central Intelligence Agency, 1996); Edgar M. Bottome, *The Missile Gap: A Study in the Formulation of Military and Political Policy* (Rutherford: Fairleigh Dickinson University Press, 1971).

[70] David Novick, *The Federal Budget as an Indicator of Government Intentions and the Implications of Intentions* (Santa Monica: RAND Corporation, 1959).

5

Military Doctrine

Toward Emphasis on Offensive Action

In contrast to the defense spending trends examined in the preceding chapter, developments in military doctrine do not capture the same level of general public attention. However, military doctrine is an important point of comparison for understanding international strategic behavior for three reasons. First, doctrine represents a vision of how a nation's military intends to fight.[1] This is important in itself, as some military doctrines have implications for key security issues such as crisis stability. For example, a strong belief among military and political leaders in the efficacy of offensive action compared to defense could exacerbate crisis instability by providing incentives for preemptive attack.[2]

Second, military doctrine alone is not a good predictor of a given state's *strategic* intentions, but it offers a guide to the state's judgment about its security environment and the *operational* challenges the state expects to face. Hence, doctrine lends some insight into the kind of wars a military

---

[1] In this section, we follow Dennis Blasko' simple definition of doctrine as "a statement of how a military fights." See Dennis J. Blasko, *The Chinese Army Today: Tradition and Transformation for the 21st Century* (New York: Routledge Press, 2006), 92. We modify Blasko's definition slightly, using "intends to fight" to capture the current gap between some Chinese and Indian aspirations and capabilities, as both of these developing countries continue to modernize their military forces. A nation's military doctrine is part of a larger (explicit or implicit) calculus that incorporates an assessment of the global and regional threat environment, national development priorities, and a domestic political process for prioritizing interests, choosing means to secure those interests, and apportioning resources toward developing those means. However, we believe choosing a simple definition of "how a military intends to fight" captures the most critical elements of interest for the purpose of this chapter.

[2] See Jack Snyder, *The Ideology of the Offensive: Military Decision Making and the Disasters of 1914* (Ithaca: Cornell University Press, 1984); Barry R. Posen, *The Sources of Military Doctrine* (Ithaca: Cornell University Press, 1986); and Stephen Van Evera, *Causes of War: Power and the Roots of Conflict* (Ithaca: Cornell University Press, 1999).

believes it will have to fight. States closely observe each other's military doctrines, so doctrinal changes in other countries can also affect a state's perceptions of the security environment. Third, in addition to spelling out the operational aspects of how a military intends to fight, doctrine also provides a foundation for many other important defense-related decisions, such as military organization, weapons procurement, and military training. These in turn affect overall military modernization goals.

The Chinese and Indian militaries have both been undertaking doctrinal reform and development programs. In both countries, doctrinal developments, like overall defense spending decisions, have been motivated by evolving security environments. Changes to the security environment include new alignments and new security challenges since the end of the Cold War, as well as the advent of new war-making capabilities demonstrated by Western weapons and military operations in the 1991 Gulf War, the late 1990s Balkans conflict, the 2003 U.S.-led invasion of Iraq, and ongoing NATO operations in Afghanistan.

A number of official and academic U.S. observers have singled out developments in Chinese military doctrine as worrisome. For some U.S. Defense Department officials, the PLA's new emphasis on offensive action suggests (or can lead to) a preference for preemptive strikes. At a minimum, these doctrinal changes are seen to raise questions about crisis stability. Possibly, they are a troubling indicator of Beijing's strategic intentions. For example, the 2009 Pentagon report, *The Military Power of the People's Republic of China*, finds that Chinese statements on PLA military doctrine "illustrate the ambiguity of PRC strategic thinking as well as the justification for offensive – or preemptive – military action at the operational and tactical level under the guise of a defensive posture at the strategic level."[3] Chinese doctrine is also seen to rely on deception. The same 2009 Pentagon report argues that "the PLA draws from China's historical experience and the traditional role that stratagem and deception have played in Chinese doctrine."[4]

With these concerns, the U.S. security establishment has greatly intensified its study of Chinese military doctrine and military modernization programs, and these are becoming much better understood. However, most studies of Chinese military doctrine lack the comparative perspective that would allow them to assess whether trends in Chinese doctrine make it "unusual" when compared to those of other states.

---

[3] *Military Power of the People's Republic of China* (Washington, DC: Office of the Secretary of Defense, March 2009), 12.

[4] *Military Power of the People's Republic of China 2009*, 16.

In comparison to China, Indian military modernization is less examined. This may reflect a belief in the United States that Indo-Pakistan and related regional security issues have been mitigated, or at least sidestepped, via Washington's new security relationships with New Delhi, Islamabad, and Kabul. Yet both India and a crisis-torn, nuclear-armed Pakistan continue to place each other at the center of strategic plans, despite India's global aspirations on the one hand and Pakistan's urgent domestic issues on the other. Hence, despite garnering less U.S. attention, Indian military development bears on U.S. security interests. India's doctrinal developments also provide comparative context for judging developments in China, and vice versa.

Chinese Military Doctrine

The 2009 Pentagon report on China's military power contains a chapter on Chinese military strategy and doctrine that pays particular attention to the PLA's "offense as defense" doctrine, and the potential for PLA preemptive strikes.[5] Analysis of China's developing military doctrine can be improved by moving away from examining Chinese doctrine in isolation. For example, comparison to the doctrines of other states will help provide a baseline for making judgments about the relative emphasis on offense. As a continental-sized, rising power with advanced land, air, and naval capabilities as well as border and territorial issues with its neighbors, India is a useful point of comparison.

Comparing military doctrines is complicated by differences in language as well as concepts. For example, there is no single word in Chinese that directly corresponds to doctrine in the way that it is used in Western militaries or in the Indian military. Further, China does not publish the same range of public documents that the United States does on national security strategy, national military strategy, and military doctrine. However, China's military doctrinal developments are not simply nontransparent. There are numerous publicly available Chinese official documents that, taken together, do describe a comprehensive military strategy and operational doctrine.[6]

---

[5] *Military Power of the People's Republic of China* (Washington, DC: Office of the Secretary of Defense, 2009), 12.

[6] To provide just a few examples of a very extensive literature, see 张玉良[Zhang Yuliang], 《战役学》 [The Science of Military Campaigns], (Beijing: National Defense University Press, 2nd edition 2006); 卢利华[Lu Lihua], 《军队指挥理论学习指南》 [Military Command Theory Study Guide], (Beijing: National Defense University Press, 2005); 薛兴林主编 [Xue Xinglin, chief editor], 《战役理论学习指南》 [Campaign Theory Study Guide], (Beijing: National Defense University Press, 2002); 中国人民解放军第二炮兵部队 [PLA Second Artillery], 《第二炮兵战役学》 [Science of Second Artillery

Unsurprisingly, most of these documents are available only in Chinese. Despite this language challenge, there is already a substantial literature in the West on Chinese military strategy and doctrine.[7] China's publication of a series of Defense White Papers since 1998, which are available in English, has also improved transparency and insight into PLA doctrinal and force modernization.[8]

The recent evolution of PLA military doctrine is one output of an extended strategic review that began in the early 1990s.[9] Both domestic and international political, economic, social, and technological factors were part of that comprehensive strategic assessment, with input from multiple civilian

---

Campaigns], (Beijing: People's Liberation Army Press, 2004); 中国空军百科全书编审委员会 [Editorial Committee of the People's Liberation Army Air Force Encyclopedia], 《中国空军百科全书"》 [China Air Force Encyclopedia], (Beijing: Aviation Industry Press, 2005); 解放军总政治部 [PLA General Political Department], 《江泽民国防和军队建设思想学习纲要》 [Outline for Studying Jiang Zemin Thought on National Defense and Army Building], (Beijing: Military Science Press, 2003); 彭光谦 [Peng Guangqian], 《中国军事战略问题研究》 [Research on Chinese Military Strategy], (Beijing: People's Liberation Army Press, 2006).

[7] The Western literature on Chinese military development is now so advanced that it is undergoing specialization – a sharp contrast with the available Western literature on modern Indian military development. This literature is not comparative, however. For a broad overview of post-1978 Chinese military developments, see David Shambaugh, *Modernizing China's Military: Progress, Problems, and Prospects* (Berkeley: University of California Press, 2003); and M. Taylor Fravel, "China's Search for Military Power," *The Washington Quarterly*, 31:3 (Summer 2008): 125–141. For an account of how the PLA might actually fight a war, see Blasko, *The Chinese Army Today*; on how doctrine has evolved to deal with border defense and border conflicts, see M. Taylor Fravel, "Securing Borders: China's Doctrine and Force Structure for Frontier Defense," *Journal of Strategic Studies*, 30:4–5 (2007): 705–737. For an examination of how doctrine interacts with decision making in China's security establishment, see John Lewis and Xue Litai, *Imagined Enemies: China Prepares for Uncertain War* (Stanford: Stanford University Press, 2006). For detailed studies of Chinese military thought and PLA doctrinal developments, including nuclear, naval, air force, and space warfare doctrines, see David M. Finkelstein and James Mulvenon, eds., *The Revolution in Doctrinal Affairs: Emerging Trends in the Operational Art of the Chinese People's Liberation Army* (Alexandria: Center for Naval Analyses, 2005); and David M. Finkelstein, "China's National Military Strategy Revisited: An Overview of the Military Strategic Guidelines," in *Right-Sizing the People's Liberation Army: Exploring the Contours of China's Military*, ed. Roy Kamphausen and Andrew Scobell (Carlisle: Army War College, 2007), 69–140.

[8] Although these English-language defense white papers leave many topics uncovered, foreign observers agree that they show a trend toward greater transparency and information sharing. See Trefor Moss, "White paper reveals insight into Chinese Defence Rationale," *Jane's Defence Weekly*, January 28, 2009.

[9] Major military reforms began even earlier, at least as far back as 1985, in line with Deng Xiaoping's broader campaign of fundamental political, economic, and social reform. See Shambaugh, *Modernizing China's Military*, 60–61. Developments in the late 1980s and early 1990s prompted more far-reaching reevaluation and reforms.

and military agencies. Civilian leaders in the Communist Party dominated the process, and subsequent changes to military doctrine have been based upon the strategic guidelines that resulted. The fall of communist regimes in Eastern Europe and Russia beginning in 1989, internal crisis in China in 1989, and the display of modern Western military power in the 1991 Gulf War all contributed to Beijing's perception that it needed new strategic guidelines (and a new military doctrine). The review process resulted in new "military strategic guidelines" (*junshi zhanlue fangzhen*) issued in January 1993.[10]

The 1993 military strategic guidelines provide a strategic assessment of the global security situation, concluding that great power global war is unlikely but local conflicts could occur. The guidelines conclude that the current period favoring peace between the great powers presents an opportunity for China to concentrate on economic development and modernization. They also find that the nature of war has changed, toward the use of precision strike weapons in integrated joint operations, prosecuted at a high tempo by mobile forces linked through wide and deep information networks. With this overall strategic assessment as the background, in 1993, the PLA was told to develop an ability to fight and win "Local Wars Under Modern High Tech Conditions."[11] Today, U.S. forces set the highest standard in this type of high-tech warfare. This factor – together with tensions over issues such as Taiwan – provides incentives for the PLA to plan with the U.S. military in mind.

In 1999, China issued detailed "operational guidelines" (*gangyao*) and "operational principles" (*zuozhan tiaoli*) that stipulated how the 1993 military strategic guidelines should be implemented.[12] Several major shifts are evident in the new doctrine of fighting "Local Wars Under Modern Informationized Conditions." Pre-1999 doctrine focused on preparation for fighting long, protracted battles of attrition deep in the Chinese mainland against a potential invader. The new doctrine calls for developing the ability to fight short-duration, high-intensity wars in or near China's border or littoral areas. The new doctrine also calls for the PLA to develop the

---

[10] David Finkelstein calls these "strategic guidelines" the highest level of national guidance and direction given to China's armed forces. Finkelstein, "China's National Military Strategy Revisited," 82.

[11] Subsequently revised in 1999 to "Local Wars Under Modern Informationized Conditions."

[12] David M. Finkelstein, "Thinking About The PLA's 'Revolution in Doctrinal Affairs,'" in James Mulvenon and David Finkelstein, eds., *The Revolution in Doctrinal Affairs: Emerging Trends in the Operational Art of the Chinese People's Liberation Army* (Alexandria: Center for Naval Analyses, 2005), 1–27.

ability to move beyond combined arms operations primarily conducted by ground forces to truly joint campaigns fought by integrated land, sea, air, and electronic warfare forces.[13]

Post-1999 doctrine shifts the PLA's task in war from a focus on destroying the enemy's weakest forces (i.e., guerrilla tactics) to attacking and destroying the enemy's most powerful critical assets. The PLA is now charged with acquiring and using more modern, accurate weapons to concentrate firepower rather than to simply mass firepower. And it is now expected to rely less on slow-moving or static defenses and more on mobile, offensive forces in combat.[14]

The doctrine of fighting local wars under informationized conditions emphasizes that once hostilities have begun, Chinese military operations will be offensive. Offensive action should not be limited by space or time, or by geographical boundaries. Increased emphasis on offensive action is evident in both the 2000 and 2006 versions of *Zhanyi Xue* (*The Science of Campaigns*), published by China's Academy of Military Sciences. In all types of campaigns, but particularly in air campaigns, gaining and maintaining the initiative is necessary for success. And in all campaigns, the best way to do that is to adopt the posture of combined offensive and defensive action. Remaining exclusively on the defensive leads to a passive posture and, therefore, defeat.[15] Even in defensive campaigns, counterattacks are critical to success, and better yet is to begin or quickly transition to the offensive campaign.

Doctrinal change has affected the way the Chinese ground forces organize, train, and equip themselves.[16] The PLA has moved to become smaller, more mobile, more capable of using electronics and information systems, and it has focused on developing a smaller number of better-armed units.

---

[13] Combined arms operations employ different branches of the same service, for example infantry, armor, and artillery in the ground forces. Joint operations are conducted by forces from different services. Like India, China is making slow progress on increased jointness and still experiences challenges in this area. See *The People's Liberation Army Navy: A Modern Navy with Chinese Characteristics* (Suitland: Office of Naval Intelligence, July 2009), 41–42.

[14] Finkelstein, "China's National Military Strategy Revisited," 69–140.

[15] Zhang Yuliang, ed., *Zhanyi Xue*, 561–562.

[16] Cortez A. Cooper III, "'Preserving the State:' Modernizing and Task-orienting a 'Hybrid' PLA Ground Force," in Roy Kamphausen and Andrew Scobell eds., *Right-Sizing the People's Liberation Army: Exploring the Contours of China's Military* (Carlisle: Army War College, 2007), 237–280; and Dennis J. Blasko, "PLA Ground Force Modernization and Mission Diversification: Underway in All Military Regions," in Roy Kamphausen and Andrew Scobell eds., *Right-Sizing the People's Liberation Army: Exploring the Contours of China's Military* (Carlisle: Army War College, 2007), 281–373.

These units are now organized in ways that optimize particular elements for specific tasks, including supporting domestic security, disaster relief, border security, and antiterrorism, as well as conventional warfare.

With the advent of new doctrine, the PLA has stepped up training for joint operations.[17] PLA ground forces are training in combined arms and joint operations, airborne assault, close-air-support operations, reconnaissance and electronic warfare operations, special operations, and engineering operations including the removal of obstacles and mine clearing.[18] In these exercises, the PLA has emphasized developing the ability to seize the initiative and go on the tactical and operational offensive.

The ground forces appear to place heavy emphasis on using conventional missile strikes and special operations forces to deliver early, possibly preemptive, strikes against an enemy's command and logistics centers. These would be followed by the deployment of combined arms forces, which would rely on area-denial (or "anti-access") operations by the Chinese air force and the Chinese navy for protection while they conducted their attacks. As important as the tactics rehearsed in training, the way in which exercises are conducted has also changed. The PLA has begun moving away from scripted exercises toward greater "free play," with an emphasis at the end on lessons learned rather than on smooth victory by red forces.

In the future, the PLA is likely to aim to make its ground forces even smaller and more mobile, and better able to concentrate firepower. The ground forces are likely to play a greater role in preparation for Taiwan-related scenarios. There are already two amphibious assault divisions within the ground forces, a substantially larger force than the two brigades of marines within the PLA Navy. Presently, amphibious lift for these forces is limited, but China does have the resources to expand its lift capacity should it feel the need.

Chinese Doctrine: Beyond the Ground Forces

With its focus on the potential for local wars in China's littoral areas, the doctrine of "local war under informationized conditions" has significant implications for China's naval, air, and strategic forces. PLA Navy (PLAN) doctrine underwent substantial change well in advance of overall PLA

---

[17] See Blasko, "PLA Ground Force Modernization." However, most foreign observers, and even PLA self-assessments, indicate that realism in PLA training is relative – it is improved but not yet at Western standards. The same appears to apply to the effectiveness of joint operations.

[18] Blasko, "PLA Ground Force Modernization," 333–334.

doctrine.[19] In February 1987, PLAN chief Admiral Liu Huaqing approved a doctrine that called for the Chinese navy to move beyond coastal defense to defense in depth.[20] As part of the defense-in-depth concept, Liu identified several areas of operation.

The first comprised China's *jin'an*, or inshore areas, including the Bohai Bay near Beijing and Tianjin, the Qiongzhou Strait in the south near Hainan Island, and the Taiwan Strait. Liu determined that the PLA Navy must be able to move beyond this zone, to be able to operate within what he called the "first island chain." According to Liu's conception, the first island chain runs north-south from the Aleutian Islands, the Kurile Islands, the Japanese Islands, the Ryuku Islands, Taiwan, the Philippines, and Indonesia. It encompasses the Yellow Sea (facing Korea), the East China Sea (bounded by Taiwan and the Ryukyu Islands), and the South China Sea (west of the Philippines and stretching as far as Indonesia). Liu envisioned the PLAN as being able to control this zone in time of war by about the year 2000.[21]

Liu also envisioned a second phase of naval development, in which the PLAN would improve its ability to conduct operations further from China's coast, into an area defined by a "second island chain," from the Kurile Islands and Japan, moving more easterly to run through the Bonin, Mariana, and Caroline Islands. Liu believed the PLAN could secure this area in time of war by about 2020. Finally, in Liu's vision, the PLAN would develop "blue water" capabilities by about 2050.[22]

Despite this expansive vision, the fighting doctrine Liu conceived stressed "stubborn defense near the shore" and "surprise guerilla attacks at sea."[23] This,

[19] On PLA Navy modernization and doctrinal developments, see Cole, "China's Maritime Strategy," 22–42; Michael McDevitt, "The Strategic and Operational Context Driving PLA Navy Building," in Roy Kamphausen and Andrew Scobell, eds., *Right-Sizing the People's Liberation Army: Exploring the Contours of China's Military* (Carlisle: Army War College, 2007), 481–522; You Ji, "China's Naval Strategy and Transformation," 71–94; Howarth, *China's Rising Sea Power*; Cole, *The Great Wall at Sea*; and John Lewis and Xue Li-tai, *China's Strategic Seapower: The Politics of Force Modernization in the Nuclear Age*, (Stanford: Stanford University Press, 1996).

[20] 刘华清 [Liu Huaqing], 《刘华清回忆录》 [Memoirs of Admiral Liu Huaqing], (Beijing: People's Liberation Army Press, 2004); see also You Ji, "China's Naval Strategy and Transformation," in Lawrence W. Prabhakar, Joshua H. Ho, and W. S. G. Bateman, eds., *The Evolving Maritime Balance of Power in the Asia-Pacific: Maritime Doctrines And Nuclear Weapons at Sea* (Singapore: World Scientific Publishing Company, 2006), 71–94.

[21] Bernard D. Cole, *The Great Wall at Sea: China's Navy Enters the Twenty-First Century* (Annapolis: Naval Institute Press, 2001), 166.

[22] Bernard D. Cole, *The Great Wall at Sea: China's Navy Enters the Twenty-First Century* 166–167.

[23] Bernard D. Cole, "China's Maritime Strategy," in Andrew S. Erickson, Lyle J. Goldstein, William S. Murray, and Andrew R. Wilson, eds., *China's Future Nuclear Submarine Force* (Annapolis: Naval Institute Press, 2007), 26.

along with the decision to delimit specific zones of operation in concentric circles moving outward from the Chinese mainland, has prompted some Western observers to note that PLAN doctrine actually reveals a strong continentalist bias, as opposed to a more purely maritime vision.[24] A number of Western analysts see China's sea-denial doctrine as optimized for Taiwan scenarios rather than as an indicator of broader offensive designs.[25]

However, given the nature of China's opponent in such a scenario – the U.S. military – the PLA feels obliged to develop capabilities for deterring or confronting U.S. forces before they can decisively intervene in the air or waters above or around Taiwan. This has led the PLA to focus on "anti-access" capabilities that could be used to deter or prevent the U.S. air or naval forces from moving close to Taiwan or China's coast. The PLA Navy has placed heavy emphasis on developing missile-armed surface ships and especially submarine forces in this context. Emerging doctrine on the use of these submarines appears to focus on sea-denial and blockade missions in a potential Taiwan conflict, although some of China's more capable nuclear submarines might engage in longer-range patrols for intelligence gathering and interdiction.[26]

The PLAN (and the PLA more generally) also appears to place great stock in being able to attack U.S. aircraft carrier battle groups, presumably to deter them from approaching Taiwan and China's coastal areas. China's increasing ability to deploy satellites and use technologies such as backscatter radar has made the long-range detection of aircraft carriers somewhat easier. However, detecting an aircraft carrier battle group in wartime would nevertheless be difficult, given the various countermeasures that might be employed.[27] The PLAN is developing its submarine doctrine in tandem

[24] Cole, "China's Maritime Strategy," pp 26–28; Peter Howarth, *China's Rising Sea Power: The PLA Navy's Submarine Challenge* (New York: Routledge Asian Security Studies, 2006), 41–56. Others disagree; for example, James R. Holmes and Toshi Yoshihara of the U.S. Naval War College find a growing "turn to Mahan" in publicly available Chinese writings on strategy, although Holmes and Yoshihara conclude that China's focus will likely remain on Taiwan and the "first island chain" rather than a limitless blue-water naval strategy. James R. Holmes and Toshi Yoshihara, *China's Naval Strategy in the 21st Century: The Turn to Mahan* (New York: Routledge Press, 2008).

[25] You Ji, "China's Naval Strategy and Transformation," 89. See also Cole, "China's Maritime Strategy," 22–24; Howarth, *China's Rising Sea Power*; and Bernard D. Cole, *The Great Wall at Sea: China's Navy Enters the Twenty-First Century* (Annapolis: Naval Institute Press, 2001).

[26] Office of Naval Intelligence, *The People's Liberation Army Navy: A Modern Navy with Chinese Characteristics*, 21.

[27] Paul H. B. Godwin, "China's Emerging Military Doctrine: A Role for Nuclear Submarines?" in Andrew S. Erickson, Lyle J. Goldstein, William S. Murray, and Andrew R. Wilson, eds., *China's Future Nuclear Submarine Force* (Annapolis: Naval Institute Press, 2007), 43–58.

with weapons such as wake-homing torpedoes and cruise missiles that can be launched while submerged. The Chinese military is also developing land-based ballistic and cruise missile capabilities for striking ships at sea, discussed later in the chapter. These weapons give China the potential to attack large U.S. surface forces. PLA and PLAN doctrinal developments remain focused on Taiwan-related scenarios, but they also give China the potential for offensive operations, sea denial, and (to a lesser extent) sea-lane security operations well beyond China's littoral areas.[28]

China's air force doctrine has also evolved as a result of the general strategic guidelines described previously. The PLAAF has been instructed to develop the capability to move from a national air defense force with a primary task of protecting mainland airspace to a force capable of conducting joint offensive air campaigns around China's periphery with fewer but more capable aircraft. Again, the primary focus is Taiwan. The PLAAF continues to suffer from several limitations, including a heavy reliance on scripted operations and the procedural control of battle space (e.g., by time and altitude). Although it is experimenting with more active and dynamic approaches, China's air force currently lacks the technical means to implement such an approach on a large scale.[29]

The PLAAF is moving toward a more independent role, one less tied to ground force control. In this it is following the course preferred by most air forces, including India's. (Paradoxically, this is occurring at the same time that "jointness" and "combined operations" are being emphasized in wider

---

[28] Office of Naval Intelligence, *The People's Liberation Army Navy: A Modern Navy with Chinese Characteristics*, 5–11; Andrew S. Erickson and Justin D. Mikolay, "Welcome China to the Fight Against Pirates," *U.S. Naval Institute Proceedings*, 135:3 (March 2009): 34–41; Andrew Erickson and Lyle Goldstein, "Gunboats for China's New 'Grand Canals'? Probing the Intersection of Beijing's Naval and Oil Security Policies," *Naval War College Review*, 62:2 (Spring 2009), 43–76.

[29] On PLAAF operational concepts, see Roger Cliff, John Fei, Jeff Hagen, Elizabeth Hague, Eric Heginbotham, and John Stillion, *Shaking the Heavens and Splitting the Earth: Chinese Air Force Employment Concepts in the 21st Century* (Santa Monica: RAND, 2011); Philip C. Saunders and Erik R. Quam, "China's Air Force Modernization," *Joint Forces Quarterly*, 47 (2007), 28–33; Erik Lin-Greenberg, "Offensive Airpower with Chinese Characteristics: Development, Capabilities, and Intentions," *Air & Space Power Journal*, 21:3 (Fall 2007); and Mark A. Stokes, "The Chinese Joint Aerospace Campaign: Strategy, Doctrine, and Force Modernization," in James Mulvenon and David Finkelstein, eds., *The Revolution in Doctrinal Affairs: Emerging Trends in the Operational Art of the Chinese People's Liberation Army* (Alexandria: Center for Naval Analyses, 2005), 221–304. For an analysis of PLAAF history and historical doctrine, as well as the emergence of new doctrine and weapons in the 1990s, see Kenneth W. Allen, "PLA Air Force Operation and Modernization" (paper presented at Conference on the People's Liberation Army, Carlisle, Pennsylvania, September 10–12, 1999); and Kenneth W. Allen, Glenn Krumel, and Jonathan D. Pollack, *China's Air Force Enters the 21st Century* (Santa Monica: RAND, 1995).

PLA doctrine.) PLAAF doctrine emphasizes offense at the operational and tactical levels, and considers surprise and seizing the initiative as important aspects of military operations. As in other areas, change is relative. In some ways, China's air force doctrine is less ambitious (or more realistic) than the air force doctrines of some other states. For example, instead of framing "air superiority" in absolute terms, PLAAF writing explicitly emphasizes the fact that air superiority can be gained within circumscribed geographical areas for limited periods of time to facilitate larger campaign objectives.[30] In principle, this concept is not at odds with U.S. thinking, but U.S. officers tend to assert the advantages of theater-wide "air superiority." The PLAAF is intent on improving important support capabilities, such as C⁴ISR, AEW, and midair refueling. PLAAF writings on air campaigns outline new functions, including an "air deterrence" capability and the ability to implement "air blockades." If successfully developed, these capabilities would significantly increase the operational range of the PLAAF, potentially beyond China's littoral areas.

China's strategic doctrine development has focused on improving the credibility of China's nuclear deterrent.[31] The emphasis has been on developing a survivable retaliatory capability in the form of strategic missile submarines and longer-range, more reliable, and more survivable ballistic missile forces in the Second Artillery Corps. This is consistent with Chinese nuclear doctrine, which emphasizes no first use of nuclear weapons, and the maintenance of "lean and effective" nuclear forces. "Lean," in this case, means small in number, and "effective" means capable of surviving a first strike and retaliating. Although the Chinese are reluctant to use the term "minimum deterrent" because the term suggests a particular threshold for retaliatory capability (and to the Chinese a high one), a number of Western analysts nevertheless believe "minimum deterrence" is an apt description of Chinese doctrine.[32] To this end, the Second Artillery is moving from liquid-fuel rockets to solid-fuel and from silo-based missiles toward mobile launchers and reloadable launchers. It is increasing the range and accuracy

---

[30] Roger Cliff et al., *Shaking the Heavens and Splitting the Earth*, 56–60.

[31] For an official statement of Second Artillery doctrine, see 中国人民解放军第二炮兵部队 [PLA Second Artillery], 《第二炮兵战役学》 [Science of Second Artillery Campaigns], (Beijing: People's Liberation Army Press, 2004).

[32] Michael S. Chase and Evan Medeiros, "China's Evolving Nuclear Calculus: Modernization and Doctrinal Debate," in James Mulvenon and David Finkelstein, eds., *The Revolution in Doctrinal Affairs: Emerging Trends in the Operational Art of the Chinese People's Liberation Army* (Alexandria: Center for Naval Analyses, 2005), 119–154. Chase and Medeiros show that there is some debate in publicly available Chinese sources about developing limited nuclear war fighting doctrine and capability, but conclude that China is actually moving toward a clearer and more explicit doctrine of credible minimum deterrence.

of its missiles, and working at a modest but steady pace to increase the number of both nuclear missiles and warheads in the inventory. It has also added a new class of more advanced ballistic missile submarines and submarine launched ballistic missiles, ending its near total reliance on a land-based deterrent.[33]

Since at least the 1990s, the Second Artillery has been charged with developing improved conventional-strike forces. To date, this effort has mainly focused on deploying large numbers of conventionally armed short-range and medium-range ballistic missiles across the straits with Taiwan, but the Chinese continue to develop new weapons with greater range and accuracy. They also appear to be developing a conventionally armed ballistic missile that could strike moving ships at sea – an anti-ship ballistic missile (ASBM).[34]

China does not yet have the latter capability, but were it to test and deploy an ASBM, it would pose new challenges to U.S. efforts to defend Taiwan in the event of war. The deployment of such a system might also undermine stability and, ironically, pose a grave (if indirect) threat to China's minimum nuclear deterrent. Deployment would provide new incentives for the United States to develop and deploy systems capable of finding and destroying mobile ballistic missile launchers. Because conventionally armed ballistic missiles are difficult if not impossible to distinguish from nuclear armed ones, any U.S. effort to destroy Chinese ASBMs (or other conventionally armed ballistic missiles) could threaten China's nuclear retaliatory capabilities, challenging Beijing's policy of nuclear "no first use."

The PLA is also developing space and counterspace capabilities.[35] Unlike other areas of PLA operations, there is little in the way of officially approved Chinese writing about space warfare doctrine. This deficit can partly be

---

[33] Kenneth Allen and Maryanne Kivlehan-Wise, "Implementing PLA Second Artillery Doctrinal Reforms," in James Mulvenon and David Finkelstein, eds., *The Revolution in Doctrinal Affairs: Emerging Trends in the Operational Art of the Chinese People's Liberation Army* (Alexandria: Center for Naval Analyses, 2005), 159–219.

[34] Roger Cliff et al., *Entering the Dragon's Lair: Chinese Antiaccess Strategies and Their Implications for the United States* (Santa Monica: RAND, 2007); Office of Naval Intelligence, *The People's Liberation Army Navy: A Modern Navy with Chinese Characteristics*; Andrew Erickson and David Yang, "On the Verge of a Game Changer," *U.S. Naval Institute Proceedings*, 135:3 (May 2009): 26–32; Andrew S. Erickson and David D. Yang, "Using The Land To Control The Sea?: Chinese Analysts Consider the Antiship Ballistic Missile," *Naval War College Review*, 62:4 (Autumn 2009): 53–86; Mark Stokes, *China's Evolving Conventional Strategic Strike Capability: The Antiship Ballistic Missile Challenge to U.S. Maritime Operations in the Western Pacific and Beyond* (Arlington: Project 2049 Institute, September 2009); and David M. Finkelstein, "China's National Military Strategy Revisited," 125.

[35] Ashley Tellis, "China's Military Space Strategy," *Survival*, 49:3 (2007): 41–72.

explained by the uncertainty surrounding the ultimate bureaucratic home for China's budding, but still nascent, space capabilities. Indeed, the two chief contenders in the fight for ownership – the PLA Air Force and the Second Artillery – have published competing visions of space operational concepts, each with semiofficial service imprimatur.[36] A wide variety of other sources by military specialists and academics are also available in book and journal form.

China's early development of space warfare doctrine appears to be largely driven by the PLA's observations of the increased U.S. military use of space, particularly during the invasion of Iraq.[37] The PLA appears to conclude that the United States could use (and depend on) American space capabilities in a confrontation over Taiwan. There are indications that China's development of space warfare doctrine and missions echoes U.S. Air Force doctrine in defining four types of operation: operations to enhance air, land, and sea forces; operations to support space-based assets; operations to control space while denying its use to the enemy; and strike operations against terrestrial targets. The PLAAF and the Second Artillery differ on the relative importance of these missions, with the PLAAF placing relatively greater emphasis on space support to other forces (especially air forces) and the Second Artillery placing relatively greater emphasis on offensive and space control functions. Despite differences in emphasis, however, PLA strategists agree that China must further develop military space capabilities.[38]

---

[36] An example from the PLAAF side is *Study of Integrated Air-Space Operations*. The book contains two forewords that endorse the work, one by the then PLAAF commander and one by its political commissar, and was penned by eight researchers from the Air Force Engineering University. On the Second Artillery side is *Advantage Comes from Space: The Space Battlefield and Space Operations*, written by a committee of eight authors assigned to the research office of the Second Artillery Headquarters and the Second Artillery Command School. The authors write, "The Second Artillery's leadership and institutions gave their highest attention and support to the writing of this book." Arguments within these and similar works by both sides suggest that the PLAAF is pushing for air force control over the space and counterspace mission. The Second Artillery, perhaps because of its relatively weaker bureaucratic position, argues for the ultimate creation of a separate service (after a period when individual components are developed within the most appropriate services). 蔡风震, 田安平, 主编 [Cai Fengzhen and Tian Anping eds.], 《空天一体作战学》 [Study of Integrated Air-Space Operations], (Beijing: People's Liberation Army Press, 2009); 杨学军, 张望新主编 [Yang Xuejun and Zhang Wangxin, eds.], 《优势来自空间--论空间战场与空间作战》 [Advantage Comes From Space: The Space Battlefield and Space Operations], (Beijing: National Defense Industry Press, 2006).

[37] Kevin Pollpeter, "The Chinese Vision of Space Military Operations," in James Mulvenon and David Finkelstein, eds., *The Revolution in Doctrinal Affairs: Emerging Trends in the Operational Art of the Chinese People's Liberation Army* (Alexandria: Center for Naval Analyses, 2005), 329–369.

[38] Pollpeter, "The Chinese Vision of Space Military Operations," 352.

Chinese Military Doctrine in Strategic Context

Preparing to fight "Local Wars Under Informationized Conditions" represents a significant shift from previous PLA doctrine. From 1935 to 1979, "People's War" was the guiding principle of the PLA and its forerunner, the Red Army. Until the 1980s, PLA doctrine emphasized homeland defense and China's force structure emphasized defensive guerrilla war or war-of-attrition campaigns while reserving only a secondary role for mechanized, air, and naval forces. However, the PLA's new doctrine does have roots in the past. The utility of offense when advantageous was captured in the concept of "active defense," as far back as Mao Zedong's 1936 essay, "The Problems of Strategy in China's Revolutionary War." Active defense emphasizes that war cannot be won by passive or defensive action alone, and that any doctrine, even an essentially defensive one, must include aspects of offense and seizing the initiative to be successful.[39]

Yet at the same time that PLA doctrine has come to emphasize the offensive at the operational level, Chinese grand strategy and foreign policy have shifted from a strategic offensive orientation prior to the reform and opening-up period toward one that supports stability and the status quo (what we refer to as a more "defensive" strategy below).[40] Where China had once sought to overturn the Western-dominated international order, as well as Western-aligned capitalist governments in the developing world, it now seeks benefits from global institutions and from its interactions with virtually all states, regardless of ideology. The process of moving China toward the strategic defensive and recognizing that global and domestic conditions generally favored great power peace was initiated by Deng Xiaoping, consolidated under Jiang Zemin, and remained constant under Hu Jintao (see Chapter 3).

Most authoritative Chinese sources do not make clear or consistent statements advocating preemptive attacks, particularly at the strategic level. Yet like all military doctrines that emphasize the efficacy of the attack, Chinese doctrine highlights the military advantages of taking the initiative at the operational level when war is judged to be imminent. Even without official endorsement of preemption, the PLA's current doctrine could work to reduce crisis stability if a PLA preference for offense is not balanced by internal political supervision, deterrence by external powers (particularly

---

[39] Blasko, *The Chinese Army Today*, 95–96.
[40] Shambaugh, *Modernizing China's Military*, 61. David M. Finkelstein, "China's National Military Strategy Revisited," 88–93; pp 105.

the United States), and improved communication and signaling procedures during crises.

However, the impact of China's military doctrine on crisis stability is a relative one. Other factors, like grand strategy and senior leaders' assessments of the national interest, are also important for resolving crises and, especially, preventing them from occurring in the first place. Since the late 1970s, contradictory trends have been evident in China's grand strategy (more defensive) and doctrinal modernization (more offensive). During this period, the impact of strategic effects outweighed doctrinal and tactical ones. As we observed in Chapter 3, China's actual use of force has declined significantly while these changes have been underway. By the same token, strategic effects also outweighed doctrinal and tactical ones under Mao, when China's foreign and strategic policy was more offensive (and sought, for example, to overturn the status quo) but China's military doctrine emphasized defensive (primarily guerrilla) operations and campaigns.

After decades as an outlier under a doctrine of operationally defensive "people's war," the PLA's doctrinal concepts are now within the mainstream. Most militaries, including the U.S. and Indian militaries, tend to favor offensive action, at least at the operational level.

China's doctrine continues to evolve, though this evolution currently focuses on refinements and additions rather than fundamental shifts. For example, as noted in China's January 2009 White Paper on national defense, in addition to preparing for "Local Wars Under Informationized Conditions," the PLA has also been instructed to develop capabilities for handling "diverse security threats" (*duozhong anquan weixie*) and "diversified military tasks" (*duoyanghua junshi renwu*) including "military operations other than war" (*fei zhanzheng junshi xingdong*).[41] These are changes that are to be expected, given China's growing economic and political power and its greater integration with the global economy and society.

Development of such doctrine and capabilities may accelerate a trend toward more distant deployments, particularly for the PLA Navy. In December 2008 PLAN surface ships were deployed to conduct escort and antipiracy operations in waters off Somalia. This type of deployment was a first for the PLAN and highlights the need (and the opportunity) to further

---

[41] 中华人民共和国国务院 [The State Council of the People's Republic of China], "2008年中国的国防" [China's National Defense in 2008], (Beijing: State Council Information Office of the People's Republic of China, 2009), 14.

integrate China into regional and international security dialogues and regimes, something that would benefit all sides.[42]

Finally, despite all of these developments, many aspects of China's military doctrine remain "aspirational." Even though doctrine calls on the PLA to fight in a certain way, the Chinese military is not yet capable of doing so in all areas. These areas include the core requirements for joint operations, integration with information systems and C[4]ISR, and development of weapons systems that are truly competitive with Western weapons – let alone development of new, secondary capabilities such as sea-lane protection or large-scale international humanitarian/relief operations.[43] It should be noted, however, that in military scenarios around China's periphery, proximity (and robust missile forces) could compensate for many operational weaknesses.

Despite modernization and professionalization, the PLA remains a servant of the CCP, not the Chinese state. Political authority in high-level military affairs is asserted through two organs: the National Security Work Leading Small Group and the Central Military Commission (CMC). The former is thought to have existed since 2000 and may be largely limited to crisis-management functions. Historically far more important is the CMC, which as of 2011 included ten military members and two civilians: Hu Jintao (chairman) and Xi Jinping (one of the vice chairmen). Perhaps the biggest difference between China and India on military-related decision making (including on doctrinal issues) is the existence in China of strong central bodies within the military that can control and coordinate the activities of the services. The CMC provides central direction at the top and is assisted by other strong central military organs, including the four "general departments" (General Staff Department, General Political Department, General Logistics Department, and General Armaments Department).

While the party asserts strong leadership over military affairs at the top of the hierarchy (which lends some predictability to Chinese strategic behavior), there have been important changes over time. The specialization, routinization, and bureaucratization of government affairs over the last three decades extend to military affairs as well. Deng Xiaoping disavowed Mao Zedong's authoritarian style within the CMC, effectively making Deng (and

[42] See Commodore Per Bigum Christensen, "Task Force 150 anti-piracy operations," MARLO Conference Report, January 25, 2009, http://www.cusnc.navy.mil/marlo/Events/ MARLO%20Conference%20speaker%20CDRE%20Christensen.ppt

[43] Blasko, *The Chinese Army Today*, 182–194; Shambaugh, *Modernizing China's Military*, 105–107, 330; see also Finkelstein and Mulvenon, *The Revolution in Doctrinal Affairs*.

his successors) the first among equals rather than autocrats. More recently, CMC representation has become thoroughly institutionalized, with particular military organizations given regular seats, diminishing the ability to establish policy through personnel selection. Moreover, unlike in past generations, the party leaders since Jiang Zemin who have served as CMC chairmen have had no military experience. All of these factors have served to limit civilian control over many day-to-day functions of the military, and may help explain the adoption of military doctrines that more closely resemble those of other nations – including greater emphasis on the efficacy of offensive action.

Indian Military Doctrine

Indian military doctrine has also undergone significant change in recent years. Like China, India has fought four wars since its independence, and, as Indian power has developed, the Indian military has attempted to incorporate lessons from its experience into its doctrine.

In 2004, the Indian army began to roll out a new military doctrine called "Cold Start."[44] Cold Start had its origins in both political and military frustration with India's ability to deter or respond to incursions (such as those in the 1999 Kargil war) and attacks (such as the terrorist assault on the Indian Parliament in December 2001). In 2001, Indian political leaders wanted to respond by quickly advancing military forces to the Pakistan border and threatening a large-scale conventional attack if Pakistan did not halt its support for Islamic terrorist attacks on India. However, Indian forces were not capable of such rapid deployment.[45]

Thus, the new doctrine stressed forward deployment, the ability to launch decisive offensive strikes from a "standing start" with little or no mobilization period, and potential preemptive attacks on enemy forces.[46] These are the areas of Chinese doctrinal development – forward deployment, offensive operational doctrine, and potential preemption – that appear to

---

[44] Walter C. Ladwig, "A Cold Start for Hot Wars? The Indian Army's New Limited War Doctrine," *International Security* 32:3 (2008): 158–190.

[45] In 2004, former Indian Army Chief Sundarajan Padmanabhan said, "When December 13 happened, my strike formations were at peace locations. At that point, I did not have the capability to mobilize large forces to go across." Quoted in Tariq Ashraf, "Doctrinal Reawakening of the Indian Armed Forces," *Military Review*, 84:6 (November 1, 2004), 53–62.

[46] Ladwig, "A Cold Start for Hot Wars?" 163–167; Subhash Kapila, "Indian Army's New 'Cold Start' War Doctrine Strategically Reviewed," No. 991 (Noida, India: South Asia Analysis Group, May 4, 2004), http://www.southasiaanalysis.org/%5Cpapers10%5Cpaper991.html

concern the United States most, although there has been much less attention paid to these more explicit developments in India.

In a shift from previous Indian military doctrine, which called for large
forces to strike deep into enemy territory with the potential to destroy a
neighboring state such as Pakistan, the Cold Start doctrine emphasized
attacking and destroying the enemy's military forces in "punishing blows"
while seizing some limited territory that might be traded for concessions
later.[47] The doctrine called for reorganizing Indian ground forces into eight
division-sized combined arms "integrated battle groups." The integrated
battle groups would be pre-positioned in forward "launch pads," ready
to rapidly embark on offensive operations. The new doctrine emphasizes
maneuver capability and calls for all eight battle groups to be able to launch
separate, simultaneous attacks along different axes.

Limited territorial objectives, combined with the emphasis on rapid mobilization and fast-paced operational tempo, were designed to avoid three
potential pitfalls. First, they avoid triggering an enemy nuclear response,
by destroying military forces but not necessarily striking into political and
population centers. Second, according to Walter Ladwig, there is a strong
implication that Cold Start was designed to create an operational tempo so
fast that once launched, India's own civilian leaders could not call it back
or halt it.[48] Finally, Cold Start aimed to secure India's objectives before the
international community could intervene. According to an unidentified
senior Indian Army officer quoted by *The Times of India*, "The idea is that
the international community should not get the opportunity to intervene.
Hence, the need for swift action starting from a 'cold start' instead of slow
mobilization."[49]

In 2010, partly as a result of pressure from U.S. officials concerned about
Pakistan's reaction to Indian doctrinal developments, the Indian government denied that the Cold Start doctrine exists.[50] India may step back from

---

[47] Ladwig, "A Cold Start for Hot Wars?" 164.

[48] Ladwig, "A Cold Start for Hot Wars?" 166. Stephen Cohen and Sunil Dasgupta agree with
Ladwig, noting the Indian military's intention to use the Cold Start doctrine timetable
to pressure Indian civilian leaders into decisive action in a crisis with Pakistan. Stephen
P. Cohen and Sunil Dasgupta, *Arming Without Aiming: India's Military Modernization*
(Washington, DC: Brookings Institution Press, 2010), 63–64.

[49] "'Cold Start' to New War Doctrine," *The Times of India*, April 15, 2004.

[50] See "No 'Cold Start' doctrine, India tells US," *Indian Express*, September 9, 2010;
and "Obama Is Not Likely to Push India Hard on Pakistan," *New York Times*, November
5, 2010. There is a question of whether India has ever had the military capability to carry

explicitly advocating some of the more provocative elements of Cold Start as it was originally conceived. Revisions now being considered may focus on strikes by air forces and other "limited" offensive options rather than invasion and occupation by ground forces.[51] Yet many doctrinal and organizational developments put in place since 2004 are likely to remain. Overall, India's evolving military doctrine seeks to improve India's ability to quickly launch offensive operations in a variety of contingencies.

Like the PLA and most other militaries, the Indian military emphasizes a form of "active defense" or "offensive defense" as a general principle of military operations. Taking the initiative through offensive action is generally preferred, and opportunities for offensive strikes are sought even in defensive campaigns. Preemption is considered a normal, fundamental aspect of military operational art in India. The official *Indian Army Doctrine* instructs Indian forces to base their plans on "offensive defence" and explicitly instructs officers that they may consider preemptive attacks. "Defensive plans at every level must be offensive in nature," and plans should be coordinated at the highest levels to "aid deception and pre-empt the enemy."[52]

Like modern PLA doctrine, Indian doctrine now also calls for joint operations, with the air force and naval aviation forces supporting army attacks through air superiority, strike, and close air support operations. In addition to joint operations, the new Indian military doctrine calls for surprise at both the strategic and operational level. Unlike Chinese doctrine, the Indian doctrine does not appear to rely heavily on conventional missile strike capabilities. Nevertheless, like PLA doctrine, it does seek to overwhelm the enemy's will and capability to fight by "unhinging" the enemy and "breaking his cohesion," presumably through attacks on command and logistics centers.[53]

The Indian military has been training to improve its ability to fight according to its new doctrine. India has conducted large-scale exercises to test and refine the new doctrine since 2004, including a thirty-day exercise in April and May 2007 that saw the deployment of brigade-level forces along

out a campaign based on Cold Start, or whether the Indian government would ever have actually allowed the Indian Army to attempt the operations Cold Start called for.

[51] See Ali Ahmed, "The advantages of 'Cold Start Minor'," IDSA Comment, Institute for Strategic and Defense Analyses, December 13, 2010.

[52] Government of India, Indian Army, *Indian Army Doctrine Part 1*, (Shimla: Headquarters Army Training Command, October 22, 2004), Section 11, 4.8, and Section 11, 4.11.

[53] Gurmeet Kanwal, "Cold Start and Battle Groups for Offensive Operations," *ORF Strategic Trends*, 4:18 (June 2006), cited in Ladwig, "A Cold Start for Hot Wars?" 165.

the Pakistan border in Rajasthan.[54] Like PLA exercises, the Indian military exercises reveal a mixed picture of improvements and gaps in capability.[55]

Indian Doctrine: Beyond the Ground Forces

While the Indian army's doctrine is primarily focused on Pakistan, the Indian navy's new Maritime Doctrine, released in 2004, is far more expansive.[56] India's Maritime Doctrine reflects India's view that the Indian Ocean is, in an important way, "Indian." This position is reinforced by the statements of senior Indian naval officers. For example, in May 2007, Indian Navy Chief of Staff told reporters, "The Indian Ocean is named after us.... If required in this Indian Ocean region, we will undertake humanitarian missions, stop piracy and gun-running, and all those kinds of things in asymmetric warfare."[57] Like China, India also takes a broad interpretation of its rights and responsibilities in its EEZ (see Chapter 3).[58]

China is clearly defined as a competitor, but India's Maritime Doctrine is also designed to maintain Indian autonomy and security against any external influence in the region.[59] Thus, in analyzing India's maritime strategy a former Indian Navy officer has recently written that the Indian Navy (IN) is required to "'provide maritime security in all directions' – the classical doctrine of 'tous azimuths.'"[60]

---

[54] "Exercise Ashwamedha," *The Nation*, May 8, 2007. According to *The Nation*, "Ashwamedha" refers to the ancient Indian ritual of a king sacrificing a horse, partly to assert sovereignty over neighboring provinces.

[55] Ladwig, "A Cold Start for Hot Wars?" 181–183.

[56] Sources used for this summary of Indian naval doctrine include *Freedom to Use the Seas: India's Maritime Military Strategy* (New Delhi: Integrated Headquarters, Ministry of Defence [Navy], May 2007); "Maritime Doctrine Envisages Formidable Blue Water Capabilities," *New Delhi Force*, July 1, 2004; "Military Responds to 'New' Challenges, Responsibilities," *New Delhi Force*, June 6, 2006; and "The Indian Navy's Monroe Doctrine," *Indian Defense Consultants*, April 11, 2004.

[57] Quoted in P. S. Suryanarayana, "No evil design behind proactive naval exercises: Admiral Mehta," *The Hindu*, May 21, 2007.

[58] See Admiral Madhvendra Singh (Ret.), "The Indian Navy in 2020," *Security Research Review*, June 21 2006, http://www.bharat-rakshak.com/SRR/2006/02/56.html. Singh describes "a total of 1197 Islands, which provide Defence in Depth and also give us a huge EEZ. At 2.01 million sq km our EEZ is 2/3rds of our land area. After demarcation of the continental shelf our EEZ is likely to be 2.54 million sq km." Some Chinese analysts claim that India's interpretation of its rights in its EEZ is similar to China's. See Ji Guoxing, "The Legality of the 'Impeccable Incident,'" *China Security*, 5:2 (Spring 2009), 16–21.

[59] *Freedom to Use the Seas: India's Maritime Military Strategy*, 41.

[60] Vijay Sakhuja, "Indian Navy: Keeping Pace with Emerging Challenges," in Lawrence W. Prabhakar, Joshua H. Ho, and Sam Bateman, eds., *The Evolving Maritime Balance of Power in the Asia-Pacific: Maritime Doctrines and Nuclear Weapons at Sea* (Singapore: Institute of Defence and Strategic Studies, Nanyang Technological University, 2006), 95–116.

India currently views the U.S. presence in the Indian Ocean as acceptable. However, a strong strain of thinking in both civilian and military circles views U.S. influence in the Indian Ocean and South Asia region as having a negative impact on Indian security interests. The specific missions for the Indian Navy in the new doctrine include[61]:

- To provide conventional and strategic nuclear deterrence against regional states;
- To raise the cost of intervention by extra regional powers;
- To exercise sea control in designated areas of the Arabian Sea and the Bay of Bengal, and at the entry/exist points of the Indian Ocean Region;
- To safeguard India's mercantile marine and seaborne trade in our SLOCs;
- To provide security to India's coastline, island territories, offshore assets and vulnerable areas from seaborne threats;
- In case of war, to carry the conflict to the enemy's territory, to strangulate his trade/oil arteries, to destroy his war waging potential and naval assets, and to ensure a decisive victory;
- To provide power projection forces, when required to land our Army;
- To counter low intensity maritime operations threats (from terrorists and insurgents);
- And to work in conjunction with the other two services to preserve, protect, and promote India's national interests.

The 2004 Maritime Doctrine highlights naval building by China and ASEAN states, particularly the acquisition of submarines by a variety of players. It also notes PLAN force developments including plans for aircraft carriers. Finally, Indian writings on maritime doctrine and strategy emphasize strike capabilities in India's littoral area, thus reaffirming the navy's commitment to western (i.e., Pakistan) missions. This is cited to provide further justification for strengthening Indian aircraft carrier forces.[62]

These missions are further refined in the Indian *Maritime Military Strategy*, released in 2007. The Maritime Military Strategy emphasizes three new issues: power projection (including the development of "expeditionary forces"); securing India's interests in a wide arc including the Indian

---

[61] This list of missions is found in "Maritime Doctrine Envisages Formidable Blue Water Capabilities," *New Delhi Force*, July 1, 2004. See also Sakhuja, "Indian Navy: Keeping Pace with Emerging Challenges," 103–106.

[62] Rahul Bedi, "India – Regional Focus: Power Play," *Jane's Defence Weekly*, July 13, 2005.

Ocean, the Middle East/Persian Gulf, and the "East" of Asia; and littoral warfare (e.g., strike capabilities) to support land forces in war.[63] The 2007 *Maritime Military Strategy* clarifies a shift in maritime strategy from defensive to offensive orientation, and from a reactive operational stance to one that favors preemption. It also emphasizes the need for India to develop a sea-based nuclear deterrent.

The new doctrine also stipulates that India "must ensure workable alliance with like-minded countries for the security of our sea-lanes, for our commercial and energy security." Like China, India also deployed warships to waters off Somalia to combat pirates in 2008. Since deploying, Indian ships have engaged and destroyed some pirate craft. Information on operational aspects of these deployments is scarce, but it appears that Indian, Chinese, Russian, and U.S.-European coalition ships operating off Somalia are in communication and are "playing by the rules."[64]

Indian air force doctrine is also undergoing revision. The Indian Air Force led the other Indian services in terms of developing and publishing a modern doctrine, with its *Air Power Doctrine* in the mid-1990s. With the publication of army and navy doctrines in recent years, and strong pressure for more joint operations especially after the experience of the Kargil War in 1999, the IAF is revising its doctrine. It circulated a draft to the other services in late 2008 and early 2009. However, the Indian air force has resisted the establishment of joint commands and strong central military institutions because of its desire (shared by most air forces worldwide) to maintain maximum operational flexibility and the ability to concentrate force. The IAF fears that "jointness" will tie it to the other services and rob it of flexibility in employing airpower. When required to support the army, the IAF appears to prefer to do so through deep interdiction and operational-level attacks rather than with close air support.[65] The acquisition of tankers and longer-range fighters (especially the Su-30) supports this conception.[66] Like the army, the IAF appears to emphasize preemption and surprise. According to an independent Indian analysis of air force operations, "the first week of

[63] *Freedom to Use the Seas: India's Maritime Military Strategy*, 101–105.
[64] Admiral Timothy J. Keating, U.S. Navy, Commander, U.S. Pacific Command, "Statement Before the Senate Armed Services Committee on U.S. Pacific Command Posture," March 19, 2009.
[65] As one astute observer notes, "The term Close Air Support (CAS) of the Tactical Battle Area (TBA) that is most important for the land commander has been re-named as Battlefield Air Support (BAS) by the IAF [Indian Air Force], implying less proximity to friendly forces and the control arrangements which are therefore needed." "Air Force, Army to Face Challenge in Operational Coordination," *New Delhi Force*, June 8, 2005.
[66] "Aerial Refuelling: IAF Quantum Leap," *Jammu Daily Excelsior*, March 2, 2003.

war will be crucial and will go in favour of the side which resorts to preemption and surprise."[67]

The IAF is also aiming to significantly expand its power projection capability. The new IAF doctrine under development in 2007–2009 is offense-oriented and "dwells on the application of military power and stresses out-of-area operations," according to one military officer.[68] If these elements become part of the official final IAF doctrine, the stress on out-of-area operations would be new, as would the delineation of a specific, expansive area for potential offensive operations that stretches from the Persian Gulf to the Malacca Strait.[69] At least in its current draft form, the IAF doctrine appears to be more forward-leaning, offense-oriented, and "expeditionary" than Chinese air force doctrine.

Like China, India is also refining its strategic doctrine. India also holds to a "no first use" nuclear weapons doctrine. Indian nuclear doctrine is "based on the principle of a minimum credible deterrent and no-first-use as opposed to doctrines or postures of launch-on-warning."[70] In contrast to conventional forces doctrine, Indian civilian leaders have been closely involved in nuclear doctrine development. Civilians have so dominated India's nuclear program that the military appears to have been left out of the Indian decision to test nuclear weapons in 1998, although there have been moves to integrate military commands for nuclear forces under civilian control since then.

Some Indian strategists have called for India to develop nuclear weapons that can reach the United States.[71] Bharat Karnad, a former member of the Indian National Security Advisory Board that developed India's nuclear weapons doctrine, has made the case for an "all azimuths" Indian nuclear deterrent. Such a deterrent specifically includes preventing a "disarming

---

[67] "Air Force, Army to Face Challenge in Operational Coordination," *New Delhi Force*, June 8, 2005.

[68] Rahul Bedi, "Indian Air Force draft doctrine envisions broader role," *Janes Defence News*, August 16, 2007.

[69] "IAF plans war doctrine to expand 'strategic reach'," *Times of India*, August 2, 2007.

[70] *Annual Report 2004–2005* (New Delhi: Indian Ministry of Defence, 2004), 14–16; George Perkovich, *India's Nuclear Bomb: Impact on Global Proliferation*, 2nd ed. (Berkeley: University of California Press, 2001), 480–488.

[71] Bharat Karnad, "India's Force Planning Imperative: The Thermonuclear Option," in D. R. SarDesai and Raju G. C. Thomas, *Nuclear India in the Twenty-First Century* (New York: Palgrave, 2002), 105–138; see also, Bharat Karnad, *Nuclear Weapons and Indian Security* (New Delhi: MacMillan India Limited, 2002). On Indian sea-launched ballistic missile development and submarine development, see Andrew C. Winner, "India as a Maritime Power?" in Toshi Yoshihara and James R. Holmes, eds., *Asia Looks Seaward: Power and Maritime Strategy* (Westport: Praeger Security International, 2008), 125–145, (137–139).

conventional or nuclear first strike, which the United States, for instance, is capable of mounting."[72] Karnad has been one of the few prominent Indian strategists to explicitly make the case for Indian nuclear weapons that can reach the United States, and he does not represent mainstream Indian views on this issue. However, he is not the only prominent Indian to link India's nuclear weapons programs to concerns about potential conflict with the United States.

One of India's most influential strategic thinkers, K. Subrahmanyam, justified India's 1998 nuclear tests on the grounds of a "deteriorating" international security environment characterized by an "interventionist" United States.[73] The former Chief of Staff of the Indian Army, General K. Sundarji, expressed similar concerns about the need for nuclear weapons to deter U.S. intervention on regional issues deemed critical to India.[74] George Perkovich notes that "other Indian elites echoed this view in public and in private, saying that India needed nuclear weapons to keep the United States from doing to India over Kashmir what it did to Serbia over Kosovo."[75] This is a debate that will continue in Indian strategic circles, particularly as India develops longer-range missiles and sea-based nuclear forces and adjusts nuclear doctrine accordingly.

There are few publicly available sources on India's view of space warfare or military space doctrine. Thus far, India's space program has focused on civilian use of space and the scientific and economic opportunities associated with launching satellites. India's Defense Research and Development Organisation (DRDO), under the Ministry of Defence, is responsible for India's missile development programs, although the civilian Indian Space Research Organisation under the Department of Space has clearly provided

---

[72] Bharat Karnad, "India's Force Planning Imperative," 105–106; 126. On Karnad's influence, see George Perkovich, *India's Nuclear Bomb*, 480.

[73] K. Subrahmanyam, "Clear and Present Danger: U.S. Path to Unipolar Hegemony," *Times of India*, May 3, 1999.

[74] In Sundarji's view, Iraq's lack of nuclear weapons had permitted the United States to invade Iraq. Rajesh Kadian, "Nuclear Weapons and the Indian Armed Forces," in D. R. SarDesai and Raju G. C. Thomas, eds., *Nuclear India in the Twenty-First Century* (New York: Palgrave, 2002), 211–227 (219).

[75] George Perkovich, "What Makes the Indian Bomb Tick?" in D. R. SarDesai and Raju G. C. Thomas, eds., *Nuclear India in the Twenty-First Century* (New York: Palgrave, 2002), 25–60 (55). Such views are not simply motivated by observing U.S. intervention in Kosovo in 1999 and the invasion of Iraq in 2003. T. V. Paul traces the inception of India's nuclear technology and weapons program back to long-standing concerns about the overall U.S. role in South Asia and the Indian Ocean region. T. V. Paul, "India, the International System, and Nuclear Weapons," in D. R. SarDesai and Raju G. C. Thomas, *Nuclear India in the Twenty-First Century* (New York: Palgrave, 2002), 85–104.

assistance to DRDO missile programs. There now appears to be an effort underway, led by the Indian Air Force, to develop greater military space capabilities and a military space doctrine. This would appear to focus on two priorities: the development of satellites to support air, land, and sea operations, and integrated air and space defenses.[76]

These efforts appear to have picked up momentum in the wake of the Chinese antisatellite weapon test in 2007 and a subsequent U.S. shoot-down of a U.S. satellite that was falling from orbit in 2008. India, like China, has taken strong public stances against the militarization of space. There is evidence that policy makers in India, like their counterparts in China, struggle with the tension between the obvious advantages of military use of space and their interest in avoiding an expensive military space race.

Indian Doctrine in Strategic Context

In its call for offensive defense, Indian military doctrine appears to have much in common with most major modern militaries, including the PLA. It is worth noting that for India, an offensive doctrine with an emphasis on preemptive attacks is not completely new. Stephen Cohen has observed that during the 1980s and early 1990s, India shifted to a strategy of "offensive defense' verging on pre-emption."[77] This was evident in April 1984, when the Indian Army made a preemptive move to seize positions at the Siachen Glacier on the border with Pakistan, setting the stage for a state of combat over the peaks that lasted for almost two decades.[78] The willingness to take offensive, preemptive action was also evident in India's attack on East Pakistan in 1971.[79]

Despite planning and training, it appears unlikely that the Indian Army would be allowed to implement Cold Start (or any derivative) against Pakistan unless India suffered a terrible provocation. India also faces gaps between its capabilities and its doctrinal aspirations, and as with China, grand strategic considerations can outweigh operational military doctrine. For example, faced with the 2008 terrorist attacks in Mumbai by militants with links to Pakistan, India refrained from launching Cold Start or any

---

[76] Jessica Guiney, "India's Space Ambitions: Headed Toward Space War?" Center for Defense Information Policy Brief, May 2008.

[77] Cohen, *India: Emerging Power*, 145.

[78] Barry Bearak, "Frozen Fury on the Roof of the World," *New York Times*, May 23, 1999.

[79] Compared to other Indian military initiatives such as against China in 1962 and in Sri Lanka in the 1980s, the 1971 East Pakistan offensive appears to have been the exception in terms of successful planning and execution. Bhashyam Kasturi, "The State of War with Pakistan," in Daniel P. Marston and Chandar S. Sundaram, eds., *A Military History of India and South Asia* (London: Praeger Security International, 2007), 146–149.

other direct military action against Pakistan. Certainly, a number of factors contributed to the Indian decision, including the relationship between Pakistan and the United States, the relatively cooperative response of a new Pakistani government, the difficulty in hitting specific militant targets in Pakistan with conventional forces, and the key background condition: Both sides possess nuclear weapons.

Doctrinal developments such as Cold Start are nevertheless worrisome. Such a doctrine could encourage a belief in a "safe" conventional war, that is, one in which decisive results could be achieved without triggering nuclear conflict. Recent doctrinal developments also appear to place Indian forces in a forward-leaning posture during crises. At the same time, an Indian doctrinal emphasis on offense and preemption also spurs similar plans, arms procurement, and balancing in Pakistan – without providing a convincing deterrent effect on militants bent on attacking India or Indian interests. There are conditions under which India might implement the doctrine for purposes other than those commonly cited. Should Pakistan begin to collapse, India might feel compelled to intervene to stabilize Pakistan, to prevent the ascent of a radical government, or to "secure" Pakistan's nuclear weapons and nuclear facilities. Such questions present a potential challenge to a U.S. crisis response and serve to exacerbate Pakistani paranoia.

Some concerns go beyond India-Pakistan alone. Whereas Cold Start has its origins in thinking about conflict with Pakistan, Indian military doctrine does not appear to have fully accounted for China.[80] Does Cold Start or a derivative of it apply to security and military planning on India's border with China? If so, it could undermine crisis stability. If not, what doctrine does apply?

A final point of comparison bears on the relationship between the formation of Indian military doctrine and the formation of India's overarching foreign policy. In India, civilian control of the military has been successful in keeping the military out of politics and asserting macro-level control over budgets and important procurement decisions. This is a profound achievement, as the unfortunate counterexample of Pakistan shows.[81]

---

[80] According to the Indian Institute for Defence Studies and Analyses, the Indian Army has been studying the potential for "two front wars," and how military doctrine must evolve. See Ali Ahmed, "Ongoing Revision of Indian Army Doctrine," Institute for Defence Studies and Analyses, January 6, 2010.

[81] For an analysis of the strong social basis for civilian control of the military in India and the avoidance of military coups, see Apurba Kundu, *Militarism in India: The Army and Civil Society Consensus* (New York: Tauris Academic Studies, 1998). Others see the extreme separation of civilian and military leadership in post-independence India as having a negative impact on India's ability to develop and deploy military power effectively. See Stephen

However, with the important exception of nuclear doctrine, civilians have exercised little influence over the development of Indian military doctrine. In the main, the Indian military services have been left free to develop and implement doctrines of their own.[82] Ashley Tellis notes the Indian military's actual ability to carry out joint operations has outstripped the development of civilian and military institutions meant to ensure doctrinal "jointness."

Integrative mechanisms within the Indian military have been weak. The Ministry of Defence deals almost exclusively with procurement issues. A small Integrated Defence Staff (IDS) was created in the aftermath of the Kargil War, but Indian Air Force opposition has prevented a Chief of Defence Staff (CDS) from being named.[83] Even if a chief is named, India is likely far from the kind of Goldwater-Nichols reform that would empower the chief vis-à-vis the individual service chiefs. Despite the official adoption of a joint doctrine in May 2006, there has been little in the way of actual joint doctrinal development.[84] Indian military doctrine is, therefore, the sum of individual army, navy, and air force doctrines, with some agreement about general principles.

Even more significantly, despite some recent reforms and improvements, Indian governments have not been as successful in developing and imposing an overarching strategic framework on the Indian armed forces. Partly as a result, Indian service doctrines have been more forward-leaning, sometimes getting ahead of India's ability to support or implement them. Although China also has difficulty in coordinating joint doctrine and operations,

P. Rosen, *Societies and Military Power: India and its Armies* (Ithaca: Cornell University Press, 1996).

[82] Cohen and Dasgupta, *Arming Without Aiming*, 143–163. See also Stephen P. Cohen, *Emerging Power: India* (Washington, DC: Brookings Institute, 2001), 146–155; and Harsh V. Pant, *Contemporary Debates in Indian Foreign and Security Policy: India Negotiates its Rise in the International System* (New York: Palgrave Macmillan, 2008), 65–90. The weak integration of civilian strategic thought and planning with military doctrine development is seen by many observers as a perennial problem in India. For both Western and Indian perspectives on this issue, see Kanti P. Bajpai and Amitabh Mattoo, eds., *Securing India, Strategic Thought and Practice: Essays by George K. Tanham with Commentarie*s (New Delhi: Manohar Publishers, 1996).

[83] "Air Force, Army to Face Challenge in Operational Coordination," *New Delhi Force*, June 8, 2005. "IAF unhappy with war doctrine," *The Hindu*, November 25, 2004.

[84] See Vinod Anand, "Evolution of a Joint Doctrine for the Indian Armed Forces," *Strategic Analysis*, 24:4 (July 2000), 733–750. There is some evidence that both the Indian military and civilian leaders are intensifying efforts to address the jointness issue. See, for example, *Freedom to Use the Seas: India's Maritime Military Strategy* (New Delhi: Integrated Headquarters, Ministry of Defence [Navy], May 2007), v. Evidence from training exercises indicates the Indian military services still find joint operations difficult. See Ladwig, "A Cold Start for Hot Wars?" 182–184.

PLA military doctrines have generally been tightly leashed to national priorities and an understanding of resource limitations, in part through relatively strong institutions such as China's Central Military Commission.

As in China, India will continue to grapple with the effect of modernization on the military as a domestic stakeholder. The Indian military has recently begun to voice public criticism of foreign policies with which it disagrees, such as the demilitarization of Jammu and Kashmir.[85] In India's more open system, this is perhaps less surprising than recent public statements on foreign policy from Chinese generals. However, as with China, it is a departure from past military-civilian practice.

Conclusions: Chinese and Indian Military Doctrines

Both Chinese and Indian military doctrines emphasize offensive action at the operational level. Most militaries worldwide prefer doctrines that emphasize offensive action.[86] Viewed from this perspective, the shift in Chinese military doctrine that emerged since the early 1990s may represent a convergence of Chinese thinking with international military norms rather than the development of something unusual. In India, offensive action and preemption have become the *sine qua non* of military operational guidelines, and this emerged earlier and more explicitly than in the case of China.

Both India and China have continuing challenges in developing "jointness" in military doctrine. In the Chinese case, the PLA has recently placed much more emphasis on jointness and joint campaigns than in the past, and there is a unified body of writing and thinking on the issue, at least at the campaign level. Problems reside primarily in the current inability, given equipment and training limitations, to implement doctrine. On the Indian side, the problems are more fundamental. There is no central arbiter within the military with the will or capacity to force service cooperation in the writing, much less execution, of joint doctrine.

Both Chinese and Indian military doctrines espouse aspirations that their respective forces cannot yet achieve. On the Indian side, it is questionable

---

[85] Cohen and Dasgupta, *Arming Without Aiming*, 63–64.

[86] On the propensity of militaries toward offensive doctrines, see Jack Snyder, "Civil-Military Relations and the Cult of the Offensive, 1914 and 1984," *International Security*, 9:1 (Summer 1984), 108–146; and Barry R. Posen, *The Sources of Military Doctrine* (Ithaca: Cornell University Press, 1986).

whether land, air, and sea forces are equipped or trained to achieve the reach or results stipulated in doctrinal or strategic statements. The mismatch may be partly explained by the lack of effective political oversight over the drafting of those documents, as well as the lack of interservice coordination. On the Chinese side, doctrine is written without reference to specific opponents. Rather, most PLA writings on "campaign theory" outline the means to achieve operational objectives that are often framed in the abstract (i.e., "achieving air superiority"). Given the relatively powerful potential opponents faced by China (surrounded by large powers and facing the possibility of U.S. interventions in some scenarios), the PLA might be unable to put many of those ideas into effective operation in the event of actual hostilities.

Compared to China, the Indian government appears to play a weaker role in providing an overarching strategic framework that would oblige the services to work more closely together. The relative lack of integrated strategy-doctrine development could undermine communication and mutual understanding between Indian political and military elites, possibly leading Indian civilian leaders to misunderstand India's relative capabilities, misjudge risks, or have difficulty signaling or otherwise availing themselves of diplomacy during crises. Civilian political authorities in China arguably have better-developed means for the direct control of military affairs, but problems exist there as well. Civilian authorities remain highly dependent on the military for analysis and information, and circumstantial evidence suggests that during some recent crises, accurate information may not have been quickly forthcoming.

There are several aspects of Chinese military doctrinal developments that could challenge U.S. interests. First, China may ultimately choose to develop a grand strategy that aims at regional or global primacy. A more offensive doctrine, accompanied by concomitant weapons procurement and training programs, could provide military capabilities that would be useful should China shift its grand strategy toward greater assertiveness or aggression. However, even though military modernization programs and doctrinal developments are giving China military capabilities it did not possess before, including some power projection capabilities and sea denial-capabilities, Taiwan scenarios remain the primary focus of PLA operational doctrine developments and military modernization programs.

Even in the case where China's military modernization and doctrinal evolution retains its focus on Taiwan, doctrinal developments could work to undermine crisis stability, particularly if China fails to join in developing effective approaches to crisis management and mutually acceptable "rules of the road" for peacetime patrolling.[87] Finally, the development of conventional missile strike capabilities, antisatellite weapons, and cyber warfare capabilities each poses new challenges for escalation control or management. But the general lack of a comparative framework and the treatment by many U.S. analysts of Chinese doctrine and doctrinal development as unusually or exceptionally troublesome leads to blanket criticisms. This, in turn, makes it more, rather than less, difficult to focus on those elements of Chinese doctrinal development that are actually unusual or dangerous.

There are also reasons for the United States to be concerned about Indian military doctrine developments. The primary near-term challenge for the United States concerns the effect of Indian doctrinal developments and military modernization on an unstable, nuclear-armed Pakistan. Pakistani strategists have claimed Pakistan may need to develop its own preemptive doctrine to counter Indian doctrine.[88] One Pakistani general has said Pakistan could resort to the use of nuclear weapons under precisely the circumstances that India's Cold Start doctrine seeks to create.[89] The combination of Indian military modernization (and the addition of new offensive strike capabilities) and offensive doctrines will likely prove to be an enduring distraction for Pakistani military and political leaders, regardless of any assurances the United States may offer. Pakistani military leaders could use issues such as provocative elements of the Cold Start doctrine to delay or dismiss calls for military and political reforms in Pakistan.

The Indian navy and air force are highly professional organizations that do many things well, often with relatively old equipment. Robust deployment posture and training, including exercises with U.S. forces, give the IN and IAF substantial experience, which could benefit the United States in the event of U.S.-India combined operations. Yet the United States should maintain sober expectations regarding the extent of potential cooperation. Changes to India's naval doctrine and openness to combined naval exercises do not necessarily imply a commitment to greater operational

---

[87] For an analysis of the intersection of doctrinal development, mutual signaling, and crisis stability, see Christopher P. Twomey, "Dangerous Differences: Crisis Management & Sino-American Naval Doctrines in the Taiwan Strait" (paper prepared for the International Studies Association Annual Meeting, March 18, 2008).

[88] Tariq M. Ashraf, "Doctrinal Awakening of the Indian Armed Forces," *Military Review*, (November–December 2004), 53–62. At the time of publication, Ashraf was an Air Commodore in the Pakistan Air Force.

[89] Lt. General Khalid Kidwai, cited in Ladwig, "A Cold Start for Hot Wars?" 168.

cooperation or collective security.[90] Whereas the United States emphasizes combined naval and air force exercises as an opportunity to develop operational expertise, integration, and combined contingency planning with a view toward actual future combined deployments, India appears to emphasize joint naval and air exercises as an opportunity to develop political contacts in all directions and with many countries.

The "all azimuths" theme also is a recurrent, common principle that appears across multiple areas of Indian strategic thinking, including maritime strategy and nuclear weapons doctrine. This is an issue that should not be simply dismissed by U.S. strategists. Even if American leaders believe U.S.-India conflict is unlikely, the fact that Indian leaders feel at pains to develop and publicize these ideas in India is evidence of domestic political constraints on India's ability to work closely with the United States in diplomatic, let alone military, affairs. Further questions about the "all azimuths" elements of Indian naval, air force, and nuclear doctrine will be raised as India develops and deploys weapons systems with interregional and intercontinental ranges.

---

[90] For example, while Indian Navy Chief of Staff Mehta acknowledged India's interest in building partnerships with neighboring countries and participating in UN-mandated operations in a 2007 interview, he also downplayed the likelihood that India would join U.S. forces to meet emergencies or engage in conventional military operations. According to Mehta, "There is no evil design [behind naval exercises], in fact no design … we are not part of any team.… We don't believe in it." See P. S. Suryanarayana, "No evil design behind proactive naval exercises: Admiral Mehta," *The Hindu*, May 21, 2007. Despite their recent history of joint naval maneuvers with U.S. ships, IN ships sent to combat pirates off Somalia in 2008 and 2009 are not part of joint commands with any other nation, although, like Chinese forces in the area, they appear to be coordinating and communicating well with other navies. See Christensen, "Task Force 150 anti-piracy operations."

6

Military Force Modernization
and Power Projection

With growing economic resources and newly developed military doctrines, India and China are both acquiring advanced weapons systems and new power projection capabilities.[1] In this chapter, we compare overall trends in force modernization in both countries, including the development of military forces that can be used to project power.[2] China's developing military capabilities have become a key focus for U.S. defense planners, and American officials have questioned the motivation for China's acquisition of power projection forces. These developments are seen as a potentially destabilizing factor in Asian military balances and as a possible indicator of an anti–status quo strategic posture.[3] According to the U.S. *National Defense Strategy 2008*, "China is one ascendant state with the potential for competing with the United States. For the foreseeable future, we will need to hedge against China's growing military modernization and the impact of its strategic choices upon international security."[4]

---

[1] The U.S. Department of Defense defines power projection as "The ability of a nation to apply all or some of its elements of national power – political, economic, informational, or military – to rapidly and effectively deploy and sustain forces in and from multiple dispersed locations to respond to crises, to contribute to deterrence, and to enhance regional stability." United States Department of Defense, *Joint Publication 1-02: Department of Defense Dictionary of Military and Associated Terms (As Amended Through 15 April 2011)*, 287, http://www.dtic.mil/doctrine/new_pubs/jp1_02.pdf

[2] In this chapter, we compare trends in the development of major weapons systems, as representative of both actual and aspirational force modernization and power projection capabilities. However, we note that actual power projection also requires a variety of other supporting capabilities, including logistical support, intelligence, communication, and command-and-control systems.

[3] *Military Power of the People's Republic of China* (Washington, DC: Office of the Secretary of Defense, March 2009), 28.

[4] *National Defense Strategy 2008* (Washington, DC: Office of the Secretary of Defense, June 2008), 3.

India too has been undertaking significant force modernization pro-grams.[5] In some ways, India's power projection forces have long been more extensive than China's. For example, India acquired its first aircraft carrier (the *INS Vikrant*, formerly *HMS Hercules*) in 1961 and has significant experience in carrier operations and naval patrolling. The Indian navy currently has one carrier in service and two under construction. For its part, China began sea trials for its first-ever aircraft carrier, a refurbished former Soviet Union ship, in 2011.[6] India is also developing new amphibious warfare and maritime patrol capabilities and is conducting major upgrades to its air force, its missile strike capabilities, and the armor and artillery striking power of its ground forces.

However, U.S. government assessments of the potential consequences of Indian force modernization stand in contrast to assessments of Chinese military development. The *2010 Quadrennial Defense Review Report* (QDR) states: "China has shared only limited information about the pace, scope, and ultimate aims of its military modernization programs.... [The] lack of transparency and the nature of China's military development and decision-making processes raise legitimate questions about its future conduct and intentions within Asia and beyond."[7] Having linked Chinese military modernization and Asian instability, the same document then makes virtually the opposite case about Indian military modernization: "India's military capabilities are rapidly improving through increased defense acquisitions .... *As its military capabilities grow, India will contribute to Asia as a net provider of security in the Indian Ocean and beyond*" (emphasis added).[8]

In contrast to China, India's force modernization (including greater power projection capability) is thus seen to lead directly to net security benefits for the United States and the rest of the world. This expectation is provided independently of an assessment of India's evolving strategic intentions and despite the potential effect of Indian military modernization on

---

[5] On Indian military modernization, see Stephen P. Cohen and Sunil Dasgupta, *Arming Without Aiming: India's Military Modernization* (Washington, DC: Brookings Institution Press, 2010).

[6] "China Begins Sea Trials of Its First Aircraft Carrier," *New York Times*, August 10, 2011. For further background, see "Chinese warship makes regional waves," *Financial Times*, April 26 2011. "Chinese State Media, in a Show of Openness, Print Jet Photos," *New York Times*, April 25, 2011. See also *The People's Liberation Army Navy: A Modern Navy with Chinese Characteristics* (Suitland: Office of Naval Intelligence, July 2009).

[7] *Quadrennial Defense Review Report* (Washington, DC: Office of the Secretary of Defense, February 2010), 31, 60.

[8] *Quadrennial Defense Review Report* (2010), 31.

security competition in Asia. Yet with its growing power and reach, India, like China, is increasingly involved in nested security dilemmas that link both region-level and system-level dynamics and that cross geographic regions (Central-, South-, and Northeast Asia).[9]

In this chapter, we employ a comparative framework to assess Chinese and Indian military force modernization programs. We base these comparisons on the best publicly available data as of early 2011, which reflect the status of force modernization programs through 2010. Although specific force structures in both nations will change, this snapshot will help refine judgments about whether either state is engaging in distinctive strategic behavior. We first compare international arms purchases and then examine modernization of naval and air forces.[10] We focus on forces that are useful in projecting power beyond each country's borders. We also briefly review strategic weapons, conventional strike, and space capability development. Strategic and space capabilities are not power projection forces in themselves, but they provide critical enablers to power projection, deterrence against homeland attack, and intelligence and communications capability.

International Arms Purchases

China and India have emerged as major buyers of weapons systems on international markets, especially since the 1990s. Between 1980 and 2010, India was the world's largest arms importer, with imports valued at about $65 billion in constant 1990 U.S. dollars (Table 6.1). China ranked fifth during this period, with arms imports valued at about $33 billion. (Except where otherwise noted, all arms import figures are Stockholm International Peace Research Institute [SIPRI] estimates for actual arms deliveries, in constant 1990 dollar equivalents representing the value – not the purchase price – of the equipment imports.[11]) During the second half of this period

---

[9] We further explore the cross-system- and cross-region-level linkages in Asian security, and the idea of "nested security dilemmas," in Chapter 9.

[10] We use standard, publicly available Western sources for data on force structure, equipment, and retirements of older units, such as the IISS *Military Balance*, and Jane's *Sentinel*. Using publicly available information, it is not possible to determine with absolute certainty at what point in time changed numbers reflect actual changes in Chinese and Indian forces, or the changed assessments of the editors of reference publications.

[11] The SIPRI arms transfers database is a consistent, inflation-adjusted data series, which tracks actual deliveries of arms. SIPRI reports arms trade data in an estimated dollar-value equivalent called Trend Indicator Values (TIV). TIV is meant to capture, in a relatively uniform way, the value of military systems imports. The calculations treat those systems where the market price is relatively well known as "core systems." In the case of systems

Table 6.1. *Delivered arms imports, top 10 recipients*

	1980–2010			1995–2010	
Rank	Importer	TIV (1990 USD billion)	Rank	Importer	TIV (1990 USD billion)
1	**India**	**65.2**	1	**China**	**29.7**
2	Japan	39.6	2	**India**	**26.9**
3	Saudi Arabia	38.4	3	South Korea	21.1
4	South Korea	34.6	4	Taiwan	16.9
5	**China**	**33.4**	5	Turkey	16.7
6	Iraq	33.1	6	Greece	15.7
7	Turkey	32.4	7	Saudi Arabia	14.0
8	Egypt	29.9	8	UAE	12.4
9	Taiwan	26.7	9	Egypt	11.5
10	Greece	26.3	10	Japan	10.8

Source: SIPRI, available at: http://www.sipri.org/databases/armstransfers/. See also http://www.sipri.org/databases/armstransfers/background

(i.e., 1995–2010), China became the world's leading arms importer, with delivered arms imports valued at $29.7 billion in constant 1990 U.S. dollars, versus $26.9 billion for India. However, in recent years, India has once again overtaken China as the world's leading arms importer. During the period from 2005 to 2010, India's arms imports were valued at $12.2 billion constant 1990 U.S. dollars, compared to $11.3 billion for China.[12]

Arms import data show distinctive patterns for the two countries over the long term since the late 1940s. China imported large quantities of weapons in the 1950s and early 1960s, primarily from the Soviet Union. A deterioration in Sino-Soviet relations (and China's own isolation) caused a precipitous drop in arms imports in the 1960s and 1970s. China imported

where the market price is unknown, the capabilities of the system (including characteristics such as size, speed, and electronic systems) are assessed relative to "core systems" and a dollar value assigned. The value is assessed whether the state buys the system at inflated prices or receives it without cost. Therefore, TIVs cannot be used to estimate the financial costs of a state's arms imports and "they are not comparable to official economic data such as gross domestic product or export/import figures." For more on SIPRI's methodology, see http://www.sipri.org/databases/armstransfers/background. In contrast to SIPRI, other sources assess both arms deliveries and the estimated financial value of arms purchase agreements, in both constant and nominal U.S. dollars. See for example, Richard F. Grimmett, *Conventional Arms Transfers to Developing Nations 2001–2008*, Congressional Research Service Report to Congress, Order Number R40796, September 4, 2009.

[12] SIPRI Arms Transfers Database, http://www.sipri.org/databases/armstransfers

some arms during the first fourteen years of its reform and opening-up period, a time of rapid economic growth. But military budgets that were flat or even declining when adjusted for inflation limited the scale of those imports (Chapter 4). China's arms imports grew rapidly after the display of modern U.S. weapons in the 1991 Gulf War and the Taiwan Strait Crisis of 1995–1996. China's arms imports then declined between 2007 and 2010.[13] About 80 percent of China's weapons imports from 1990 to 2010 came from Russia.

Indian weapons imports were relatively low in the 1950s and early 1960s. During that period, imports came primarily from the West. Yet India saw almost three decades of large increases in delivered arms imports during the period following the 1962 border war with China up to 1990. During this time, India purchased most of its arms from the Soviet Union (about 73 percent by value).[14] Indian arms imports declined significantly in the 1990s, partly due to stagnant economic growth and government budget cutbacks. Arms deliveries to India began to increase again by about 2003, particularly as economic reforms gained traction. As its strategic relationship with the United States developed, India began importing more weapons from the West, although Russia has remained its most important arms supplier overall.

Beijing and New Delhi have also imported similar types of weapons. This reflects similar goals for gaining advanced weapon capabilities and similar challenges in producing these weapons domestically (Table 6.2). Aircraft have been the largest category of delivered imports by value for both countries, accounting for 59 percent of deliveries to China and 49 percent of deliveries to India from 1950 to 2010. Warships and missiles have also been a major focus of arms imports for both. In comparison to China, India is also dependent on arms imports for less complex weapons such as armor and artillery. China and India import similar types of major weapons systems (and in some cases the same systems) from Russia.

The relative decline in Chinese arms imports beginning in 2007–2008 reflects several developments. First, China may have met some of its force modernization goals and must absorb the systems it has already purchased. Second, the leveling-off of arms imports also likely reflects China's improving ability to develop and manufacture advanced weapons itself.[15] Finally, a

---

[13] SIPRI Arms Transfers Database, http://www.sipri.org/databases/armstransfers

[14] SIPRI Arms Transfers Database, http://www.sipri.org/databases/armstransfers

[15] China's ability to produce weapons and defense equipment has improved markedly in the last decade. See Evan S. Medeiros et al., *A New Direction for China's Defense Industry* (Santa Monica: RAND Corporation, 2005). Nevertheless, Chinese industry still finds it

Table 6.2. Selected major Chinese and Indian arms imports, 2000–2010

	China			India		
	Number	System	Year	Number	System	Year
Ground Forces	200	Mi-17 transport helicopters	2005–	310	T-90 tanks	2004–2008
				347	T-90 tanks	2007–
Air Forces	28	Su-27 UBK trainer aircraft (add. 36 Su-27SK purchased pre-2000; 200 under local production)	2000	18	Su-30K fighter	2000–2007
	48	Su-30MKK fighter (add. 76 purchased prior to 2000)	2004	230	Su-30MKI fighter (some may be co-produced)	2000–2007
	8	IL-78 tanker aircraft	2005–	57	MiG-29 fighter-bomber	2000–2006
	30	IL-76 transport aircraft	2005–	40 upgrades	for MiG-27 fighter-bomber	2002–
	500–1000	SA-20/S-300 surface-to-air missile (with radars)	2004–2008	6	C-130J transport aircraft	2008–
	2	A-50E *Mainstay* AEW/AWACS aircraft with domestic radar		3	A-50E *Mainstay* AEW/AWACS aircraft with Israeli *Phalcon* radar	2003–
				2	EMB-145 AEW aircraft	2008–
				66	*Hawk* Mk-132 trainer aircraft	2003–
Naval Forces	8	*Kilo* 877 and *Kilo* 636 diesel-electric submarines (some *Kilo* purchased from 1985–)	2002–2007	1	*Admiral Gorshkov* aircraft carrier (long delays)	2004–
	2	*Sovremenny* II guided missile destroyer (add. 2 purchased prior to 2000)	2006–2007	16	MiG-29 naval fighter-bomber	2004–

(continued)

Table 6.2 (*continued*)

	China				India	
	Number	System	Year	Number	System	Year
	24	Su-30MKK fighter aircraft (may order more)	2002–2007	6	*Scorpene* submarines	2005–
				3	*Krivak* III guided missile frigate	2006–
				10 upgrades	for *Kilo* 877 submarines	2006–
				1	*Trenton* amphibious transport dock	2007
				6	SH-3 *Sea King* helicopters	2008–
				8	P-81 maritime patrol aircraft	2009–
Other	n/a	HARPY unmanned aerial vehicle (Israel)	2008–	n/a	*BrahMos* antiship missiles (joint with Russia)	2008–
		Jet engines for new version of H6 bomber (Russia)		12	AN-TPQ/37 *Firefinder* counterbattery radar	2003–2007
		Jet engines for FC-1 fighter bomber (Russia)			Artillery technology from United Kingdom and Singapore	2008–
		Antiship missile technology from Russia; sea-based antiaircraft missile technology from France; radar technology from Sweden and Russia				

Note: Joint/local production not included in this table except where noted. The list includes only programs in production or that have already begun deliveries. This table is based on available public data, and may be incomplete. See International Institute for Strategic Studies (IISS), *The Military Balance 2011*, March 7, 2011, 284–286.

relative decline in China's arms imports may be partly explained by the souring of China's arms relationship with its primary supplier, Russia. Moscow has come to view Chinese efforts to absorb Russian technology with suspicion. Unlike China's defense industry, India's defense industries have yet to emerge as reliable suppliers of modern weapons and equipment.[16] Thus for India, new arms deals reflect both the relative failure of Indian defense industries to provide timely delivery of competitive weapons systems and New Delhi's new determination to rearm and reequip its forces.[17] At the same time, India's arms relationship with Russia appears to be entering a new phase, with efforts to jointly develop sophisticated missiles and fighter aircraft.

Even as India and China improve their ability to manufacture weapons platforms, both must still import key components, manufacturing equipment, support systems, and other technologies. Priority areas for military system imports for both countries include jet aircraft engines, some avionics, advanced machine tools, and a wide range of support technologies (e.g., communication equipment and radar). Catching up to continuously improving Western capabilities in these technologies is a challenge. Both countries continue to rely largely on imports for certain major combat systems, such as advanced long-range surface-to-air missile systems.

Indian and Chinese foreign arms imports also come in the context of military developments in Pakistan and in Taiwan. Security planning in India and Pakistan still focuses on preparing for conventional war on their mutual border.[18] Many of the weapons India and Pakistan purchase are

---

challenging to build weapons and support systems that can compete with the performance of Western systems. See Tai Ming Cheung, *Fortifying China: The Struggle to Build a Modern Defense Economy* (Ithaca: Cornell University Press, 2009), especially 235–262. Western defense industries are not standing still – in some areas they are maintaining or extending their lead in deployed capabilities, such as missile defense, undersea warfare, robotics/unmanned vehicles, situational awareness in space (earth orbit), and special forces operations and technologies.

[16] Cohen and Dasgupta, *Arming Without Aiming*, 30–39; Vinay Shankar, "Defence Industry," *Indian Defence Review*, 23:1, September 11 2008; Richard A. Bitzinger, "India's Once and Future Defence Industry," *RSIS Commentaries*, Nanyang Technological University Singapore, October 8, 2007; and Deba R. Mohanty, *Changing Times? India's Defence Industry in the 21st Century*, Bonn International Center for Conversion, 2004.

[17] "Land of Gandhi Asserts Itself as Global Military Power," *New York Times*, September 22, 2008, http://www.nytimes.com/2008/09/22/world/asia/22iht-22india.16352927.html

[18] "India deploys fighter jets in Kashmir," *Times of India*, September 17, 2008, http://timesofindia.indiatimes.com/India/India_deploys_fighter_jets_in_Kashmir/rssarticleshow/3493057.cms; see also "Indian Air Force to Setup First Sukhoi Squadron in Punjab by 2011," http://www.india-defence.com/reports/4082; "Frontline Sukhoi SU-30 jet deployed in Jammu and Kashmir," *Indo-Asian News Service*, September 17, 2008,

deployed on or near each other's borders, despite a recent revival of Indian security preparations on its borders with China.[19]

Pakistan's advanced weapons imports increased significantly during the same period when India's arms purchases also rose rapidly.[20] According to the U.S. Congressional Research Service, Pakistan secured arms import agreements worth $11 billion between 2005 and 2008, trailing only Saudi Arabia, India, and the United Arab Emirates (UAE) among all developing nations in terms of the current financial value of arms import agreements in that period.[21]

The bulk of Pakistan's arms imports were conventional warfare systems (such as fighter-bombers from China and AWACs from Sweden) rather than equipment better suited for domestic counterinsurgency. Of Pakistan's 2001–2007 U.S. weapons imports, more than 75 percent (current dollar

http://www.thaindian.com/newsportal/uncategorized/frontline-sukhoi-su-30-jet-deployed-in-jammu-and-kashmir_10096710.html; Sandeep Unnithan, "Phalcon inducted 'quietly' in IAF." *India Today*, January 13, 2009, http://indiatoday.intoday.in/index.php?option=com_content&task=view&id=25156&sectionid=4&issueid=88&Itemid=1; "IAF plans missile base near Pakistan border," *Daily News and Analysis*, January 6 2009, http://www.dnaindia.com/report.asp?newsid=1219153

[19] India has reopened some of its former airfields near border areas with China and plans to locate some of its newest fighter planes to bases near the Chinese border. However, overall Indian deployment and operational planning still focuses on Pakistan. See "Air Force to Reactivate Nyama Airfield Near Chinese Border," *India Defence*, November 13, 2008, http://www.india-defence.com/reports-4079; "Air Force Su-30 MKI Fighter Jets to be Stationed at Tezpur Air Base Assam," *India Defence*, August 15, 2008, http://www.india-defence.com/reports-3963; "Additional Su-30 MKI Fighter Jets Deployed to Kashmir's Avantipura Air Force Base," *India Defence*, September 17, 2008, http://www.india-defence.com/reports-4024; and "Indian Air Force to set up first Sukhoi Squadron in Punjab by 2011," *India Defence*, November 16, 2008, http://www.india-defence.com/reports-4082

[20] See Christopher Bolkcom et al., *Combat Aircraft Sales to South Asia: Potential Implications*, Congressional Research Service Report to Congress, Order Code RS22148, May 19, 2005; Craig Cohen and Derek Chollet, "When $10 Billion Is Not Enough: Rethinking U.S. Strategy Towards Pakistan," *The Washington Quarterly*, 30:2 (Spring 2007): 7–19; K. Alan Kronstadt, *Major U.S. Arms Sales and Grants to Pakistan Since 2001*, Congressional Research Service Report to Congress, Order Code RS22757, April 23, 2008; "U.S. Officials See Waste in Billions Sent to Pakistan," *New York Times*, December 24, 2007; "Pakistan Fails to Aim Billions in U.S. Military Aid At Al-Qaeda," *Los Angeles Times*, November 5, 2007; "Plan Would Use Anti-Terror Aid on Pakistani Jets," *New York Times*, July 24, 2008; "Pakistan Is Rapidly Adding Nuclear Arms, U.S. Says," *New York Times*, May 17, 2009; Robert S. Norris and Hans Kristensen, "Pakistani Nuclear Forces 2009," *Bulletin of the Atomic Scientists* (September/October 2009); "U.S. Says Pakistan Made Changes to Missiles Sold for Defense," *New York Times*, August 29, 2009; Michael F. Martin and K. Alan Kronstadt, "Pakistan's Capital Crisis: Implications for U.S. Policy," Congressional Research Service Report for Congress, Order Code RS22983, November 7, 2008; and Julide Yildrim and Nadir Ocal, "Arms Race and Economic Growth: The Case of India and Pakistan," *Defence and Peace Economics*, 17:1 (February 2006): 37–45.

[21] Richard F. Grimmett, *Conventional Arms Transfers to Developing Nations 2001–2008*.

financial value) were for conventional warfare systems. These included F-16 fighter planes, AMRAAM air-to-air missiles, Harpoon antiship missiles, P-3C maritime patrol aircraft, TOW antitank missiles, and M-109 mobile artillery systems.[22] The United States began to shift its arms supplies and military aid to Pakistan away from conventional weapons and toward counterinsurgency in 2008. However, Pakistan has other options, including Chinese and European suppliers. Pakistan also accelerated its nuclear-weapons program at the same time the United States was concluding its nuclear cooperation agreement with India.[23]

Islamabad's determination to balance New Delhi's arms imports (and its ability to develop options for doing so) poses multiple risks. It could further weaken Pakistan's economy, distract Islamabad from its domestic insurgency, and exacerbate internal instability.[24] The determination (and some ability) to balance against India will likely remain an enduring feature of any Pakistani regime.

In contrast to the Indo-Pakistan arms competition dynamic, Taiwan has no nuclear weapons, is more stable, and has better financial resources to sustain military modernization relative to its great-power neighbor. But Taiwan has appeared to move fitfully in its arms imports because of Beijing's pressure on potential suppliers and Taiwan's own internal politics.[25] After a surge in arms deliveries in 1997 and 1998, actual deliveries of arms imports to Taiwan declined sharply and were nearly zero in 2007 and 2008. However, the United States approved major arms sales packages in October 2008 and January 2010, with financial values (current dollars) of $6.6 billion and $6 billion, respectively.[26] These included PAC-3 Patriot missiles, *Black Hawk* helicopters, *Osprey*-class mine-hunting vessels, and *Harpoon* antiship missiles.

The links between Indian and Chinese force modernization and the balancing reactions produced in Pakistan and Taiwan pose different risks

[22] K. Alan Kronstadt, *Major U.S. Arms Sales and Grants to Pakistan Since 2001*.
[23] "Pakistan is Rapidly Adding Nuclear Arms, U.S. Says," *New York Times*.
[24] Michael F. Martin and K. Alan Kronstadt, "Pakistan's Capital Crisis: Implications for U.S. Policy"; and Julide Yildrim and Nadir Ocal, "Arms Race and Economic Growth: The Case of India and Pakistan."
[25] See Alan D. Romberg, "Cross-Strait Relations: 'Ascend the Heights and Take a Long-term Perspective,'" *China Leadership Monitor*, 27 (Winter 2009); and Andrew N. D. Yang, "Taiwan's Defense Preparation Against the Chinese Military Threat," in Michael D. Swaine, Andrew N. D. Yang, and Evan S. Medeiros, eds., *Assessing the Threat: The Chinese Military and Taiwan's Security* (Washington, DC: Carnegie Endowment for International Peace, 2007), 265–284.
[26] U.S. Defense Security Cooperation Agency, Arms Sales Notifications, available at: http://www.dsca.mil/PressReleases/36-b/36b_index.htm

to U.S. interests. Indian military modernization remains a key focus for Pakistan. Yet Pakistan's military programs threaten to distract attention and resources from its own internal instabilities. Islamabad's recent acceleration of strategic weapons programs is particularly worrisome given those internal crises.[27] Taiwan's sluggish domestic political support for modernizing its military forces risks a growing imbalance with China, which could undermine cross-Strait deterrence and stability. On the other hand, arms transfers to Taiwan could intensify emerging regional security competition between China and the United States.

Naval Forces

While the Indian Navy (IN) has long been a blue-water force, the PLA Navy (PLAN) has become one over the last decade. PLAN ships have become larger and more capable, incorporating modern air defenses (the lack of which has historically been a notable weakness), more sophisticated antiship missiles, and combat control systems.[28] The Indian navy has also continued to update and modernize its fleet.

China's naval modernization is sometimes characterized as an expansion or buildup.[29] However, neither China nor India is emphasizing growth in the overall numbers of ships, submarines, and naval aircraft in their inventories. Instead, both navies have primarily focused on improving quality, developing naval forces with fewer but more capable units. PLAN capabilities have improved markedly in just the last decade.[30] American naval officers have noted, however, that PLAN forces still suffer from a number of weaknesses compared to the U.S. Navy and some other navies in Asia.[31]

---

[27] "Pakistan Is Rapidly Adding Nuclear Arms, U.S. Says," *New York Times*, May 17, 2009.

[28] A useful, balanced assessment can be found in *The People's Liberation Army Navy: A Modern Navy with Chinese Characteristics* (Suitland: Office of Naval Intelligence, July 2009).

[29] Richard D. Fisher, *China's Military Modernization: Building for Regional and Global Reach* (Westport: Praeger Security International Press, 2008), vii, 1–2.

[30] Office of Naval Intelligence, *The People's Liberation Army Navy: A Modern Navy with Chinese Characteristics* (Suitland: Office of Naval Intelligence, July 2009).

[31] Office of Naval Intelligence, *The People's Liberation Army Navy: A Modern Navy with Chinese Characteristics*. For comments by a U.S. admiral on PLAN undersea warfare disadvantages relative to U.S. capabilities, see Charles Snyder, "New Pacific Commander Vows Commitment to Taiwan," *Taipei Times*, March 10, 2007. For analysis of China's military and naval capabilities relative to U.S. capabilities, see Michael D. Swaine and Oriana Skylar Mastro, "Assessing the Threat," in Michael D. Swaine, Andrew N. D. Yang, and Evan S. Medeiros, eds., *Assessing the Threat: The Chinese Military and Taiwan's Security* (Washington, DC: Carnegie Endowment for International Peace, 2007), 337–366.

China's defensive naval doctrines (the so-called "people's war at sea") and its strategic focus on Taiwan have limited the amount of attention it has paid to naval power projection capability in the past, although this began to change in the early twenty-first century. Compared to China, Indian naval leaders have historically placed greater relative emphasis on power projection capabilities. Despite the smaller size of India's economy and military budget, New Delhi continues to maintain greater naval power projection capabilities than Beijing in some categories. The Indian Navy is also an important part of India's regional military diplomacy, conducting naval exercises with numerous countries, including the United States and China, and deploying on humanitarian missions as well as naval patrols. In contrast, Beijing has recently embraced military diplomacy but has limited experience and capability in this area.

Aircraft Carriers

The IN has operated at least one aircraft carrier since 1961. India has one operational carrier, the *Viraat*. The ship is the former HMS *Hermes*, originally commissioned in 1959. *Viraat* entered IN service in 1987, displaces 29,000 tons, has a range of 5,000 nautical miles (nm), and can carry up to 30 total aircraft, including 12 to 18 fighter-bombers and additional helicopters.[32] The ship carries new air defenses, upgrades to its propulsion and electronic systems, and aircraft that have modern strike, airborne early warning, and search-and-rescue capabilities. Its air wing includes FRS-Mk51 *Sea Harrier* vertical/short takeoff fighter-bombers, and Ka-27 *Helix* and SH-3 *Sea King* helicopters. Among Asian navies, this one carrier, its support ships, and the IN's experience in operating it give India a leading power projection capability. *Viraat*'s retirement has been delayed to allow completion of procurement programs for newer aircraft carriers. The Indian Navy has said it plans to retire *Viraat* in 2012.[33]

India purchased the former Russian *Admiral Gorshkov* (originally commissioned as the Soviet *Baku* in 1987) in 2004. Renamed *Vikramaditya*, the ship is being refitted in Russia, although there have been a number of delays in the acquisition process and frictions between the Indian and Russian sides over costs. Western sources indicate the ship may be ready

---

[32] According to the International Institute for Strategic Studies (IISS), India's Naval Aviation force has one squadron of six MiG-29K Fulcrum fighter-bombers and one squadron of nine FRS MK51 Sea Harriers, plus two Sea Harrier T-4N trainer aircraft. IISS, *The Military Balance 2011*, March 7, 2011, 240.

[33] IISS, *The Military Balance 2011*, 214.

for commissioning between 2012 and 2013.[34] When India finally commissions *Vikramaditya*, it could potentially embark sixteen MiG-29K aircraft, as well as eight Ka-31 antisubmarine and AEW helicopters.[35] At 45,000 tons, *Vikramaditya*, with its MiG-29Ks and a 14,000-nm range, will be a significantly more capable ship than *Viraat*.

Finally, India is building an aircraft carrier of domestic design, potentially a 37,500 ton vessel that may be able to carry up to 20 modern aircraft and 10 helicopters. The keel of the new ship, *Vikrant*, was laid down in February 2009.[36] According to Western sources, the carrier should be commissioned around 2015 (although historically, such Indian programs have often experienced delays).[37]

China's first aircraft carrier began sea trials in 2011. This vessel is the former Soviet *Varyag*, a 53,000-ton *Kuznetsov*-class aircraft carrier that underwent more than a decade of refurbishment after China purchased it in 1998. The ship will likely serve as a testing and development platform for some time.[38] U.S. Navy sources indicate that a domestically designed Chinese aircraft carrier could be operational sometime after 2015.[39]

In the past, some Chinese strategists have highlighted the risks of developing even a single aircraft carrier both in terms of the total cost of the program (including all necessary ships, aircraft, and support systems) and in terms of the potential reaction such a development could spark among China's neighbors.[40] Nevertheless, calls for expanded PLAN missions (and consideration of national prestige) appear to have overridden fears of a negative reaction and potential balancing responses among other states in Asia.

---

[34] IISS, *The Military Balance 2011*, 214. Plans for commissioning have been delayed numerous times.

[35] Donald L. Berlin, "India in the Indian Ocean," *Naval War College Review*, 59:2 (Spring 2006): 80.

[36] This project was formerly known as the Air Defence Ship (ADS). "Keel-laying of indigenous aircraft carrier in December," *The Hindu*, Monday, September 29, 2008, http://www. hindu.com/2008/09/29/stories/2008092955681400.htm

[37] IISS, *The Military Balance 2011*, 214. According to Western sources, India has plans to build at least two of these domestically designed vessels.

[38] Office of Naval Intelligence, *The People's Liberation Army Navy: A Modern Navy with Chinese Characteristics*, 19.

[39] Office of Naval Intelligence, *The People's Liberation Army Navy: A Modern Navy with Chinese Characteristics*, 19.

[40] See for example, 林立民[Lin Limin],"航母: 不敢说爱你"[Aircraft Carrier: I Don't Dare Say I Treasure You], 《北京世界知识》 [Beijing World Affairs], Volume 18, 2005; Andrew F. Diamond, "Dying With Eyes Open or Closed: The Debate over a Chinese Aircraft Carrier," *Korean Journal of Defense Analysis*, 18:1 (Spring 2006): 35–58.

Naval Aviation

The PLAN operates a large land-based naval aviation force of mixed quality. The PLAN naval aviation bomber force comprises fifty aircraft. Thirty of these are H-6s, an upgrade of the Soviet-era Tu-16 medium-range bomber design with relatively short range and poor penetration capabilities. However, H-6s are capable of carrying an air-launched version of the DH-10 cruise missile, providing a stand-off strike capability. Twenty aircraft in the bomber force are antiquated torpedo bombers. Many of the PLAN's 222 fighters and fighter-bombers are older aircraft, including 48 J-8, 36 J-7, and 30 Q-5 aircraft, based on the Cold War Soviet Su-15, MiG-21, and MiG-19, respectively. Many of these older aircraft are being retired. However, PLAN naval aviation has eighty-four relatively modern JH-7 fighter-bombers configured for maritime attack and twenty-four modern Su-30MK2 fighter-bombers. China's maritime patrol and antisubmarine aviation capabilities are relatively weak. The force is comprised of only four Y-8 (An-12) maritime patrol aircraft and four older SH-5 ASW flying boats.[41]

The Indian Navy's combat aviation forces consist of a squadron of *Sea Harriers* deployed on the *Viraat* and a squadron of MiG-29Ks, which will presumably be deployed on its newer carriers when they enter service. Unlike the PLAN, the IN does not have land-based fighter-bombers in its inventory, although the Indian Air Force has ten *Jaguar* IM aircraft armed with *Sea Eagle* missiles for maritime strike.[42] The IN has better maritime patrol and ASW capabilities than China. The IN has five Il-38 *May* and fourteen Do-228 maritime patrol aircraft, as well as four Tu-142M *Bear* F ASW aircraft. This capability will be greatly enhanced by a $2 billion deal to buy eight Boeing P-8I maritime patrol aircraft from the United States, approved by Washington in March 2009. The P-8I is a variant of the P-8A (based on the Boeing 737 commercial jet), the same aircraft that will be replacing the P-3 *Orion* maritime patrol/ASW aircraft for the U.S. Navy. India is the first international buyer of this system.

Surface Warships

China has more principal surface combatants than India – seventy-eight versus twenty-three (Tables 6.3 and 6.4). By tonnage, the Chinese fleet of major surface warships is about twice as large as India's (253,870 tons vs.

---

[41] Data from IISS *Military Balance 2011*, 233.
[42] *Military Balance 2011*, 240–241.

Table 6.3. *China's major surface warships: Destroyers, 2010*

Operational	Type/Class	Commissioned	Tons Displac.	Main Armament (SSM Range km/Speed Mach)	Air Defense (SAM Range km/Speed Mach)	Aircraft
2	Type 051C *Luzhou*	2005–2006	7,100	8 YJ-83 (180km/M 1.5) / 1 100mm gun	48 S-300F RIF (150km/M 10)	1 Ka-28 Helix ASW
2	Type 052C *Luyang* II	2004–2005	6,500	8 YJ-62 (280km/M 0.8) / 6 324mm TT / 1 100mm gun	48 HQ-9 (150km/M 6)	1 Ka-28 Helix ASW
2	Type 052B *Luyang*	2004	6,500	16 YJ-83 (180km/M1.5) / 6 324mm TT / 1 100mm gun	48 SA-N-7 (30–45km/M 3)	1 Ka-28 Helix ASW
4	Type 956 *Hangzhou* (Sovremenny)	2000	7,625	8 3M80E (120–200km/M 2–3) / 4 533mm TT / 4 130mm guns	44 SA-N-7 (30–45km/M 3)	
1	Type 051B *Luhai*	1998	6,100	16 YJ-83 (180km/M1.5) / 6 324mm TT / 2 100mm guns	8 HQ-7 (15km/M 2)	
2	Type 052A *Luhu*	1994	4,800	16 YJ-83 (180km/M1.5) / 6 324mm TT / 1 100mm gun	8 HQ-7 (15km/M 2; 16 missiles stored)	2 Ka-27 or Z-9 (Dauphin)
1	Type 051 *Luda* III	1991	3,730	16 YJ-83 (180km/M1.5) / 3 Whitehead TT / 2 130mm guns		
2	Type 051DT *Luda* Mod	1987–1990	3,670	8 YJ-83 (180km/M1.5) / 2 130mm guns	8 HQ-7 (15km/M 2; 16 missiles stored)	
1	Type 051 *Luda* II	1971	3,670	8 YJ-8 (40km/M 0.9) / 1 130mm gun		2 helo
9	Type 051 *Luda*	1971	3,670	6 HY-2 (95km/M 0.9) / 2 130mm gun		

26

Sources: Jane's Fighting Ships 2010; IISS, *The Military Balance 2011*. Note that as of 2011, IISS categorizes the Type 051 *Luda*, *Luda* Mod, *Luda* II, *and Luda* III classes of ships as frigates, based on tonnage. IISS formerly categorized these ships as destroyers. In this table, we retain the classification for *Luda* series ships as destroyers, which is consistent with the ships' original design and the Chinese classification.

Table 6.4. *China's major surface warships: Frigates, 2010*

Operational	Type/Class	Commissioned	Tons Displac.	Main Arm. (SSM Range km/Speed Mach)	Air Defense (SAM Range km/Speed Mach)	Aircraft
7	Type 054A *Jiangkai* II	2007	4,500	8 YJ-83 (180km/M1.5) 6 324mm TT 1 76mm gun	32 VLS HQ-16 (42km/M 4+)	Ka-28 Helix or Z-9C Panther helo
2	Type 054 *Jiangkai* I	2005	3,400	YJ-83 (180km/M1.5) 6 324mm TT 1 100mm gun	8 HQ-7 (15km/M 2; 16 missiles stored) or 32 VLS HQ-16 (42km/M 4+)	Ka-28 Helix or Z-9C Panther helo
10	Type 053H3 *Jiangwei* II	1999	2,250	8 YJ-83 (180km/M1.5) 6 324mm TT 2 100mm guns	8 HQ-7 (15km/M 2; 16 missiles stored) 8 37mm AA guns	2 Z-9C Panther helo
6	Type 053H1G *Jianghu* V	1993	1,700	6 SY-1 (100km/M 0.8) 2 100mm guns	8 37mm AA guns	1 Z-9C Panther helo
4	Type 053H2G *Jiangwei* I	1992	2,250	6 YJ-8 (40km/M 0.9) 6 324mm TT 2 100mm guns	6 HQ-61B (10km/M 3) 8 37mm AA guns	2 Z-9C Panther helo
3	Type 053H2 *Jianghu* III	1986	1,960	8 YJ-8 (40km/M 0.9) 2 100mm guns	8 37mm AA guns	1 Z-9C Panther helo
1	Type 053HTH *Jianghu* IV	1985	1,960	6 SY-1 (100km/M 0.8) 2 100mm guns	8 37mm AA guns	1 Z-9C Panther helo
8	Type 053H1 *Jianghu* II	1984	1,700	6 SY-1 (100km/M 0.8) 2 100mm guns	8 37mm AA guns	
11	Type 053H *Jianghu* I	1974	1,660	6 SY-1 (100km/M 0.8) 2 100mm guns	8 37mm AA guns	

52

Source: IISS, *The Military Balance 2011.*

127,470 tons).[43] However, a significant number of China's surface warships have extremely limited air defenses and no effective defense against submarines. These outmoded ships, including eleven *Luda* destroyers and twenty-nine *Jianghu* frigates, account for about half of all Chinese major surface combat ships and would contribute little in a modern naval battle. These ships are being retired as newer PLAN ships are brought into service.

Modern naval platforms must have sensors and weapons that allow them to survive to complete their missions in a combat environment. These include (but are not limited to) advanced radar systems such as planar arrays, and an adequate supply of surface-to-air missiles (SAMs) capable of protecting the ship from aircraft and missile attack. Most modern ships also include at least some defenses against submarine attack, including active and passive sonar and helicopters that can attack subs. Flexible and rapid-reloading vertical launch systems (VLS) for both defensive and offensive missiles are also becoming standard.[44] Western sources report that the focus of new PLAN surface ship development appears to be better radars, antiair defenses, and anti-surface weapons.

By 2011, about half of the PLAN's twenty-six destroyers and slightly less than half of its fifty-two frigates could be considered modern, up from 20 percent and 25 percent, respectively, in 2000.[45] Some of these, however, do not meet all elements of the relatively strict definition outlined above. China's destroyer fleet has dramatically improved in recent years. Newer PLAN destroyers are larger and have more capable systems, particularly

---

[43] This comparison is based on commissioned surface ships over 1,000 tons, and includes the 28,700-ton Indian aircraft carrier *Viraat*. IISS, *The Military Balance 2011*, and *Jane's Fighting Ships* 2010. Relative per-ship tonnage (ship size) is an indicator of potential ship capabilities. Other things being equal, larger ships have greater range, can carry more equipment, can accommodate a larger variety of systems, and are easier to upgrade through on-board system replacement or enhancement.

[44] There is no universally accepted standard definition for what constitutes a "modern" weapons system. Military technology constantly changes. Judgments about relative advances often focus on sensors, defenses, and weapons, as well as the performance characteristics (speed, ease of detection) of the vehicle, ship, or aircraft platform itself. For one source that makes an assessment of which Chinese weapons systems are considered modern, see Anthony Cordesman and Martin Klieber, *Chinese Military Modernization: Force Development and Strategic Capabilities* (Washington, DC: Center for Strategic and International Studies, 2008).

[45] Modern frigates include the Type 053H2G *Jiangwei* I, Type 053H3 *Jiangwei* II, Type 054 *Jiangkai* I, and Type 054A *Jiangkai* II. For further analysis of the modern characteristics of China's surface fleet, see Anthony Cordesman and Martin Klieber, *Chinese Military Modernization: Force Development and Strategic Capabilities*, 117–144. See also James C. Bussert and Bruce A. Elleman, *People's Liberation Army Navy: Combat Systems Technology, 1949–2010* (Annapolis: Naval Institute Press, 2011), 17–61.

in air defense, radar, and hull design. The PLAN appears to continue to experiment with destroyer designs, recently building only two of each class before moving on to the next class. China also appears to continue to experiment with the outfitting of these ships, with an intriguing reversion to more imported weapons systems in the *Luzhou* class after having used domestic systems in the *Luyang II*.[46] The PLAN seems to be more comfortable with series production of recent frigate designs, including its *Jiangkai* and *Jiangwei* frigates, than it is with series production of recent destroyer designs.

India's fleet of major surface warships consists of three Type 15 *Delhi*-class destroyers and five older *Rajput*-class destroyers (based on the former Soviet *Kashin* class).[47] The IN frigate fleet has two Type 17 *Shivalik*, three Type 1135.6 *Talwar*-class, three Type 16A *Brahmaputra*-class, three Type 16 *Godavari*, and three older *Nilgiri* -class ships (based on the UK *Leander* class, now being retired). Unlike some of China's older ships, all of India's guided missile destroyers and guided missile frigates have at least some SAM and ASW capability (Table 6.5). Eight of the newer Indian ships (including the *Delhi* and *Talwar* destroyers and the *Shivalik*-class frigates) are equipped with planar array radar (*Top Hat*) and vertical-launch missile systems.

Among India's destroyers, the Type 15 *Delhi*-class ships have modern antiship missiles and air defenses. By that standard, less than half of India's destroyer fleet was composed of modern ships as of early 2011 (although a new class of destroyers is under construction and older ships are being retired). Among the IN's frigates, the Type 17 *Shivalik*, the Type 1135.6 *Talwar* (an updated version of the Russian *Krivak* III, built in Russia), the *Brahmaputra*-class, and the *Godavari*-class ships possess modern offensive and defensive capabilities, including vertical-launch SAM systems. By that standard, almost 80 percent of India's frigate fleet can be considered modern.

Like China, India continues to modernize its surface fleet. India recently retired four older *Nilgiri* frigates.[48] New ships under construction in India include three Project 15A *Kolkata* destroyers being built in India as a

---

[46] We thank Michael Nixon for this observation.

[47] As with some Chinese ships, standard Western references such as the IISS *Military Balance* have recently recategorized some Indian vessels, based on ship size (tonnage). The Indian Navy *Shivalik* class, formerly categorized as a frigate, is now listed as a destroyer in IISS *The Military Balance 2011*, 239. As with Chinese ships such as the *Luda* series noted earlier, we retain the original classification for these ships, consistent with the practice of that nation's own navy. In this case, we use the original classification of the *Shivalik*-class as frigates.

[48] IISS *Military Balance 2009*, February 3, 2010.

Table 6.5. *India's major surface warships, 2010*

	Operational	Type/Class	Commissioned	Tons Displac.	Main armament (SSM Range km/Speed Mach)	Air defense (SAM Range km/Speed Mach)	Aircraft
Aircraft Carriers	**1**						
	1	*Viraat*	1959 (as UK *Hermes*)	28,700 (full)		16 *Barak 1* (12 km/ M 2)	30 *Sea Harrier* FRS- Mk51 7 Ka-27 Helix ASW or *Sea King* Mk 24B ASW
Destroyers	**8**						
	3	Type 15 *Delhi*	1997	6,700	16 SS-N-25 (130 km/ M 0.8) 5 533 mm TT 1 100 mm gun	24 *Barak 1* (12 km/ M 2) or 24 SA-N-24 (6 km/ M 1.2)	2 SH-3 *Sea King* or *Alouette*
	5	*Rajput*	1980	4,974	4 PJ-10 BrahMos ASM (290 km/ M 2) 4 SS-N-2C (80 km/ M 0.9) 5 533 mm TT 1 76 mm gun	16 SA-N-1 (15 km/ M 3.5)	1 Ka-25 or Ka-28
Frigates	**14**						
	2	Type 17 *Shivalik*	2008	5,000	8 SS-N-27 (200+km/ M 2.2) or 8 BrahMos (290 km/ M 2) 533 mm TT 1 76 mm gun	6 SA-N-7 (30–40 km/ M 3)	1 SH-3 *Sea King*

3	Type 1135.6 Talwar	2003	4,000	8 SS-N-27 (200 + km/ M 2.2) or 8 PJ-10 BrahMos (290 km/ M 2) 4 533 mm TT 1 100 mm gun	24 SA-N-12 (42 km/ M 3.5) 8 SA-N-16 (5 km/ n.a.; portable) 32 SA-N-11 (8 km/ n.a.) CIWS SAM (n.a.) 2 CIWS gun system	1 Ka-31 AEW or Ka-28 ASW or Alouette ASW utility helo
3	Type 16A Brahmaputra	2000	3,850	16 SS-N-25 (130 km/ M 0.8) 6 324 mm TT	24 Barak 1 (12 km/ M 2)	2 SH-3 Sea King or Alouette
3	Type 16 Godavari	1983	3,850	4 SS-N-2D (80 km/ M 0.9) 6 324 mm TT 2 57 mm gun	24 Barak 1 (12 km/ M 2) or 20 SA-N-4 (10–15 km/ M 2)	2 SH-3 Sea King or Alouette
3	Nilgiri (based on Leander)	1972–1981	2,900	4 114 mm guns 6 324 mm TT 2 30 mm guns 2 20 mm guns	n/a	1 SH-3 Sea King or Alouette

Source: IISS, The Military Balance 2011. Note that as of 2011, IISS categorizes the Type 17 Shivalik class of ships as destroyers. IISS formerly categorized these ships as frigates. In this table, we retain the classification of these ships as frigates.

follow-on to the Project 15 *Delhi* class, as well as three Project 17 (*Shivalik*) frigates and seven Project 17A frigates (a follow-on to the *Shivalik* class).[49] India also has plans to build three *Advanced Talwar* guided missile frigates and four Project 28 *Kamorta* class ASW frigates. The new ships will have greater offensive capability. For example, the Type 15A destroyers will have the joint Indo-Russian-developed *BrahMos* cruise missile. There is also a possibility that some of India's new destroyers will eventually be equipped with an American air defense radar and missile targeting/management system.[50] (Even if it is not actually able to purchase U.S. radars, the IN may benefit from American technology transfer in this area.)

Although the striking power and the air defenses of surface ships in both navies are rapidly improving, antisubmarine warfare (ASW) capabilities appear to remain a challenge for the PLAN and the IN. Both navies are building surface ships that now embark helicopters, but effective ASW also requires advanced sonar, data processing, and networking capabilities.

Submarines

India and China both have modern submarine forces and are continuing to develop new types of boats. The PLAN has given submarine development special attention in recent years and has made significant improvements in its overall submarine capabilities (Tables 6.6 and 6.7).[51] The challenge from Chinese submarine force modernization has recently been singled out by senior U.S. officers as "the number one priority" for U.S. Pacific Fleet readiness.[52]

According to standard Western reference sources, the number of PLAN submarines has declined from more than 100 in the mid-1980s to 71 as of early 2011.[53] Of China's fleet of seventy-one submarines, about 60 percent may be considered modern, and that percentage is rising rapidly with

---

[49] IISS *Military Balance 2011*, 285.

[50] "India-US Ties in Focus," *Jane's Intelligence Digest*, July 29, 2005.

[51] Office of Naval Intelligence, *The People's Liberation Army Navy: A Modern Navy with Chinese Characteristics*, 20–23; Andrew S. Erickson, Lyle J. Goldstein, William S. Murray, and Andrew R. Wilson, eds., *China's Future Nuclear Submarine Force* (Annapolis: Naval Institute Press, 2007).

[52] Admiral Timothy J. Keating, U.S. Navy Commander U.S. Pacific Command, "Testimony Before the Senate Armed Services Committee on U.S. Pacific Command Posture," Senate Armed Services Committee, March 19, 2009.

[53] IISS, *Military Balance 2011*, 231. As with other weapons systems, assessing "in service" submarines can be difficult. We cannot determine with certainty that these numbers reflect actual change in PLAN forces or changed public-source western evaluations of "in service" submarines.

Table 6.6. China's submarine forces, 2010

	In service	Operational	Type	Commissioned	Displacement (tons, submerged)	Main armament
SSBN	**3**	**2**				
	2	0	Type 094 *Jin*	2004	8,000–9,000	JL-2 6 533mm TT
	1	0	Type 092 *Xia*	1987	6,500–7,000	JL-1 6 533mm TT
SSN	**6**	**6**				
	2	2	Type 093 *Shang*	2006	6,000–7,000	YJ-82 ASM LACM? 6 533mm TT
	4	4	Type 091 *Han*	1980	5,500	YJ-82 ASM 6 533mm TT
SSG	**1**	**1**				
	1	1	Project 033G *Romeo Mod*	1962	2,110	YJ-1 ASM 8 533mm TT
SSK	**60**	**60**				
	2	2	Type 041 *Yuan*	2006	n/a (may be similar to *Kilo*)	YJ-82 ASM 6 533mm TT
	16	16	Type 039/039G *Song*	1999	~2,250	YJ-2 SSM 6 533mm TT
	12	12	Type 877EKM *Kilo* Type 636 Kilo	1985/ 1995	3,000–4,000	SS-N-27 6 533mm TT
	20	20	Type 035 *Ming*	1971	2,110	8 533mm TT
	8	8	Type 033 *Romeo*	1962	2,110	8 533mm TT
SS	**1**	**1**				
	1	1	Type 031 *Golf*	1966	2,700–3,500	

Source: IISS, *The Military Balance 2011*. Data on submarines is sometimes contradictory across different public sources.

185

Table 6.7. *India's submarine forces, 2010*

	In service	Operational	Type	Commissioned	Tons Diplac. (Sub.)	Main Armament
SSN	**1**	**0**				
	1	0	*Chakra* (former Nerpa, Project 971A / 971M Akula II)	2011–2012 (est.)	7,900–9,500	SS-N-27 6 533mm TT
SSK	**15**	**14**				
	0	0	*Scorpene*	2012+	1,600–1,900	ASM 6 533mm TT
	10	10	Type 877 *Kilo* (*Sindhugosh*)	1986	3,000–4,000	SS-N-27 (on 7 of 10 boats) 6 533mm TT
	4	4	Type 209/1500 (*Shishumar*)	1986	1,400–1,850	8 533mm TT
	1	1 (?)	Type 641 *Foxtrot* (Vela)	1970	2,475	10 533mm TT

Source: IISS, *The Military Balance 2011.*

the retirement of legacy craft.[54] Diesel-electric submarines continue to represent the primary focus for PLAN development, although new nuclear-powered classes are also coming into service. The PLAN currently operates twelve *Kilo* diesel-electric submarines, having taken delivery of the final two *Kilos* ordered from Russia in 2007. These are likely the PLAN's quietest submarines.[55]

China had four domestically built Type 041 *Yuan*-class diesel-electric submarines. The first two of these began sea trials in 2008 and 2009.[56] The *Yuan* class is said to incorporate lessons from the experience with the *Song* class and the *Kilo* class, although some Western sources speculate that these submarines may continue to experience technical problems. These difficulties

[54] Chinese submarines considered modern by Western analysts include the Type 092 *Xia* and Type 094 *Jin* SSBNs, Type 093 *Shang* SSN, and the Type 041 *Yuan*, Type 039 *Song*, and Type 877 and Type 636 *Kilo*-class diesel-electric submarines. *The Military Balance* 2009, February 3, 2010. For further analysis of the modern characteristics of China's submarine fleet, see Anthony Cordesman and Martin Klieber, *Chinese Military Modernization: Force Development and Strategic Capabilities,* 117–144. See also James C. Bussert and Bruce A. Elleman, *People's Liberation Army Navy: Combat Systems Technology, 1949–2010,* 62–81.

[55] Office of Naval Intelligence, *The People's Liberation Army Navy: A Modern Navy with Chinese Characteristics,* 22.

[56] IISS *Military Balance 2009,* February 3, 2010.

may concern the propulsion system, which is said to include air-independent propulsion (AIP). If operational, AIP would allow these submarines to operate more quietly and for longer periods submerged (albeit at slower speeds) than boats equipped only with diesel-electric engines.[57]

A new Chinese nuclear-powered attack submarine (SSN) class, the Type 093 *Shang*, is currently in production. Two of these submarines were operational as of early 2011. Publicly available sources indicate that these subs may borrow design characteristics from the former Soviet Union *Victor III* class.[58] Like the *Yuan* class, the *Shang* class will be equipped with antiship missiles (ASMs) and may also be able to carry land-attack cruise missiles (LACMs) when and if those become available.

China also has three ballistic missile submarines (SSBNs). One, the Type 092 *Xia*, has been plagued by technical difficulties from the start and its operations have been extremely limited. China is now deploying a new-design SSBN, the Type 094 *Jin*. Two had been completed and two more were under construction as of 2011. Public sources indicate these will carry a new submarine-launched ballistic missile, the JL-2, which began testing and trials in 2009.

China's domestic submarine development and manufacturing program has improved markedly, although it is still dependent on some Russian technologies. China's domestic submarine design, development, and construction capabilities appear to be superior to India's. Although the PLAN has been modernizing its submarine fleet, it has only begun to increase its historically very low operational tempo.[59] China's own antisubmarine warfare capabilities appear to lag in development.[60]

The Indian Navy submarine fleet comprises sixteen vessels. Of these, fifteen can be considered modern. These include four German-built Type 209s, ten Russian-built *Kilo*-class boats, and a nuclear attack submarine leased from Russia, the *Chakra* (the former Russian *Nerpa*, an *Akula II*-class SSN).[61] One of India's fifteen diesel-electric submarines – an older

---

[57] See, for example, http://www.globalsecurity.org/military/world/china/yuan.htm

[58] "Type 093 (Shang Class)," *Jane's Underwater Warfare Systems*, July 3, 2006.

[59] Publicly available data appears to indicate that realistic training and active patrolling for Chinese submarine forces has been relatively rare. If that is true, operational experience and tactical skill could be challenges for Chinese submariners. "Chinese submarine patrols increase," *Jane's Defence Weekly*, February 6, 2009; Office of Naval Intelligence, *The People's Liberation Army Navy: A Modern Navy with Chinese Characteristics*, 40.

[60] Office of Naval Intelligence, *The People's Liberation Army Navy: A Modern Navy with Chinese Characteristics*, 1–2, 18.

[61] India's plan to bring *Chakra* into operational service suffered a setback in 2008 when the boat (then still the Russian *Nerpa*) suffered a deadly accident while on sea trials. See

Foxtrot-class boat – is considered outdated. Six of the Indian *Kilo* subs have the SS-N-27 *Club* antiship missile system, and the four older *Kilos* are being retrofitted to accommodate that missile.[62]

India recently signed a contract with France for six *Scorpene* diesel-electric submarines. All six will be built in the Mazagon Dockyard, Mumbai. Construction began in May 2007, and deliveries are planned for 2013, although construction appears to face delays.[63] When completed, the *Scorpene* program will result in a significant gain in Indian access to advanced submarine technology and manufacturing know-how, including air-independent propulsion. The *Scorpene* program may also include a design capable of accepting a nuclear reactor.[64]

Despite both Russian and French assistance with its domestic submarine building program, India has struggled to develop an operational nuclear-powered submarine, something China achieved (with mixed effectiveness) in the late 1970s.[65] India has its own domestic nuclear-powered submarine project, the Advanced Technology Vessel (ATV). That program too has experienced years of development delays. The first vessel from the project was launched in July 2009 as INS *Arihant*.[66] The ATV may be the foundation for India's future sea-based nuclear deterrent, possibly armed with the *Sagarika* K-15 submarine-launched ballistic missile (SLBM). However, this program still faces many technical and budgetary challenges, as well as competition for resources from other Indian naval and military programs.

Amphibious and Support Capability

Despite China's focus on Taiwan as its most important external security issue, the PLAN's amphibious assault capabilities have been relatively under-developed. According to public sources, China has 87 amphibious assault vessels: 61 landing ships (LSM; capacities ranging from two to five tanks and up to 250 troops) and 26 landing ship tank (LST; capacity of 10 tanks

---

IISS, *Military Balance 2011*, March 7, 2011, 214. India has experience operating a Soviet *Charlie*-class nuclear-powered guided missile submarine, which it leased from 1988 to 1991.

[62] There may be delays to this retrofit program. IISS, *Military Balance 2009*, February 3, 2010.

[63] IISS, *Military Balance 2009*, February 3, 2010. See also, "Scorpene construction work begins in Mumbai," *The Hindu*, May 24, 2007.

[64] Bharat Karnad, "Putting Bang in the Bomb," *Indian Express*, November 13, 2002.

[65] On the Chinese nuclear submarine program, see John Wilson Lewis and Xue Litai, *China's Strategic Seapower: The Politics of Force Modernization in the Nuclear Age* (Stanford: Stanford University Press, 1994).

[66] IISS, *Military Balance 2009*, February 3, 2010.

and 250 troops, and in some cases two helicopters or four smaller personnel landing craft).[67] However, the PLAN is developing new ships that may give it the ability to initiate over-the-horizon amphibious assault operations.

The first *Yuzhao* class Type 071 amphibious transport dock (LPD) became operational in 2007. This is a 17,600-ton vessel that can carry up to 800 troops, 15 to 20 amphibious combat vehicles, two to four assault hovercraft (LCACs), and two assault helicopters over short voyages. China's mainstay LCAC, the Type 724, is a relatively small craft. China has discussed importing larger LCACs from Russia, and public sources indicate a deal was finalized in July 2010, although no date has yet been set for deliveries.[68] Some Western sources say a domestic LCAC design is under development, which may carry a 60-ton to 70-ton load (equivalent to about 180 troops or one main battle tank). Other reports indicate that China is developing a class of helicopter assault ships, or LHDs.[69]

Support ships have been historically neglected, but China is also developing new multiproduct underway replenishment ships, which would be critical to power projection. The PLAN's recent antipiracy operations in the Gulf of Aden, where it has only limited local options for resupply, have highlighted the need for such support. The PLAN has commissioned two of the 23,000-ton 886 *Fuchi*-class support ships.[70] In 2008, China commissioned its first hospital ship, the 20,000-ton Type 920 *Daishandao*, which may have capacity for up to 600 beds, plus two helicopters for medical evacuation.[71]

India's amphibious capabilities are also relatively modest, with fewer but larger ships than China's mainstay landing craft. India has five LSMs, each with capacity for five main battle tanks or 160 troops, and five LSTs, each with capacity for 15 tanks, two helicopters, and 500 troops. India's amphibious warfare ability was significantly improved in 2006 with the acquisition of the former USS *Trenton*, a 16,500-ton, flat-rear-deck LPD (originally commissioned in 1971), along with six *Sea King* helicopters. The vessel was renamed the *Jalashwa*, and, in addition to the six helicopters, can carry nine landing craft (LCM) with capacity of about 50 tons each, or about 1,000 troops.[72] The *Jalashwa* is currently the second-largest combat vessel in the IN, after the *Viraat*.

[67] IISS, *Military Balance 2011*, 233.
[68] IISS, *Military Balance 2011*, March 7, 2011, 284.
[69] *Jane's Sentinel*, "China Procurement," February 7, 2008.
[70] IISS, *Military Balance 2011; Janes Sentinel 2008*
[71] IISS, *Military Balance 2011; Janes Sentinel 2008*
[72] IISS, *Military Balance 2008*, 343.

Historically the IN has also had to make do with a relatively under-developed fleet of support vessels, and modernization of this part of the IN lags in comparison to recent PLAN developments. At 39,000 tons, the underway replenishment ship *Jyoti* is the largest vessel in the IN, built in Russia and commissioned in 1996. The IN also has the 24,000-ton *Aditya*, which became operational in 2000 after a thirteen-year development and construction period. *Aditya* is a modified version of the older 15,000-ton *Deepak*-class replenishment ships. (One was recently decommissioned; one remains in service.)

Air Forces

India and China are also modernizing their air forces, and each possesses limited but growing capability to project air power. Compared to India, China has a larger total number of combat aircraft, more fourth-generation fighters, a larger bomber force, and airborne (parachute) units. China also has a more advanced indigenous aircraft production capability. India appears to have comparable or superior capabilities in ground-attack aircraft, military airlift, in-flight refueling, and AWACS.

Indian Air Force (IAF) combat aircraft include a mix of MiG-29B, MiG-27M, *Mirage* 2000-M, *Jaguar* (one squadron has *Sea Eagle* missiles for maritime strike), and Su-30 (Table 6.8). The IAF operates 122 Su-30MKI aircraft in six squadrons. A Su-30MKI production line (as distinct from kit assembly) opened in India in 2007 and will produce 140 aircraft through 2020.[73] Like the PLAAF, the IAF has been retiring some of its older aircraft, such as its MiG-23s, as newer planes become available.

Among IAF fighters and fighter-bombers, the Su-30MKI, MiG-29B, and Mirage 2000 are considered modern. Modern multirole fighters made up about 37 percent of India's fighter and fighter-bomber fleet as of early 2011. New Delhi will buy a large number of new fighter-bomber aircraft over the next several years. Candidates included the Eurofighter *Typhoon*, the French *Rafale*, the Russian Su-35, the Swedish JAS-39 *Gripen*, and advanced versions of the U.S. F/A-18 *Hornet* and F-16 *Fighting Falcon*.[74] In April 2011, the Indian government announced a short list for the final procurement competition, which rejected the U.S. aircraft and retained only the Eurofighter *Typhoon* and the French

---

[73] "Air Force, India," *Jane's Sentinel Security Assessment*, March 3, 2008.
[74] Public reports indicate that India could purchase as many as 126 modern fighters. "Air Force, India," *Jane's Sentinel Security Assessment*, March 3, 2008.

Table 6.8. *India's air force, 2010*

	In service	Type	NATO designation or derivative	Aircraft generation
Fighter	**112**			
	64	MiG-29B *Fulcrum*	MiG-29B *Fulcrum*	4
	48	MiG-21FL *Fishbed*	MiG-21FL *Fishbed*	3
Fighter/ Ground Attack	**526**			
	122	Su-30MKI *Flanker*	Su-30MKI *Flanker*	4
	52	*Mirage 2000* H/E/ TH/ED	*Mirage 2000* H/E/ TH/ED	4
	36	MiG-27ML *Flogger*	MiG-27ML *Flogger*	3
	83	*Jaguar* S Int'l	*Jaguar* S Int'l	3
	10	*Jaguar IM* (maritime attack)	*Jaguar* M	3
	152	MiG-21bis L/N *Fishbed*	MiG-21bis L/N *Fishbed*	3
	71	MiG-21 M/MF/ PFMA *Fishbed*	MiG-21 M/MF *Fishbed*	2
AEW/ AWACS	**2**			
	2	IL-76TD *Phalcon* (1 more on order)	IL-76 *Mainstay*	
Tanker	**6**			
	6	IL-78 *Midas*	IL-78 *Midas*	
Transport	**217**			
	0	C-130J *Hercules* (6 on order)	C-130J Hercules SF configuration	
	24	IL-76 Candid	IL-76 Candid	
	105	An-32 Cline	An-32 Cline	
	6	B-707	B-707	
	4	B-737	B-737	
	20	HS-478	BAE-748	
	51	Do-228	Do-228	
	4	EMB-135BJ	EMB-135BJ	
	3	Boeing BBJ	Boeing BBJ	

Source: IISS, *The Military Balance 2011*, 241.

Rafale.[75] Either of these aircraft would represent a significant upgrade to India's air power capabilities.

[75] "India rejects US fighters: Envoy Roemer resigns," *Asia Tribune*, April 28, 2011, http:// www.asiantribune.com/news/2011/04/28/india-rejects-us-fighters-envoy-roemer-resigns; "India spurns U.S. for fighter jet order," *Reuters*, April 29, 2011, http://in.mobile.

The PLA air force (PLAAF) operates a larger number of fourth-generation fighters and fighter-bombers than India (483 vs. 238; Tables 6.8 and 6.9).[76] On the Chinese side, these include Su-30s and Su-27s, as well as the J-10 (an aircraft design influenced by the Israeli *Lavi* and possibly the F-16), and the indigenously designed JH-7 (a fighter-bomber). More of all these aircraft types, including as many as 300 license-produced SU-27/J-11 aircraft, will be brought on-line in the years to come.[77]

Although China has larger numbers of fourth-generation aircraft, the variance in quality of its aircraft is much greater than in the Indian case. Relatively more of China's total inventory is comprised of older planes. For example, China still has about 570 J-7 and J-7 variant aircraft, based on the MiG-21 (which entered Soviet service in 1959). Many of the J-7s have been updated, and many are also being retired. The PLAAF also maintains around 120 Q-5C/D fighter-bombers based on the even older MiG-19 airframe. The IAF's smaller force of legacy aircraft is comprised mainly of updated MiG-21s.

China maintains a significant bomber force. The PLAAF's bomber force consists of more than eighty H-6 (Tu-16) aircraft. By modern standards, these aircraft are relatively modest in range and payload, and would have difficulty penetrating modern air defenses. The H-6 has a range of 6,000 km and can carry a 9,000-kg payload, including an air-launched version of the DH-10 cruise missile. For comparison, the U.S. B-2 bomber has a range of 11,100 km and a payload of 23,000 kg.

Although India does not possess dedicated long-range bombers, it has recently upgraded its *Jaguar* attack aircraft to enhance their ability as nuclear-strike platforms.[78] The IAF has proposed to lease three long-range Tu-22M3 *Backfire* bombers from Russia.[79] The *Backfires* have a range of

reuters.com/article/businessNews/idINIndia-56625520110428; and "U.S. 'deeply disappointed' by thumbs down to fighter jets," *The Hindu*, April 29, 2011, http://www.hindu.com/2011/04/29/stories/2011042966311500.htm

[76] On the Indian side, this includes MiG-29, SU-30, and Mirage M-2000H variants; on the Chinese side, this number includes J-10, SU-27, SU-30, and JH-10 aircraft. Numbers from IISS, *Military Balance 2008*.

[77] Some 300 SU-27/J-11 fighters may be acquired through licensed production, although disputes continue about component supply from Russia. Meanwhile, China is moving ahead with production of the J-10 and the JH-7. "Procurement, China," *Jane's Sentinel Security Assessment*, June 13, 2007.

[78] Pulkit Singh, "India Bolstering Jaguar Fleet, Phasing Out Some Older MiGs," *Journal of Electronic Defense*, October 2002.

[79] The deal is currently stalled over terms, but whether this particular arrangement is completed or not, it indicates Indian interest in long-range bombers. "Armed Forces, India," *Jane's Sentinel Security Assessment*, February 2, 2007.

Table 6.9. *China's air force 2010*

	In service	Type	NATO designation or derivative	Aircraft generation
Bomber	**~82**			
	~82	H-6A/E/H/M	Tu-16 *Badger*	1960s design, updated
Fighter	**986**			
	576	J-7 and variants	MiG-21 *Fishbed*	3
	240	J-8 and variants	Based on MiG-21 and Su-15 *Flagon*	2
	170	J-11 and variants	Su-27SK/ UBK *Flanker*	4
Fighter/ Attack	**433+**			
	73	Su-30MKK *Flanker*	Su-30MKK *Flanker*	4
	72	JH-7/JH-7A (FBC-1) *Flying Leopard*	JH-7 *Flounder*	4
	144+	J-10 *Menglong*	J-10 *Swift Dragon*	4
	24+	J-11B *Flanker*	Su-27 *Flanker*	4
	120	Q-5C/D *Fantan*	Based on MiG-19 *Farmer*	2
AEW/ AWACS	**8+**			
	4	KJ-2000	Beriev A-50 *Mainstay* (IL-76)	
	4	Y-8	An-12 *Cub*	
Tanker	**10**			
	10	HY-6	Tu-16 *Badger*	
	8	IL-78M (all are on order)	IL-78M	
Transport	**336**			
	15	B-737–200	B-737–200	
	5	CL-601 *Challenger*	CL-601 *Challenger*	
	2	IL-18 *Coot*	IL-18 *Coot*	
	18	IL-76MD *Candid* (30 more on order)	IL-76MD *Candid*	
	17	Tu-154 *Careless*	Tu-154 *Careless*	
	40	Y-8	An-12	
	20	Y-11		
	8	Y-12		
	170	Y-5	An-2 *Colt*	
	41	Y-7/Y-7H	An-24 *Coke*/An-26 *Curl*	

Source: IISS, *The Military Balance 2011*, 234.

almost 7,000 nm, can fly at supersonic speeds, and can carry a 21,000-kg payload (either bombs or stand-off missiles such as the air-launched variant of the *BrahMos*).[80] However, no such agreement had been finalized, according to public sources.

In the airlift category, Indian capabilities roughly equal those of China. The IAF has 159 aircraft capable of lifting 40 or more troops, whereas the PLAAF has 133 such aircraft, of slightly larger average capacity.[81] Based on the original specifications of these aircraft, the total one-sortie lift capacity they provide is comparable, despite the greater number of Indian aircraft: about 12,000 troops for India and approximately 13,900 for China. Given the age of most of the transports on both sides and the need to carry some equipment, actual personnel capacity would presumably be lower. The longest-range transport aircraft for both air forces are their Il-76s, with a range of 3,650 km. In 2007, India signed a deal with the United States to acquire six C-130J transport aircraft. These planes have a range of 5,250 km and capacity for up to 128 troops. Delivery of the C-130Js is scheduled to begin in 2012.[82]

China has placed orders with Russia for up to thirty more IL-76 transports. However, PLAAF plans for IL-76s and aircraft based on the IL-76 (such as IL-78 tankers and A-50/KJ-2000 AWACs) have been delayed because of production problems in Russia. (The IAF has also suffered similar delays related to Russian IL-76 production reorganization, as well as quality problems and price disputes.) India may also seek new transport aircraft. The U.S. C-17, with a larger capacity and longer range than the IL-76, is one possibility.[83] Both India and China have substantial commercial airline fleets that could, depending on circumstances, be used for military or other security-related operations. China has 823 commercial aircraft, and India has 166. The commercial aircraft fleets in both countries are growing.[84]

India and China are both actively developing force multiplier and support capabilities, including tankers and AWACS aircraft. India acquired

---

[80] "External Affairs, India," *Jane's Sentinel Security Assessment*, March 9, 2006.

[81] Chinese lift aircraft with this capacity include 15 B-737s, 2 Il-18s, 18 Il-76s, 17 Tu-154s, and 41 AN-24/26s. India's include 112 AN-32s, 24 Il-76s, 6 B-707s, 6 B-737s, and 20 BAE-748s. IISS, *Military Balance 2009*.

[82] IISS, *Military Balance 2011*, March 7, 2011, 286.

[83] IISS, *Military Balance 2009*; Gulshan Luthra, "IAF chooses Boeing's latest C-17 for heavy-lift transport aircraft," *South Asia Monitor*, June 14, 2009, accessed at http://www.southasiamonitor.org/2009/June/news/15ip1.shtml

[84] Data from http://www.airfleets.net. India used its commercial air fleet to successfully carry out one of the largest airlifts in history in 1990–1991, returning many Indians home before the outbreak of the Gulf War.

its first squadron of six Il-78 tanker aircraft in 2003. The IAF has already used them to demonstrate an extended reach, conducting refueling operations to permit nonstop flights of Su-30s from Pune (near Mumbai) to Car Nicobar in the Bay of Bengal. The Indian Il-78s are more advanced than the PLAAF's ten converted H-6 tankers. China signed a contract for a squadron of eight Il-78 tankers in September 2005, though delivery has been delayed for many years.[85] For comparative perspective, the United States operates some 475 tankers in its active and reserve components, a figure which highlights America's global posture.

India has taken delivery of two IL-76 AWACs aircraft equipped with the Israeli *Phalcon* AEW radar, with at least one more on order.[86] *Phalcon* is the same system that the United States forced Israel to refrain from selling to China in 2000. The *Phalcon* system can conduct 360-degree surveillance and manage target assignments to a range of approximately 350 nm. China, having been denied the *Phalcon*, has since acquired four Russian A-50 early warning and control aircraft (with a Chinese radar, these are designated KJ-2000). The radar performance and range, at 200–215 nm, is inferior to *Phalcon*. China also has four KJ-200 AEW aircraft, based on the domestic Y-8 transport airframe (itself a derivative of the Soviet-era An-12), also with a domestic radar. Both countries continue to explore AEW and AWACs options, including foreign and domestic designs.

The IAF's training and power projection capabilities have been significantly enhanced by several years of continuous combined training and exercises with U.S. forces. Also notable in terms of power projection capability, India has access to an air base at Farkhor in Tajikistan, about 130 kilometers (80 miles) southeast of Dushanbe, close to the Tajik-Afghan border.[87] It is the only Indian military base in a foreign country.

Nuclear Forces

Nuclear forces are strategic weapons, not power projection forces. We include a brief overview of nuclear forces here to compare relative emphasis on force modernization overall and because these forces play a role in enabling conventional power projection by acting as a final security guarantee against potential retaliation.

---

[85] "Air Force, China," *Jane's Sentinel Security Assessment*, November 7, 2005; IISS, *Military Balance 2011*, March 7, 2011, 234.

[86] IISS, *Military Balance 2009*.

[87] "Tajik air base is ready, gives India its first footprint in strategic Central Asia," *Indian Express*, February 25, 2007, http://www.indianexpress.com/news/Tajik-air-base-is-ready,-gives-India-its – first-footprint-in-strategic-Central-Asia – -/24207/

Publicly available information on Chinese and Indian nuclear-weapons programs and strategic forces is scarce, incomplete, and sometimes contradictory. Neither country makes public any detailed information about its nuclear forces or nuclear-weapons programs. Chinese nuclear weapons and delivery systems are more numerous, more varied, longer-ranged, and more advanced than India's (Table 6.10).

Both China and India are modernizing their strategic forces. Both countries appear to be focusing modernization efforts on developing credible deterrent forces that could survive a first strike. Both have lacked a credible sea-based nuclear deterrent, and both are seeking to develop this capability as it is believed to be the most survivable type of system in the event of a first strike.

Estimates of China's nuclear forces have varied widely. One standard source places the number of Chinese warheads at 240, though other estimates range from fewer than 200 to about 400.[88] Putting China in the context of the other four original nuclear-weapons states, this range compares to fewer than 160 deployed strategic nuclear warheads for the United Kingdom, about 350 for France, 4,138 for Russia, and 5,951 for the United States.[89] Under the terms of the 2010 New START treaty, Russia and the United States will be limited to 1,550 deployed nuclear warheads. Warheads in storage will not count against this limit. The size of the Chinese warhead inventory is almost certainly growing. China is also adding new ballistic missiles to its force.

Land-based strategic rocket forces of the PLA Second Artillery Corps are the backbone of China's nuclear deterrent. According to the IISS *Military Balance 2011*, China has 442 "strategic" missiles (including both conventionally armed and nuclear ballistic missiles), of which 204 are short-range ballistic missiles (SRBM). According to publicly available sources, the short-range ballistic missiles, as well as approximately thirty-six medium-range DF-21C missiles, are not believed to be dedicated to nuclear-strike missions.[90] China's strategic nuclear missile force consists of approximately

[88] Robert S. Norris & Hans M. Kristensen, "Chinese Nuclear Forces 2010," *Bulletin of the Atomic Scientists*, 66:6 (2010): 134–141; see also Anthony Cordesman and Martin Klieber, *Chinese Military Modernization: Force Development and Strategic Capabilities* (Washington, DC: Center for Strategic and International Studies, 2008), 167–182; and *Jane's Sentinel*, 2008. In 2003, the Council on Foreign Relations reported that China had between 410 and 440 nuclear weapons. See Harold Brown et al., *Chinese Military Power: Report of an Independent Task Force* (New York: Council on Foreign Relations, 2003), 51.

[89] Data from Arms Control Association, http://www.armscontrol.org

[90] Norris and Kristensen, "Chinese Nuclear Forces 2010," 139. DF-21C missiles may be dual-capable – able to carry both conventional and nuclear warheads.

Table 6.10. Chinese and Indian strategic weapons, 2010

	China					India				
	No.	Type	Range (km)	Deployed	Warheads*	No.	Type	Range (km)	Deployed	Warheads*
Land-Based										
ICBM	~10	DF-4	~5,400	1980	~10					
	20	DF-5A	~13,000	1981	20					
	~12	DF-31	~7,200	2008	~12					
	~24	DF-31A	~11,200	2008	~24					
IRBM	~2	DF-3A	3,100	1971	~2	n/a	Agni III	3,000	Testing	0
MRBM	80	DF-21	2,100	1991	80	~20–25	Agni II	2,000	Development	0
						~80–100	Agni I	700	Development	0
SRBM						~15–30	Prithvi-I***	150	1998	0
Cruise Missile	~54	DH-10	~2,000	2007(?)	~15					
Sea-Based	0	JL-1	~1,000	1986	0	0	Dhanush (naval Prithvi II, surface launched)		Development	0
	0	JL-2**	~7,200	Testing/Trials	0	0	K-15 (sub-launched cruise missile)		Development	0
Aircraft	20	H-6	3,100	1965	~20	~20	Mirage 2000H	1,800	1985	~20
						~36	Jaguar IS/IB	1,600	1981	~30
Total Warheads					~175 to 240					~60 to 80

Sources: Robert S. Norris and Hans M. Kristensen, "Nuclear Notebook: Worldwide deployments of nuclear weapons, 2009," *Bulletin of the Atomic Scientists*, 65:86 (November/December 2009); Robert S. Norris & Hans M. Kristensen, "Chinese Nuclear Forces 2010," *Bulletin of the Atomic Scientists*, 66:6 (2010): 134–141; Robert S. Norris and Hans M. Kristensen, "Indian Nuclear Forces 2010," *Bulletin of the Atomic Scientists*, 66:5 (2010): 76–81. Some data on numbers of Chinese and Indian missiles are from IISS, *The Military Balance 2011*. This table is based on publicly available information and may be incomplete.

* Both China and India appear to store nuclear warheads separately from delivery systems. There is no clarity on numbers of warheads that are fully operational.

** According to public sources, the JL-2 has not reached full operational capability as of early 2011.

*** Of India's total of ~150 Prithvi I missiles, possibly only 15 of 30 are assigned to the strategic role.

sixty-six intercontinental ballistic missiles (ICBM), two intermediate range ballistic missiles (IRBM), and eighty medium-range ballistic missiles (MRBM).[91] Beijing has undertaken significant improvements to its strategic rocket forces, including focusing on solid-fuel rockets with quick-launch capabilities, more survivable mobile missiles, greater accuracy, and missiles with longer ranges. These include new solid-fuel rockets with the ability to reach the continental United States, such as the DF-31A with a range of between 10,000 and 12,000 kilometers. Several public sources speculate that China has the ability to put multiple warheads on its missiles, although it has not been confirmed that it has done so.

The PLA Navy has three ballistic missile submarines (SSBN). Its first one, the *Xia*, has always had doubtful operational status. However, the PLAN has launched two new *Jin*-class SSBNs, with two more under construction. Each *Jin*-class SSBN is designed to carry twelve JL-2 sea-launched ballistic missiles (SLBM). In the future, the PLA Air Force may develop some nuclear-weapons capability for its H-6 bomber fleet, possibly including a nuclear-armed version of the DH-10 cruise missile.[92]

Public sources estimate that India has a total stockpile of sixty to eighty nuclear warheads, of which about fifty are operationally deployed.[93] The number of Indian nuclear warheads is expected to grow. This may be enabled in part by the U.S.-India nuclear cooperation agreement of 2008, which will allow India to dedicate scarce domestic resources (including nuclear fuel) to its military program while importing civilian fuel and technology from international suppliers.

Unlike China, which relies primarily on strategic missiles, fighter-bomber aircraft are the mainstay of India's nuclear-strike forces. IAF Jaguar IS/IB and Mirage 2000H aircraft are likely to be nuclear-weapons capable. These aircraft have a range of about 1,600 to 1,800 km and can carry payloads of up to 4,700 to 6,300 kg, respectively. Some of India's MiG-27 fighter-bombers may also be capable of nuclear-strike missions. India may seek to augment its nuclear-capable air forces, possibly by developing an air-launched cruise missile suitable for its newly purchased Su-30 fighter-bombers.

---

[91] Norris and Kristensen, "Chinese Nuclear Forces 2010," 139; IISS, *The Military Balance 2011*, 230. There is some inconsistency in categorization of missiles across different public sources. For example, in recent years, IISS appears to have modified its categorization of the DF-5 missile, to an ICBM from a previous categorization as an IRBM. IISS does not differentiate between IRBMs (typically defined as range between 3,000 km and 5,500 km), and MRBMs (typically defined as range between 1,000 km and 3,000 km).

[92] Norris and Kristensen, "Chinese Nuclear Forces 2010," 138.

[93] Norris and Kristensen, "Indian Nuclear Forces 2010," 76.

The second leg of India's nuclear dyad is comprised of land-based missile forces. According to publicly available sources, India has approximately 150 liquid-fuel *Prithvi* I and about 25 *Prithvi* II missiles with a range of about 150 kilometers. About half of the *Prithvi* I missiles may be reserved for strategic missions. New Delhi is developing and testing longer-range land-based missiles, including the *Agni* I, which has been tested and is now undergoing further operational testing, and the *Agni* II, a longer-range version of the *Agni* I. The *Agni* III missile, a solid-fuel, rail-mobile missile designed for a 3,000-km range, had mixed results in early testing. However, successful tests were conducted in 2009 and in February 2010.[94] India has yet to develop missiles with intercontinental range, although the Agni V, currently under development, will approach that range.[95]

India is also developing sea-based nuclear forces. Development programs include the ATV, the *Sagarika* missile, and potentially nuclear-armed versions of submarine-launched cruise missiles (see the Naval Forces section earlier in the chapter).[96] Like China, India will also face new command, control, operational, and safety issues if the IN puts nuclear weapons at sea.

Conventional Strategic Strike Capability

China appears to have placed relatively greater emphasis than India on conventional-strike capability (Table 6.11). In addition to the deployment of large numbers of short-range conventional ballistic missiles opposite Taiwan, China is developing missile systems that could give it a capability to launch precision conventional-weapon attacks against distant land targets and possibly even moving ships at sea.[97] These programs include a

[94] "India Successfully Tests Nuclear-Capable Missile," *New York Times*, February 7, 2010, http://www.nytimes.com/aponline/2010/02/07/world/AP-AS-India-Missile-Test.html

[95] Norris and Kristensen, "Indian Nuclear Forces 2010," 77.

[96] As with other military modernization programs, Pakistan watches India's nuclear weapons and strategic force development closely. Pakistan's Navy chief Muhammad Afzal Tahir claimed that India's test of sea-based, nuclear-capable missiles in February 2008 could start a new arms race, although Pakistan can ill-afford to conduct such an effort given its urgent domestic issues. "'India's undersea missile test may trigger arms race,'" *Times of India*, February 27, 2008, http://timesofindia.indiatimes.com/Indias_undersea_missile_test_may_trigger_arms_race/rssarticleshow/2819272.cms

[97] Roger Cliff et al., *Entering the Dragon's Lair: Chinese Anti-access Strategies and Their Implications for the United States* (Santa Monica: RAND, 2007); Office of Naval Intelligence, *The People's Liberation Army Navy: A Modern Navy with Chinese Characteristics*; Andrew Erickson and David Yang, "On the Verge of a Game Changer," *U.S. Naval Institute Proceedings*, 135:3 (May 2009): 26–32; Andrew S. Erickson and David D. Yang, "Using The Land To Control The Sea?: Chinese Analysts Consider the Antiship Ballistic Missile," *Naval War College Review*, 62:4 (Autumn 2009): 53–86; Mark Stokes, *China's Evolving*

Table 6.11. *Conventional strike: Selected missile programs circa 2010*

Name	Type	Payload	Range	Status	Est. #
India					
Prithvi I	Ballistic, road-mobile, liquid fuel	1,000 kg	150 km	Operational	~120–135
Prithvi II	Ballistic, road-mobile, liquid fuel	500 kg	250 km	Trials	~25
Prithvi III	Ballistic, ship-based, liquid fuel	unknown	350 km	Testing	–
BrahMos	Cruise, land-, sea-, air-based versions, solid booster, liquid	200 kg–300 kg	~300 km	Testing/initial deployment	–
Sagarika	Ballistic, sub-launched	600 kg	700 km	Testing	–
Shaurya	Ballistic, silo-based	~500 kg	600 km	Testing	–
Nirbhay	Cruise, land, sea-, air-based versions	unknown	~1,000 km	Development	–
China					
DF-11	Ballistic, road-mobile, solid fuel	800 kg	300 km	Operational	~700–750
DF-15	Ballistic, road-mobile, solid fuel	500 kg	600 km	Operational	~350–400
DF-21	Ballistic, road-mobile, solid fuel	500 kg	~1,750 km	Operational	~85–95
DF-21 "ASBM"	Ballistic, road-mobile, solid fuel	500 kg	1,500 km	Development	–
DH-10	Cruise, land- solid booster, turbofan (air- and sea-launched cruise missiles in development)	unknown	~2,000 nm	Operational	200–500

conventional-strike version of the DF-21 medium-range ballistic missile and cruise missiles such as the DH-10. The DH-10 has a range of roughly 2,000 km. China may already have an air-launched version of the DH-10, and it may develop submarine-launched versions. To carry out precision strikes against mobile targets (e.g., aircraft carriers), missile systems require advanced over-the-horizon (OTH) surveillance, tracking, communications, and guidance. Chinese capabilities in these areas are improving rapidly, but they are not yet sufficiently robust to provide a reliable combat capability.[98]

India's missile programs are not as well developed as China's, but India is also working on conventional-strike systems. India's primary operational short-range conventional-armed ballistic missile is the *Prithvi* I, which is operated by the Indian Army. A smaller number of Prithvi II missiles (with a slightly longer range) have been developed, primarily for the Indian Air Force. Variants with longer ranges are undergoing tests.

India is beginning to deploy a conventional/nuclear-capable cruise missile developed with Russia, called *BrahMos*. India is also developing a longer-ranged cruise missile, called *Nirbhay*.[99] In November 2008, India successfully tested two missiles that may be based on the same design, the *Sagarika* submarine-launched ballistic missile (which may be nuclear-armed), and a land-based ballistic missile, called *Shaurya*.[100] Indian missile developments are driven in large part by its views of Pakistan, which has its own ballistic- and cruise missile programs, though China's missile developments are also a factor.[101]

New missile-based conventional-strike capabilities being developed by both countries are potentially destabilizing. These systems are difficult to

---

Conventional Strategic Strike Capability: The Antiship Ballistic Missile Challenge to U.S. Maritime Operations in the Western Pacific and Beyond (Arlington: Project 2049 Institute, September 2009); and Ian Easton, *The Assassin Under the Radar: China's DH-10 Cruise Missile Program* (Arlington: Project 2049 Institute, September 2009)

[98] Eric Hagt and Matthew Durnin, "China's Antiship Ballistic Missile: Developments and Missing Links," *Naval War College Review*, 62:4 (Autumn 2009), 87–115. China has deployed operational OTH radar and is increasing the number of its imaging satellites.

[99] "BrahMos test-fired 'successfully,'" *Times of India*, March 30, 2009.

[100] "India successfully test fires Shaurya missile," *Times of India*, November 13, 2008.

[101] "Army raising a special BrahMos missile regiment," *Times of India*, April 3, 2006; "Pak's 'India-specific' nuke arsenal exposed," *Times of India*, September 1, 2009; "Agni-III, with China in range, to be tested," *Times of India*, June 20, 2009; "India's new missile is able to attack China's Harbin," *People's Daily*, October 14, 2009; "India surprised by Chinese fuss over Agni-V," *Times of India*, October 17, 2009; and "India Successfully Tests Nuclear-Capable Missile," *New York Times*, February 7, 2010, http://www.nytimes.com/aponline/2010/02/07/world/AP-AS-India-Missile-Test.html

distinguish from strategic nuclear-weapons systems, and their use or preparation for use may send confusing signals to adversaries. This could be particularly dangerous in a crisis. If conventional-strike weapons are aimed at an enemy's strategic nuclear-weapons systems, their employment or even outward mobilization could force that adversary to make a "use them or lose them" decision about the use of those strategic weapons. Further, these conventional-strike systems are themselves often dual conventional/ nuclear assets. If an adversary decides to eliminate the risk from these strike systems by attacking them or their supporting systems on the ground, those attacks may force a similar "use them or lose them" decision on the owner.

Space Capabilities

Both China and India have robust space capabilities. According to one estimate based on publicly available information, by late 2009, China had fifty-three active earth-orbiting satellites, and India had twenty-two.[102] Both countries have domestic satellite and launch vehicle programs, and both appear to have singled out space technology development as a national priority.[103] China's space program is more advanced.

Of China's fifty-three active earth-orbiting satellites at the end of 2009, twelve were dedicated to military purposes.[104] Some commercial and government satellites could potentially be used for military purposes. (For comparison, the United States was operating 435 earth-orbiting satellites, of which 111 were military, and Russia was operating 90 satellites, of which 57 were military.[105]) Not all of China's space programs are military. China has set up a civilian space agency, the China National Space Administration (CNSA), although the space program is still dominated by the PLA.[106] China's satellite program has benefited from significant foreign cooperation, particularly in its communications satellite program. Seven of China's fourteen communications satellites were developed with American contractors, including Loral, Lockheed Martin, and Boeing. China also has

---

[102] Publicly available information may be incomplete. However, a detailed satellite database is kept by the Union of Concerned Scientists. See Union of Concerned Scientists, "Satellite Database," accessed October 19, 2009, http://www.ucsusa.org/nuclear_weapons_and_global_security/space_weapons/technical_issues/ucs-satellite-database.html

[103] "India's space ambitions taking off," *Washington Post*, November 3, 2009.

[104] Based on publicly available information. See Union of Concerned Scientists, "Satellite Database."

[105] Union of Concerned Scientists, "Satellite Database."

[106] Jeffrey Logan, *China's Space Program: Options for U.S.-China Cooperation*, Congressional Research Service Report for Congress, Order Code RS22777, May 21, 2008.

three shared remote sensing and research satellites, two with Brazil and one with the European Space Agency. China also has satellite reconnaissance and surveillance capabilities.

China is developing a range of counterspace capabilities. These anti-satellite (ASAT) weapons include jammers that could impede the function of satellites, lasers that could blind or "dazzle" them, and kinetic kill vehicles that could shoot down satellites in low earth orbit. Most of these capabilities are in the research or development stages, though in some cases, research systems could be employed in actual military operations. In January 2007, a Chinese ballistic missile launched from a mobile transport/launch platform carried a "kinetic kill vehicle" into low earth orbit, intercepting and destroying a Chinese weather satellite. This sparked an intense international reaction.[107]

India has also concentrated more on space applications than exploration, with its main emphasis thus far on technologies to support economic development. India has a fledgling space exploration program and has also developed a commercial satellite launch business. Indian leaders acknowledge competition with China as a motivator for this science and exploration program.[108]

The Indian Space Research Organisation (ISRO), under the Department of Space (DOS) focuses on developing civilian use satellites for remote sensing applications such as meteorology, disaster relief, and communications. ISRO also operates India's commercial satellite launch program. India's missiles are designed and built by the Defence Research Development Organization (DRDO) under the Ministry of Defence.[109] DRDO and ISRO have separate mandates, although they have cooperated on joint programs.[110]

---

[107] Bruce W. MacDonald, *China, Space Weapons, and U.S. Security*, Special Report No. 38, Council on Foreign Relations, September 2008; Ashley J. Tellis, "China's Military Space Strategy," *Survival*, 49:3 (September 2007), 41–72; Phillip C. Saunders and Charles D. Lutes, "China's ASAT Test: Motivations and Implications," Institute for National Strategic Studies Special Report, National Defense University, June 2007; Larry M. Wortzel, *The Chinese People's Liberation Army and Space Warfare: Emerging United States-China Military Competition*, American Enterprise Institute, October 2007; Ashley J. Tellis, "Punching the U.S. Military's 'Soft Ribs': China's Antisatellite Weapon Test in Strategic Perspective," Carnegie Endowment, June 2007.

[108] "India Launches Unmanned Orbiter to Moon," *New York Times*, October 22, 2008.

[109] DRDO has been the subject of much criticism for inefficiency and ineffectiveness, including in government of India evaluations. See Stephen P. Cohen and Sunil Dasgupta, *Arming without Aiming: India's Military Modernization* (Washington, DC: Brookings Institution Press, 2010), 32–36.

[110] The United States applied sanctions on ISRO in the early 1990s for missile technology proliferation.

By late 2009, three of India's twenty-two active satellites were dedicated to military use. Compared to China's satellite program, India has had less foreign cooperation: Only one of its satellites (a military satellite) was developed with a foreign contractor. India has sometimes used foreign launch vehicles, primarily Ariane rockets. Until recently, India has not emphasized military applications in space. Instead, most Indian military space applications have depended on using India's civilian satellites and launch capabilities.[111] However, several factors have caused India to accelerate development of its military space capabilities, including concerns about terrorist infiltrations after the Mumbai terror attacks in late 2008, and renewed lobbying by the IAF for the space mission.[112] Statements by Indian officers on the military applications of space capabilities (including reconnaissance satellites) indicate that Kashmir and border areas with Pakistan are the main focus for the Indian military, although presumably these capabilities would also be useful on India's other border areas.[113]

India's near-term focus appears to be on military reconnaissance satellites and space-based communications (in other words, space support for terrestrial operations). India is, however, embarking on the development of a counterspace capability. This move has been spurred in part by New Delhi's fears that it will be left permanently behind if the international community moves to control the further development or testing anti-satellite or military space weapons. That fear was heightened by evidence of Chinese and U.S. advances, marked in part by the 2007 Chinese ASAT test and the early 2008 U.S. shoot-down of a defunct American satellite in a decaying orbit.

Conclusions: Force Modernization

China and India devote similar levels of effort toward military force modernization. This is a notable finding given China's relatively larger economy. Many of the focus areas for modernization are also similar. Both countries have used large-scale imports to improve advanced air, sea, strike, and support capabilities. Both are developing advanced domestically produced

---

[111] Guiney, "India's Space Ambitions"; "India takes on old rival China in new Asian space race," *The Times of London*, June 20, 2008, http://www.timesonline.co.uk/tol/news/world/asia/article4182216.ece

[112] "India takes on old rival China in new Asian space race"; Guiney, "India's Space Ambitions"; Vincent G. Sabathier and G. Ryan Faith, *India's Space Program*, Center for Strategic and International Studies, January 25, 2008.

[113] K. K. Nair, *Space the Frontiers of Modern Defense* (New Delhi: Knowledge World, 2006), cited in Guiney, "India's Space Ambitions."

weapons systems. In this regard, China has seen greater success, particularly in ballistic missiles, submarines, and fighter aircraft. Despite a significant budgetary gap, Indian power projection capabilities are roughly comparable to China's in a number of areas. In some cases, such as in aircraft carriers and long-distance naval patrols, India's capabilities are superior. However, there are important differences in Chinese and Indian force modernization programs.

In India, force modernization generally has followed doctrinal development, which is left to the individual military services and, in comparison to China, lacks tight coordination. Both interservice and civilian-military coordination is weak in India.[114] Indian doctrine emphasizes offense, expeditionary capability, and a wide geographical area of potential operations, from the Persian Gulf to the Malacca Straits. Despite its relatively weaker material capabilities, India is more readily inclined to see itself as both a regional and global great power in need of requisite power projection capabilities. India also sees its power projection forces (especially its navy) as a key component of its regional diplomacy. In comparison, China appears more cautious, without a grand vision about the role its modernizing military forces might play beyond Taiwan. However, the dispatch of PLAN forces to antipiracy patrols off the coast of Somalia, and the new emphasis on military operations other than war mentioned in China's January 2009 Defense White Paper, suggest that Beijing is beginning to develop a vision of the role of military forces in diplomacy.

Indian leaders have treated India's nuclear-weapons program primarily as a prestige- and autonomy-enhancing capability. However, like China, India is working to develop a more effective, diverse, and survivable minimum deterrent. Both countries have developed some ballistic missile-based conventional-strike capability. China has made greater progress in this area. Relative to China, India has weaker industrial manufacturing capabilities, and India experiences significant political and bureaucratic disputes and delays in implementing procurement and force modernization programs.[115]

---

[114] Stephen P. Cohen and Sunil Dasgupta, *Arming without Aiming: India's Military Modernization*, 143–157.

[115] A number of Indian strategists argue that political, bureaucratic, and military interests face perennial misalignment in India, with negative impact on the integration of grand strategy, doctrine, and foreign policy, as well as implementation of force modernization plans and budget spending. See, for example, comments by of C. Uday Bhaskar, former director of New Delhi's Institute for Defence Studies and Analyses (IDSA), and Ajai Sahni of New Delhi's Institute for Conflict Management in Bappa Majumdar, "India's defence budget rises, but problems remain," *Reuters India*, February 29, 2008, http://in.reuters.

Most aspects of China's force modernization appear to fit its military doctrine closely. China is improving offensive forces generally, with a heavy focus on Taiwan and power projection capability in the air- and sea-space around Taiwan and the approaches to Taiwan. This pattern fits the Chinese grand strategy and foreign policy outlined in Chapter 3. Offensive capabilities provide a powerful deterrent against a Taiwanese move toward de jure independence. In the future, military modernization may provide China with greater offensive options against Taiwan, although the prospect of possible war with the United States will remain a powerful restraining influence on China's thinking. China's military is clearly embracing both new missions and military diplomacy. These will provide incentives to acquire lift and support capabilities that will contribute to power projection.[116]

Another important difference is that China's military modernization includes development of access denial capabilities such as new submarines, antisatellite weapons, cruise missiles, and conventionally armed ballistic missiles (including systems potentially capable of hitting moving ships at sea). These could directly challenge U.S. forces in a Taiwan-related crisis, and they could also present challenges to the United States and its allies in the event of escalation of maritime disputes in Asia.[117] Even absent a crisis, continuing preparations on both sides could intensify Sino-U.S. security competition.

Ironically, further intensive development of some of these capabilities could undermine a central aim of China's own foreign policy: avoiding anti-China balancing that could undermine China's goal of focusing on economic and social development. Beijing's focus on anti-access capabilities aimed at American aircraft carriers and Asian air bases is not a panacea for Chinese security. China remains vulnerable to alternative responses from

com/article/topNews/idININdia-32228720080229. Similar arguments by Indian analysts can be found in papers by leading Indian policy research institutes such as IDSA and Institute for Peace and Conflict Studies.

[116] On Chinese military diplomacy, see 肖天亮[Xiao Tianliang], 《军事力量的非战争运用》 [The Non-War Use of Military Power], (Beijing: National Defense University Press, 2009); 王明武, 常永志, 徐戈, 章楠 [Wang Mingwu, Chang Yongzhi, Xu Ge, Zhang Nan], 《非战争军事行动》 [Non-War Military Activities], (Beijing: National Defense University Press, 2006); "2006年9月22日曹刚川出席全军外事工作会议时提出: 研究军事外交战略, 深化对外军事合作," [Cao Gangchuan said at the September 22, 2006 PLA Foreign Affairs Conference: "Study Military Diplomacy, Deepen Foreign Military Cooperation"], 新华社 [Xinhua News], September 23, 2006.

[117] For a comprehensive analysis of the implications of Chinese military developments for American strategic interests in Asia, see Michael D. Swaine, *America's Challenge: Engaging a Rising China in the Twenty-First Century* (Washington, DC: Carnegie Endowment for International Peace, 2011), especially 147–182.

the United States that might raise the overall cost of security for China.[118] Even more worrisome, a number of the potential defenses and counter-measures the United States and its allies (such as Japan) could develop to counter growing Chinese anti-access capabilities might also pose a latent threat to China's nuclear deterrent or its strategic surveillance and intelligence assets.[119]

New Delhi's efforts to upgrade its power projection forces – in line with its offense-oriented military doctrines – could also pose problems for American interests. India is procuring additional aircraft carriers, more modern surface ships and submarines, modern maritime patrol aircraft, and new fighter-bomber aircraft. Indian force modernization has benefited from U.S. weapons sales and combined training with U.S. forces and may also benefit from U.S. technology transfer. Together with support capabilities such as air-to-air refueling and AWACS, these will give India the ability to deploy naval and air "expeditionary forces," as called for in Indian doctrines. In theory this could provide the basis for mutually beneficial combined deployments and operations with U.S. forces (although there remain formidable political obstacles in India to such combined operations).

However, Indian force modernization could exacerbate security dilemmas in South Asia and potentially beyond. For example, India's recent development of an air base in Tajikistan appears to come primarily in the context of New Delhi's ongoing competition with Islamabad for influence in Afghanistan.[120] Major changes to the balance of power in the region, combined with more offense-oriented doctrinal changes, could spark responses from India's rivals, such as Pakistan or China, that are inimical to American interests.

There are also potentially positive aspects to Chinese and Indian military force modernization. More capable Chinese and Indian forces may improve the potential for cooperation in collective security, as has already happened with antipiracy operations off Somalia. These operations have seen extensive

---

[118] These could include shifting the role of aircraft carrier battle groups while leveraging the capabilities of land-based aircraft, submarines, and other ships, and developing longer-range antiaircraft and strike weapons. Other options for the U.S. could include highly cost-effective, difficult-to-counter strategies such as a maritime blockade using naval mines against mainland Chinese ports.

[119] Cliff et al., *Entering the Dragon's Lair*, 104–105; 107. Options that have been discussed or are under development include highly capable anti–ballistic missile defenses (including airborne ABM systems), systems for tracking and striking mobile missile launchers on the ground, and antisatellite weapons as part of missile defense.

[120] See Rajat Pandit, "Indian Forces Get Foothold in Central Asia," *Times of India*, July 17, 2007, http://timesofindia.indiatimes.com/India/Indian_forces_get_foothold_in_Central_Asia/articleshow/2208676.cms

communication and de facto cooperation between Western, Indian, and Chinese forces, despite being formally independent deployments. Both militaries already participate actively in a wide range of UN-sponsored peacekeeping missions. India has shown it is capable of supporting significant humanitarian assistance and disaster relief missions with its naval and military forces, and China's growing capabilities could also open the potential for such cooperation.[121] Somewhat paradoxically, force modernization and the acquisition of new weapons may reveal that all major powers in Asia have a common interest in increased security dialogue, potentially including both conventional and nuclear arms control discussions.

---

[121] Writings on the new Chinese "Type 920" hospital ship, for example, suggest that it will be used for disaster relief as well as in operational military applications.

7

Economic Strategic Behavior

Trade and Energy

The West is nervously puzzled by the nature of rising Chinese and Indian economic might. In the space of a few months, pundits seem as likely to produce book titles that proclaim the coming "Indian Century" and the looming prospect of a China that "Rules the World" as they are to produce headlines warning that China and India are "Two Vulnerable Economies" facing a potential "Economic Crash."[1] How each country negotiates its domestic political-economic vulnerabilities over the near and medium term will largely determine their respective potential for global economic leadership. The way Beijing and New Delhi manage their economies will also influence their relations with trading partners, including the United States.

India and China have each undertaken programs of economic reforms and opening aimed at promoting domestic development and rising national power. Reforms and opening have produced stunning economic results. Perhaps the most important of these are rising household incomes and poverty alleviation in both countries. Greater wealth also provides greater resources that can be devoted to security and other international goals. However, despite their rapidly growing economies, both China and India will likely remain preoccupied powers for decades to come. Entering the second decade of the twenty-first century, they remain poor or at best modestly developed countries on a per-capita basis and face potential social and political turmoil as a result of domestic development imbalances.

---

[1] Kamal Nath, *India's Century: The Age of Entrepreneurship in the World's Biggest Democracy* (New York: McGraw-Hill, 2007); Martin Jacques, *When China Rules the World: The End of the Western World and the Birth of a New Global Order* (New York: Penguin Press, 2009); "China and India: Suddenly Vulnerable," *The Economist*, December 11, 2008, http://www.economist.com/node/12773135; and "Contrarian Investor Sees Economic Crash in China," *New York Times*, January 7, 2010.

These problems consume the lion's share of leadership attention in each country. Domestic challenges make New Delhi and Beijing cautious about the pace of further reforms, but they also provide powerful incentives to continue with reform and global economic integration. Domestic vulnerabilities are also likely to draw limits around the ability of China and India to influence the international system – both in terms availability of resources and leadership attention as well as appetite for risk.[2]

Growing bilateral trade and investment opportunities are a core element of U.S. common interest with both countries. As the leading power in the international system, the United States also enjoys significant indirect benefits from the role China and India play as active participants in a rules-based, relatively open international trade and financial system. These indirect benefits include the rising powers' general acceptance of liberal institutions for global economic governance, implicit reinforcement of American economic leadership, and the continued leading role of the U.S. dollar.

However, rising Chinese and Indian economic power has also contributed to international trade and investment disputes. The United States has been vexed by a large and growing bilateral trade deficit with China. Washington has also criticized China's currency policy, which is seen to contribute to that imbalance. Many trading partners have complained about market access and barriers to investment and trade in both China and India. The growing Chinese and Indian economies have also placed new demands on global commodities markets, contributing to rising prices, market volatility, and fears about continued access to resources such as oil and gas supplies.

In this chapter, we compare Chinese and Indian international economic behavior. In the first part, we compare the two economies in terms of economic scale, international trade and direct investment, and bilateral trade relations with the United States. In the second part, we compare Chinese and Indian competition for international energy resources. In this we include their dealings with unsavory regimes with which the United States does not do business, such as Iran, Sudan, and Myanmar.

Economy, Trade, and Investment

China and more recently India have both enjoyed sustained periods of high economic growth since each began market reforms. Both have become

---

[2]   On the limits of China's ability to take on international economic leadership, see Elizabeth C. Economy and Adam Segal, "The G2 Mirage," *Foreign Affairs*, 88:3 (May/June 2009).

major players in international trade, as well as targets for substantial foreign direct investment. Reforms and greater integration with the global economy were initiated more than a decade apart, in December 1978 for China, and July 1991 for India.[3] However, the leadership in both countries made the decision to liberalize economic policy for similar reasons. Each faced domestic economic stagnation and thus potential social and political crisis. Leaders in Beijing and in New Delhi also came to believe that renewed economic development was necessary to maintain sufficient military power and diplomatic influence for security.

Economic Growth and Domestic Preoccupations

The two countries started at about the same level of development in 1980, but by 2010, the Chinese economy was four times the size of the Indian economy at market exchange rates. Table 7.1 provides a snapshot of the two economies in 2010, with some comparisons to the United States for additional context. China's twelve-year head start on economic reforms may account for much of the difference in recent Chinese and Indian development performance.[4] Over the period from 1980 to 2010, China's compound annual average real GDP growth rate was 10.1 percent. India's compound annual average growth rate was 6.2 percent over the same period.

According to International Monetary Fund estimates, at the end of 2010, China's GDP was nearly $5.8 trillion and India's GDP was about $1.43 trillion at market exchange rates.[5] At market exchange rates, Chinese GDP/capita was about $4,280 in 2010, and India's GDP/capita about $1,180. At purchasing power parity (PPP) exchange rates, China's 2010 GDP/capita was about $7,500 and India's GDP/capita was about 3,300.[6] United States GDP/capita was more than $47,000 in 2010.

China's head start on market reforms and the resulting divergence in the size of the two economies could have long-lasting consequences. India may

---

[3] Although both countries saw some earlier periods of economic experimentation, the initiation of breakthrough market reform programs can be traced to December 1978 in China and July 1991 in India. On China, see Barry Naughton, *Growing Out of the Plan: Chinese Economic Reform 1978–1993* (New York: Cambridge University Press, 1995), 74–76. On India, see Arvind Panagariya, *India: The Emerging Giant* (New York: Oxford University Press, 2008), 103–109.

[4] Arthur Kroeber, "China & India: Friends, Rivals, or Just Two Different Countries?" Dragonomics Research & Advisory, Presentation to British Chamber of Commerce Beijing, April 2, 2008.

[5] Market exchange rates are more appropriate for comparing relative international trade, financial, industrial, and military power and capability. See Chapter 4 and Appendix.

[6] PPP exchange rates are appropriate for comparing total domestic production and relative living standards across countries. See Chapter 4 and Appendix.

Table 7.1. *2010 snapshot: Population and economy*

	India	China	United States
Population (billion persons)	1.22	1.34	0.31
GDP (billion current USD)	1,430	5,745	14,624
GDP per capita (current USD)	1,176	4,283	47,132
GDP (PPP, billion USD)	4,001	10,084	14,624
GDP per capita (PPP USD)	3,291	7,518	47,132

Source: International Monetary Fund, *World Economic Outlook Database*, October 2010.

soon reach or even surpass GDP growth rates in China. Nevertheless, based on reasonable expectations for GDP growth and barring crises in either country, China's economy could still be about three times larger than the Indian economy in 2030.[7]

Yet with significant domestic risks in both countries, it is unlikely that either will see a smooth, linear pattern of growth in coming decades. Even as India and China gain influence in international trade and in geopolitics, the leadership in both countries will be obliged to focus on domestic economic, social, and political challenges for many years.

At the broadest level, both countries have populations with rapidly rising expectations but with current standards of living that remain low or at best modest for all but a privileged few. The United Nations compiles an international index of human development that illustrates the challenge. It considers factors including health, education, incomes, inequality, the incidence of poverty, and social stability. According to that human development index, of 169 countries, China ranked 89th and India 119th in 2010.[8]

[7] A reasonable long-term outlook for GDP growth would see China's real annual GDP growth rate of about 10.5 percent in 2010 decline to about 6 percent by 2020, and about 5 percent in 2030. Similarly, a reasonable outlook for India would see real GDP growth of more than 8 percent per annum in 2010 remain at that level (or somewhat higher) for much of the next decade, then decline to about 6 percent from 2020, and to slightly more than 5 percent by 2030. In the long run, both countries will tend to slow down from recent high rates of growth, as the relatively easy returns from initial reforms and investments are secured. Over the next decade, India may grow relatively faster than China, reflecting both China's maturing economy and India's relatively later entry into a period of reform and rapid growth. However, business cycles and potential political, social, or economic crises could also affect the outlook for both countries.

[8] See World Bank, *2010 World Development Indicators* (Washington, DC: World Bank, 2010); and United Nations, *Human Development Report 2010: The Real Wealth of Nations: Pathways to Human Development* (New York: United Nations, 2010). For a detailed analysis of urban living standards, see UN-Habitat, *State of the World's Cities 2008/2009 – Harmonious Cities* (New York: United Nations, October 2008).

Poverty alleviation has been the most important overall achievement secured by recent growth in both countries.[9] China reduced poverty levels from 84 percent of its population in 1981 to about 16 percent in 2005. India reduced poverty from about 60 percent of its population in 1981 to about 42 percent of its population in 2005. [10] Nevertheless, in absolute terms, this means a great number of people are still living in poverty in both countries. According to the United Nations, in 2005, the population living on less than the equivalent of $1.25 per day amounted to more than 500 million people in India and more than 200 million people in China.[11]

Beyond poverty, both countries face other severe challenges including growing disparities of wealth, growth and investment imbalances, environmental degradation, and official corruption.[12] China is in the midst of a historic urbanization process, and India may be on the cusp of one. The rural-urban transformation will put pressure on both governments to deal with socially and politically sensitive issues such as land reform and the integration of rural migrants into urban society. Governments in both countries already struggle to provide adequate employment, education, health care, social welfare, and public services.[13]

Demographic trends will make resolving these issues more difficult.[14] China's population is aging. India will see a growing youth and working-age

[9] Shaohua Chen and Martin Ravallion, "The Developing World Is Poorer than We Thought, but No Less Successful in the Fight against Poverty," Development Research Group, World Bank, August 26, 2008.

[10] Martin Ravallion, "A Comparative Perspective on Poverty Reduction in Brazil, China and India," Policy Research Working Paper 5080, World Bank, October 2009.

[11] United Nations, *International Human Development Indicators 2010*, http://hdrstats.undp.org

[12] For an overview of imbalances, risks, and government "accountability gaps" in both economies, see Pranab Bardhan, *Awakening Giants: Feet of Clay* (Princeton: Princeton University Press, 2010). Environmental damage is economically and socially disruptive in both countries. See Elizabeth C. Economy, *The River Runs Black: The Environmental Challenge to China's Future* (Ithaca, NY: Cornell University Press, 2004); and Elizabeth Economy, "Asia's Water Security Crisis: China, India, and the United States," in Ashley J. Tellis, Mercy Kuo, and Andrew Marble eds., *Strategic Asia 2008–2009: Challenges and Choices* (Seattle, WA: National Bureau of Asian Research, 2008), 365–390.

[13] Shubham Chaudhuri and Martin Ravallion, "Partially Awakened Giants: Uneven Growth in China and India," in L. Alan Winters and Shahid Yusuf, eds., *Dancing With Giants: China, India, and the Global Economy* (Washington, DC: World Bank, 2007), 175–210.

[14] Richard Jackson et al., *The Graying of the Great Powers: Demography and Geopolitics in the 21st Century* (Washington, DC: Center for Strategic and International Studies, 2008); Julie DaVanzo, Harun Dogo, and Clifford Grammich, "Demographic dividend or demographic drag?: A net assessment of population trends in China and India, 2020–2025, and their implications," paper presented at International Union for Scientific Study of Population Seminar on Demographics and Macroeconomic Performance, Paris, France,

population. Demographic shifts will be relatively abrupt in China, but smoother in India.[15] In China, dependency ratios will begin to increase as early as 2012 and old-age dependency will become pronounced by 2030 – just as China becomes a middle-income country but before it reaches high per-capita income levels.[16] An aging population could drag growth down from recent high levels. An older population will also require greater resource allocation for pensions and health care. India's population is younger, and this wave of youthful workers could contribute a "demographic dividend" to growth in India.[17] However, Indian labor market experts argue that as much as 40 percent of India's youth bulge will be comprised of poorly educated people from impoverished regions.[18] India will need to devote greater resources and attention to education, the creation of entry-level jobs, and affordable urban housing.

Both economies are also vulnerable to business cycles, investment bubbles, and inflation. In some ways, China and India are more vulnerable to economic volatility than advanced economies because of their relatively weaker social safety nets and concerns about social stability. Integration with the global economy through increased trade and investment will help promote continued growth, but leaders in New Delhi and Beijing are keenly aware that international trade and financial flows are also potential sources of instability.

International Trade, Foreign Direct Investment, and Trade Disputes

China plays a larger role in global trade and investment than India. China conducted nearly $2.5 trillion in total international trade in 2009. By the end of 2009, China was the world's largest exporter of merchandise.[19] At the same time, China was the world's second-largest merchandise importer. Between 2007 and 2009, China's total international trade was equivalent to nearly 60 percent of its GDP.

June 4–5, 2010; Markus Jaeger, "Demographic outlook for BRIC countries differs sharply," Deutsche Bank Talking Point, February 26, 2010.

[15] DaVanzo et al., 13–16.

[16] Jackson et al., 171; DaVanzo et al., 16; Helen (Hong) Qiao, "Will China Grow Old Before Getting Rich?" Goldman Sachs Global Economics Paper 138, February 14, 2006.

[17] Navi Radjou, "Can India Reap Its Demographic Dividend?" Harvard Business Review Blog, 10:43 A.M. Tuesday, November 10, 2009, http://blogs.hbr.org/radjou/2009/11/can-india-reap-its-demographic.html#

[18] TeamLease and Indian Institute of Job-Oriented Training, *India Labour Report 2009*, June 2010.

[19] China has overtaken Germany to become the world's largest exporter, accounting for about 10 percent of world exports. "China Trade Review," GavKalDragonomics, Dragonomics Advisory Services, January 2011, 4.

India's total international trade in 2009, at $580 billion, was less than one-quarter the size of China's total trade. Although it is only a medium-sized exporter of goods, India is a relatively large exporter of services to the global economy.[20] India accounted for slightly more than 1 percent of total world exports in 2009, but it accounted for nearly 3 percent of total world services exports.[21] Between 2007 and 2009, India's total international trade was equivalent to about 46 percent of Indian GDP. Table 7.2 shows a comparison of Chinese and Indian international trade in 2009.[22] Data for the United States is provided for additional context.

The pattern of China's international trade differs from India's, and it also differs from that of other East Asian countries that preceded China on the path to rapid economic growth, such as Japan and South Korea. With the help of policies that encouraged foreign direct investment and export processing, China has become highly integrated with the global manufacturing and technology supply chains that emerged in Asia from the 1980s onward. Reflecting the depth of these links, about 60 percent of China's total exports are accounted for by foreign-invested firms operating in China, many engaged in the import of parts and components for processing, assembly, and reexport.[23] In addition to imported component technologies, most of these firms also use imported designs, software, and manufacturing equipment.[24] In contrast to China's mix of capital-intensive and labor-intensive exports, Indian exports have been dominated by capital-intensive and skill-intensive goods such as iron and steel products and jewelry, with relatively smaller exports from labor-intensive sectors such as light manufacturing.[25]

---

[20] There are some signs that India could become a larger player in manufactured goods trade in the future. Although still far behind China, India has been rapidly increasing its imports of capital equipment, a necessary precursor to increased manufacturing capability. See Philip Wyatt, "India: A Sea Change for Trade?" UBS Investment Research South Asia Focus, April 26, 2011.

[21] India's success in services industries may not be sufficient to drive India's continued overall growth. Less than 1 percent of Indian workers are employed in India's information technology services sector. See Bardhan, *Awakening Giants: Feet of Clay*, 6–7.

[22] As of early 2011, the most recent complete WTO annual data on trade are for 2009. Where available, we have provided more recent data in the text.

[23] People's Republic of China State Administration of Customs, Customs Statistics, http://www.customs.gov.cn/publish/portal0/

[24] On China's place in the global technological and industrial system and how this affects Western economic and corporate interests, see Edward S. Steinfeld, *Playing Our Game: Why China's Rise Doesn't Threaten the West* (New York: Oxford University Press, 2010).

[25] Panagariya, 259–266.

Table 7.2. *International trade, 2009*

Million 2009 USD except where noted	India	China	United States
Merchandise Trade			
Merchandise exports, f.o.b.	162,613	1,201,534	1,056,043
Merchandise imports, c.i.f.	249,590	1,005,688	1,605,296
Share in world total merchandise exports (%)	1.30	9.62	8.45
Services Trade			
Commercial services exports	87,434	128,600	473,899
Commercial services imports	79,774	158,200	330,590
Share in world total services exports (%)	2.61	3.84	14.15
Total Trade			
Exports	250,047	1,330,134	1,529,942
Imports	329,364	1,163,888	1,935,885
Balance	−79,317	166,246	−405,943
Trade-to-GDP ratio (2007–2009) (%)	46	59	27

Source: World Trade Organization.

Partly as a result of its role in manufacturing assembly and reprocessing trade, China runs a large trade surplus. China's current account surplus was about 4.7 percent of its GDP in 2010, down from its recent peak of 8.7 percent of GDP in 2007.[26] A current account surplus equivalent to about 4 percent of GDP is similar to the highest levels reached by Japan in the mid-1980s (about 4.4 percent).[27] However, China's trade surplus is qualitatively different from the trade surpluses of Japan in its heyday. In addition to exporting final assembled products, Japan was (and still is) a large exporter of high-value-added producer goods such as manufacturing equipment and intermediate goods such as advanced semiconductors, touch screens, and automotive and aerospace components.[28] Although it

[26] The current account is the sum of the balance of trade, net factor income (such as interest and dividends), and net transfer payments (such as foreign aid). China's large trade surplus accounts for the lion's share of its current account surplus. Likewise for India, a large trade deficit contributes to the overall current account deficit. International Monetary Fund, *World Economic Outlook Database*, October 2010, http://www.imf.org/external/pubs/ft/weo/2010/02/weodata/index.aspx. The 2007–2010 decline in China's overall current account surplus is partly attributable to rising domestic investment and consumption in China, as well as rising imports. "Dragon Week," GavKalDragonomics, Dragonomics Advisory Services, January 17, 2011; "China Trade Review," GavKalDragonomics, Dragonomics Advisory Services, January 2011, 4.

[27] Bela Belassa and Marcus Noland, *Japan in the World Economy* (Washington, DC: Institute for International Economics, 1988), 77.

[28] On the Chinese technological and economic development model in comparison to Japan and other northeast Asian industrial economies, see Arthur Kroeber, "Developmental

is improving incrementally, China remains at the tail end of many global production chains, engaged in relatively low-value-added processing and assembly of components sourced from other countries.[29]

Standard measures of bilateral merchandise trade flows are misleading.[30] Official statistics measure trade in terms of the total value of final goods for export.[31] The Apple iPhone can be used as an example to illustrate some of these issues. The estimated total cost of an Apple iPhone assembled in and exported from China in 2009 was about $179 dollars.[32] Standard trade statistics do not capture the fact that China contributed only 3.6 percent of the total cost of the phone, while components imported from Japan, Germany, and Korea then assembled in China accounted for nearly two-thirds of the total costs of the phone.[33] Instead, official trade data assign the entire value of the finally assembled phone to China's exports when accounting for the balance of trade. Nothing is recorded against Japan's bilateral trade account with the United States, despite the fact that Japanese components in iPhones imported by the United States are valued at roughly ten times the value added from China. Given China's position at the end of many global production chains, bilateral trade statistics tend to provide a systematically inflated picture of China as a source of U.S. imports. Bilateral trade data also paint a distorted picture of the balance of global production and leadership in technology, and the benefits from trade overall.

Dreams: Policy and Reality in China's Economic Reforms," in Scott Kennedy, ed., *Beyond the Middle Kingdom: Comparative Perspectives on China's Capitalist Transformation* (Stanford: Stanford University Press, 2011), 44–65. For further comparison, see the definitive account of the rise of Japan's technological and industrial system: Richard J. Samuels, *"Rich Nation, Strong Army": National Security and the Technological Transformation of Japan* (Ithaca: Cornell University Press, 1994).

[29] China faces numerous obstacles to becoming a technological innovation and global industrial leader, despite ambitious government policies. Still, Chinese firms have made incremental technological and industrial advances. See Dan Breznitz and Michael Murphree, *Run of the Red Queen: Government, Innovation, Globalization, and Economic Growth in China* (New Haven: Yale University Press, 2011).

[30] Andreas Maurer and Christophe Degain, "Globalization and trade flows: what you see is not what you get!" World Trade Organization Staff Working Paper ERSD-2010–12, June 2010.

[31] These include data reported by the U.S. government and international organizations such as the WTO and the United Nations.

[32] See Andrew Rassweiler, "iSuppli Apple iPhone 3G S 16GB Teardown Analysis," iSuppli Press Release, June 24, 2009; Yuqing Xing and Neal Detert, "How the iPhone Widens the United States Trade Deficit with the People's Republic of China," ADBI Working Paper Series No. 257, Asian Development Bank Institute, December 2010.

[33] Components from Japan (34%), Germany (17%), and Korea (13%) comprised about 64% of the value of the phone. See Rassweiler, "iSuppli Apple iPhone 3G S 16GB Teardown Analysis."

American companies contributed components accounting for about 6 percent of the total costs of the iPhone – more than the value added during assembly in China.[34] A study by the Asian Development Bank has shown that if trade data were collected on a value-added basis – adjusting the national trade accounts for the origin and value of intermediate goods comprising a final product – the $1.9 billion U.S. deficit with China in iPhone-related trade would actually become a $48 million surplus.[35] Another study by the World Trade Organization (WTO) estimated that if value-added trade data were used instead of current methods of trade accounting, China's overall bilateral trade surplus with the United States would be lowered by 21 percent.[36]

China's deliberate policy of attracting foreign direct investment contributed to the emergence of the pattern of trade described earlier. Many foreign investments have been aimed at establishing manufacturing operations in China as a platform for exports to other markets. Between 1995 and 2005, foreign direct investment (FDI) flows into China averaged $48.8 billion per year.[37] In 2009, China attracted $95 billion in FDI. India opened up to FDI later and moved slower once it began opening. Between 1995 and 2005, India averaged about $4 billion per year in FDI.[38] Foreign direct investment has increased rapidly in India, however, with more than $34 billion of FDI going to India in 2009.

In addition to its effect on the composition of trade through globalized production, FDI can also affect a nation's trade policy preferences and overall trade openness. Foreign investment helps create constituencies within the recipient country – including firms, banks, investors, and employees – that have an ongoing interest in freer trade and investment. These groups want relatively free trade and investment policies to maintain access to international markets as well as sources of capital, components, services, and equipment.

---

[34] Although not strictly related to balance of trade, it is also worth noting that the phone's designer and software provider, U.S.-based Apple, had a profit margin on an iPhone estimated to be between 55% and 65% in 2009. This is an indicator of some of the relative benefits from globalized production and international trade regardless of trade balances. See Andreas Maurer and Christophe Degain, "Globalization and trade flows," June 2010.

[35] Xing and Detert, 5.

[36] Maurer and Degain, 20–21.

[37] UN Conference on Trade and Development, *World Investment Report 2010, Country Fact Sheet: China*, July 22, 2010, http://www.unctad.org

[38] UN Conference on Trade and Development, *World Investment Report 2010, Country Fact Sheet: India*, July 22, 2010, http://www.unctad.org

Table 7.3. *Inward foreign direct investment*

	India	China	Japan	United States
Total FDI stock 2009 (Million current USD)	163,959	473,083	200,141	3,120,583
Total FDI stock as share of GDP (%)	12.9	10.1	3.9	21.9

Source: UN Conference on Trade and Development.

A lack of receptiveness to FDI was a primary U.S. complaint about the developmental model pursued by other East Asian states, especially Japan and South Korea, during the decades when they were undergoing their most rapid growth. In this regard, China and, to a lesser extent, India have broken with the East Asian model and opened their economies to global investors (Table 7.3).[39] According to UN data, by 2009, India's $164 billion stock of FDI had already surpassed Korea's FDI stock of $111 billion and was approaching the level of Japan's $200 billion.[40] China's stock of FDI in 2009 was nearly $1.4 trillion if Hong Kong ($912 billion) and Macao ($13 billion) are included. The total stock of FDI in mainland China alone was more than $473 billion in 2009.[41] Proportional to the size of their economies, FDI in both India and China has been significantly greater than FDI in South Korea and Japan.

By many indicators, China is more open to trade and investment than India, although India has been opening rapidly. The broadest gauges of

[39] Competition for foreign direct investment access and its effect on domestic protectionist policies in rival markets is underexamined in the Chinese case. Studies of Japan revealed that Japan's relative closure to FDI in the 1970s and 1980s was a key enabling factor for its trade protectionism in the 1980s and 1990s, whereas openness to FDI in Western markets contributed to strong political coalitions supporting freer trade. See Dennis J. Encarnation, *Rivals Beyond Trade: America Versus Japan in Global Competition* (Ithaca: Cornell University Press, 1993); Mark Mason and Dennis Encarnation, eds., *Does Ownership Matter? Japanese Multinationals in Europe* (New York: Oxford University Press, 1995).

[40] Most of Japan's inward FDI has come in the decade between 2000 and 2010, well after Japan's era of high-speed growth and export dominance. In 1995, Japan's total FDI stock was equivalent to only 0.6 percent of GDP. As recently as 2000, Japan's total stock of FDI was only $50 billion. UN Conference on Trade and Development, *World Investment Report 2010, Country Fact Sheet: Japan*, July 22, 2010, http://www.unctad.org. Similarly for Korea, total FDI stock was less than 2 percent of GDP in 1995, with a total stock of only $38 billion as recently as 2000. UN Conference on Trade and Development, *World Investment Report 2010, Country Fact Sheet: Republic of Korea*, July 22, 2010, http://www.unctad.org

[41] UN Conference on Trade and Development, FDI Statistics Interactive Database, http://www.unctad.org

relative openness are simply the difference in the two countries' scale of international trade, links to processing trade and FDI, and the ratio of total trade to GDP, all of which are greater for China than for India. Tariff levels are another indicator. India was a founding member of the General Agreement on Tariffs and Trade (GATT) in 1947. India joined the successor to the GATT regime, the WTO, at its inception in 1995, six years earlier than China's own WTO accession. However, China's tariffs on imports are lower than India's, particularly in the agricultural sector and in key industry sectors such as automobiles and textiles (Table 7.4). Tariffs in both countries have been falling, although both countries erect significant nontariff barriers to trade and investment.

China and India share some similarities in terms of trade disputes within the WTO regime. Although China's international trade is much larger than India's, the two countries were respondents in the same number of WTO disputes as of November 2010.[42] China was the respondent in twenty complaints brought against it by trade partners. Half of the complaints against China have been brought by the United States. India was also the respondent to twenty disputes filed against it at the WTO, most of these from European countries (Table 7.5).

Trade complaints against China and India are also similar in nature. Most are related to domestic protection policies limiting market access for foreign firms and goods in industrial, services, and agriculture sectors. In fewer cases, complaints against both countries have cited intellectual property and patent protections, as well as unfair export practices ("dumping"). According to WTO data, India has been found to be noncompliant or has had arbitration findings against it slightly more often than China.

Despite its smaller volume of international trade, India appears more likely to file trade complaints at the WTO than China, with nineteen cases brought by India as of late 2010, compared to seven brought by China (Table 7.6). India and China are also third parties in a large number of multiparty disputes.

The increased role both India and China are playing within the rules-based WTO marks a victory for long-standing American policies aimed at bringing these large emerging economies into liberal international regimes. In some respects, the United States has actually worked harder to convince China of the benefits of liberal global governance regimes than it has with

[42] Data from the World Trade Organization, http://www.wto.org/english/tratop_e/dispu_e/dispu_maps_e.htm

Table 7.4. *Simple average MFN applied tariffs on international trade goods (percent), 2009*

	Total	Agricultural	Nonagricultural	WTO Member Since
China	9.6	15.6	8.7	2001
India	12.9	31.8	10.1	1995

Source: World Trade Organization.

Table 7.5. *WTO trade complaints against China and India*

As of November 2010	China	India
European Union	4	10
Switzerland	–	1
Canada	4	1
United States	10	4
Mexico	3	–
Guatemala	1	–
Taiwan	–	1
Bangladesh	–	1
Australia	–	1
New Zealand	–	1
Total	**20**	**20**

Source: World Trade Organization.

Table 7.6. *Comparison of WTO trade dispute cases*

As of November 2010	Complainant	Respondent	Third Party
China	7	20	71
India	19	20	63
United States	96	110	80

Source: World Trade Organization.

India. India's performance within many global governance regimes is not appreciably better than China's from a U.S. perspective.[43]

Action within multilateral regimes such as the WTO is unlikely to resolve all of America's trade disputes with either China or India. Temporary bilateral trade restrictions or duties may be required in some cases. Such temporary

---

[43] See Barbara Crossette, "The Elephant in the Room: How India Gives Global Governance the Biggest Headache," *Foreign Policy*, January/February 2010.

policies have been used before to secure reciprocal market access and relief for American firms and workers from unfair trade practices. In some cases, temporary bilateral discrimination can ultimately lead to greater trade and investment openness overall.[44]

Bilateral Trade and Investment Relations with the United States

Although trade and investment generate huge benefits for consumers and for workers in all three countries, the magnitude of Sino-U.S. trade works to ensure intense political focus on bilateral imbalances. At nearly $457 billion in 2010, total U.S.-China trade was almost ten times the $49 billion in U.S.-India trade the same year (Table 7.7).[45] The United States has a large bilateral trade deficit with China, reaching $273 billion in 2010. The 2010 U.S. bilateral trade deficit with India was about $10 billion.

The bilateral trade deficit with China is a source of considerable political friction between Washington and Beijing.[46] However, as described earlier, the rise of globalized production in the 1980s and 1990s calls into question the utility of current official trade statistics in measuring the relative benefits from trade. Current official data focus attention on bilateral trade in final goods for export rather than the role of intermediate goods and the share of value added in a multicountry production system. As low-value-added assembly and processing of imported components shifted from countries such as Korea, Taiwan, Singapore, and Malaysia to China during the 1990s, China's share of U.S. imports increased, and the share of U.S. imports from traditional Asian suppliers decreased.

[44] Kenneth A. Oye, *Economic Discrimination and Political Exchange: World Political Economy in the 1930s and 1980s* (Princeton: Princeton University Press, 1993).

[45] U.S. Census Bureau, Foreign Trade Division, Data Dissemination Branch, Washington, DC 20233, http://www.census.gov/foreign-trade/index.html

[46] Eswar S. Prasad, "The U.S.-China Economic Relationship: Shifts and Twists in the Balance of Power," Testimony to the U.S. China Economic and Security Commission, revised March 10, 2010. There are various estimates of the bilateral U.S.-China trade deficit. One study estimates how Chinese exports affect China's domestic value-added and employment; see Chen, Xikang, Cheng, Leonard, Fung, K.C., Lau, Lawrence J., Sung, Yun-Wing, Yang, C., Zhu, K., Pei, J. and Tang, Z., "Domestic Value Added and Employment Generated by Chinese Exports: A Quantitative Estimation," Unpublished monograph, 2008, accessed at http://mpra.ub.uni-muenchen.de/15663/1/MPRA_paper_15663.pdf. Another study estimates trade balances using value-added data, which is arguably the most meaningful measure. See Lau, Lawrence J., Xikang Chen, Leonard K. Cheng, K. C. Fung, Yun-Wing Sung, Cuihong Yang, Kunfu Zhu, Zhipeng Tang, and Jiansuo Pei, 2006c, "Estimates of U.S.-China Trade Balances in Terms of Domestic Value-Added," Working Paper No. 295, Stanford Center for International Development, Stanford University.

Table 7.7. *U.S. trade with India and China, 2010*

Million USD	Total Trade	U.S. Exports	U.S. Imports	U.S. Trade Balance
India	48,754	19,223	29,531	−10,309
China (including Hong Kong)	456,822	91,878	364,944	−273,066

Source: U.S. Census Bureau, Foreign Trade Statistics.

Accordingly, a significant portion of America's former bilateral trade deficits with multiple Asian countries was shifted to China. China's share of total U.S. imports grew from 3 percent in 1990 to 14 percent in 2005, whereas the rest of East Asia's share (Japan, Korea, Taiwan, and ASEAN) fell from 36 percent to 19 percent.[47] This reduced attention on American trade deficits with other Asian countries and focused more attention on China.[48]

However, the globalization of production and the resulting trade flows, surpluses, and deficits are not immutable trends. Factors such as rising energy and transportation costs or the advent of new production technologies could slow or even reverse the flow of some manufacturing production from advanced economies to low-cost producers in Asia, and therefore affect merchandise trade flows.[49] The United States and other advanced countries still have considerable competitive advantages, from product and process technologies to management and political-economic institutions

---

[47] Thomas Lum and Dick K. Nanto, "China's Trade with the United States and the World," Congressional Research Service Report to Congress, Order Code RL31403, January 4, 2007, 13.

[48] The structure of bilateral trade is the product of many factors in addition to the globalization of production, including comparative advantage as well as trade and exchange rate policies. Of course, the fundamental cause of America's overall trade deficit remains the same as it ever was: The United States spends more than it saves.

[49] New manufacturing technologies such as three-dimensional printing (also known as additive manufacturing) could present a challenge to currently dominant systems of trade and production. Rather than shipment of components between many nations for assembly by unskilled laborers, new production technologies may favor mass customization of production in the hands of a few highly skilled worker-designers, performed close to end-user markets. See B. Joseph Pine, *Mass Customization: The New Frontier in Business Competition* (Cambridge, MA: Harvard University Press, 1992); Neil Hopkinson, "Additive Manufacturing: What's happening and where are we going with printing in the third dimension?" British Educational Communications Technology Association, October 2010; "The printed world," *The Economist*, February 10, 2011; "Print me a Stradivarius," *The Economist* February 10, 2011.

that promote innovation.[50] Trade relations among China, India, and the United States will remain dynamic and far from zero-sum.

The focus on bilateral deficits sometimes overshadows the role of China and India as growing markets for U.S. exports, especially from advanced-technology industries that support high-paying American jobs. In 2010, China was the third-largest U.S. export market for all products and services, after U.S. neighbors Canada and Mexico. Total U.S. exports to China were about $92 billion in 2010, and advanced-technology exports to China were more than $21 billion in the same year.[51] Although trade is growing quickly, India was not yet among the top fifteen U.S. export markets in 2010. Total U.S. exports to India were $19 billion in 2010. India is also a smaller export market for advanced-technology goods than China. American advanced-technology exports to India were about $3 billion in 2010.

In addition to friction over trade deficits, China's exchange rate policy has emerged as a contentious issue in U.S.-China economic relations. Beijing intervenes heavily in currency markets to keep its currency, the yuan, pegged to the U.S. dollar.[52] This makes China's exports cheaper in foreign markets (and imports more expensive for Chinese consumers) than they would be if the value of the yuan were determined by market forces. However, there is disagreement among economists about the extent to which any reasonably likely Chinese currency appreciation would affect the bilateral United States-China trade deficit and contribute directly to shifting jobs to American workers.[53]

The Apple iPhone again helps illustrate the issue. The total 2009 manufacturing cost for an iPhone was about $179 dollars, and assembly

---

[50] On American relative technological advantages, see Adam Segal, *Advantage: How American Innovation Can Overcome the Asian Challenge* (New York: W.W. Norton, 2011).

[51] The United States defines Advanced Technology Product (ATP) sectors as biotechnology, life science, opto-electronics, information and communications, electronics, flexible manufacturing, advanced materials, aerospace, weapons, and nuclear technology. U.S. Census Bureau, Foreign Trade Statistics 2010, http://www.census.gov/foreign-trade/statistics/product/atp/select-ctryatp.html#2010

[52] C. Fred Bergsten, "Correcting the Chinese Exchange Rate: An Action Plan," Testimony before the Committee on Ways and Means, U.S. House of Representatives, March 24, 2010, http://www.iie.com/publications/papers/paper.cfm?ResearchID=1523; Morris Goldstein and Nicholas R. Lardy, *The Future of China's Exchange Rate Policy*, Peterson Institute for International Economics, Policy Analyses in International Economics 87, July 2009.

[53] See Joseph E. Stiglitz, "No Time for a Trade War," Project Syndicate, April 6, 2010, available at http://www.project-syndicate.org/commentary/stiglitz124/English; and Paul R. Krugman, "Immaculate Transfer Strikes Again," *New York Times*, April 6, 2010.

in China comprised about $6.50 of that cost.[54] A 20 percent increase in the value of the yuan would therefore only result in a $1.30 increase of China-related costs. This would amount to an increase in total manufacturing costs for the phone of less than 1 percent. The difference obtained from that level of appreciation is not likely to be sufficient to justify moving assembly work to the United States, although it might create incentives to shift low-value assembly work from China to other countries with even lower cost levels. Because Japan, Korea, and Taiwan contribute much more to the value of an iPhone, any appreciation of their currencies (which are also considered to be undervalued) would have a much greater effect than a similar level of Chinese yuan appreciation.[55]

Despite this, yuan appreciation might still deliver significant benefits to the United States as well as to China. It would benefit American exporters and workers if it contributed to increased consumer demand in China and therefore to increased overall global demand. Yuan appreciation might also indirectly benefit the United States, China, and the world because it would help China avoid excessive domestic inflation and other imbalances that could lead to domestic economic instability.[56]

India's exchange rate policy shares some similarities with China's. Notionally, the value of the Indian rupee is determined by market exchange rates, but in fact the Reserve Bank of India (RBI) also engages in substantial U.S. dollar trading to dampen exchange rate volatility and to shield Indian exporters.[57] From the mid-1980s to the early 1990s, India pursued a policy of rupee depreciation to promote Indian exports.[58] Since then, the RBI has allowed the rupee to appreciate in a "managed float" against the U.S. dollar (not strictly a peg). India's managed float of the rupee to the dollar is not a

---

[54] See Andrew Rassweiler, "iSuppli Apple iPhone 3G S 16GB Teardown Analysis," iSuppli Press Release, June 24, 2009. See also Xing and Detert, "How the iPhone Widens the United States Trade Deficit with the People's Republic of China," December 2010, 6.

[55] Xing and Detert, "How the iPhone Widens the United States Trade Deficit with the People's Republic of China," December 2010.

[56] Allowing greater scope for market forces to determine the value of the yuan would be in China's interest as it would help Beijing address significant economic imbalances at home. See Arthur Kroeber, "Rising inflation and a possible currency surprise," GavKalDragonomics China Insight, December 18, 2009; Nicholas R. Lardy, "China: Towards a Consumption-Driven Growth Path," Peterson Institute for International Economics, Policy Brief Number PB06–6, October 2006. China's twelfth five-year plan, announced in March 2011, includes policies to promote consumption and rebalance China's economy. See Arthur Kroeber, "12th Five Year Plan Proposal Released," in *Dragon Week 1 November 10*, GavKalDragonomics November 1, 2010.

[57] "India May Shield Exporters from Rupee, Minister Says," *Bloomberg News*, September 26, 2007; Panagariya, *India: The Emerging Giant*, 203.

[58] Panagariya, *India: The Emerging Giant*, 202.

Table 7.8. *China and India: Similar American trade and investment complaints*

U.S. Concerns on Trade and Investment Issues	
China	India
• Limits on foreign investment	• Restrictions on foreign investment
• Intellectual property protection regime	• Weak enforcement of intellectual property rights
• Transparency, "administrative regulation"	• Excessive government interference
• Rule of law	• Questions about "sanctity of contract"
• Integrity of trade and product safety	• Substandard infrastructure
• Previous policies giving preferential tax treatment to foreign firms being revised to equal treatment with domestic firms	• Discriminatory tax rates against foreign companies
• Exchange rate policy	• High tariffs and excessive indirect taxes
• Financial sector reform	

Sources: U.S. Embassy Beijing, "U.S. Fact Sheet: Third Cabinet Level Meeting of the U.S. China Strategic Economic Dialogue," December 13, 2007; U.S. Embassy New Delhi, Economic Section, "The Indian Economy," presentation, 2007, p. 46, "U.S. Business Complaints," accessed at http://newdelhi.usembassy.gov/uploads/images/AlTyKr7Arq_hdF7ONZeGMg/econindeco.pdf

highly contentious issue, because India's overall exports and its trade surpluses with the United States remain relatively small. However, a number of Indian officials and economists continue to see the need for capital controls and a managed currency for the purpose of maintaining a "competitive exchange rate" for years to come.[59] Such policies could become more controversial as India's economy and international trade grow, or if India sees large inflows (or outflows) of foreign investment.

Bilateral trade deficit numbers and exchange rate policy debates garner most headlines, but issues of market access and the protection of intellectual property are central to maintaining relative American benefits from economic relations with both China and India. These issues may get less attention than they should. Table 7.8 shows a comparison of separate but contemporary presentations, one from the U.S. Embassy in Beijing and one from the U.S. Embassy in New Delhi, summarizing American views about trade and investment access in China and India. Comparing the two reveals a number of similar complaints.

[59] Panagariya, *India: The Emerging Giant*, 209, 207–213.

Table 7.9. *Business and investment environment, rank among 183 economies, 2011*

	China	India
Overall Doing Business 2011 Rank	79	135
Starting a business	151	165
Dealing with construction permits	181	177
Registering property	38	94
Getting credit	65	32
Protecting investors	93	44
Paying taxes	114	164
Trading across borders	50	100
Enforcing contracts	15	182
Closing a business	68	134

Source: World Bank, International Finance Corporation, Doing Business Rankings, http://www.doingbusiness.org/rankings

Despite these similar concerns, surveys performed by the World Bank and the International Finance Corporation show that international business leaders rank China ahead of India in terms of market access and ease of investment. Firms also give higher marks to China's legal system, especially with regard to enforcing contracts (Table 7.9).

In theory, India's democratic politics and more highly developed legal system should be an advantage in attracting trade and investment. However, in current practice, foreign firms find bloated bureaucracy, regulatory restrictions, slow and uneven law enforcement, and corruption in India to be as great (or even greater) than in China.[60] Corruption is a serious problem in both countries, but it is seen to be worse in India than in China. In Transparency International's 2007 global corruption perception report, China ranked 73rd and India ranked 75th out of 180 countries (where 1 is cleanest and 180 most corrupt).[61]

Despite China's advantage in these rankings, concerns about market access for foreign firms in key Chinese industrial sectors emerged in late 2008 and early 2009. Beijing imposed policies ostensibly aimed at promoting "indigenous innovation." These included measures discriminating

---

[60] In the view of one Indian investor, "I prefer investing in China because its legal system is much more dependable and transparent." Arthur Kroeber, "China & India: Friends, Rivals or Just Two Different Countries?" Dragonomics Research & Advisory, Presentation to British Chamber of Commerce Beijing, April 2, 2008, 15.

[61] See ranking at http://www.transparency.org

against foreign firms competing to win Chinese government procurement contracts for advanced-technology products and equipment.[62] The protectionist elements of China's indigenous innovation policies met stiff resistance from China's trade partners, including the United States.[63] Perhaps as important, such policies raised concerns at foreign companies operating within China and among their domestic Chinese customers, suppliers, and partners.[64] Together, intense pressure from within and outside China caused Beijing to back away from the most protectionist elements of its technology policies.[65] However, market access issues such as this will remain a recurring problem in Sino-U.S. relations.

Some of India's innovation and industrial policy goals are similar to China's.[66] The Indian government has made the transfer of advanced industrial and defense technologies a condition for deepened trade, investment,

---

[62] In recent years, China's total public-sector purchases have been an approximately $90 billion annual market. The key document is *National Indigenous Innovation Product Accreditation System* (Circular 618), jointly issued by China's Science and Technology Ministry, Finance Ministry, and its economic planning commission, the National Development Reform Commission (NDRC), on November 15, 2009.

[63] "Tech Firms Complain About New Chinese Procurement Rules," *PC World*, December 11, 2009; "German Executives Push Back in China," *The Wall Street Journal*, July 19, 2010.

[64] One Chinese academic has noted, "In the short term, the implementation of Circular 618 may have some negative impacts on China's technology trade." See Jingxia Shi, "China's Indigenous Innovation and Government Procurement," International Centre for Trade and Sustainable Development, China Programme, 14:3 (September 16, 2010). See also statements of senior Chinese leaders promising that China's exporters and export-processing firms would not be cut off from foreign technology; "China Vows Fairness for Foreign Companies, *Industry Week*, April 29, 2010.

[65] In September 2010, Chinese Premier Wen Jiabao said that some of the indigenous innovation policies were "not clear" and had to be "improved." Further, contrary to earlier documents, Wen said all foreign companies registered in China would be given equal treatment under procurement and indigenous innovation policies. See "Wen Says Indigenous Innovation Complaints Due to Unclear Rules," *Bloomberg Businessweek*, September 13, 2010. and International Centre for Trade and Sustainable Development, "China Relaxes Innovation Standard," International Centre for Trade and Sustainable Development, *China Programme*, 14:3 (September 16, 2010).

[66] See Department of Science and Technology, *Science and Technology Policy 2003* (New Delhi: Department of Science and Technology, 2003); Department of Science and Technology, *Annual Report 2009–2010* (New Delhi: Department of Science and Technology, 2009); Ministry of Defence, Defence Research Development Organisation, "Policies," http://www.drdo.gov.in/drdo/English/index.jsp?pg=policies.jsp. See also Charles W. Wessner and Sujai J. Shivakumar, eds., *India's Changing Innovation System: Achievements, Challenges, and Opportunities for Cooperation: Report of a Symposium* (Washington, DC: National Academies Press, 2007); and Carl Dahlman and Anuja Utz, *India and the Knowledge Economy Leveraging Strengths and Opportunities* (Washington, DC: World Bank, 2005).

and geostrategic relations with the United States.[67] India has not attempted protectionist policies similar to China's indigenous innovation policy. However, Organisation for Economic Co-operation and Development (OECD) studies find that Indian regulations such as restrictions on FDI, labor policies, and policies that govern the entry and exit of firms from the market are an obstacle to trade and investment in manufacturing and high-technology industries.[68] Indian government procurement processes are also plagued by problems including corruption and policies aimed at promoting domestic technology firms.[69] Disputes over market access and trade in technology and industrial goods could intensify as India gains industrial might.

For the United States, a number of intense international trade and investment disputes involve intellectual property rights (IPR). The International Intellectual Property Association (IIPA), a private-sector coalition of trade associations representing U.S. copyright-based industries, claims that U.S. companies lost $3.5 billion to IPR violations in China in 2007.[70] Levels of piracy are high in India as well, prompting the IIPA to place India on its priority watch list, along with China. Estimates of losses from piracy and copyright theft in India, at $1.2 billion in 2007, were more than one-third of estimated losses in China. The Indian economy is about one-fourth as large as the Chinese economy, and Indian per-capita incomes are about one-fourth to one-third of China's. Thus far, IPR violations and losses – particularly in software, music, and books – are roughly proportional to the size of the two economies.

[67] "US lifts curbs on ISRO, DRDO," *Times of India*, January 25, 2011; "India-U.S. Joint Statement," The White House, Washington, DC, July 18, 2005. See also K. Alan Kronstadt, *U.S.-India Bilateral Agreements in 2005*, Congressional Research Service Report for Congress, Order Code RL33072, September 8, 2005; and Paul K. Kerr, *U.S. Nuclear Cooperation with India: Issues for Congress*, Congressional Research Service Report for Congress, Order Code RL33016, September 30, 2010.

[68] Mark A. Dutz, ed., *Unleashing India's Innovation: Toward Sustainable and Inclusive Growth* (Washington, DC: World Bank, 2007), 1–48; Carl Dahlman and Anuja Utz, *India and the Knowledge Economy: Leveraging Strengths and Opportunities* (Washington, DC: World Bank, 2005), 21–44; Sean M. Dougherty et al., "India's Growth Pattern and Obstacles to Higher Growth," OECD Economics Department Working Paper No. 63, August 11, 2008.

[69] "India Scandal Threatens 'Pure' Premier," *Wall Street Journal*, November 18, 2010; "India Stocks Sink on Telecommunications Scandal," *New York Times*, November 19, 2010; "Eight executives arrested in latest Indian financial scandal," *Cable News Network CNNWorld*, November 26, 2010, http://articles.cnn.com/2010-11-26/world/india.scandals_1_singh-s-congress-indian-premier-league-federal-investigators?_s=PM:WORLD

[70] International Intellectual Property Alliance, "IIPA 2008 'Special 301' Recommendations: 2006 and 2007 Estimated Trade Losses Due to Copyright Piracy and 2006–2007 Estimated Levels of Copyright Piracy," November 5, 2008.

IPR losses may actually increase in both India and China as per-capita incomes increase and consumers can afford a greater range of products (although they may level off or even decline after a certain level of wealth is attained and product quality becomes a greater consideration). According to the IIPA, intellectual property violations have grown faster in India than in China in recent years – up nearly 60 percent in 2007 over 2006 levels, compared to an increase of 44 percent over the same period for China. As the U.S.-India trade and investment relationship grows, the significance of these similar trade and investment frictions may also grow.[71]

Beyond trade in merchandise and services, China and India are large markets for U.S. direct investment. However, American companies have invested nearly ten times more in China than in India, with cumulative direct investment of more than $65 billion in China and about $7 billion in India.[72] Despite its smaller economy, India is a larger direct investor in the United States than China. India had about $4 billion in FDI in the United States as of 2008, compared to $1.2 billion Chinese FDI in 2008.[73] Direct investment from both countries into the United States will probably continue to grow. Whether this contributes to trade disputes or mitigates them will largely depend on whether this investment is seen to create good jobs in America. For their own part, both China and India are looking beyond merely accepting inward FDI. They are becoming larger outward investors. Nowhere has this activity captured more attention than in global energy and resources industries.

International Energy Competition

Reform, economic growth, and integration with the global economy have made both China and India hungrier for international energy resources. Both countries have contributed to intensified volatility in global energy demand and prices in the early twenty-first century. Governments and

---

[71] "EU concerned over 'rising protectionism in India'" *The Business Standard*, February 9, 2010; U.S. International Trade Commission, "Very High Tariff Barriers Impede U.S. Agricultural Exports to India, Says USITC," news release No. 09–104, December 11, 2009; on intellectual property protection reforms and other barriers to manufacturing investment in India, see Office of Industries, U.S. International Trade Commission, *Competitive Conditions for U.S. Foreign Direct Investment in India*, publication 3931, July 2007.

[72] Estimates based on data from China Ministry of Commerce and Indian Ministry of Finance.

[73] Year 2008 data were the latest official data available as of early 2011. Office of U.S. Trade Representative, "India," http://www.ustr.gov/countries-regions/south-central-asia/india; Office of U.S. Trade Representative, "China," http://www.ustr.gov/countries-regions/china

consumers in the West have observed the growing competition for resources and investment opportunities with concern, especially as the price of oil and natural gas rose sharply after 2002.[74]

Tightening markets and higher oil and gas prices, combined with a wave of outward investment from newly profitable state-owned energy firms, have given rise to fears about resource scarcity and energy security. Senior U.S. officials have expressed a view that Chinese state-owned firms and the Chinese government are pursuing a coherent strategy for "locking up" international energy resources, especially oil and natural gas resources.[75] By early 2009, when commodities prices fell dramatically, many international energy and resources firms were in need of cash while Western banks were seriously weakened. Both Indian and Chinese state firms and financial institutions had significant cash on hand for loans and investments in energy resource projects.

In this section, we examine whether either India or China threaten to "lock up" energy resources in a way that might significantly affect international markets. To do so, we first look at the two countries in the context of global oil supply and demand. We then compare the role their state-owned energy firms play in total world oil production and merger and acquisition (M&A) activities in global petroleum industries. We also compare Chinese and Indian energy investments in states governed by authoritarian governments noted for abuses of their own people, sometimes called "rogue regimes." Finally, we examine broad patterns of Chinese and Indian trading in international energy markets.

Chinese and Indian Energy Competition in Global Context

A first step is to place China and India in the context of world energy markets (Table 7.10). We focus on oil demand and production because it is at the center of global energy trading, and it is also the focus of world energy geopolitics. In this section, we employ several terms that are commonly

---

[74] Oil and natural gas prices moderated with the global financial crisis of 2008–2009, but by late 2010, they had recovered to pre-crisis levels, with Brent crude in the region of $83 to $87 per barrel. Oil prices again passed the $100-per-barrel mark in early 2011 with revolutions and unrest in the Middle East.

[75] See U.S. Economic and Security Review Commission, *Annual Report to Congress 2005*, Chapter 4, p. 167. Deputy Secretary of State Robert B. Zoellick, Speech at the National Committee on US-China Relations, New York, September 2005, see "U.S. Says China Must Address Its Intentions How Its Power Will Be Used Is of Concern," *Washington Post*, September 22, 2005; and Senator Joseph I. Lieberman, "China-U.S. Energy Policies: A Choice of Cooperation or Collision – Remarks at Council on Foreign Relations Washington, DC, November 30, 2005.

Table 7.10. *Oil demand, production, and reserves, 2010 (E)*

	World	China	India
Oil demand* (million barrels/day)	86.1	8.9	3.4
Oil production* (million barrels/day)	86.8	3.9	0.9
Oil reserves** (billion barrels)	~800	19.7	3.8

(E) – Estimate

* Demand and supply numbers include conventional oil, natural gas liquids, gas-to-liquids, coal-to-liquids, and biofuels.
** Reserves are for conventional oil only, proved and probable, in billions of barrels. This estimate excludes yet-to-be-found resources, as well as any estimate for resources in the Arctic. Reserve estimates vary widely; this one is provided to give a sense of overall context and scale for Chinese and Indian share of world crude oil markets.

Source: Authors' estimates for full year 2010 based on interview responses and data from Wood Mackenzie and Cambridge Energy Research Associates. Some data are subject to future revisions as national accounts are revised or corrected.

used in the energy industry. Both China and India have national oil companies (NOCs), which are oil and gas companies that are wholly or majority-owned by the national government. NOCs contrast with international oil companies (IOCs), which are private or publicly listed companies that lease or own the rights to develop petroleum resources. We also discuss merger and acquisition (M&A) activity in the oil and gas industry, which refers to the sale and purchase of petroleum resources such as oil and gas fields (or the right to develop them), as well as the sale and purchase of companies that own such resources or such rights.

China is a significant oil-producing country, with production within China of about 3.9 million barrels per day (mbd) in 2010, accounting for about 4 percent of world production of about 87 mbd that year.[76] China has three large state-owned national oil companies. Despite their expertise and recent growth, Chinese firms account for a modest share of international oil production. China's largest crude oil producer is China National Petroleum Corporation (CNPC), with total production of about 3.2 mbd in 2010 (Table 7.11). In 2010, CNPC's non-China production of 1.03 million

---

[76] Interviews with Cambridge Energy Research Associates, and Wood Mackenzie, February 6, 2009 and August 9, 2010. Chinese company data from company annual reports. CNPC is the wholly state-owned parent company of PetroChina, which is partially listed on international and domestic stock markets. CNPC owns about 90% of PetroChina. Sinopec and CNOOC are also state-owned firms with partially listed subsidiary companies. In this section, for simplicity, we do not differentiate between state-owned parent companies and their partially listed subsidiaries, although there are differences in commercial and corporate governance practices.

Table 7.11. *Chinese and Indian NOC crude oil production, 2010 (E)*
(Million barrels per day)

	Total production	Overseas equity production
CNPC	3.177	1.026
Sinopec	1.157	0.374
CNOOC	0.712	0.157
ONGC	0.733	0.152

(E) – Estimate
Source: Estimates for full year 2010 based on interviews with Wood Mackenzie and Cambridge Energy Research Associates. Some data are subject to future revisions as company annual reports are issued.

barrels per day accounted for 32 percent of its total production, up from about 21 percent in 2009. However, this increase was largely the result of the addition of 390,000 barrels per day of production in Iraq under a service contract (as distinguished from equity-owned production). To put these figures in context, Exxon Mobil's 2010 non-U.S. production was more than double CNPC's non-China production, at approximately 2.4 mbd, and Chevron's 2010 non-U.S. production was nearly double CNPCs' non-China production, at 1.9 mbd.[77]

Almost half of CNPC's 2010 non-China equity production came from operations in Kazakhstan. (CNPC bought Canada's PetroKazakhstan in 2005.) Sinopec, China's second-largest NOC, had about 374,000 barrels per day of non-China oil production in 2010, mainly in Russia and Latin America. CNOOC, the third Chinese NOC, had about 157,000 barrels per day of international oil production in 2010.

This makes a total 2010 Chinese overseas crude oil production of about 1.5 million barrels per day, comprising less than 2 percent of total world production in 2010. China's overseas equity oil production is set to grow as its investments increase, and as recently established overseas projects begin producing. However, building from 2 percent of total world production in 2010, no reasonable estimate of overseas production growth would find Chinese companies emerging as dominant international oil producers.

India is an even smaller player in global oil production. Indian domestic production was only about 870,000 barrels per day in 2010, about 1 percent of world production. India has two large state-owned national oil

---

[77] Estimates from Wood Mackenzie; these estimates are subject to revisions as company reports are issued in 2010 and 2011.

and gas companies, Oil and Natural Gas Corporation (ONGC) and Gas Authority of India Limited (GAIL). Only ONGC has significant crude oil production, with about 733,000 barrels per day in 2010, of which about 152,000 barrels per day was overseas equity production. ONGC's overseas equity production thus accounted for less than 1 percent of world crude oil production in 2010.

Both India and China will become increasingly dependent on energy imports over the next several decades. In a scenario where both economies avoid crises and maintain expected GDP growth rates (as described earlier in this chapter), and under current and expected economic and energy reform policies, India will come to depend on imports for more than 90 percent of its oil by 2030, up from about 74 percent in 2010. In the same scenario, China's oil import dependency will rise to about 85 percent in 2030, up from about 56 percent in 2010.[78]

Overseas Energy Investments

Concern over rapidly rising energy import dependency has underpinned both Chinese and Indian government support for overseas oil and gas investment. In both cases, this has been led by their respective NOCs. Despite state ownership, these companies have their own reasons for seeking such investments, including commercial interests in growth and profits as they confront the consequences of their relatively limited resource bases at home.

China's first forays into purchasing upstream oil and gas assets occurred in the mid-1990s. In the fifteen-year period from 1994 to 2008, Chinese firms conducted about $38.8 billion in international upstream M&A activity, purchasing petroleum reserves of about 7.8 billion barrels of oil equivalent (boe). China's investments have been focused on the former Soviet states in Central Asia, which account for about 41 percent of China's M&A activity. But China is also investing in the Middle East, Africa, South America, Canada, and Australia.

Even though China's upstream asset purchases have grown rapidly, especially in a period of high activity in 2005 and 2006, they remain

---

[78] Authors' estimates based on the economic outlook described in footnote 7 of this chapter and interviews with Wood Mackenzie, August 9, 2010, and Cambridge Energy Research Associates, November 11, 2010. This is a simplified outlook for the purpose of illustrating current trends and geopolitical concerns. Actual outcomes will be highly sensitive to economic performance, political stability, energy policies, and energy-related technology developments. Another method for producing long-term economic and energy outlooks can be found in International Energy Agency, *World Energy Outlook 2010* (Paris: IEA, 2010).

modest by comparison to the activity of established international oil companies. For example, between 1994 and 2008, a group of only seven IOCs conducted nearly \$612 billion in M&A – more than fifteen times larger than Chinese total M&A (Figure 7.1).[79] International firms acquired a correspondingly larger share of total oil and gas reserves over that period (Figure 7.2). The international upstream oil and gas M&A market during the 1994–2008 period totaled more than \$1.4 trillion. Thus, China's international upstream acquisitions represented less than 3 percent of the international upstream M&A market for oil and gas reserves over that fifteen-year period.

India's two state-owned oil companies, ONGC and GAIL, are also active on international markets. Over the same period between 1994 and 2008, Indian NOCs invested about \$4.8 billion in international upstream M&A, acquiring about 1 billion boe in reserves. In contrast to the Chinese firms, Indian firms have focused most of their efforts to date on Africa, although like China, India is planning large new investments in the Middle East, including in Iran.

Both China and India greatly expanded international upstream M&A activity in the period between 2004 and 2006 (Table 7.12). Even during this period, Chinese NOCs accounted for only 7 percent of world upstream M&A of \$392 billion. Two Western firms, Conoco-Phillips of the United States and state-owned Statoil of Norway, each individually accounted for more M&A activity in 2004–2006 than the three Chinese NOCs combined. Indian firms accounted for less than 1 percent of world upstream oil and gas M&A in the 2004–2006 period.

Chinese and Indian upstream M&A should also be seen in the context of long-term patterns of oil and gas industry M&A activity. IOCs typically conduct greater levels of M&A when oil prices are low because there is a perception that resources are "cheaper" to buy. Chinese and Indian firms too have learned more about astute purchasing. Acquisitions by Chinese and Indian firms have not followed a simple, rising trend. For example, Chinese M&A activity slowed when oil prices rose and opportunities became scarce. Compared to twenty-one deals amounting to nearly \$22.5 billion in 2005 and 2006 (accounting for 58 percent of total Chinese M&A for the entire fifteen-year period), Chinese NOCs secured only nine deals worth \$4.8 billion in 2007 and 2008.

---

[79] This not meant to be a representative sample – these seven firms have been chosen only to give a sense of scale. These seven, primarily from Europe and North America, are among the most recognizable international oil companies and are among the largest.

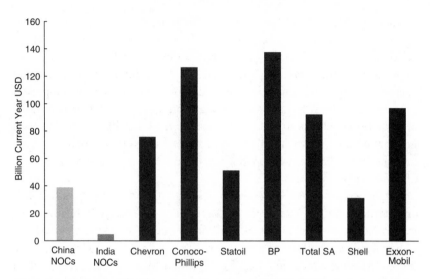

Figure 7.1. Upstream oil and gas acquisitions by value, 1994–2008, selected companies.
Source: Estimates compiled from oil and gas industry media.

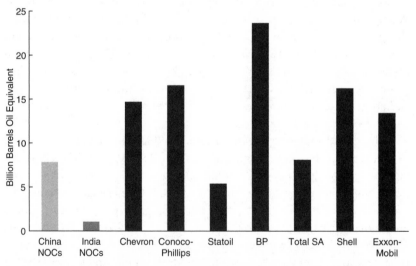

Figure 7.2. Upstream oil and gas acquisitions by reserves, 1994–2008, selected companies.
Source: Estimates compiled from oil and gas industry media.

In the wake of the financial crisis of 2008–2009, Indian and especially Chinese NOCs again increased the intensity of their overseas investment activities (unsurprising given the fall of oil prices and the relatively distressed condition of many energy projects and companies). For example, in

Table 7.12. *Chinese and Indian NOC's "going out" 2004–2006 in context*

	Acquisitions, USD Billion	Share of World Total (%)
China NOCs	26.96	7
India NOCs	1.87	0.5
Chevron	20.51	5
Conoco-Phillips	43.70	11
Statoil	36.42	9
World	391.84	100

Source: Estimates compiled from oil and gas industry media.

January 2009, India's ONGC finalized its $2 billion acquisition of Imperial Energy Plc., a London-listed firm with oil production in Western Siberia and Central Asia.

China's CNPC, Sinopec, and CNOOC committed nearly $25 billion to asset and corporate acquisitions between mid-2009 and mid-2010. Chinese companies accounted for only about 11 percent of total M&A in 2009, but their share rose significantly in 2010. Even so, the total investments of all three Chinese NOCs combined reached only about 20 percent of total world oil and gas M&A activity in 2010. Data from earlier in the decade had shown that Chinese NOCs did not pay an undue premium for oil and gas acquisitions. However, data from 2010 indicated a different outcome. Chinese companies paid significantly higher prices for 2010 asset acquisitions when compared to prices implied by standard Western financial valuation models.[80]

These bursts in M&A activity may be difficult to sustain. The 2009–2010 experience was partly the result of unique post–financial crisis conditions. Moreover, paying a premium for assets is neither commercially nor politically sustainable for long. Significant asset upside (i.e., more petroleum resource contained in the oil or gas field than was known or expected at the time of purchase) or significantly higher oil prices must be forthcoming to make such investments economically viable. Further, revelations about state firms overpaying for international assets are politically embarrassing, and no leader would want to be associated with investments seen in this light.

Competition from other NOCs, including from the national companies of countries with significant oil and gas resources, will also place limits to the oil and gas acquisition activities of Chinese NOCs. For example, in 2009, the Libyan government used its preemption rights to acquire Verenex in

---

[80] Wood Mackenzie, "Chinese NOCs step-up international expansion," May 2010.

Libya, blocking CNPC's $462 million bid for the assets. Angola's Sonangol preempted a joint Sinopec/CNOOC offer to buy a 20 percent stake in an offshore asset from Marathon for $1.3 billion. Notably, Sonangol has started to develop a partnership with India's ONGC, and in January 2010 signed a cooperation deal with the Indian NOC. Also in 2009, the Iraqi government blocked China's Sinopec from participating in the 2009 oil and gas asset-licensing round, citing Sinopec's acquisition of assets in Iraqi Kurdistan.

Beyond access to resources, the search for attractive investments for their large foreign exchange reserves has been another motivation for Chinese and Indian oil and gas M&A.[81] But some recent deals are poorly understood. For example, elite Western media report deal figures that conflate Chinese and Indian loans with equity ownership investments. More than half of the Chinese energy "investments" reported in early 2009 were actually loans.[82] China Development Bank's loan of $10 billion to Brazil's Petrobras actually highlights the refusal of Petrobras and the Brazilian government to allow foreign companies to take direct equity ownership stakes in Brazil's huge, newfound oil deposits. Instead of selling equity, Petrobras secured a Chinese loan that helped it deal with near-term debt as well as underwriting a significant portion of its new investment requirements. In exchange, Petrobras will supply up 160,000 bpd of oil to Sinopec and CNPC at market prices.[83] That represented less than one-tenth of Brazil's 2009 production of about 2 million barrels per day. Meanwhile, the Chinese financing helped fund Petrobras's plan to increase Brazilian production to nearly 6 million barrels per day over the next decade (thereby increasing total world supply). Similarly, Chinese loan deals of up to $25 billion to Russia's Rosneft and Transneft in early 2009 also reflect the refusal of Russian firms and the Russian government to permit foreign acquisition of major equity stakes in Russia's petroleum resources.[84]

---

[81] Andrew Batson, "China Looks at Using Foreign Exchange Reserves to Boost Overseas Investments," *The Wall Street Journal*, February 18, 2009.

[82] "China Starts Investing Globally," *New York Times*, February 21, 2009.

[83] In the Petrobras announcement, a spokeswoman noted that crude sales would be at "market prices." See "Petrobras says inks supply deal with Sinopec, MOU for $10 bil loan," *Platt's Commodity News*, February 19, 2009. Details of the deal are not public, but there are established market practices for negotiating a market price for future energy supplies. Both sides have a strong interest in using such practices because they are relatively transparent, ensure that neither side is afraid it has gotten a bad deal, and help justify these deals to respective leaders at home.

[84] Rosneft said crude oil supplies would be "at market prices at the time of delivery"; see "Rosneft to start newly agreed oil supplies to China in Jan 2011," *Platt's Commodity News*, 2009.

In both of these loan deals, China obtained an opportunity to buy energy resources at market prices, secured supply diversification away from the Middle East, and gained the prospect of a higher return than alternative investments such as U.S. Treasury bonds. The world benefited from these deals, because Chinese money helped key oil producers (and their Western bankers) avoid default on debt – Rosneft alone had $19 billion in debt at the time, about 60 percent of which was reportedly owed to non-Russian banks. Chinese finance also enabled Russian and Brazilian exploration and production activities, thereby helping increase global energy supplies. The world did not lose energy supply from the combined 460,000 barrels-per-day commitments to sell to China at market prices because these commitments freed up supply from other producers, which might otherwise have been purchased by China.

Chinese and Indian diplomatic support for overseas investment has also gained international attention, and there is little doubt that firms from both have moved in to countries where Western firms are unwilling or unable to invest or do business. Yet contrary to public perception, China's track record of UN diplomacy is not determined principally by its trade interests and its energy strategy.[85] Further, in many ways, the Chinese and Indian experience operating in major resource-holding countries ranging from Indonesia to Iran, Nigeria, and Venezuela actually echoes the experience of the IOCs who preceded them there. Many major resource-holding countries are simply difficult places to operate for any outside investor, whether IOC or NOC. Despite diplomatic support from Beijing and New Delhi, and despite large investments, Chinese and Indian NOCs have also suffered from difficulties in negotiating and preserving access to investment opportunities, erosion of the financial terms for their investments, and delays and cancellation of projects in host countries.

Resource Holdings and Limits on Chinese and Indian Investment

Chinese and Indian companies have grown from being small players in international oil and gas M&A to becoming major, though not dominant, players. Their role in the market will continue to evolve, as they seek to add technology and skills to their portfolios, not merely upstream resources. Yet most of the world's petroleum resources may be off limits to Chinese and Indian investment. The world's largest conventional oil and gas resources

---

[85] Trevor Houser and Roy Levy have shown that China's UN diplomacy is more closely linked to its fundamental security strategy, particularly its position on sovereignty and noninterference in the internal affairs of other nations. Trevor Houser and Roy Levy, "Energy Security and China's UN Diplomacy," *China Security* 4:3, Summer 2008.

are under the control of the national oil companies of major resource-holding nations, such as Saudi Arabia, Russia, Qatar, Iran, Venezuela, Kuwait, and Nigeria.

These seven countries (all of which have dominant national oil companies controlled by authoritarian governments) account for about 60 percent of proven and probable global conventional oil reserves, and more than 75 percent of global conventional natural gas reserves.[86] These countries severely restrict private investment in their upstream industries and place most reserves completely off limits to foreign investment. Where foreign investment is permitted, it is restricted to minority stakes. The combined politics and mathematics of resource deposits mean that neither Western publicly listed oil companies nor Chinese and Indian state-owned oil companies are able to invest in the majority of the world's conventional petroleum reserves, much less control them.

Chinese and Indian oil and natural gas demand is growing fast, and both countries have firms that are entering markets in which they have not previously participated. Yet the scale of their upstream activities is not large enough to disrupt global oil and gas markets. Actually, the overall effect of their activities is opposite to the concerns typically expressed about them. Rather than taking energy off the market, Chinese and Indian global upstream investment generally increases global energy supply. The volatility in world energy demand and energy prices – to which China and India contribute by dint of their own cycles of domestic reform, investment, and growth – is a more important issue for global energy security than the illusionary threat that either country will disrupt markets by "locking up resources."

Rogue Regimes and Energy

Some American leaders have objected that China's behavior in international energy markets undermines both norms of acceptable international political behavior and the accepted rules of market-based competition. China has oil and gas investments in a number of countries with governments that oppress their own people. [87] This includes Cuba, Syria, Sudan, Iran, and Myanmar (Burma). International oil companies, including American and European companies, have a long history of working in developing countries and dealing with unsavory regimes. Since the mid-1990s, however, Western companies have been subject to greater pressures from public

---

[86] British Petroleum, *BP Statistical Review of Energy 2008*, http://www.bp.com/sectionenericarticle.do?categoryId=9023753&contentId=704410

[87] Elaine Kwei, "China, India, and Energy Security: Implications for the United States," presentation, August 9, 2006.

opinion, transmitted by a combination of new and old media, and have been forced to retreat from many of these states. Neither Chinese nor Indian NOCs are subject to the same degree of pressure. NOCs from both countries are pursuing similar investments in what are now sometimes termed "rogue" states (Table 7.13).

China is a focus for international criticism of these investments. For example, on Sudan, human rights organizations typically concentrate their ire on China (or Western firms that hold stock in PetroChina), while often overlooking the Indian and Malaysian investments there.[88] In Sudan, China has a 40 percent stake in the Greater Nile Petroleum Operating Company (GNPOC), and India's ONGC has a 25 percent stake in the same company. India's ONGC has a 24 percent stake in White Nile Petroleum Corp, and Malaysia's Petronas has a 68 percent share of that company.

Both China and India have pursued energy interests in Myanmar. In the wake of the 2007 uprising by monks and civilians against the Burmese military junta, India's response was similar to China's. New Delhi did not align with U.S. calls for tougher sanctions against the regime. The Indian government described Myanmar as its "close and friendly neighbor" and said it would aid in its national reconciliation.[89] New Delhi argued that it must secure access to important energy supplies, maintain a dialogue with the Burmese junta rather than isolate it, and continue to compete for influence in Myanmar rather than cede influence to a competitor such as China.

India has its own views of how best to achieve its energy security and regional influence in Myanmar, and these do not always mesh with the policies of Western countries. Similarly, India intends to maintain a close relationship with Iran.[90] New Delhi sees the Iran relationship as serving Indian interests in energy security and enhanced Indian diplomatic status in the Middle East and Central Asia. The Iran relationship is also one way for India to balance what some see as excessive Western and especially U.S. power. Indian energy security experts at the prestigious Jawaharlal Nehru University see New Delhi's special relationship with Tehran as a way for India and Iran to "empower each other" in the context of an "emboldened

---

[88] See "Calls for Sudanese Divestiture Grow Louder: Fidelity, Berkshire Hathaway Continue to be Targeted," *Investment Dealers Digest*, May 21, 2007.

[89] "India Agrees to Help Sides Reconcile in Myanmar," *New York Times*, October 24, 2007.

[90] C. Christine Fair, "India and Iran: New Delhi's Balancing Act," *Washington Quarterly*, 30:3 (Summer 2007): 145–159; Robert M. Hathaway et al., "The 'Strategic Partnership' Between India and Iran," Asia Program Special Report, Woodrow Wilson Center, April 2004.

Table 7.13. *Chinese and Indian energy investments in "rogue" states*

	China	India
Sudan	• CNPC has 40% in Greater Nile Petroleum Operating Company, which produces about 200,000 bpd of oil from concession blocks 1, 2, and 4 (Malaysia's Petronas has 30% of GNPOC, and India's ONGC has 25%, Sudan's Sudapet has 5%). • CNPC has 41%, and Sinopec has 6%, in Petrodar, which produces about 230,000 bpd oil from concession blocks 3 and 7 (Petronas has 40%, Sudapet 8%, and Tri-Ocean Energy, controlled by Kuwaiti interests, has 5%) • CNPC helped expand the Khartoum refinery from 50,000 bpd capacity to 100,000 bpd capacity in 2006, and owns 50% of the refinery (Sudan Energy Ministry owns 50%). • CNPC has invested about $4 billion in Sudan since 1995. Sudan production accounts for about 40% of CNPC total overseas equity production. • Sinopec has interests in exploration blocks (with Malaysia's Petronas).	• ONGC has 25% stake in GNPOC • ONGC 23.5% in Block 5a operated by White Nile Petroleum Operating Company, with production about 60,000 bpd oil (Malaysia's Petronas has 68%, and Sudapet has 8%) • ONGC has 23.5% in Block 5b, also operated by WNPOC, where a drilling campaign apparently produced unsatisfactory results in 2008 (Petronas has 39%, Sweden's Lundin has 24.5%, Sudapet has 13%). Drilling services are provided by Dietswell Engineering of France. • ONGC has 32.5% of Block Ba in southern Sudan, where it is conducting an exploration drilling program (Total SA of France has 32.5%, Kufpec of Kuwait has 25%, and Nilepet of Sudan has 5%).
Myanmar	• CNPC concluded a deal for a gas pipeline and gas supply from Myanmar to southern China in December 2008. The pipeline will deliver 2 billion cubic meters (bcm) per year to 4 bcm per year of natural gas from blocks A1 and A3 to Yunnan in southwestern China, for 30 years. CNPC will own 50.9% of the pipeline and operate the pipeline. Korea's Daewoo is the operator of blocks A1 and A3 and owns 51%, India's ONGC has 17%, India's GAIL has 8.5%, Korea Gas has 8.5%, and Myanmar's MOGE has 15%.	• India's ONGC has 17%, India's GAIL has 8.5%, in Blocks A1 and A3 which will supply gas to Yunnan province via a CNPC operated pipeline. Korea's Daewoo is the operator of blocks A1 and A3 and owns 51%, Korea Gas has 8.5%, and Myanmar's MOGE has 15%. • GAIL has 30% of gas field A-7, and 10% in other smaller fields.

	China	India
	• CNPC will build a 400,000-bpd capacity oil pipeline along the same route as the gas pipeline; oil will be offloaded from tankers from the Middle East and Africa, thus avoiding transit of the Malacca Straits. • CNPC has three deepwater exploration blocks in Bay of Bengal and Andaman Sea, AD-1, AD-6, and AD-8. • CNOOC has a joint venture with Singapore and Chinese companies that secured exploration blocks in 2004 and 2005, and in 2008 did a swap with Thailand's PTTEP for additional blocks.	
Iran	• CNPC signed a 25-year deal to develop the North Azedegan oil field in January 2009. Production could reach 75,000 bpd by 2013; CNPC cannot own equity, will be paid from sale of oil. Japan's INPEX was involved in this project but withdrew when Japan agreed to join U.S. sanctions on Iran in late 2010. • CNPC has 10% of Pars LNG project (with Malaysia's Petronas). Total of France was involved but withdrew from the project in 2008. The project is delayed, although CNPC has agreement to purchase up to 4 million tons per year LNG from the project if it is built. • Sinopec secured a deal to develop the Yadavaran oil field in late 2007; Sinopec cannot own equity, will be paid from it 50% share in sale of oil (300,000 bpd planned production; oil field development plan originally performed by Shell).	• ONGC has sought to negotiate a $22 billion deal for development rights in Jufeyr oil field, and 10% to 20% of Yadavaran oil field in exchange for agreement to purchase 5 mtpa LNG for 25 years. • ONGC (40%) Indian Oil Corp. (40%) and Oil India (20%) announced a discovery at its Farsi exploration block in May 2007. • ONGC has engaged in talks with National Iranian Oil Company to develop oil and gas fields in Caspian. • ONGC and GAIL have long-running negotiations with NIOC for a proposed gas pipeline from Iran to India, which would transit Pakistan; price and security remain issues. • India's Essar has sought to participate in a 300,000-bpd-capacity refinery in Bandar Abbas

(continued)

Table 7.13 (*coninued*)

China	India
• Sinopec provided technical and engineering services to upgrade the Teheran and Tebriz refineries in 2000–2003. • CNOOC secured a deal in late 2008 to develop the North Pars gas field and build a gas liquefaction facility (LNG). CNOOC cannot own equity, will be paid from its 50% share of production. CNOOC must purchase 10 million tons of LNG from the project over 25 years as part of the deal (this purchase obligation may possibly be shared with Sinopec as part its conditions for getting the Yadavaran deal). Iran LNG projects have seen significant delays.	• Indian External Affairs Minister called for greater Indian investment in Iran's energy and industrial sectors in a November 2008 speech in Teheran; Indian government supported ONGC for more upstream investment in Iran.

	China	India
Cuba[91]	• Sinopec has joint heavy crude production with Cuba Petroleum onshore in Pinar del Rio province. • CNPC has oil services and equipment support agreements with Cuba's Cupet. • China has additional offshore exploration agreements under discussion with Cuba.	• ONGC is a partner in a consortium in six Gulf of Mexico E&P blocks opened by Cuba to foreign companies.[92] ONGC's partners include Spain's Repsol YPF and Norway's Norsk Hydro. Drilling commenced in late 2007. • ONGC has 100% in two other Cuban E&P blocks. • India's Minister of Renewable Energy signed an agreement for wind, biomass, and solar energy technology and training exchanges with Cuba's Minister of Science and Technology in May 2007.

[91] Canada's Sherritt was the most active foreign company in Cuba, with nine fields operating onshore and five exploration or appraisal blocks being drilled in 2007. See "China, Cuba Plan Joint Ventures," *Reuters News Wire*, March 28, 2007. Malaysia's Petronas also secured four E&P blocks in Cuba.

[92] "Cuba, India sign energy agreement," *Indo-Asian News Service*, May 26, 2007. India discussed these energy ties and forgave $62 million in Cuban debt during a meeting between Cuban Foreign Minister Felipe Perez Roque and Indian Prime Minister Manmohan Singh in New Delhi in April 2007.

	China	India
Syria	• CNPC has 50% of the Kokab oil project with Syrian Petroleum Company, which owns the other 50%. This is a project to re-develop the Qubibe oil field. • CNPC with India's ONGC jointly bid to take Petro-Canada's 38% stake in Al-Furat Production Company, Syria's largest producer with about 60,000 bpd, in late 2005. The two companies manage their 38% share in Al-Furat through a 50–50 joint-venture company called Himalaya Energy (Syria). • CNPC has an MOU with Syria to build a 100,000-bpd-capacity refinery in Deir-al Zour; feasibility study has been completed.	• ONGC (50%) in JV with CNPC for oil production in Syria, own 38% of Al-Furat, production about 60,000 bpd. • Indian firms in negotiations for seven oil exploration blocks following a visit of Indian Oil Minister in April 2007.[93] • GAIL in negotiations for compressed natural gas (CNG) processing and distribution. • Engineers India Limited (EIL) negotiating to perform upgrade to Syria's Banias Refinery.

Note: This table is based on best available public information at the time of publication, and may not be comprehensive or complete. Investment positions are subject to change, with some companies exiting and new ones entering these markets. In some cases, preliminary agreements may never be fully implemented. For example, both India and China have encountered difficulties in fully implementing investment plans in Iran.

dominant power" (i.e., the United States) that has greatly increased its military presence in the Middle East.[94]

The Indo-Iran relationship is not limited to government-to-government relations. Many Indian or Indian-invested private firms, such as Hindujas, Essar, and Reliance, have long histories of mutually beneficial investment and trade with Iran. New Delhi might find it politically difficult to restrict the activities of private Indian firms in Iran even if it believed this was good foreign policy. Currently, rather than restricting investment, Indian officials promote Indian investment in Iran and Indo-Iranian trade at the highest levels. For example, External Affairs Minister Pranab Mukherjee specifically

---

[93] "Syria will preferentially allot exploration blocks to Indian firms," *The Hindu*, April 21, 2007. The Indian Oil Minister was accompanied on this visit by a number of officials including the Petroleum Secretary and the chairmen of four Indian oil and gas companies.

[94] S. D. Muni and Girijesh Pant, *India's Energy Security: Prospects for Cooperation with Extended Neighbourhood* (New Delhi: Rupa & Company Publishers, 2005), 265.

requested Iranian approval for further investments in Iran by ONGC and other Indian energy companies at a high-profile conference with Iranian Foreign Minister Manoucher Mottaki in Teheran in November 2008.[95]

India is not the only American friend or ally to cooperate with China in investments in "rogue regimes."[96] Companies from U.S. partners and allies also invest (or have attempted to invest) in energy and resource projects in these countries. Although some have ultimately withdrawn, at various times these have included companies from Korea, Japan, France, Italy, and Canada, as well as from friendly European states such as Sweden.

India has invested in nearly every "rogue" nation where China is involved. This evidence does not provide political or moral justification for collaboration with repressive regimes, nor does it amount to a unique indictment of India. It does suggest, however, that U.S. policy should target the behavior – cooperating with a regime that pursues policies contrary to U.S. interests in human rights and universally accepted political norms – rather than seeking to single out particular nations and punish that nation disproportionately. Further, the United States might be more successful in persuading China to alter its behavior (and to agree that some values are truly "universal") if American policies and rhetoric on this issue were more balanced and consistent.

Disrupting International Markets?

In addition to support for unsavory regimes, some in the West question whether China will undermine the accepted rules of international market competition. Most governments see international energy supply as a major strategic concern. India, for example, has sought to coordinate international M&A activity with China to prevent market competition between their respective companies from bidding up the price of resources.[97] The anti-competition agreement came at India's initiative, after India's ONGC lost out to Chinese rivals in competition to acquire oil and gas fields in Angola, Nigeria, Kazakhstan, and Ecuador.[98] China initially rejected many of India's collaborative overtures for anti-market competition, but in January 2006,

---

[95] Address by H. E. Mr. Pranab Mukherjee, Minister of External Affairs, Seminar on "India and Iran: Ancient Civilizations and Modern Nations," Teheran, November 2, 2008, http://meaindia.nic.in/speech/2008/11/02ss01.htm

[96] "China, Rivals Join in Search for Energy," *Dow Jones Energy Service*, April 4, 2007; see also "OVL, CNPC set off on joint oil hunt again," *The Economic Times of India*, April 7, 2007.

[97] Richard MacGregor et al., "China and India forge alliance on oil," *Financial Times*, January 12, 2006.

[98] "India Yet to Match China's Cash, Political Clout," *Petroleum Intelligence Weekly*, October 24, 2005; also *Petroleum Intelligence Weekly*, November 15, 2005.

Indian Petroleum Minister Mani Shankar Aiyar and the head of China's National Development Reform Commission, Ma Kai, signed an agreement to cooperate in securing international petroleum resources. This eventually helped support collaborative Indian and Chinese investments in Syria, Colombia, Angola, and Venezuela.

Another question about respect for accepted market rules centers on the way firms purchase international energy supplies. In the view of some members of the U.S. Congress, Chinese firms exhibit a unique pattern of energy trade. In this view, China does not buy oil and gas on international markets. It attempts to "lock up" resources through equity investments and ship production back to China.[99] According to its 2005 annual report to Congress, members of the U.S.-China Economic and Security Review Commission (USCC) believe that "China increasingly is focused on acquiring petroleum at the source, rather than purchasing it – as the United States and most other nations do – on international markets."[100]

Contrary to such claims, China's principal mode of international oil market behavior is to purchase crude oil on international markets at international market prices. For example, in 2008, only about half of Chinese firms' total overseas equity production was shipped back to China. That represents a small fraction of China's total crude oil imports. In total, about 90 percent of China's total oil imports of 4 mbd that year came from international market purchases. Furthermore, there is little evidence that even this trade activity is closely coordinated from Beijing. Decisions on sales of Chinese equity crude are typically made on the basis of commercial incentives, and many of these decisions are made on a daily basis by subsidiary companies, not coordinated by state oil company headquarters in Beijing.[101]

For example, China's imports from Sudan demonstrate a response to market conditions and price rather than to political mandates alone. Chinese imports from Sudan declined in 2006, from a mid-year high of more than 150,000 barrels per day to less than 30,000 barrels per day, before

---

[99] Statement of Hon. C. Richard D'Amato, Chairman, U.S.-China Economic and Security Review Commission, "National Security Dimensions of the Possible Acquisition of UNOCAL by CNOOC and the Role of CFIUS," Before the House Committee on Armed Services, July 13, 2005.

[100] U.S.-China Economic and Security Review Commission, *Annual Report to Congress*, 2005, 168.

[101] Julie Jiang and Jonathan Sinton, "Overseas Investments by Chinese National Oil Companies: Assessing the Drivers and Impacts," International Energy Agency, February 2011; interview with NDRC official September 2007; interview with China National Petroleum Corporation official, September 2007.

recovering in December 2006. Japan was offering a higher price for Sudan crude in 2006 as it needed to increase fuel oil supplies for electricity generation to replace nuclear power that had been shut down for safety reasons. Japan's imports from Sudan increased from about 45,000 barrels per day in March 2006 to more than 150,000 barrels per day in June, before stabilizing at slightly less than 100,000 barrels per day at the end of the year.[102]

This pattern of trading and importing oil at market prices according to general international market norms is unlikely to change for either Chinese or Indian firms. In general, because international oil markets are well developed and integrated, it is neither profitable nor practical to pursue a long-term strategy of shipping all of one's own physical production back to one's home country. It is wiser to sell at the highest price in the market. Doing so minimizes transport costs and maximizes returns.

Crude oil trade flows are heavily influenced by freight costs and the specific match between different crude oil qualities (such as sulphur content) and the technical requirements of specific refiners. These factors determine the price and the availability of crude supply. Sudan crude fits requirements at some Chinese refineries.[103] A substantial portion (though not all) of Chinese equity production from Sudan is sold to refiners in China for this reason. However, in general, like their IOC counterparts, Chinese and Indian national oil companies sell most of their international crude oil production for the highest possible price, and they purchase crude by seeking the lowest delivered cost in comparison to the next best supply alternative.[104]

It may, however, be useful to consider a worst-case scenario, in which Chinese firms are instructed to ignore costs and logistical constraints and are ordered to ship all of their overseas production back to China. Some Chinese government officials do believe that the physical ability to ship equity production back to China (on Chinese-owned ships) does augment China's energy security, even if only in theory and as a last resort.[105]

---

[102] For a useful introduction to the logic behind these oil trade movements, see Daniel H. Rosen and Trevor Houser, "China Energy: A Guide for the Perplexed," Center for Strategic and International Studies and Peterson Institute for International Economics, May 2007.

[103] China has built a number of refineries with the ability to handle lower quality crude oil, such as high-sulphur Sudan crude. India has also built new, highly complex refineries capable of handling low quality crude oil. This allows these Chinese and Indian refiners to scour international markets for crude oils that have very few market alternatives, and are therefore relatively cheap. Interview with international oil company crude oil trader, October 2010.

[104] Interview with international oil company crude oil trader, October 2010.

[105] Interview with NDRC official; interview with China National Petroleum Corporation official, September 2007.

If China could execute such a strategy over the long term and sustain the commercial and economic penalties associated with it, would this appreciably disrupt international oil markets? Even in the unlikely (and expensive) hypothetical case where all of China's equity oil production was shipped back to China, this oil would not come close to meeting China's domestic demand. Total Chinese overseas equity crude oil production in 2010 was equivalent to only about 30 percent of China's 2010 crude oil imports of about 5 million barrels per day. Reliance on overseas equity production, therefore, would not satisfy China's import needs.[106]

From the perspective of American interests, even if China's firms did ship all their international oil production back to China, this would only free up an equivalent amount of oil on international markets because China would not be purchasing that amount of crude. In such a case, Beijing would pay higher-than-usual costs to transport the oil to China, and the absence of Chinese firms from regular oil-trading markets might cause spot prices to temporarily decline for everyone else.

In India, as in China, there is an ongoing debate about the best way to achieve and maintain energy security. For example, in a December 2006 speech, the Secretary of India's Ministry of Power, R. V. Shahi, said that one component of Indian energy security strategy should be to access "cheap" natural gas supplies and set up "captive" fertilizer or gas liquefaction plants in those countries to "augment energy availability for India."[107] Similar concepts for securing supply through diplomacy and state-supported direct investments have been criticized in the West when proposed or implemented by Chinese firms. Yet Shahi's 2006 speech also recognized that for India, energy security is "primarily about ensuring the continuous availability of commercial energy at competitive prices to support its economic growth." Thus far, the dominant view of industry and political leaders in both New Delhi and Beijing is that, despite the political and commercial attractions of some outward investment in energy resources, energy security remains contingent on participation in diverse markets according to international market practices.[108]

---

[106] China also imported 959,000 bpd of oil products in 2006, so its equity oil production as a percent of total oil imports was lower than 20 percent.

[107] R. V. Shahi, "India's Strategy Towards Energy Development and Security," Ministry of Power, paper presented to the Board of International Energy Agency at Sydney on December 12, 2006 in the Seminar on "Energy Insights from Asia Pacific."

[108] Shahi, "India's Strategy Towards Energy Development," 8.

Conclusions: Economic Strategies and Energy Competition

Compared to India, China has a larger economy, a more developed industrial sector, and a greater role in both global trade and bilateral trade and investment with the United States. Both countries are growing fast but both also have large-scale poverty, populations with rising expectations, and significant domestic risks to continued growth. China's manufacturing firms are more closely integrated with global technology supply chains than India's. Indian manufacturing firms may have potential, but thus far the closest international supply chain relations for Indian firms are in services and software industries. By some measures, China's economy is more open to international trade and investment than India's. The frequency and the nature of WTO trade disputes are similar for the two countries, despite China's much larger scale of trade.

Bilateral disputes with the United States are similar in nature, albeit not in scale. Structural impediments to market access are present in both countries. Some trade disputes, such as losses from IPR violations and piracy, are proportional to the two economies' relative size. In 2008 and 2009, Beijing announced technology promotion policies, which, if maintained, would represent a shift away from its relatively open trade and investment regime and toward protectionism. Such measures have been attempted before, and most have failed, because China's domestic firms are embedded in global supply chains. Dependence on international trade for revenue, growth, and employment, as well as access to key resources and technology mean that protectionism and trade conflict hold the potential for heavy economic and social costs to China and, increasingly, to India.

Chinese and Indian behaviors do not appear to be markedly different in international energy markets. Both Chinese and Indian firms are active investors and collaborators with states that the United States considers rogue regimes, but in general they are joining international energy markets on the terms and according to the market practices established by their IOC predecessors. Like companies from developed economies, Chinese and Indian firms are unable to "control" upstream resources in any way that threatens to significantly disrupt global energy trade. Nor does it appear that they are seeking to do this. Both India and China import energy resources on international markets, and their upstream acquisitions are not greatly different from the activities of other international energy companies.

8

India, China, and Democratic Peace Theory

Side-by-side comparisons in the preceding chapters have revealed broad similarities in Indian and Chinese international strategic behavior. Despite some important specific differences that come into focus through structured comparison, neither state can be described as generally more prone than the other to foreign policy *realpolitik*, the use of force, and a preference for offensive military doctrine. Neither is more intent on modernizing its military forces, pursuing trade protectionism, or working with rogue regimes to secure energy interests. But what of the future? The two states have starkly different domestic regimes – India has a vibrant democracy, China has an adaptive but enduring authoritarian state. Is the difference in regime type a useful predictor of future international strategic behavior? Can projections based on regime type help U.S. leaders determine how the two powers will behave relative to U.S. interests?

In this chapter, we explore two claims made by scholars and policy makers about the relationship between regime type and a state's international security behavior. The first claim is that democracies are more prone to peace than nondemocracies. The core of this argument is that democracies do not fight wars with one another, although in public and policy debates, the argument is frequently broadened to assert that democracies are more peaceful in general. The second claim is that shared political values (specifically democracy and rule of law) tend to cause the security interests of democratic states to converge. These ideas have broad appeal among both elites and the general public in the United States, and are frequently cited in debates about U.S. policy toward both China and India.

In the first section, we briefly review the role ideas about democracy have played in U.S. foreign policy since the 1990s. Political leaders may not believe in a simple causal relationship between regime type and a state's international behavior, even if some academic arguments verge on making such a link. However, for American leaders, the broad popularity and the intuitive appeal of the connection between democracy and peace make these ideas a powerful mental image.[1] These images may shape leadership views of other states, not only in terms of what behaviors to expect, but also in terms of what is (and is not) achievable in bilateral relations. Thus, we take these views seriously, including statements about them by senior U.S. policy makers. In the second section of this chapter, we evaluate both the theoretical and empirical basis for the two claims, and offer conclusions about the extent to which U.S. leaders can rely on democratic peace theory as a predictor of the security behavior of other states.

Democratic Peace and American Foreign Policy

The cause of "democracy" as a concern for American foreign policy has roots that go at least as far back as Woodrow Wilson. In 1917, in 1941, and during the Cold War, American leaders argued that the United States had an interest in preventing wealthy and powerful democratic states from being conquered and absorbed by even more powerful authoritarian states. In the 1980s, Ronald Reagan argued that U.S. foreign policy should promote democratic values, not merely prevent established democracies from being destroyed. In the 1990s, Bill Clinton took an approach similar to Reagan's, limiting his vision to U.S. support for democratization rather than promotion of regime change. Yet Clinton also believed that, "Ultimately, the best strategy to ensure our security and to build a durable peace is to support the advance of democracy elsewhere. Democracies don't attack each other."[2]

The George W. Bush administration took the ideological and policy commitment to democracy further. Beginning in 2001, the U.S. government made the international promotion of democracy a central pillar of its foreign policy across regions as diverse as Eastern Europe, the Middle East, and Central Asia. Promoting democracy was identified with promoting peace and security.[3] The U.S. Congress also provided bipartisan support to

---

[1]   We thank Stephen P. Cohen for this point.

[2]   Bill Clinton, "1994 State Of The Union Address," January 25, 1994.

[3]   George W. Bush explained, "[T]he reason why I'm so strong on democracy is democracies don't go to war with each other. It's a duty to our own country ... to help secure the peace by promoting democratic societies." "President and Prime Minister Blair Discussed Iraq, Middle East," The White House, Office of the Press Secretary, November 12, 2004, http://www.whitehouse.gov/news/releases/2004/11/20041112-5.html

democracy promotion on the grounds that it would promote international peace and support American interests.[4]

There have been important differences in policies across these administrations. Yet a common belief linking all of them, Democratic and Republican, is that democracies and nondemocracies act differently on the international stage. Leadership views have been heavily influenced by a specific set of ideas associated with "democratic peace theory," the central claim of which is that democracies do not fight wars against one another.

Some U.S. leaders have added an extension to that core idea: Even more than relative power and its interests, a state's regime type (democratic or nondemocratic) should be the guideline for the U.S. foreign policy and security approach to that nation.[5] This approach characterized much U.S. foreign policy from 2001 to 2008, and these principles remain popular with leaders in both U.S. political parties. These views also underpin recent conservative and liberal critiques of any "turn to realism" in U.S. foreign policy.[6]

Democracy in U.S. India and China Policy

Liberal values rightly form a guide for America's own behavior. Liberal values also form a powerful interpretive filter for American leaders trying to understand and predict the behaviors and strategies of other states. Over the last decade, U.S. policies toward China and India appear increasingly to reflect an underlying assumption that India, a democracy, is more likely to pursue foreign policies commensurate with U.S. interests than China, an authoritarian system with roots in both imperial traditions and communism. Extrapolating from democratic peace theory, the lack of common

---

[4] In 2005, Congress passed the Advance Democracy Act, which states: "There is a correlation between nondemocratic rule and other threats to international peace and security.... Wars between or among democratic countries are exceedingly rare, while wars between and among nondemocratic countries are commonplace, with nearly 170,000,000 people having lost their lives because of the policies of totalitarian governments." "Advance Democratic Values, Address Nondemocratic Countries, and Enhance Democracy Act of 2005," 109th Congress, 1st Session, S. 516, March 3, 2005.

[5] Condoleezza Rice, "The Promise of Democratic Peace," *The Washington Post*, December 11, 2005.

[6] Michael J. Green, "Obama's self-defeating 'realism' in Asia," *Foreign Policy*, October 6, 2009, http://shadow.foreignpolicy.com/blog/12381; Robert Kagan "Foreign Policy Sequels," *Washington Post*, March 9, 2009; Daniel Blumenthal, "Obama's Asia trip: a series of unfortunate events, *Foreign Policy*, November 18, 2009, http://shadow.foreignpolicy.com/posts/2009/11/18/obamas_asia_trip_a_series_of_unfortunate_events; "During Visit, Obama Skirts Chinese Political Sensitivities," *New York Times*, November 17, 2009; and Stephen Zunes, "Human Rights: C+," *Foreign Policy in Focus*, January 25, 2010, http://www.fpif.org/articles/human_rights_c

values and institutions is said to make international conflict with China more likely than with India. For some, shared democratic values are also seen as facilitating the convergence of Indian and U.S. foreign policy and security interests – a viewpoint that is a departure from the more limited claims made by the academic proponents of democratic peace theory.

Referring to China, U.S. Senator John McCain summed up a view common to much of the American foreign policy establishment: "[U]ntil China moves toward political liberalization, our relationship will be based on periodically shared interests rather than the bedrock of shared values."[7] Recent statements on U.S. India policy reflect the opposite side of the same theoretical coin. Since the late 1990s, American leaders have highlighted the power of common democratic political institutions and values to help shape common U.S.-India foreign policy interests.[8] Democracy has been viewed by both Indian and U.S. leaders as the foundation for a new U.S.-India relationship as "natural allies."[9]

Although often only vaguely articulated, such justifications for U.S. policy posit two links between democracy and United States-India security interests. The first appeals to the idea of democracy and peace. However, it goes beyond the idea that "democracies do not fight one another" to suggest that democracies are both more pacific and more inclined to protect the peace than nondemocracies.[10] A second and even broader extension of ideas on democracy and international politics suggests that because the United States and India are both democracies, they share values and their foreign policy interests will therefore tend to converge.[11]

---

[7] John McCain, "An Enduring Peace Built on Freedom: Securing America's Future," *Foreign Affairs*, 86:6 (November/December 2007), 19–34.

[8] In the late 1990s, Bill Clinton saw India's intrinsic importance as a large democracy with great economic potential as a principal factor leading him to want to develop a new relationship with India. See George Perkovich, *India's Nuclear Bomb: The Impact on Global Proliferation*, 2nd ed. (Berkeley: University of California Press, 2001), 490; and Strobe Talbott, *Engaging India: Diplomacy, Democracy and The Bomb* (Washington, DC: Brookings Institution, 2004), 44–45.

[9] Indian Prime Minister Atal Bihari Vajpayee first used the term "natural allies" in 1998. Vajpayee described the United States and India as natural allies during his visit to the White House in November 2002. That sentiment was echoed by American officials preparing for George W. Bush's state visit to India in March 2006. See "The great Indian hope trick – India and America," *The Economist*, February 25, 2006.

[10] "President, Indian Prime Minister Singh Exchange Toasts," Washington, DC: The White House Office of the Press Secretary, July 18, 2005; and "Remarks by President Bush and Prime Minister Manmohan Singh of India in Joint Press Availability," Washington, DC: The White House Office of the Press Secretary, July 18, 2005.

[11] Winston Lord, U.S. ambassador to China during the Clinton administration and Assistant Secretary of State for Asian and Pacific Affairs under Clinton, summarized the

In a 2008 essay, then-U.S. Secretary of State Condoleezza Rice outlined a comprehensive argument for the role of democratic political ideals as the proper guidelines for American foreign and security policy.[12] Rice's arguments represent an enduring perspective on American foreign policy that will continue to play an important role in debates about America's response to rising Chinese and Indian power for many years to come. In this view, relations with China are "rooted more in common interests than common values" and are "characterized simultaneously by competition and cooperation." In contrast, India is seen as a "democratic nation [that] promises to become a global power and an ally in shaping an international order rooted in freedom and rule of law."[13] Further, regime type is seen to be the major determining factor in future balances of power in Asia, as well as determining future security alignments.[14] India as a democracy is seen as playing a critical role in ensuring that the balance of power will favor U.S. interests. The United States should, therefore, actively work to support rising Indian relative power.[15]

It is possible that American statements on democracy as the basis for common interest (or conflict) between the United States and other states might simply be rhetorical cover for a realist policy. Certainly, disentangling the causal links between common values and common foreign policy interests is difficult. And for some leaders, the influence of democratic peace theory and related notions may operate at a subconscious level, in competition with other ideas. Yet there are four reasons to take statements about regime type and expected behavior seriously and to properly distinguish these arguments from the perspective of realist international relations theory (a theory that focuses on relative power and interest as principal determinants of state behavior).

First, senior U.S. leaders have been consistent in their stated views over time. There appear to be links between these stated preferences and actual U.S. policies across regions including Eastern Europe, the Middle East, and

---

contrasting American views of potential security interests and relations with India and China: "(T)here is a limit to our relations with China because we share only interests, not values. The fundamental reason for India and the US coming together is our shared values." Winston Lord, quoted in Sharif Shuja, "The realignment of India-US relations: strategic dimensions," *Contemporary Review*, October 2005. See also *Quadrennial Defense Review Report* (Washington, DC: Office of the Secretary of Defense, February 2010), 31.

[12] Condoleezza Rice, "Rethinking the National Interest: American Realism for a New World," *Foreign Affairs*, 87:4 (July/August 2008): 2–26.
[13] Rice, "Rethinking the National Interest," 5.
[14] Rice, "Rethinking the National Interest," 7.
[15] Rice, "Rethinking the National Interest," 8.

Asia. Second, both statements on democracy as a criterion for forming foreign policy, as well as the policies themselves, have found support in both Republican and Democratic administrations. Third, even if such statements are merely rhetoric, they have been used to justify a number of important policies to the American people, and they shape expectations about U.S. policy both among U.S. citizens and in the international community.

Finally, if arguments about democracy as a basis for common international security interests are merely rhetorical cover for a realist policy, the rhetoric itself threatens to obscure real, specific conflicts of interest, as well as specific areas ripe for cooperation. These ideas represent a perennial debate in U.S. foreign policy circles. Their application to democratic India and authoritarian China is likely to attract attention over the next several decades, so it is useful to review the debate on "democratic peace" and evaluate the extent to which this knowledge may be a reliable guide to policy making.

Democratic Peace Theory

Democratic peace theory has its roots in Immanuel Kant's 1795 essay, "Perpetual Peace." Kant argued that republican states will not fight one another, and that a "zone of peace" will emerge and widen as more states become democratic. Modern political science has rediscovered Kant, most famously in a 1986 essay by Michael Doyle.[16] The modern advocates of democratic peace theory limit their claim to an argument about international relations *between* democracies. They argue that democracies rarely – if ever – fight wars against each other.

This limited claim is the core idea of the "democratic peace." Even the theory's strongest academic proponents do not argue that it helps predict the frequency of war between individual democratic and nondemocratic states. Indeed, it is widely acknowledged that, because of the frequency with which democracies fight nondemocracies, democratic states are just as prone to engage in war as any other type of regime.[17]

Modern students differ on what might explain the democratic peace phenomenon. Some emphasize shared political norms. The practices of

---

[16] Michael W. Doyle, "Liberalism and World Politics," *American Political Science Review*, 80:4 (December 1986): 1151–1169.

[17] Michael W. Doyle, "Kant, Liberal Legacies, and Foreign Affairs, Part 1," *Philosophy and Public Affairs*, 12:3 (1983): 205–235; and Edward D. Mansfield and Jack Snyder, "Democratization and the Dangers of War," *International Security*, 20:1 (Summer 1995): 18.

adjudication and bargaining characterize domestic politics in democratic states, and negotiated agreements are recognized as a more attractive and workable solution to disputes than war. Between democracies, these methods are mutually recognized as working well to resolve conflicts of interest in domestic politics, and therefore are incorporated into foreign policy.[18] Other theorists place greater emphasis on structural explanations. Democracies are characterized by systems of checks and balances. Average citizens, who are most likely to fight, suffer and die in war, have the power to oppose decisions (through legislatures, courts, and the media) or sanction leaders (through elections). Leaders, therefore, are cautious about launching wars.[19]

Advocates of democratic peace theory must explain why democracies, despite the values and structures outlined above, fight as many wars as nondemocracies even if they do not fight each other. Here, at the risk of some oversimplification, theorists suggest that the citizens of democratic states project their own values onto potential democratic adversaries and are more inclined to accept that the issues raised by democratic adversaries are legitimate or "just," even if unpalatable.[20] Conversely, issues and concerns raised by nondemocratic states are implicitly less "just," and conflict of interest is therefore more likely to lead to war.

Analytical Issues

Democratic peace theorists have tested their propositions by examining the correlation between different types of regime types and war. In doing so, they have employed both data sets that categorize (or "code") states according to their regime type and other data sets that code international conflicts according to their nature and intensity.[21] They conclude that there is substantial empirical evidence to support the argument that democracies tend to not fight wars with one another. However, even many proponents of the theory do not propose that there is a law of international relations that

---

[18] Zeev Maoz and Bruce M. Russett, "Normative and Structural Causes of Democratic Peace, 1946–1986," *American Political Science Review*, 87:3 (September 1993): 624–638; and Henry S. Farber and Joanne Gowa, "Polities and Peace," *International Security*, 20:2 (Fall 1995): 125.

[19] T. Clifton Morgan and Sally Howard Campbell, "Domestic Structure, Decisional Constraints, and War: So Why Kant Democracies Fight?" *Journal of Conflict Resolution*, 35:2 (June 1991): 187–211; Farber and Gowa, "Polities and Peace," 128.

[20] Doyle, "Kant, Liberal Legacies, and Foreign Affairs, Part 1," 230.

[21] See Michael E. Brown, Sean M. Lynn-Jones, and Steven E. Miller, *Debating the Democratic Peace* (Cambridge: MIT Press, 1996).

democracies *never* fight each other, partly due to doubts about the quality of evidence for such a strong claim.[22]

Critics have raised a number of questions about democratic peace theory. They focus on three areas: its logic, its dependence on hotly disputed definitions and "coding" necessary to produce statistically significant evidence in support of the theory, and the persuasiveness of the theory in contrast to other theories that may better account for the same empirical results.

Both the "shared norms" and "checks and balances" arguments about why democracies tend to not fight one another have logical problems. The argument that shared norms explain the democratic peace faces the difficulty of showing that norms, or values, are somehow distinct from interests. All values are held to be valuable because they are, after all, in our interest. It is therefore difficult to construct a test of the idea that norms, rather than interests, explain behavior.[23] The idea that shared liberal norms and values act to align interests and spur us to choose negotiation rather than combat does engage a strong, self-confirming feeling of "rightness," especially among citizens of post–World War II, advanced industrial democracies. However, the weakness of the logical explanation of how shared norms might operate in a distinct way from shared interests raises doubts about the power of this variant of democratic peace theory.[24] The checks-and-balances argument is on even shakier ground because it does not explain why democracies fight just as often overall as other countries.

In short, advocates of democratic peace theory are left in the uncomfortable position of claiming the theory is "right," even though they have not yet satisfied themselves or their critics that they can explain why or how it works. With a less-than-compelling logic, the real value of democratic peace theory appears to depend on the empirical evidence that can be marshaled in its support. The historical track record is the source of most of the theory's persuasive power.

Empirical Disputes

The empirical evidence does not present an open-and-shut case for democratic peace theory. Instead, a number of important qualifications are

---

[22] Bruce Russett, "The Democratic Peace – and Yet It Moves." *International Security*, 19:4 (Spring 1995): 164–175 (169).

[23] Farber and Gowa, "Polities and Peace," 126.

[24] Specifically, the theory appears to perform best in explaining post–World War II relations among advanced industrial democracies in a world where the great powers also have nuclear weapons.

required to make the theory work. The strongest claims for a separate peace among democratic states come from individuals who have coded their own data prior to their statistical analysis. In other words, these analysts personally determined key definitions for historical data used to test their own theories, such as exactly what constitutes a "democratic state" and what qualifies as a "war." This opens their arguments to charges of selective or biased coding, particularly since until quite recently, the number of democratic states has been small, and the chances that any two given states will be at war at any particular time are low.[25] With the odds of war between any two democracies (a subset of "states") being even smaller, the entire empirical basis for democratic peace theory turns on definitions and the coding of a handful of individual cases. This has produced a lively debate on whether the War of 1812, the Spanish-American War, Germany's role in World War I, Finland's joining Nazi Germany against the Allies during World War II, and Israel's 2006 invasion of Lebanon might constitute wars between democracies.[26]

Elaborate definitional and methodological debates have resulted in less-than-fully satisfying answers. The War of 1812 is a case in point. Advocates claim that the war between Britain and the United States does not constitute a war between democracies because Britain was not yet a democracy, with only one-seventh of the British population enjoying political suffrage at that time. Yet the same analysts are willing to code Britain as a democracy only a few years later, in 1832, when suffrage was expanded to include a total of only one-fifth of the population. Such a small difference seems a negligible hook on which to hang the fate of a "law" of international politics.

Other researchers have analyzed the relationship between regime type and war using third-party databases originally created for other purposes. (These databases are therefore less susceptible to conscious or unconscious manipulation in support of particular findings.) These analysts have found weaker support for a separate democratic peace or, depending on how the data are parsed, they have found no statistical relationship between regime type and the propensity to war.[27]

---

[25] Farber and Gowa, "Polities and Peace," 137.

[26] For a more thorough discussion of possible exceptions, see David E. Spiro, "The Insignificance of the Liberal Peace," *International Security*, 19:2 (Autumn 1994): 50–86.

[27] See, for example, Edward D. Mansfield and Jack Snyder, "Democratization and the Dangers of War," *International Security*, 20:1 (Summer 1995): 5–38; Farber and Gowa, "Polities and Peace"; and comments by Christopher Layne and David E. Spiro, in "Correspondence: The Democratic Peace," *International Security*, 19:4 (Spring 1995): 169.

The important issue here is not specific detail, such as exactly when Britain, or Finland, or Lebanon "qualifies" as a democracy. The point is that the utility of the empirical evidence is highly dependent on careful study of definitions and historical context. This raises questions about the universality of the democratic peace concept. Can a theory that depends so heavily on shared norms and the detailed configuration of domestic checks and balances be extended beyond a particular, historically derived form of democracy to a more diverse set of regimes in Latin America, Africa, and Asia?

Notably, all of these concerns and qualifications apply to the theory's core, limited argument about war between democracies. Extensions of the core theory – including ideas about the potential for shared regime type and shared political values to produce common foreign policy preferences or even convergent security interests – have no logical support from democratic peace theory, and have yet to be empirically tested.

Competing Theories

A final problem confronting democratic peace theory is that there are alternative explanations for the phenomenon of the democratic peace. Indeed, the most convincing empirical evidence cited to support the theory may actually suggest that an alternative explanation is superior. Henry S. Farber and Joanne Gowa, for example, find that between 1816 and 1980, "war between democracies occurs at a significantly lower rate than does war between members of other pairs of states." This result, however, applies primarily to the post-1945 period. Farber and Gowa find that "what seems to have become the conventional wisdom about the relationship between democracies and war applies, in fact, *only* to the Cold War years [italics in original]."[28]

The Cold War period, however, was characterized by a particular structure of international relations: a bipolar system ruled by hegemons that forced their allies to emulate their own regime types, with international system structure thus partly "selecting" regime type. The advent of nuclear weapons in this period may also have significantly reduced the chances of major powers going to war. This finding suggests that relative power, and the common interest states in the West had in opposing a threat from states in the East, is at least as powerful an explanation for the post-1945 peace between the democracies as either shared democratic norms or the ability of democracies to check executive power.

[28] Farber and Gowa, "Polities and Peace," 142.

Finally, another difficulty with democratic peace theory is that in concentrating on the experience of the post–World War II era modern industrial democracies, proponents have tended to overlook the track record of immature democracies and states in the process of democratization. Edward Mansfield and Jack Snyder have shown that democratizing states and immature democracies are actually more prone to war than other states.[29] For the period from 1811 to 1980, Mansfield and Snyder found that democratizing states were about two-thirds more likely to go to war than states that had experienced no regime change. This offers further reason for caution about the utility of regime type as a predictor of international strategic behavior. Further, this historical record indicates that democratic India may struggle to maintain good relations with South Asian neighbors who are democratizing or trying to consolidate democracy. In East and North Asia, democratization in China may not necessarily be the sole answer to regional peace and stability.

Expansive Claims

The core of democratic peace theory thus rests on shaky theoretical and empirical ground. Yet some U.S. scholars and officials argue that further extensions of the theory can be built on these foundations.[30] Perhaps the most questionable suggestion made about the link between democracy and international behavior is that democracy may endow states such as India and the United States with common or converging foreign policy interests.[31] Democratic peace theory says nothing on the issue of potential convergence of foreign and security policy preferences and interests among democracies. It is intuitively appealing to believe that common political values should encourage common foreign policy views, but these are untested assertions.

As we have seen from side-by-side comparison of the strategic behavior of democratic India and authoritarian China, the empirical record of the relationship between democracy and peace, and regime type and common

---

[29] Mansfield and Snyder, "Democratization and the Danger of War"; Edward D. Mansfield and Jack Snyder, *Electing to Fight: Why Emerging Democracies Go To War* (Cambridge, MA: MIT Press, 2005).

[30] Condoleezza Rice, "The Promise of Democratic Peace," *The Washington Post*, December 11, 2005.

[31] American officials often imply a link between democracy and peace but do not specify how this linkage operates. *Quadrennial Defense Review Report*, 2010, 31. Colin Powell, confirmation hearings, *Washington File*, January 17, 2001, cited in Amit Gupta, *The U.S. India Relationship: Strategic Partnership or Complementary Interests?* (Carlisle: U.S. Army War College, 2005).

interest, is mixed at best. Even the necessarily high-level review of only two states presented in this book shows there is little reason to believe, *a priori*, that regime type will necessarily dictate the outcome of individual cases. The post–Cold War history of U.S. relations with democracies such as France and Israel demonstrates that regional balances of power and specific circumstances can result in divergent security interests and policy approaches, even among formal allies.

India and the United States are both democracies, but they are different societies with different politics and regimes. More importantly, they face different domestic, regional, and global challenges. The United States is embedded in North American, Northeast Asian, and European relationships that surround it with stable and mature democracies. It faces no major security threats from within its own region, and it has no core territorial disputes with its neighbors. In contrast, India is embedded in a South Asian region with states that have a mixed experience with political liberalism at best, and India confronts a number of regional security challenges. Different levels of economic development and the particulars of national resource endowment shape the two countries' material interests in international regimes and organizations, as well as in their relations with a host of individual states. It is not clear that democracy or common democratic values will help the United States and India see common interests in South Asia, or in Asia generally.

Conclusions: An Uncertain Guide to Future Behavior

The democratic peace – even the restricted definition as a separate peace between democratic states – is hotly debated. Among experts, it is now most often discussed in probabilistic rather than absolute terms. Hopes that India will, by dint of its democratic politics, inevitably serve as a pacifying force in South Asia are not supported in any direct or unequivocal way by the literature on the democratic peace. Indeed, the sometimes arcane debate over specific cases – whether, for example, Britain in 1812, Spain in 1898, Imperial Germany in 1914, or Lebanon in 2006 were democratic states – highlights the uncertainty of applications to the South Asian subcontinent. Ultimately, the democratic peace appears to be limited to a particular kind of relationship: relations between mature, modern democracies (and perhaps mainly those with stable nuclear-deterrent relations).

India is surrounded by weak states, several of which constitute fallen or faltering democracies, making the applicability of a separate democratic peace questionable on the subcontinent. Moreover, India itself is a well-established democracy, but one with high levels of electoral violence, endemic ethnic and religious tension, rising levels of inequality, and government institutions that struggle to provide public goods and protect the rights of disadvantaged citizens. In many ways, India's democratic achievement is all the more remarkable and laudatory because of the challenges it has overcome and continues to surmount. With respect to China, democratic peace theory may offer some hope that if China liberalizes in the future, it might be better able to manage crises and correct foreign policy misadventures. However, the troubled history of states undergoing democratization contradicts simple assumptions that political change will produce a more peaceful China – at least until such change is consolidated.

There appears to be strong intuitive and moral appeal to a theory of "democratic peace," but our analysis shows that the practicability and safety of pursuing a foreign policy based on these values is questionable. The empirical basis for the theoretical claim that democracies "never fight each other" is disputed. The logic of the democratic peace argument has critical weaknesses. And there is no empirical basis at all for claims that democracies are fundamentally more peaceful than other regimes, or that the security interests of democracies in different regions facing different challenges will tend to converge simply because they share similar domestic political institutions and values.

9

Meeting the Dual Challenge

A U.S. Strategy for China and India

The growth of Chinese power has inspired alarm in the United States. India, too, is gaining relative power and influence. Yet most assessments of rising Chinese and Indian power and American interests suffer from three limitations. First, they often assume smooth, uninterrupted growth for both China and India despite the many internal challenges these emerging powers face. They also often fail to account for America's proven track record of revitalization, adaptation, innovation, and growth, especially when faced with new challenges. Second, most recent studies focus on one or the other country in isolation or, less helpfully, as an amalgamated "Chindia." Examining the rising power of each nation in relation to its own recent past puts the scale and pace of domestic change in sharp relief. It says little, however, about what matters most for international politics: capability and behavior relative to other states. Third, many studies draw conclusions about the potential threats and opportunities China and India may present without careful examination of the empirical track record of their actual strategic behavior. A lack of empirical comparison raises the risk that either country will appear to be an outlier in its international behavior, which in turn could lead the United States to exaggerate its response to that power.

This book has examined Chinese and Indian international strategic behavior, revisiting commonly held assumptions in comparative context. Past behavior does not guarantee that either country will continue along recent policy trajectories. However, international strategic behavior is "sticky" – with powerful bases in the structure of international politics, the long-term challenges faced by the state, the state's own core interests, and the bureaucratic inertia imposed by domestic political and military traditions and preferences. Broad patterns of strategic behavior can change, but only in response to major (and usually observable) developments.

Many aspects of Chinese and Indian international strategic behavior are similar. Certainly, evidence from a wide cross-section of foreign policies over a period of several decades does not support a view of one or the other nation as an outlier in its strategic behavior. Both India and China have strategic cultures influenced by classic texts that acknowledge the utility of force and duplicity in interstate relations. Those texts also caution rulers about the dangers of war and urge a focus on domestic development and legitimate government. China and India have been involved in the same number of wars since the founding of their modern states, and they have been involved in the use of force the same number of times since China's reforms began in 1978–1979.

Both countries have military doctrines that emphasize offense at the operational level. Both are modernizing their militaries and acquiring power projection capabilities. Both are raising overall defense spending in line with economic growth. Both pursue their interests in energy security through resource investments in "rogue" regimes. Both Beijing and New Delhi have undertaken large-scale domestic social and economic reform programs and have chosen to join the liberal, rules-based international trade, investment, and financial system.

Both countries are following grand strategy and foreign policy trajectories that emphasize domestic development and integration with the global economy while seeking to avoid great power conflict. Both are preoccupied powers, confronting domestic challenges that absorb the lion's share of leadership attention and state resources. Chinese and Indian foreign policy trajectories are generally in line with U.S. interests. Indeed, the United States has similar common interests with both China and India. All three countries oppose religious extremism and terrorism, support the continued deepening of global economic integration, and are explicitly committed to a peaceful, stable, and prosperous environment in Asia, conducive to pursuing further economic and social development.

Washington also has conflicts of interest with New Delhi and Beijing. Both China and India are unwilling to support U.S.-preferred approaches to countries such as Iran and Myanmar, and for similar reasons. Beijing and New Delhi may recognize some benefits from Washington's global leadership, but both would like to see more constraints on American power, and both believe they will benefit from a shift away from a U.S.-led unipolar system to a multipolar international system. The two countries also have similar trade and investment disputes with the United States, and the scale of these disputes is roughly proportional to the size of their economies and the volume of bilateral trade. China's larger economy makes any Chinese trade protection a greater challenge. India also maintains some policies that discourage direct investment and aim to support favored domestic firms. These may become more problematic as India becomes a larger trade and investment partner. Finally, and most distinctively, the issues of Kashmir and Taiwan both challenge U.S. interests but to different degrees and in different ways. A Taiwan crisis might bring the United States and China into war with each other. The Indo-Pakistan conflict over Jammu and Kashmir does not involve the United States directly, but it is an essential backdrop to the urgent challenge of stability in nuclear-armed Pakistan.

There are some important differences in Chinese and Indian strategic behavior. China's economic reform and trade strategies have differed from India's. China has done more to encourage foreign direct investment, integration with global manufacturing, and infrastructure development. This has contributed to more advanced industrial capabilities and a greater share of global merchandise trade compared to India. China still remains relatively more open to international trade and foreign direct investment than India. However, recent Chinese government efforts to reinforce the position of state firms and exclusively promote domestic technologies could strengthen domestic monopolies and lead to more trade protection.

Other differences bear on foreign and military policies. China is developing military capabilities specifically designed to counter U.S. forces that might intervene in a Taiwan conflict. Some of these have potential for use beyond Taiwan, representing a potential challenge to U.S. interests in the wider Asia Pacific. China's planning and preparations for military modernization thus have an underlying adversarial focus on U.S. forces that is absent in U.S.-India relations. China also has more maritime disputes, with more parties, farther away from its shores than India.

India acts as a regional hegemon within South Asia, whereas China has yet to do so in East and Northeast Asia. India has used force to absorb some territories and to eliminate threats such as East Pakistan. India has conducted military interventions in neighboring states and used its political and military influence to control the foreign policies of neighbors such as Nepal. India also asserts a right to a large sphere of influence in South and Central Asia and the Indian Ocean area. As is the case with China's maritime disputes, this hegemonic behavior is related to political geography. India is surrounded by relatively weak neighbors. China's neighbors are relatively strong.

Both countries have moved toward more offense-oriented operational military doctrines. However, India's doctrine is even more explicitly reliant on preemption and offensive strikes than China's. India's military doctrine is also developed primarily by the individual military services, with a relatively weaker role for civilian-imposed strategic frameworks. Both of these characteristics could exacerbate crisis instability in South Asia. Finally, India spends a somewhat greater percentage of GDP on defense and military modernization than China does, and it gives equal, if not greater, attention to developing power projection and "expeditionary" capabilities. The difference here is one of degree, but it is notable because India is a poorer country.

What is remarkable about the differences in behavior, however, is the degree to which most of them are related to specific circumstances of history, geography, and the relative size of the Chinese and Indian economies. Nowhere is this truer than in the case of Taiwan, a historical legacy that differentiates the relationship between the United States and China from that of the United States and India. Taiwan is a critical concern for U.S. policy. The United States must maintain military superiority in Asia, including a robust deterrence capability across the Taiwan Strait. However, American leaders should exercise caution in extrapolating general trends in Chinese strategic behavior from its conduct regarding Taiwan.

Based on our findings from comparison of Chinese and Indian strategic behavior in the preceding chapters, we provide eight recommendations for U.S. policies toward China and India. These aim to maximize U.S. interests with both countries, as well as in East and South Asia more generally. The first three recommendations concern the analytical and theoretical perspectives that inform strategic assessments and U.S. leadership expectations. The other five represent specific proposals for U.S. foreign policy. The final section of this chapter offers our concluding thoughts on comparative Chinese and Indian strategic behavior and American interests.

Institutionalize a Comparative Approach to Assessment

Analysis of evolving Chinese and Indian power should incorporate greater comparative perspective, moving beyond examination of one country in isolation. Both government and academic work would benefit from this perspective. One example on the government side is the U.S. Defense Department annual review of Chinese military power.[1] In recent years, this

---

[1]   Office of the Secretary of Defense, *The Military Power of the People's Republic of China*, various years.

report has already begun to incorporate comparative analysis of Chinese defense budgets, but this could be improved by making the budget comparisons more consistent. For example, off-budget items should be included for all countries that are compared, according to the same methodology that is used to derive an estimate for China. Comparison of doctrinal developments, force modernization, and power projection capabilities can also be given greater comparative context without sacrificing the report's focus on China.

Other U.S. government assessments of China and India will also benefit from comparative analysis. These could include reviews of human and civic rights,[2] relations with "rogue" regimes, international trade, market access, intellectual property, technology development, arms sales, proliferation, and participation in international institutions. Trend analysis and threat assessment will benefit from including other states in addition to India, such as Brazil and Russia. Comparison to developed countries in Asia could also provide important context. The extensive research and testimony solicited by U.S. Congressional commissions on Chinese military developments, trade practices, human rights, and social development should also be enhanced with comparative perspectives.

Academic studies of Chinese and Indian foreign policy and rising power can also be improved by greater attention to comparison. This book has taken one approach – there are certainly other possibilities.[3] Some of the best comparative studies currently available can be found in the area of development economics. There are significant academic research opportunities for better comparative analysis in areas including (but not limited to) traditional and nontraditional security, participation in international regimes, relations with Middle East, African, and Latin American countries, technological innovation, studies of defense industries, international arms purchase behavior, civil-military relations, comparative grand strategy, and the relationship between domestic politics and foreign policy.

Not every study must be explicitly comparative. Focused assessments of threats and opportunities emanating from China should continue. Yet in the field of Asian security studies and assessment, attention to China should not crowd out other analysis. Taking India seriously means considering the challenges rising Indian power may present to the United States and to Asia,

---

[2]   These include political rights, but also the rights of women, ethnic and religious minorities, and children.
[3]   For an example of explicitly comparative analysis, see Alastair Iain Johnston, "Is China a Status Quo Power?" *International Security* 27:4 (2003): 5–56.

not simply focusing on India as a counterweight to China. India's growing power and influence merits increased official and scholarly attention in its own right, as do developments in a number of other regional states.

Comparative metrics should also be improved. In Chapter 4 we showed that many comparisons of international defense spending are inconsistent. We offered a template for including similar spending items and an improved method of PPP calculation. Similarly, Chapter 7 showed that current measures of bilateral trade balances do not fully capture the mutual benefits and vulnerabilities from trade in a world of globalized production. U.S. official trade statistics should include data on the value-added at each stage of international trade rather than tracking trade in final assembled goods alone. At a minimum, government reports should highlight the questions associated with current accounting methods and the impressions they may convey. Estimates of the number and types of jobs created through foreign trade and foreign direct investment should become part of official government statistics. Developing such methodologies would keep the American people informed of the benefits derived from international trade, and signal to them how they can prepare themselves to secure jobs in a globalized economy.

Finally, adopting a comparative approach to assessment will help combat "stove piping" (the failure to share information) in government, private sector, and academic communities. Expertise on countries as large and diverse as China and India is far-flung, and often separated by bureaucratic and other organizational barriers. Specialization can breed barriers to sharing data and analysis, while bureaucratic interests and competition can also undermine inter-area and interagency coordination.[4] Both the Defense and State departments, as well as other key policy-making institutions such as the National Security Council, already conduct policy coordination and integration activity, both internally and with each other. Encouraging comparison in major policy assessments would provide incentives for specialist groups and diverse organizations to share information and insights. A greater role for comparative analysis and information sharing could help the United States avoid surprises.

---

[4] Recent reviews of U.S. intelligence analysis and processes have concluded that additional area expertise is required to improve U.S. intelligence and strategic assessments. We support these recommendations, and we would add that area expertise must become more explicitly comparative. Requirements for comparison will help with other recommendations on breaking down stovepipes in intelligence, analysis, and policy making. See, for example, Kenneth Lieberthal, *The U.S. Intelligence Community and Foreign Policy: Getting Analysis Right* (Washington, DC: Brookings Institution, 2009).

Realism for the Long Run

U.S. policy toward China and India – and in Asia more broadly – should be based on a nuanced, pragmatic realism.[5] Empirical comparison provides little support for the notion that the stark difference in regime type between India and China offers a reliable guide to their international strategic behavior as it bears on American interests. American expectations about Chinese and Indian strategic behavior should instead be grounded in an assessment of the two countries' material interests in prosperity and security and in the evolving regional and global balance of power. The realist perspective provides guidelines that will see American foreign policy interests through the long run, as China and India continue to undergo significant domestic political and economic change and as relations with both countries experience ups and downs.

Contrary to some critical views, a realist concern for core interests and balances of material and military power need not be "impoverished." Nor does realism force the United States to surrender the benefits America gains from behaving according to its own values.[6] The United States gains both material power and moral influence from its political and cultural values. Unlike some modern realist approaches that focus overwhelmingly on international system structure, a nuanced political realism that has been recognized by political thinkers from Thucydides to E. H. Carr is deeply concerned with politics, values, and moral suasion.[7] A nuanced realism also recognizes the influence of history, contingency, and domestic politics on foreign policy choices. However, a nuanced realism does not view values as superior to interests or regime type as more important than balances of

---

[5] Our discussion of "nuanced realism" is consistent with what international relations theorists call "classical" or "neoclassical" realism. For an application to Asian international relations, see George J. Gilboy and Eric Heginbotham, "Getting Realism: U.S. Asia (and China) Policy Reconceived," *The National Interest*, 69 (Fall 2002): 99–109.

[6] Michael J. Green, "Obama's self-defeating 'realism' in Asia," *Foreign Policy*, October 6, 2009, http://shadow.foreignpolicy.com/blog/12381; Stephen Zunes, "Human Rights: C+," *Foreign Policy in Focus*, January 25, 2010, http://www.fpif.org/articles/human_rights_c

[7] Three examples in Thucydides illustrate this nuanced view of the balance between values and interests in shaping international political outcomes: the Mytilenean debate, the Melian dialogue, and the Sicilian expedition (especially with reference to the role and fate of Alicibiades and Nicias in Sicily). See Thucydides, *History of the Peloponnesian War*, translated by C. F. Smith (Cambridge, MA: Loeb Classical Library, Harvard University Press, 2003), especially Book III 36–50, Book V 84–116, Book VI 1–105, and Book VII 42–87. For a modern classic in the tradition of nuanced realism, see E. H. Carr, *The Twenty Years' Crisis: An Introduction to the Study of International Relations* (New York: Macmillan Press, 1939).

power in predicting the behavior of other states. Our comparisons of China and India demonstrate this point in areas such as resource policy, use of force, and the settlement of international boundaries. Realism also recognizes that states possess few effective tools for imposing their value systems on one another, and that seeking to do so can be costly.

In Chapter 8, we examined the perennial debate about the role of democracy and regime type in determining international strategic behavior. This debate is once again being played out in contrasting American views of the rise of democratic India and authoritarian China. As our review of democratic peace theory shows, popular expectations about the relationship between regime type and international strategic behavior rest on shaky theoretical and empirical foundations. Justifying policies this way raises expectations among both elites and the broader American public that may not be met in U.S.-India relations. American leaders must resist the impulse to allow "common values" to become a metaphor for common interests and alignment. The latter will not automatically proceed from the former. To the contrary, ensuring a stronger relationship based on common interests will require leaders in New Delhi and Washington to confront squarely their divergent views and interests.

A realist policy does not underestimate conflicts in Sino-U.S. relations. Far from ignoring the Taiwan issue as a central problem in Sino-U.S. relations, a realist approach, with its focus on material balances of power, calls attention to the need for robust deterrence across the Taiwan Strait. However, realism recognizes unique features of the Taiwan issue, as well as the larger context of American and Chinese interests beyond Taiwan. Realism also highlights the dangers of unrestrained security competition in the region.

Various critics from both the left and the right of American politics have accused Washington of edging toward realism and away from an emphasis on American values in foreign policy. Some viewed this as coming at India's expense.[8] Yet in some ways, U.S. India policy still appears to be grounded primarily in shared values and expectations of future behaviors based on those values, as reflected in the assessment of India in the *2010 Quadrennial Defense Review*. Despite shared values, America's interests with India are still relatively untested and underexamined. New Delhi's definition of its

---

[8] "Meeting Shows U.S.-India Split on Emissions," *New York Times*, July 19, 2009; "India Fears Pressure From U.S. to Mend Ties With Pakistan," *New York Times*, July 17, 2009; "China Gains in U.S. Eyes, and India Feels Slights," *New York Times*, November 23, 2009; "Hopes for India-Pakistan peace talks are modest," *The Washington Post*, February 24, 2010.

own interests in the Middle East, Central Asia, and South Asia, as well as in trade and energy/environment policy, may run counter to American expectations.

A realist perspective that takes into account the empirical record of Indian interests and strategic behavior will recognize the benefits of broadening and deepening good relations with India, especially by developing stronger common economic interests through trade and investment and by encouraging greater political and diplomatic cooperation. But taking India and its interests and capabilities seriously will also alert American leaders to potential challenges. Some of these emanate from the current U.S. policy of supporting India's rise to great power status (with commensurate capabilities). U.S. arms and geostrategic support provided to India could exacerbate Asia's security dilemmas. These security dilemmas are nested in relationships that link China, India, Pakistan, and Afghanistan, as well as China, Japan, and South Korea.

There is also another sense in which "realism for the long run" is desirable for U.S. policy. American foreign policy success is largely determined by "hard power." This includes technological and economic capabilities that underpin diplomatic and military power. Hard power is the essential base on which "soft power" rests and without which soft power is ineffective.[9] Any long-term strategy for dealing with a more powerful China and India must recognize the need to maintain America's relative advantage in technological, economic, and military capabilities. This requires getting the basics right at home, including education, health care, financial sector stability, energy policy, R&D and innovation incentives, a competitive industrial economy with healthy employment levels, and a balanced approach to budget deficit reduction. Material power generated from wise choices at home will be essential for maintaining U.S. international leadership.

[9] For more on the relationship between capabilities and moral influence in international politics, see Kurt M. Campbell and Michael E. O'Hanlon, *Hard Power: The New Politics of National Security* (New York: Basic Books, 2006); and Joseph S. Nye, *Soft Power: The Means to Success in World Politics* (New York: Public Affairs Press, 2004). Both the nuanced realist tradition (represented by ancient and modern classics from Thucydides to E. H. Carr) and sophisticated neoliberal approaches (represented by Robert Keohane's *After Hegemony*) recognize that any choice between developing hard capabilities and developing moral influence is a false choice. Both are mutually supporting and both are necessary for success in world politics. Robert O. Keohane, *After Hegemony: Cooperation and Discord in the World Political Economy* (Princeton: Princeton University Press, 1984). For more on technological and industrial capabilities as a basis for relative international power and prosperity, see Stephen S. Cohen and John Zysman, *Manufacturing Matters: The Myth of the Post-Industrial Economy* (New York: Basic Books, 1987); and Eamonn Fingleton, *In Praise of Hard Industries: Why Manufacturing, Not The Information Economy, Is the Key To Future Prosperity* (New York: Houghton Mifflin, 1999).

Recognize and Mitigate Asia's Nested Security Dilemmas

Beijing and New Delhi are primarily enmeshed in regional security concerns. However, because each is a rising power with increasing extra-regional influence, Chinese and Indian responses to security challenges could have effects beyond their immediate periphery. Washington must respond to these developments, but it must also recognize and mitigate the potential effect of its own policies on wider security dynamics in Asia. This is a challenge because security dilemmas involving major states in Asia are nested.

The security dilemma describes a paradox in international relations. A state's efforts to make itself more secure could actually undermine its own security because these efforts may elicit balancing responses.[10] By describing Asia's security dilemmas as nested, we mean that these security dynamics simultaneously operate across both hierarchical *levels* (region-level and international system-level politics) and across geographical *regions* (such as South and Northeast Asia).[11] Conceptualizing Asian security in terms of nested security dilemmas offers analytical insights that complement a nuanced, pragmatic realist theory.[12] This framework also offers a model for

[10] The security dilemma emerges from the effects of an anarchic international system. States must rely on "self-help" to ensure their security. Under anarchy, an increase in one state's security (perhaps by arming itself) may pose a potential threat to the security of other states, because there is no guarantee that increased power cannot be turned against other states. With no guarantee of good behavior, any effort by one state to increase its security capabilities could produce countermeasures on the part of other states, which could make all states worse off than before. This dilemma is aggravated when defensive measures are not distinguishable from offensive capabilities and when offense has, or is perceived to have, the advantage over defense. See Robert Jervis, "Cooperation under the Security Dilemma," *World Politics*, 30:2, (January 1978): 167–214; and Stephen Van Evera, "The Cult of the Offensive and the Origins of the First World War," *International Security*, 9:1 (Summer 1984): 58–107.

[11] Standard approaches to international relations theory emphasize dyadic relations between major states (or sometimes between rival alliance groups) and the distinctiveness and even separateness of regions, both from each other and from the system level of international politics. For an excellent summary of approaches in this vein, see Amitav Acharya, "Theoretical Perspectives on International Relations in Asia," in David Shambaugh and Michael Yahuda, eds., *International Relations of Asia* (New York: Rowman and Littlefield, 2008): 57–84.

[12] The concept of nested security dilemmas differs from other concepts of regional security, such as the notion of "regional security complexes" first developed by Barry Buzan in "New Patterns of Global Security in the Twenty-First Century," *International Affairs*, 67:3 (1991): 431–451. Buzan and Ole Wæver have since further developed regional security complex theory (RSCT), a useful and instructive approach to regional security dynamics. Unlike nested security dilemmas, RSCT takes an explicitly constructivist view of security and primarily limits its focus to dynamics within regions rather than between regions or

understanding the connections between region-level security competition and rivalry at the international system level.[13]

For example, viewing China as a potential challenger not only in East Asia, but also as a challenger for international system-level power, America has responded to Chinese military modernization with measures to strengthen alliances across Asia and provide geostrategic support and arms to India. Yet providing support to India has the potential to cause major shifts in the South Asian military balance, which could increase instability at the subregional level.

The two graphics that follow illustrate the difference between a traditional view of security and a view that emphasizes nested security dilemmas. The dominant American approach to Asian security relations reflects the standard view of security dynamics (Figure 9.1).

According to this view, the United States is engaged in nascent security competition with China and is hedging against China's rise. The standard view also recognizes security competition between China and Japan in Northeast Asia and between China and India in South Asia. One element of Washington's hedging policy toward China thus involves strengthening the existing alliance with Japan and developing a new security-enhancing relationship with India. From Washington's perspective, viewing Asian security this way makes sense. As the sole superpower in the current international system, the United States has global interests and, more than most states, tends to interpret local challenges as global problems.[14]

---

between the international system level and regional level politics. See Barry Buzan and Ole Wæver, *Regions and Powers: The Structure of International Security* (New York: Cambridge University Press, 2003), 45, 71.

[13] Even though we have not developed a formal model here, our approach helps address a weakness in standard models of international relations such as power transition theory, which has difficulty specifying the circumstances under which great powers compete for system level influence. See Jack S. Levy, "Power Transition Theory and the Rise of China," in Robert S. Ross and Zhu Feng, eds., *China's Ascent: Power Security, and the Future of International Politics* (Ithaca: Cornell University Press, 2008), 11–33. Power transition theory traces its roots to A. F. K. Organski, *World Politics* (New York: Knopf, 1958); Robert Gilpin, *War and Change in World Politics* (New York: Cambridge University Press, 1981); Robert Gilpin, "The Theory of Hegemonic War," *Journal of Interdisciplinary History*, 18 (Spring 1988): 591–614; and Ronald L. Tammen et al., *Power Transitions: Strategies for the 21st Century* (New York: Chatham House, 2000). Power transition theory has recently resurfaced as a popular approach to analyzing international relations in Asia, especially U.S.-China relations. See Robert S. Ross and Zhu Feng, eds., *China's Ascent: Power Security, and the Future of International Politics* (Ithaca: Cornell University Press, 2008); and Aaron L. Friedberg, "The Future of U.S.-China Relations: Is Conflict Inevitable?" *International Security*, 30 (Fall 2005): 7–45.

[14] Even though today the United States is the sole superpower, this tendency to view local challenges as threats to America's system-level interests is also influenced by more than

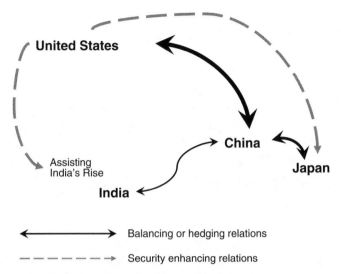

Figure 9.1. Standard view of security dilemmas in Asia.
Note: The relative intensity of the security competition relationship is indicated by the thickness of the double-headed solid black line. The position of the states indicates relative system-level influence. States listed toward the top of the graphic have greater system-level power than those listed lower down.

However, American policies could have unintended consequences at the regional level. Figure 9.2 illustrates the challenge by providing a more complete picture. Security dilemmas are nested across hierarchical levels and between geographic regions.[15] The United States tends to focus on system-level challenges to U.S. primacy, but other powers are more likely to see security issues as primarily local or regional problems. Indeed, most states give priority to security issues closest to their territory.[16] Some American efforts to hedge against China's rising power by strengthening geopolitical alignments with major powers, such as Japan and India, could exacerbate instabilities in South Asia and Northeast Asia.

Within South Asia's subregional hierarchy, major-power India is involved in security dilemma dynamics with a relatively weaker Pakistan. In the Northeast Asian region, a similar subregional security hierarchy involves

sixty years of experience as one of two global superpowers. It has shaped U.S. responses to challenges in Korea, Vietnam, and Iraq, as well as post-9/11 terrorism. These and other experiences serve as reminders of the way local politics and priorities – even among nominal allies – can clash with U.S. interests and intentions.

[15] To simplify and focus the analysis here, we have not included either Taiwan or North Korea in this representation.

[16] Buzan and Wæver, *Regions and Powers*, 3–5.

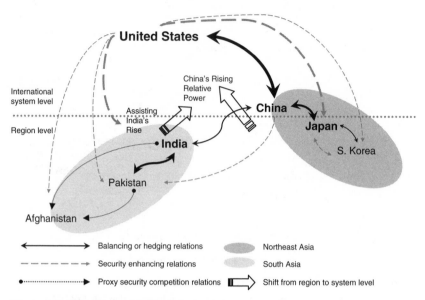

Figure 9.2. Nested security dilemmas in Asia.
Note: Although security-enhancing relations are often mutual, most are represented here by single-headed gray lines, because in this analysis we are focused primarily on the provision of security assistance from one power to another – this largely defines U.S. relations with Japan, South Korea, India, Pakistan, and Afghanistan, for example.

major-power Japan and a junior (but in many ways more vigorous) player, South Korea.[17] In both Northeast Asia and South Asia, American policies are reinforcing the more powerful player. However, for deep-rooted historical and political reasons, both Pakistan and South Korea have proved themselves determined to continue security competition with their larger and wealthier rivals. Pakistan, for example, will likely seek to keep pace with India, even if that entails greater risks to its own internal security. Indo-Pakistan security competition has long been played out in their support for competing factions and forces within an even weaker Afghanistan, and this tendency has intensified since 2001. Pakistani fears of India's growing military lead give Pakistan even greater incentives to compete for influence and "strategic depth" in Afghanistan. A South Korea that feels threatened by Japan, for its part, could escalate conflicts over disputed islands, seek closer relations with China, or explore its own nuclear options.

---

[17] Japan and South Korea have a mixed security relationship that involves both security cooperation and security competition. Japan-South Korea security cooperation was strengthened by a perception of increased Chinese assertiveness after 2009, but mutual security concerns and politically charged territorial disputes remain.

Careful observers have seen the potential connections among multiple states with tendencies toward strong bilateral security competition.[18] Nevertheless, most analyses of security dynamics in East Asia assume that a dominant United States will act in ways that will dampen middle power security competition.[19] Viewing Asia's security dilemmas as nested raises a question about whether certain actions by the United States could instead exacerbate subregional security competition.

This does not mean that U.S. policy must forever remain hostage to rivalry between America's allies (whether India-Pakistan or Japan-South Korea). But policy should be calibrated to recognize these nested dilemmas and avoid exacerbating them. Many modern weapons systems have both offensive and defensive capabilities, and in some cases these are difficult to separate. However, the United States has options in what it can provide. For example, fighter planes sold to partners and allies can be optimized for air combat and long-range precision attack packages can be withheld. Antiship cruise missiles may be less destabilizing than land-attack variants. Other items are particular to local conditions. For example, further extending India's lead in numbers and quality of artillery on the Pakistan border may be destabilizing. Missile defenses, while nominally defensive weapons, are potentially deeply destabilizing in Asia. India, Pakistan, and China all possess relatively small and unsophisticated nuclear deterrent forces, and missile defenses held by a rival could denude them of retaliatory capability in the event of a nuclear first strike against them.

Nested security dilemma dynamics may become more intense as Chinese and Indian relative power increases and as the scope of their regional and global activities expands. American policy makers must prepare for a long-term, sustained challenge. In the near and medium term, South and Central Asia is the place where American interests face the greatest potential risks from the effects of nested security dilemmas.

Account for Pakistan in U.S. India and China Policy

The United States should take a comprehensive approach to South Asian security. Under a comprehensive approach, Washington will not only

---

[18] Thomas J. Christensen, "China, the US-Japan Alliance, and the Security Dilemma in East Asia," *International Security*, 23:4 (Spring 1999): 49–80.

[19] Christensen, "China, The US-Japan Alliance, and the Security Dilemma in East Asia"; G. John Ikenberry and Michael Mastanduno, "Images of Order in the Asia Pacific and the Role of the United States," in G. John Ikenberry and Michael Mastanduno, eds., *International Relations Theory and The Asia-Pacific* (New York: Columbia University Press, 2003), 421–439.

consider the effect its support for rising Indian power may have on the China-India balance. It will also consider the effect support for India will have on a fragile Pakistan and, via Pakistan, the effect on security and stability in Afghanistan. A comprehensive strategy also balances traditional military approaches to security with appropriate political and economic policies.

Beginning in the last year of the George W. Bush administration and continuing with the Obama administration, U.S. military leaders in Central Command undertook a comprehensive political and military approach to security and stability in Afghanistan that broke with U.S. policy from 2001 to mid-2008. Part of this new policy also shifted most American military assistance to Pakistan away from conventional weapons and toward anti-insurgency assistance, while urging India to moderate security competition with Pakistan. Yet the United States still faces an unresolved contradiction between the goal of building up Indian technological and military capabilities relative to China on the one hand and the goal of promoting security and stability in Pakistan (and Afghanistan) on the other. The risks are on three main dimensions: security and stability within Pakistan itself, crisis stability between India and Pakistan, and the destabilizing effects of Indo-Pakistani rivalry within Afghanistan.

Post-2001 U.S. military and geostrategic assistance to India has aimed at helping India become a great power. An underlying expectation is that rising Indian power will help balance rising Chinese power. Yet some of these policies have the potential to aggravate the security situation within Pakistan. Pakistan can little afford an arms race – indeed, military competition with India could further impoverish and destabilize the country. Competition with India could also divert scarce resources and leadership attention away from economic and social reform, which is essential for Pakistan's internal stability.[20] The United States has recognized Pakistan's tendency to shift resources toward competing with India and has tailored aid and military assistance to Pakistan to focus on anti-insurgency capabilities since 2008. However, this issue is likely to remain a chronic problem because Pakistan has alternative (i.e., non-U.S.) sources of conventional arms to match U.S. arms sales to India.

Analysis in Chapter 5 showed that as India's arms purchases rose between 2000 and 2010, Pakistan tried to keep up, diverting resources (including

---

[20] For evidence that both Pakistani and Indian economic development have been retarded by their security competition and arms-racing behavior, see Jülide Yildirim and Nadir Öcal, "Arms Race and Economic Growth: The Case of India and Pakistan," *Defence and Peace Economics*, 17:1 (February 2006): 37–45.

U.S. aid) away from fighting its domestic insurgency to focus on procuring major conventional weapons systems.[21] After major domestic shocks, the Pakistani military and intelligence services finally turned their attention toward internal insurgents in 2009 but have not yet effectively countered the threat.[22]

Pakistan still deploys most of its forces on the Indian border (with some units returning to these border areas after temporary deployments to fight insurgents), and the Pakistani military still retains a core focus on its security competition with India.[23] Islamabad appeared to shift forces away from urgent internal counterinsurgency operations and back to the India border in March 2009, apparently in response to Indian army deployments.[24] According to published accounts, in January 2010, Pakistani Army chief Ashfaq Parvez Kiyani told the commander of U.S. and NATO forces in Afghanistan, Stanley McChrystal, that the Pakistani army still regarded India as its primary enemy and was stretched too thin to open a new front against Taliban forces in North Waziristan, as the United States desired.[25]

In addition to worsening security within Pakistan itself, Pakistan's responses to growing Indian power and India's Cold Start doctrine could also undermine stability in South Asia. Since Washington concluded a civilian nuclear technology cooperation deal with New Delhi that provides both geopolitical and technological benefits to Indian nuclear programs, Pakistan has accelerated its own nuclear weapons program.[26] The Pakistani leadership may have domestic political reasons for doing this, but developments in India's nuclear programs also influence Pakistan's calculus. Pakistan's perception of the shifting conventional military

[21] See "U.S. Officials See Waste in Billions Sent to Pakistan," *New York Times*, December 24, 2007; "Pakistan Fails to Aim Billions in U.S. Military Aid At Al-Qaeda," *Los Angeles Times*, November 5, 2007; "Plan Would Use Anti-Terror Aid on Pakistani Jets," *New York Times*, July 24, 2008.

[22] "White House Assails Pakistan Effort on Militants," *New York Times*, April 5, 2011.

[23] "Pakistani Army will remain India-centric, says Kayani," *Indo-Asian News Service Rawalpindi*, February 05, 2010; "Pakistan's Swat offensive leaves India sceptical," *Reuters India*, May 17, 2009.

[24] "Pull back troops from Pak border: US to India" *The Times of India*, March 19, 2009.

[25] Kayani specifically cited India's Cold Start doctrine as one reason Pakistan could not divert more forces away from the Indian border toward fighting Taliban and Al-Qaeda forces in Pakistan. "Pakistan Is Said to Pursue Role in Afghan Talks with U.S.," *New York Times*, February 9, 2010. Even though Pakistani leaders may have multiple reasons for making such statements, Pakistan does have some legitimate security concerns. On Pakistan's determination to seek "strategic depth" in Afghanistan versus India, see interview with Pakistan's army chief; "Kayani spells out terms for regional stability" *The Dawn*, February 2, 2010.

[26] "Pakistan Is Rapidly Adding Nuclear Arms, U.S. Says," *New York Times,* May 17, 2009.

balance with India may be another element in its decision to add more nuclear weapons to its arsenal despite its growing domestic instabilities. If the conventional balance tips too far against it, Pakistan could deploy its nuclear weapons closer to the Indian border. Such a "chicken" strategy, in which Pakistan would be effectively announcing that it would be forced to "use or lose" forward-deployed nuclear weapons in the event of war, could buttress deterrence. However, it would also make wartime escalation dynamics extraordinarily dangerous and substantially increase the probability of a nuclear exchange. Alternatively, Pakistan could seek to escalate conflicts with India to signal its dissatisfaction with a widening gap in relative power or with a failure to reach acceptable compromise on core issues.

Ongoing India-Pakistan military competition may also have a direct and damaging effect on U.S. security interests in Afghanistan.[27] Pakistan's intelligence services and its military have multiple reasons for pursuing influence in Afghanistan (some related to Pakistani domestic politics). Pakistan has undermined some American goals in Afghanistan and its military and intelligence services have been linked to attacks on Americans.[28] However, Pakistan's interests in Afghanistan are largely defined by its security relationship with India, and its behavior is exacerbated by competition with India for influence there. Indian support for the regime in Kabul strengthens Pakistan's determination to preserve its influence via the Taliban and groups such as the Haqqani network.[29]

Pakistan sees Indian influence in Afghanistan as a threat to its vital security interests, and it is likely to behave accordingly despite pressures to the contrary.[30] Islamabad believes that New Delhi is using its diplomatic facilities in Afghanistan to train and recruit anti-Pakistan insurgents and that it is leveraging Indian reconstruction funds to build Indian political influence in Afghanistan.[31] For its part, New Delhi appears determined to deny

---

[27] Pakistani security and intelligence services also compete for influence in Afghanistan with China and Iran, but most intensely with India. "Missile Kills Militant's Brother in Pakistan," *New York Times*, February 19, 2010.

[28] "Pakistan's Spy Agency Is Tied to Attack on U.S. Embassy," *New York Times*, September 22, 2011.

[29] "Militant Group Expands Attacks in Afghanistan," *New York Times*, June 16, 2010.

[30] Michael Scheuer, "India's Strategic Challenge in Pakistan's Afghan Hinterland," Jamestown Foundation, *Global Terrorism Analysis*, 5:30, August 12, 2008; Robert D. Kaplan, "Behind the Indian Embassy Bombing," *The Atlantic Monthly*, August 1, 2008; Soutik Biswas, "India: Afghanistan's influential ally," *BBC News* July 7, 2008.

[31] Kenneth Katzman, "Afghanistan: Post-Taliban Governance, Security and U.S. Policy," Congressional Research Service Report to Congress, Order Code RL30588, February 9, 2009, 43–44.

Pakistan "strategic depth" in Afghanistan. Some see the Indian presence in Afghanistan as a way to combat Pakistan's links to forces used against India in Kashmir, as well as a means to extend Indian influence in Central Asia.[32] New Delhi's efforts run the gamut from investments in Afghan education and health care, to an Indian-built road from Afghanistan's Nimruz province to the Iranian border, to securing India's only foreign military base, an airfield at Farkhor in Tajikistan.[33] India's effort to develop influence in Afghanistan culminated in the October 2011 signing of a strategic partnership agreement with the Afghan regime of Hamid Karzai.[34] India can play a constructive role in Afghanistan. The question for U.S. policy is how to help ensure that the benefits of Indian activity are not outweighed by the negative consequences of Pakistani reaction to greater Indian involvement.[35] This question could take on heightened importance as U.S. forces are withdrawn from Afghanistan.

[32] James Lamont, "New Delhi seeks to bolster Afghan role," *Financial Times*, March 24, 2009; Kenneth Katzman, "Afghanistan: Post-Taliban Governance, Security and U.S. Policy," Congressional Research Service Report to Congress, Order Code RL30588, February 9, 2009, 47–48. See also James Lamont, "New Delhi seeks to bolster Afghan role," *Financial Times*, March 24, 2009. For more on India's goals in Afghanistan, see Scheuer, "India's Strategic Challenge in Pakistan's Afghan Hinterland."

[33] See Rajat Pandit, "Indian Forces Get Foothold in Central Asia," *Times of India*, July 17, 2007. According to Western analysts, the new Indian air base in Farkhor may have intensified Indo-Pakistani competition in Afghanistan by stoking Pakistan's fears of encirclement. See Raja Karthikeya Gundu and Teresita C. Schaffer, "India and Pakistan in Afghanistan: Hostile Sports," *South Asia Monitor*, 117, Center for Strategic and International Studies, April 03, 2008.

[34] "Afghanistan Favors India and Denigrates Pakistan," *New York Times*, October 4, 2011; "Pak in mind, Karzai signs pact with Manmohan Singh," *The Times of India*, October 4, 2011. This agreement may allow India to train Afghan security forces. It could reinforce existing ethnic divisions within Afghanistan that pit ethnic majority Pashtuns (many of whom support the Taliban, associated with Pakistan) versus Tajiks (who dominate the Karzai government, which is becoming closer to India). Even if the agreement remains largely symbolic, it is certain to cause further tensions between India and Pakistan.

[35] Bomb attacks on the Indian embassy in Afghanistan have been linked to forces close to Pakistani military and intelligence officers. Kaplan, "Behind the Indian Embassy Bombing." See also "Top Indian Diplomat in Afghanistan after Blast," *Reuters*, October 9, 2009. U.S. pressure on Pakistan to simply accept India's growing role is unlikely to guarantee U.S. interests, given the intensity of Pakistani views on this issue across the full spectrum of Pakistani elites and society. See Kenneth Katzman, "Afghanistan: Post-Taliban Governance, Security and U.S. Policy," Congressional Research Service Report to Congress, Order Code RL30588, February 9, 2009, 47–48; see also "CIA Outlines Pakistan Links With Militants," *New York Times*, July 30, 2008; "Time Is Short as U.S. Presses Pakistan, a Reluctant Ally," *New York Times*, April 6, 2008; Barnett R. Rubin, "Saving Afghanistan," *Foreign Affairs*, 86:1 (January/February 2007): 57–78; Barnett R. Rubin and Abubakar Siddique, "Resolving the Pakistan- Afghanistan Stalemate," United States Institute of Peace, Special Report No. 176, October 2006.

These three issues – security and stability within Pakistan itself, crisis stability between India and Pakistan, and the destabilizing effects of India-Pakistan rivalry within Afghanistan – are long-term problems that will persist regardless of any near-term outcome in Afghanistan.[36] These issues are also likely to persist whether or not a new regime (either civilian or military) comes to power in Pakistan. Given these security dynamics, Washington has already taken steps to narrow the scope of military aid to Pakistan and increase Pakistan's focus and accountability for its own internal security. In the same context, the United States should also move cautiously and deliberately in providing weapons, defense assistance, and geopolitical support to India.[37]

In the first instance, there may be opportunities to avoid or limit some arms sales.[38] Some items of concern may not be high-profile systems. For example, one of Washington's earliest moves in consolidating its military relationship with India was to sell sophisticated AN-TPQ/37 counter-battery (i.e., counter-artillery) radars to the Indian army. Yet the most common form of low-intensity warfare between India and Pakistan has been shelling across the line of control, and the sale was far more likely to be felt in Islamabad than Beijing. If counter-battery radars give India a decisive advantage, Pakistan will have two options in a conflict: withdraw or escalate. This and other sales that increase India's existing advantage in ground-force capabilities are candidates for some restraint.

Second, the United States could urge changes to Indian military doctrine and reinforce its appeals through the terms of arms sales agreements and

---

[36] On the enduring nature of the rivalry between nuclear-armed India and Pakistan and the implications for regional security, see Peter R. Lavoy, "Introduction: The Importance of the Kargil Conflict,"in Peter R. Lavoy, ed., *Assymetric Warfare in South Asia: The Causes and Consequences of the Kargil Conflict* (New York: Cambridge University Press, 2009), 1–38. This volume also contains a number of valuable essays on strategic lessons learned by the two sides and implications for American interests.

[37] On trends in U.S. arms sales policy and their impact on South Asia, see Richard F. Grimmett, "Conventional Arms Transfers to Developing Nations, 2000–2007," Congressional Research Service Report to Congress, Order Code RL34723, October 23, 2008, 10; Christopher Bolkcom, Richard F. Grimmett, and K. Alan Kronstadt, "Combat Aircraft Sales to South Asia: Potential Implications," CRS Report RL33515, May 19, 2005; Andrew Feickert and K. Alan Kronstadt, "Missile Proliferation and the Strategic Balance in South Asia," Congressional Research Service Report to Congress, Order Code RL32115, October 17, 2003; and Andrew Feickert, "Missile Survey: Ballistic and Cruise Missiles of Selected Foreign Countries," Congressional Research Service Report to Congress, Order Code RL30427, July 26, 2005.

[38] See "Raytheon Delivers Twelve Firefinder Radars to Indian Army," *India Defence*, March 5, 2007, http://www.india-defence.com/reports/3117. See also U.S. Defense Security Cooperation Agency, Arms Sales Notifications, http://www.dsca.mil/PressReleases/ 36-b/2010/India_09–79.pdf

through existing joint training exercises. With better overall capabilities, New Delhi can afford to abandon doctrinal guidelines that call for blitz-krieg victory before diplomacy can intervene. The United States can avoid providing offensive weapons and training that would make such doctrines more destabilizing. Ultimately, the United States should place defense coop-eration and arms sales to either India or Pakistan in a broader political and diplomatic context that emphasizes regional security dialogue.

There are two potential objections to taking this comprehensive approach to South Asian security. First, some might argue that such an approach will undermine recent gains in U.S.-India relations. In this view, breaking the link between U.S.-India policy and U.S. policy toward Pakistan was the essential success factor in U.S.-India relations since the late 1990s, primarily because this decision permitted changes in U.S. policy that satisfied Indian requirements for closer relations. Thus, the United States is faced with a choice between building on its new relationship with India or "re-hyphen-ating" India and Pakistan in U.S. policy, which could potentially reverse these gains.[39]

This is a false choice. Intense, ongoing Indo-Pakistan security compe-tition and emerging Pakistani instability are facts. These facts challenge U.S. interests. Recognizing these issues – as well as Pakistan's intention and ability to pursue security competition with India – does not imply a moral judgment equating Pakistani and Indian behavior, nor does it pre-clude building closer relations with India. The United States can continue to enhance relations with India while adjusting U.S. defense assistance to avoid aggravating security dilemmas in South Asia. The American policy debate on China has already moved beyond the false dichotomy between engagement and containment policies. Likewise, the U.S. India policy debate should move beyond the false dichotomy between a "hyphenated" versus a "de-hyphenated" India policy.

A second potential objection is that U.S. restraint in its relations with India will not by itself end Pakistani insecurity (or paranoia). Pakistani security competition with India is driven by domestic political causes, as well as legitimate security concerns. Further, Pakistani leaders are not above using the threat of intensified Indo-Pakistan conflict to attempt to constrain U.S.-India relations. The United States should use all available political, eco-nomic, and diplomatic pressure to reduce or eliminate Pakistani support for extremists and terrorists. Washington should also employ appropriate economic incentives and military assistance to encourage Islamabad to

[39] C. Raja Mohan, "How Obama Can Get South Asia Right," *The Washington Quarterly*, 32:2 (April 2009): 173–189.

focus on internal stability and to behave responsibly and cooperatively in South and Central Asia. However, not all of Pakistan's security concerns are "illegitimate" – at least to the extent that such distinctions can be made in international politics. The United States can seek to mitigate Pakistan's legitimate security concerns by calibrating its geopolitical and military support to India and by placing defense cooperation in a broader political and diplomatic context that supports stability in the region.

The New U.S.–India Relationship: Avoid Buyer's Regret

Washington is buying into a new U.S.–India geostrategic relationship. American expectations must be managed to avoid regrets from the buildup of capabilities that, once transferred to New Delhi, cannot be controlled from Washington. Furthermore, the United States should be wary of "buying in" based on excessively optimistic expectations for diplomatic alignment with India. New Delhi has its own strategic interests in South Asia, Central Asia, and the Middle East. Beyond the challenge of regional security competition, another issue with the potential for U.S. regrets involves New Delhi's relationship with Tehran. India's relationship with Iran is important in itself, but it also symbolizes India's reluctance (or inability) to align with U.S. foreign policy goals.

India believes it has an interest in maintaining close relations with Iran, and it has made it clear that it will not give up this relationship.[40] The New Delhi Declaration of January 2003 commits India and Iran to "explore opportunities for cooperation in defense and agreed areas, including training and exchange of visits."[41] India has assisted Iran in upgrading its *Kilo*-class submarines, including developing submarine batteries, and Iran has sought Indian help to upgrade its MiG-29 aircraft.[42] India may also help

---

[40] Robert M. Hathaway et al., "The 'Strategic Partnership' Between India and Iran," *Asia Program Special Report*, Woodrow Wilson Center, April 2004; K. Alan Kronstadt and Kenneth Katzman, "India-Iran Relations and U.S. Interests," Congressional Research Service Report for Congress, Order Code RS22486, August 2, 2006; and C. Christine Fair, "India and Iran: New Delhi's Balancing Act," *The Washington Quarterly*, 30:3 (Summer 2007): 145–159. From New Delhi's perspective, India-Iran relations have seen some disappointments. See Harsh V. Pant. "India's Relations with Iran: Much Ado about Nothing," *The Washington Quarterly*, 34:1 (Summer 2007): 61–74. However, India seeks to strengthen its ties to Iran, and many of the limits of the relationship are through no fault of New Delhi. See Pant, "India's Relations with Iran," 62–65.

[41] Text of the India-Iran 2003 New Delhi Declaration, http://meaindia.nic.in/declarestatement/2003/01/25jd1.htm

[42] Anthony H. Cordesman and Martin Kleiber, *Iran's Military Forces and Warfighting Capabilities: The Threat in the Northern Gulf* (New York: Praeger, 2007), 114. See also

Iran develop port facilities in Chahbahar, perhaps in the hope of gaining access to naval facilities there. The Chahbahar issue may be driven in part by New Delhi's fear that China may gain naval access to Pakistan's port of Gwadar and in part by Indian commercial interests. But this and other collaborations with Iran also find support within some Indian security circles because the Iran relationship is seen as a key lever for balancing against American power and policies.[43]

A November 2008 speech by India's external affairs minister Pranab Mukherjee (a principal architect of the U.S.-India nuclear deal when he was defense minister) offers insight into persistent, fundamentally different Indian and American perspectives. Only four weeks after the U.S.-India nuclear cooperation agreement was finalized, Mukherjee addressed a high-profile audience in Teheran that included Iran's Foreign minister Manoucher Mottaki. Mukherjee described India's first and foremost foreign policy principle as independence and freedom of thought and action, and said, "[W]e are instinctively multipolar ... we are conscious of the manipulation of international law by those who drafted it." He went on to describe India's resistance to international pressure to restrict its own nuclear weapons program as opposition to "unequal treaties," which was "ultimately vindicated." Mukherjee then characterized the India-Iran relationship as one where the impulse toward "similar positions on a range of economic, political, and strategic issues" remains strong.[44]

India's Iran policy also reflects what one strategist describes as India's "atavistic desire for autonomy."[45] The pursuit of strategic autonomy as an end in itself (as opposed to a means to an end) has broad support across the

Center For Strategic and International Studies, "India and Iran: Limited Partnership, High Stakes," *South Asia Monitor*, 114, December 20, 2007; Kronstadt and Katzman, "India-Iran Relations and U.S. Interests"; Anthony Cordesman, *Iran's Developing Military Capabilities* (Washington, DC: Center for Strategic and International Studies, 2004); Vijay Sakhuja, "Iran Stirs India-US Waters," Article No. 1986, Institute for Peace and Conflict Studies, New Delhi, April 10, 2006; and Jehangir Pocha, "Concern increases over ties between India, Iran: Nuclear arms proliferation worries U.S.," *San Francisco Chronicle*, Tuesday, October 14, 2003.

[43] Two Indian political scientists summarize this view in the context of Indian opposition to U.S. hegemony and interventionism; see S. D. Muni and Girijesh Pant, *India's Energy Security: Prospects for Cooperation with Extended Neighborhood* (New Delhi: Rupa & Co, 2005), 265.

[44] Address by Pranab Mukherjee, Minister of External Affairs, Seminar on "India and Iran: Ancient Civilizations and Modern Nations," Teheran, November 2, 2008, http://meaindia.nic.in/speech/2008/11/02ss01.htm

[45] Sumit Ganguly, "India's Alliances 2020," in Michael R. Chambers, ed., *South Asia in 2020: Future Strategic Balances and Alliances* (Carlisle: U.S. Army War College, 2002), 329–384, especially 374.

entire Indian political spectrum and could be an obstacle to closer alignment with the United States, even in areas of common interest.[46] For example, although Indian strategists are, like the United States, concerned about rising Chinese power, New Delhi has made it clear that India is not the solution. On the contrary, Indian strategists may prefer that the United States recognize Indian primacy in South Asia and the Indian Ocean, refrain from interventions in South Asia, and play a role as an "offshore balancer, keeping Chinese threats at bay."[47] India also intends to develop closer trade and investment ties with China while avoiding direct security competition.

More broadly, India (like China) remains a strategic work in progress. Some of the recent U.S. affinity for India appears to be based on what India is not, rather than on what it is. India has a rapidly developing economy with a low-cost labor force, but as yet it has no politically sensitive trade surplus with the United States. India's principal territorial conflict, in Kashmir, does not directly involve U.S. interests (unlike Taiwan). India does not neighbor critical U.S. allies like Japan or South Korea, and its expanding role in Asia does not appear to challenge Japanese or South Korean interests. India has nuclear weapons but no delivery systems currently capable of reaching the United States.

Some of these conditions, however, may change in the not-too-distant future. For example, the sometimes paranoid view of some Indian pundits and officials toward the United States could appear more significant to Americans as New Delhi's nuclear reach grows, particularly as India updates its nuclear doctrine and operational procedures to include intercontinental ballistic missiles and nuclear-armed ballistic missile submarines. India's economic relationship with the United States promises benefits for both, but as it grows, that part of the relationship is also likely to experience conflict. These uncertainties highlight the need for restraint in the transfer of weapons and defense technologies. They also reveal the need to build more broad-based and deeper mutual interests with India, beyond security cooperation.

Build Broader, Stronger Common Interests with India

The United States should continue to build on improved relations with India. Washington should, however, bring greater balance to the relationship, which has been centered on security relations and on mutual concerns

---

[46] Ganguly, "India's Alliances 2020," 377.
[47] Ganguly, "India's Alliances 2020," 374–375.

about China's rise in Asia. India has a unique identity and unique attractions. These are not captured in an approach that views India primarily as China's alter ego. Both Washington and New Delhi will miss out on the full potential of the new relationship if it becomes primarily defined in terms of security relations, high-profile dual-use technology transfer, or in terms of India's contrasts with China.

The United States has already begun some efforts at broadening and deepening its economic, political, cultural, and diplomatic relations with India.[48] By increasing the strength of mutual interests, these engagements will give greater substance to the potentially powerful logic for closer U.S.-India security relations.

Both India and the United States would benefit from lowering trade barriers, increasing bilateral trade and investment, and encouraging continued market and regulatory reforms. Washington and New Delhi should encourage bilateral trade and investment beyond the services sector. Trade and investment in industrial and technology sectors such as manufacturing, construction, engineering, energy, telecommunications and information technologies, and environmental protection should be a priority for both sides. To secure these mutual benefits, however, New Delhi must provide a more attractive environment for direct investment in India. For example, although United States policies ended India's isolation from civilian nuclear technology markets, American companies have lost sales opportunities to state owned firms from France and Russia because New Delhi has not reformed its corporate liability regulations. Greater agricultural trade and investment would benefit both consumers and farmers in India and the United States. A U.S.-India free-trade agreement (FTA) would enrich both countries, and negotiations for an FTA would provide a positive platform for airing and working through differences on trade and investment. Certainly, policy reforms and increased bilateral trade and investment will lead to sometimes painful social and economic adjustments in both countries. However, U.S. encouragement for greater trade, investment, and market reforms in India will help reduce poverty and make India wealthier. Economic strength would, in turn, be the strongest and most sustainable support to India's goal of becoming a great power.

Political and cultural ties should also be strengthened. The United States has much to learn from India's great civilization and culture. America also has much to offer. Both Washington and New Delhi should follow up on

---

[48] "Clinton Urges Stronger U.S.-India Ties," *New York Times*, July 20, 2009; "Seeking Business Allies, Clinton Connects With India's Billionaires," *New York Times*, July 18, 2009.

their rhetoric about common democratic values with pragmatic steps to strengthen political, legal, and social institutions in both countries. Indian states would benefit from exchanges on the operation of political parties and legislatures, especially with regard to organization, fund raising, transparency, and ethical standards. Exchanges on administrative and judicial reform and efficiency would also benefit both sides. Law enforcement has already become a focus of intergovernmental cooperation, but this could be expanded beyond antiterrorism and antinarcotics to include anticorruption and anti–white-collar crime.

The United States and India stand to gain from the promotion of cultural ties as well. Education should be made a priority for both public- and private-sector exchanges. Many wealthy Indians already enjoy access to higher education in the United States. But U.S. educational programs and institutions should also be brought to India. The transfer of educational technologies and approaches should aim to reach beyond the sons and daughters of India's richest families, helping enhance both middle and higher education. Both governments should consider funding and hosting additional programs (akin to the Marshall scholarships) to promote graduate and postgraduate fellowships in areas of common interest, including security studies.

Building on U.S.-India political and cultural interests is an end in itself. However, a secondary effect of greater political, cultural, and educational exchange may be the reduction of lingering suspicions of U.S. intentions among Indian elites, paving the way for establishing common views on key international political and economic issues, and therefore greater diplomatic alignment.

Improving U.S.-India diplomatic alignment on multilateral approaches to security, global trade, finance, and climate change issues should also be a priority. In the security realm, Washington should encourage New Delhi to continue to move away from a view that sees bilateral and multilateral cooperation as a challenge to Indian autonomy. Washington and New Delhi should explore greater participation in multilateral security regimes and bilateral or multilateral military deployments (not merely exercises). The United States could also consider engaging India on regional security issues and confidence building in South Asia on a multilateral basis. This might be done through the South Asian Association for Regional Cooperation (SAARC), which includes Pakistan. Counterterrorism is an obvious candidate for greater bilateral and multilateral cooperation. However, Washington should be cautious about creating the appearance that cooperation with New Delhi is directed against Islamabad.

Currently, Indian views on international trade and multilateral institutions differ markedly from the views of the United States and most of its allies. India's role (with China) in the July 2008 collapse of the Doha round trade talks highlighted this difference. Differences were again on display during the 2009 Copenhagen conference on climate change, as India and China collaborated to undermine U.S. and European proposals. Washington should encourage New Delhi to focus on supporting existing global institutions with universal appeal, such as the WTO, rather than separate "South-South" forums, with their adversarial overtones toward the developed nations. (The India-Brazil-South Africa [IBSA] initiative is an example of a forum that seeks to build South-South alignment.) As it has already done with Beijing since early 2009, Washington should increase engagement with New Delhi on climate change, greenhouse gas emissions, and new energy technologies. The United States should encourage India to take, at a minimum, a stance on energy and emissions that is at least as positive as China's.[49] As with Sino-U.S. engagements on this issue, the United States will ultimately have to lead by example if it is to make collaboration successful.

Finally, the United States should take a measured approach on military cooperation and dual-use technology transfer, the areas where Washington and some American and Indian constituencies have recently been pushing hardest and fastest. The United States should recognize that Indian leaders prize status-related achievements even more than many other U.S. partners. Geopolitical, nuclear, military, and technological cooperation are America's trump cards in its relations with India. The United States should ensure that the two sides are focused on building common ground on basic economic, diplomatic, and strategic interests before delivering status and material benefits.

Consistent Approach on Values

The United States should apply consistent standards in its policies and statements on value-related goals. This includes human rights policies and opposition to regimes that systematically persecute their own people. One

---

[49] Indian leaders appear to recognize that New Delhi's international reputation as a deal breaker on global climate change agreements could backfire. This is particularly so as Beijing has moderated its own position. China has also committed to considerable domestic energy efficiency gains which in turn limit emissions growth. See "New Script for India on Climate Change: Altering Its Tactics to Protect Its Interests," *New York Times*, October 3, 2009.

area where the United States fails to hold countries to the same standard is support for rogue regimes, particularly rogue regimes with oil. On this issue, India's behavior is virtually indistinguishable from China's. Nevertheless, most American critics focus on Beijing while making little, if any, mention of New Delhi. Reflecting its larger companies and greater financial wherewithal, China is a larger investor in projects that benefit unsavory regimes, but it is hardly less discriminating in its choice of friends. India has been just as eager to invest in Myanmar, Iran, Syria, Sudan, and Cuba. New Delhi has provided equally important state support and diplomatic facilitation to those deals. The engagement of these regimes by national oil companies from the developing world (and in some cases by companies from the developed West) is a global problem. The United States cannot expect international support for its policies on these regimes when it appears to give some states a free ride on the issue while singling out others for criticism.

A similar principle applies to the issue of human rights. The Chinese regime engages in widespread human rights violations, including the use of its legal system to persecute people for political crimes. In contrast, India is notable among nations for its protection of political rights and rights to speech. However, violations of the rights of women and children remain widespread in India, as does violence against religious minorities. Recognizing India's achievements on political freedom, Washington should continue to constructively engage New Delhi on these issues. This will make U.S. diplomacy more consistent, and therefore more convincing. Progress in these areas will also promote social stability within India and deepen common U.S.-India interests.

China Policy: Prioritize Challenges, Build on Mutual Benefits

To manage China's rising relative power and secure U.S. interests, Washington should shift its China policy in five ways: meet the Chinese techno-economic challenge by revitalizing American manufacturing and innovation; work to reconstruct an element of trust in the Sino-U.S. relationship; prioritize the issues on which it seeks to confront Beijing; respond appropriately to Chinese military developments; and create both incentives and disincentives for specific behaviors instead of simply criticizing Chinese policy. The recommendations presented here should have bipartisan appeal and are aimed at securing American interests with China (and in Asia) over the long run. Some will produce short-term results. Others may take years to produce their full potential benefits.

Meet the Chinese Techno-Economic Challenge

A realist perspective recognizes that America's long-term relationship with China will be determined largely by the balance of relative techno-economic power between the two countries. Technological and economic prowess not only determines relative wealth and affects trade balances; it also underpins relative military power. Perhaps the most important steps the United States can take to meet the long-term challenge posed by rising Chinese power will be domestic: revitalizing American manufacturing industries and innovation and continuing to ensure that the United States remains the world's most attractive home for capital and human talent. The United States must also get other major domestic policies "right" if it is to maintain global leadership as China's relative power increases. These will include policies to improve performance and stability in America's energy, education, health care, and financial sectors.

Reconstruct and Maintain an Element of Trust

Washington and Beijing distrust each other's long-term intentions. Distaste for China's authoritarian regime intensifies American suspicions about China's growing relative power and its aims in Asia. Chinese leaders, for their part, fear the United States seeks to undermine their regime and constrain the growth of Chinese wealth and power.

Trust is not an end in itself. However, an absence of trust is a serious problem with practical consequences. Mutual suspicion is self-reinforcing, and it threatens to prevent Sino-U.S. cooperation even when such cooperation would be mutually beneficial. The responsibility for framing the relationship properly lies on both sides of the Pacific. From the U.S. side, simply maintaining moderate rhetoric on China policy can be a helpful foundation. Framing Sino-U.S. relations in terms of mutual benefits and shared responsibilities (as Robert Zoellick's 2005 "responsible stakeholders" speech did) met with positive responses in China and continues to hold promise. Chinese rhetoric is also important. American officials should seek commitments from Chinese leaders to halt the practice of using the official propaganda machine to encourage a xenophobic nationalism based on negative views of the United States and its allies (including Japan).

Another promising approach is to raise the profile of selected issues that could produce clear benefits for both sides. Small, discrete steps can help reestablish a minimum basis of trust. American efforts to elevate the importance of clean energy technology cooperation with China ran into roadblocks when Beijing implemented protectionist trade and direct investment policies in the wake of the 2008–2009 financial crisis.[50] Yet the logic of the American approach is sound, and persistence is required to secure the benefits for both sides. The principles of building trust in small steps by constructing non-security-related, "win-win" engagements should be extended to issue areas beyond energy. As part of this effort, the U.S. should consider actively promoting some types of Chinese direct investment in the United States.

Prioritize Challenges and Engagements

Rebuilding trust in selected areas will not be enough. It must be followed by action, both to confront challenges and to achieve mutual benefit. But the United States should first prioritize both challenges and opportunities with China. For Washington, priority should be given to the issue areas that could produce the greatest harm to U.S. interests, on the one hand, and to those that hold out the potential for generating greatest benefit, on the other. These are: engaging on cross–Taiwan Strait security, securing Chinese cooperation for weapons of mass destruction (WMD) anti-proliferation and strategic arms control, bringing China into regional security dialogue while preventing Beijing from excluding the United States from regional fora, maximizing U.S. economic interests with China, and ensuring a firm response to any Chinese tendency toward expansive diplomatic or territorial claims, or aggression.

The danger of being drawn into war makes the Taiwan Strait a top priority in Sino-U.S. relations. Even barring other considerations, the possibility of conflict with China over Taiwan would drive a different U.S. approach to China than toward India. The United States must continue to maintain the difficult balancing act of deterring mainland use of force against Taiwan without encouraging moves by Taipei toward *de jure* independence.

Deterrence will require the United States to maintain its relative military superiority in Asia. Given the geographic realities of Taiwan's location 100 miles off the Chinese coast and the attenuation of military power across the vast distances of the Pacific Ocean, this task is inherently challenging. However, American political and military leaders must make it clear to their

---

[50] "U.S.-China Joint Statement," November 17, 2009, http://www.whitehouse.gov/the-press-office/us-china-joint-statement; Kenneth Lieberthal and David Sandalow, *Overcoming Obstacles to U.S.-China Cooperation on Climate Change* (Washington, DC: Brookings Institution), 2008; Richard Holbrooke et al., *A Roadmap for U.S. China Cooperation on Energy and Climate Change* (Washington, DC: Asia Society, 2008); and Kenneth Lieberthal, *U.S. China Clean Energy Cooperation: The Road Ahead* (Washington, DC: Brookings Institution, 2009).

Chinese counterparts that Washington has many options, and the United States will impose steep costs on China if it engages in unconstrained security competition.

Conflict over Taiwan is not in the interest of either side. Yet the dangers of escalation and conflict are growing with time as the line between conventional and nuclear weapons is blurred by the development and deployment of new categories of conventionally armed ballistic missiles. In addition to ensuring robust American military options and deterrent capability and helping Taiwan prepare defenses that are resilient and effective, American leaders should encourage both sides to improve crisis stability across the Strait by enhancing the reliability and clarity of signaling under potential crises.

Another high priority for engagement, and one where Washington and Beijing might work together, is controlling the spread of weapons of mass destruction (WMD).[51] Establishing a senior-level official dialogue on strategic nuclear issues could provide a useful forum.[52] Beijing has expressed interest in gaining membership in the Missile Technology Control Regime (MTCR).[53] An official bilateral WMD dialogue would enable Washington to address at a higher level its concerns about weak Chinese export control standards, which have prevented Beijing's membership in the MTCR. It would also facilitate discussions about what an expanded MTCR might look like in a world of long-range high-speed cruise missiles, dual-use technologies, and growing civilian (and even private) space programs. The United States should also continue to push China on steps that will build toward a Fissile Material Cutoff Treaty (FMCT). Washington might address issues such as transparency on fissile material stocks, creating international stockpiles, and moving toward a safer and more secure international fuel cycle. Despite Washington's frustration with Beijing's lack of decisive action on North Korea's WMD programs, the United States should continue to

[51] Thanks to Chris Twomey for sharing a number of insights with us on the potential for U.S.-China cooperation on strategic nuclear issues. See also Christopher P. Twomey, ed., *Perspectives on Sino-American Strategic Nuclear Issues* (New York: Palgrave Macmillan, 2008).

[52] Regular track 2 (nongovernmental) and track 1.5 (nonofficial but with some government participation) dialogues have been held on strategic issues since 2000 and have contributed to mutual understanding of respective national positions. Without track 1 dialogue, however, it is impossible to progress toward more concrete cooperation. A single track 1 (official government-to-government) meeting was held in 2008, but the Chinese have been reluctant to hold official meetings since then. In late 2010 and early 2011, however, there were some signs the Chinese side was becoming more receptive to such meetings.

[53] China is not a member of the MTCR, but has made a commitment to abide by the MTCR guidelines signed in 1987. It has not agreed to abide by subsequent MTCR agreements.

take advantage of China's role in facilitating and hosting discussions and continue to encourage Beijing to take more meaningful action in response to North Korean provocations.

Washington might also consider ways to integrate China further into regional security architectures. China has already joined a number of regional political and economic forums and has generally played a positive role in these regimes.[54] However, Beijing has also sometimes worked to enhance its influence in Asia in ways that are not in U.S. interests. China has encouraged the development of security-related regimes that exclude the United States, such as the East Asia Summit and the Shanghai Cooperation Organization. Washington must work to ensure that Beijing is brought into regional dialogue, and that the United States is not kept out of key institutions. This is a reminder that the United States must compete for influence in Asia. America should not become so focused on traditional security issues that it cedes the realm of economic development and trade to Chinese influence.

Economic issues should also be prioritized. Since the 1990s, the U.S. policy debates on Sino-American economic relations have focused on a number of issues on which compromise is difficult to achieve and the prospects for direct benefits to the U.S. economy are low, such as the value of China's currency. China will ultimately have its own reasons to adjust its currency policy, and when it does so, the greatest direct effect on trade and jobs may be felt in low-cost competitor nations, such as Vietnam, Indonesia, and Mexico, rather than in the United States. American economic diplomacy with China should focus on areas where Chinese trade and finance policies pose the greatest threat to U.S. interests and on areas where U.S. firms and workers stand to garner the greatest benefit. These include intellectual property and trademark protection, enforcing product safety and quality standards, reducing China's investment in excess industrial production capacity, and ensuring trade and investment market access in China for U.S. companies (especially for advanced technology goods and services). The U.S. should encourage Chinese financial sector reforms that will permit greater capital flows to both foreign and domestic private firms in China.

The United States should also vigorously fight Chinese protectionist policies, such as unreasonable demands placed on foreign firms for technology

---

[54] See Marc Lanteigne, *China and International Institutions: Alternate Paths to Global Power* (New York: Routledge, 2005); Alastair Iain Johnston, *Social States: China and International Institutions 1980–2000* (Princeton: Princeton University Press, 2007); and Stephen Olson and Clyde Prestowitz, "The Evolving Role of China in International Institutions," The Economic Strategy Institute, January 2011.

transfer; unreasonable technical standards, such as the "Green Dam" censorship software; and unfair government procurement policies, such as those imposed to promote "indigenous innovation" in clean energy. While economic relations are mutually beneficial, United States and Western markets are much more important to China than China's cheap manufactured goods are to the world.[55] The United States has considerable bilateral trade policy levers at its disposal to ensure access to Chinese markets and protection of U.S. intellectual property. These include temporary sector-level trade sanctions, which could be linked to requirements for trade and investment openness, fairness, and reciprocal access.

Human rights issues will always have a high priority for American citizens and have a place in U.S. diplomacy with China. However, high-profile reports and speeches on the human rights situation in China have lost effectiveness because most Chinese people (including the growing educated middle class) have come to perceive ulterior motives in U.S. criticisms. Washington should continue to deplore China's use of its legal system to prosecute political crimes, continue to inquire about the status of persons prosecuted for political crimes, and continue to support their release. However, Washington should find more effective, pragmatic ways to engage on human rights. One possibility is to increase support for initiatives in areas that are not formally labeled "human rights," but where significant practical improvements to civil and human rights can be achieved. These could include promoting greater police, legal, and judicial exchanges. Another potential area for greater support is in capacity building for municipal governance (especially in secondary cities).[56]

---

[55] In recent years, the value-added of exports directly contributes 15 percent to 18 percent of the level of China's GDP. At least 30 million people are directly employed in China's export sector. (An additional 25 to 30 million jobs are linked to the export sector indirectly.) Trade is essential to China's technological upgrading and productivity growth through technology transfer. Cheaper Chinese goods help Westerners save on the cost of many imports, yet most of these products are available from other exporters in Asia and elsewhere. China itself is an increasingly important growth market for many Western firms. On balance, however, given its need to maintain high growth, employment, and access to markets and technology, China still needs its trading partners more than they need China.

[56] On the potential for (and limits to) municipal governance and legal system reform in China, see Young Nam Cho, *Local People's Congresses in China: Development and Transition* (New York: Cambridge University Press, 2009); Joseph Fewsmith, "Staying in Power: What Does the Chinese Communist Party Have to Do?" in Cheng Li, ed., *China's Changing Political Landscape: Prospects for Democracy* (Washington, DC: Brookings, 2008), 212–226; Jacques deLisle, "Legalization without Democratization in China Under Hu Jintao," also in Li, *China's Changing Political Landscape*, 185–211; and Jerome Cohen, "Law in Political Transitions: Lessons from East Asia and the Road Ahead for China,"

Respond Appropriately to Evolving Chinese Military Capabilities

China's development of anti-access capabilities – including submarines, ballistic missiles, antiship ballistic missiles, antisatellite weapons, and other long-range strike systems – appears designed to discourage U.S. intervention in a Taiwan conflict. Many of these capabilities have potential applications in Asia beyond Taiwan.[57] U.S. military planners will need to explore a variety of responses to maintain American superiority while minimizing excessive regional security competition where possible. These steps should include new regional basing options, continued investments in unmanned vehicle technologies, stealth technologies, long-range strike, new ways of capitalizing on superior submarine forces, and new operational concepts.

U.S. bases in Asia should be prepared for dispersal. As part of this effort, the United States should secure access to alternative bases in current host nations, as well as access to both permanent and contingency bases in other nations in Asia. Some of these may need to be further away from China than existing large forward bases, such as Kadena on Okinawa. In addition to raising the costs to any attacker and enhancing survivability, dispersal will reduce America's relative dependence on a few large bases in Japan. Further, in the event of a conflict, base options in a number of countries around Asia would present Beijing with a diplomatic dilemma: Attacking all of them would increase the likelihood of a unified Asia-wide response, with attendant military, diplomatic, and economic consequences. Experience in Europe shows these preparations can be effective, but securing access will require Washington to conduct intense, long-term regional diplomacy.[58]

Bases in Asia should also be hardened so that key assets and personnel are more likely to survive attack. The ability to repair runways and other facilities quickly should be improved. The United States should also ensure that aerial refueling capacity for U.S. forces is robust even in cases where bases are attacked. The demand for refueling will increase if fighters must fly increased distances from aircraft carriers and land bases farther to the rear. Yet forward-based tanker aircraft and the runways to support them would be particularly vulnerable in a conflict. Fuel depots should be hardened and

---

written statement before the U.S. Congressional Executive Commission on China, July 26, 2005.

[57] Roger Cliff, et al., *Entering the Dragon's Lair: Chinese Antiaccess Strategies and Their Implications for the United States* (Santa Monica: RAND Corporation, 2007).

[58] On regional responses to rising Chinese power, see Evan S. Medeiros et al., *Pacific Currents: The Responses of U.S. Allies and Security Partners in East Asia to China's Rise* (Santa Monica: RAND Corporation, 2008).

dispersed. Base access far from the battle lines for aerial refueling aircraft will be particularly important, as forward bases lie within range of developing Chinese military capabilities.

In addition to improved regional base options, improved defenses for Taiwan are also required. These should aim to enhance Taiwan's ability to resist missile and aircraft attack as well as submarine and sea mine attacks against Taiwan's ports and shipping. In addition, survivable systems to strike Chinese invasion forces massed at landing areas in Taiwan might also be developed. Robust and resilient defenses are preferred to the development of any long-range Taiwanese offensive strike capabilities.[59]

The United States has many advantages in military technology relative to China. The Pentagon should continue to invest in unmanned aerial and undersea vehicle technologies and further develop ways to leverage its relative superiority in undersea warfare. Long-range strike capabilities should be further developed, including cruise missiles that can penetrate modern air defenses. Some new technologies and options will likely produce "Billy Mitchell moments" for the American military and U.S. defense industries, challenging traditional preferences and operational concepts.[60] For example, the United States faces choices about continued traditional reliance on large aircraft carriers as opposed to development of greater numbers of smaller surface ships and submarines.

Debates on the development of new U.S. operational concepts, such as AirSea Battle, have already touched on many of the issues discussed earlier. As initiated by the Pentagon, AirSea Battle aims to enhance integration of U.S. Air Force and Navy capabilities and operations, much as the AirLand Battle sought to improve the coordination and integration of U.S. Army and Air Force elements during the 1980s and 1990s. Closer integration would undoubtedly improve U.S. deterrence and war-fighting capabilities in the Pacific. However, some recent nongovernment discussions marry the "doctrine" (which is not yet fully defined) to specific procurement requirements for new large-scale weapons programs and operational concepts. Those

---

[59] See Michael D. Swaine and Oriana Skylar Mastro, "Assessing the Threat," in Michael D. Swaine et al., eds., *Assessing the Threat: The Chinese Military and Taiwan's Security* (Washington DC: Carnegie Endowment for International Peace, 2007), 337–366; and David A. Shlapak et al., *A Question of Balance: Political Context and Military Aspects of the China-Taiwan Dispute* (Santa Monica: RAND Corporation, 2009), especially 123–149.

[60] In the interwar period, a senior U.S. Army officer, William L. "Billy" Mitchell, conducted a prominent, albeit divisive, campaign to secure support for military and naval airpower relative to traditional forces such as large naval surface fleets.

concepts are largely offensive and involve the early destruction or disabling of key targets on the Chinese mainland or in space.[61]

These studies provide a valuable baseline for what might be required to win a war with relatively few adjustments to current U.S. operational concepts. Yet with new budgetary realities in the United States, purchasing all of the capabilities that some recommend for the new AirSea Battle concept may prove prohibitively expensive. Further, forward-leaning operational concepts may not fully capitalize on U.S. strengths and may instead play into Chinese geographic advantages. Preparation and deployment of such a forward-leaning force and operational plan could also undermine crisis stability and exacerbate arms-racing behavior in Asia. In responding to Chinese military developments, the U.S. should consider all options, particularly those that would allow it to negate the advantages accruing to China from proximity to areas of potential conflict. These might include ensuring robust and resilient defenses for U.S. and allied forces and counterattack capabilities based on the U.S. dominance of air and sea spaces at greater distances.[62]

Some of these suggestions hark back to another period of strategic and operational ferment, between the late 1890s and 1941. As American planners considered "War Plan Orange" against Japan, a recurring internal debate emerged between those who favored a forward-leaning strategy of offensive attacks from the start of a conflict and those who preferred a strong initial defensive position, followed by counterattacks aimed at the enemy's weaknesses.[63] Having emerged from a decades-long period when there was no military problem that could not be solved with more money and technology, the United States may once again be entering a period when a broader range of strategic options should be assessed in considering how best to buttress deterrence and war-fighting potential in Asia.

Incentives and Disincentives

Any policy must also have both a carrot and a stick to create incentives and disincentives for specific behaviors. U.S. policy has tended to focus on

---

[61] Andrew F. Krepinevich, *Why AirSea Battle?* (Washington, DC: Center for Strategic and Budgetary Assessments, 2010); Jan Van Tol et al., *Air Sea Battle: A Point-of-Departure Operational Concept* (Washington, DC: Center for Strategic and Budgetary Assessments, 2010).

[62] Many of these advantages are explained in Barry Posen, "Command of the Commons: The Military Foundation of U.S. Hegemony," *International Security*, 28:1 (Summer 2003): 5–46.

[63] Edward S. Miller, *War Plan Orange: The U.S. Strategy to Defeat Japan, 1897–1945* (Annapolis: Naval Institute Press, 1991).

stick, whether sanctions or other forms of enforcement, and has underutilized the potential for creating incentives that will attract support from key political or corporate constituencies in China. In each priority issue area where the United States seeks to engage China, policies should construct both incentives and disincentives for specific behaviors.

For example, in areas of great interest to the United States, such as IPR, energy, and environment, China has many good regulations and laws on its books, but the costs Chinese companies pay for cheating are low. This is an opportunity for U.S. economic diplomacy. One example will serve to illustrate the principle of creating positive incentives. U.S. government agencies could encourage the development of independent industry associations that vet Chinese companies and periodically certify them as "IPR protectors," or "energy efficient," or "carbon care" companies, in much the way U.S. manufacturers were once awarded the "Good Housekeeping Seal." These Chinese companies will have an advantage that is marketable, which would be an incentive for them and their local government backers to comply with policies and regulations. There is precedent in such evaluations and awards in the International Organization for Standardization ISO 9000 quality certification process, the U.S. Green Building Council's Leadership in Energy Efficiency and Environmental Design (LEED) certification process for energy-efficient buildings, and the Energy Star program for appliance makers, managed by the U.S. Department of Energy and the Environmental Protection Agency. All such processes, awards, and their host organizations must be carefully monitored to prevent corruption and ensure compliance.

Chinese and Indian Strategic Behavior and American Interests

The review of Chinese and Indian behavior in this book demonstrates that the broad patterns of Indian and Chinese strategic behavior are not widely divergent. The finding that these two large emerging powers share important similarities in strategic behavior does not minimize the importance of idiosyncratic differences. However, the differences do not reveal a Beijing consistently more prone than New Delhi to pursue its own narrow self-interests, use force, or build military power to secure its objectives. In the twenty-first century, the United States faces a complex, dual challenge from Asia's rising powers, rather than a simple, singular challenge of balancing China's growing relative power.

Washington and Beijing share a varied bilateral agenda, which is now expanding to include regional and global issues. These include trade and finance, energy and climate change, Korean peninsula security, and Iran, among others. The U.S.-India agenda is not yet as expansive, primarily because India is not yet as large an economy or as important a trading partner. Yet the U.S.-India agenda too is becoming more varied and complex. U.S.-India relations are evolving to include bilateral direct investment, military cooperation and arms sales, and development in Afghanistan. Washington and New Delhi are also continuing to search for common ground on issues that still pose challenges in the bilateral relationship. These include stability and security in Pakistan and on the Indo-Pakistan border, global trade and climate change regimes, and Iran.

Domestic politics in China, India, and the United States also affect cycles of cooperation and conflict across these agenda items. This is most evident on perennial issues such as the criminalization of peaceful expression and violations of human rights in China; lingering mistrust of Western firms and Western foreign policy motives in India; the relations New Delhi and Beijing both maintain with regimes in Iran, Sudan, and Myanmar; trade disputes; and, most distinctively, the issue of Taiwan. It is tempting to simplify expectations about Chinese and Indian strategic behavior. However, the empirical record of international strategic behavior is a complex mix of both similarities and differences. Assessments of these rising powers should remain grounded in pragmatism and a comparative analysis of capabilities, interests, and balances of power. This nuanced realist perspective will help the United States secure its interests in each bilateral relationship and more broadly throughout Asia.

Defense Spending, Selected Additional Data

This appendix contains additional data supporting the analysis of defense spending in Chapter 4. The first section provides details of the calculation for the upper boundary to our baseline full defense spending estimates. The second section provides detailed data on PPP exchange rates, as well as detailed calculation of defense spending in appropriate PPP terms. We also list the local currency GDP estimates that we used to calculate defense spending as a percentage of GDP in Chapter 4.

Defense Spending: Upper Boundary Value

Table A.1 shows details of the calculation for the upper boundary for each country's defense spending in 2005 and 2010. We emphasize that this material is provided as a theoretical upper boundary for the purposes of framing the analysis; the upper boundary value is not an alternative defense spending estimate comparable to our baseline full spending estimate. This estimate almost certainly exaggerates spending in several important categories, but is provided as a theoretical limit.

The subtotals for published defense spending are taken from Chapter 4, Tables 4.7 and 4.8. Additional upper boundary items are described in Chapter 4, and data for these items is provided in the table below. Combined with the subtotal for published defense spending, these items represent our upper boundary value for defense spending in China and India.

Defense Spending: Appropriate PPP Calculation

As we have shown in Chapter 4, international defense spending is usually best compared using market exchange rates. PPP-adjusted estimates cannot

Table A.1. *Defense spending upper boundary calculation*

Billion				
Nuclear weapons, space, and intelligence programs not included	2005		2010	
	Rupees	USD	Rupees	USD
India				
Subtotal Category A. Published Defense Spending	1,036	23.5	2,090	42.2
Total Government R&D	193	4.4	453	9.2
Total direct subsidies to state-owned industrial firms	5	0.1	7	0.1
INDIA UPPER BOUNDARY VALUE	**1,234**	**28.0**	**2,550**	**51.5**
	Yuan	USD	Yuan	USD
China				
Subtotal Category A. Published Defense Spending	301	36.8	682	100.6
Total Government R&D	65	7.9	163	24
Total direct subsidies to state-owned industrial firms	4	0.5	–	–
Arms Imports	11.5	1.4	10.2	1.5
Arms Sales Profits	2	0.2	4.0	0.6
CHINA UPPER BOUNDARY VALUE	**384**	**46.9**	**859**	**126.7**

be interpreted to mean that a country is hiding spending, or "spending more" than an announced figure.

However, if employed properly, PPP methods can help improve the accuracy of detailed defense spending estimates. There are a limited number of defense spending items that could be underestimated if using market exchange rates alone. These are typically related to personnel costs and are the least lethal components of modern conventional military power.

This appendix provides data and calculations for properly using PPP to estimate the limited elements of defense spending to which it may apply. Our goal is twofold. First, we provide transparency regarding our methods and estimates presented in Chapter 4. Second, we hope this will encourage constructive criticism and future work by others aimed at making comparative defense spending estimates more transparent and consistent.

Table A.2 provides market exchange rates and PPP exchange rates for various sectors of the Indian and Chinese economies for 2005 and 2010.

Table A.2. *Market exchange rates and PPP exchange rates to*
1 U.S. dollar, 2005 and 2010

	2005		2010	
	China	India	China	India
Market Exchange Rate (MER)	8.19	44.26	6.78	49.50
GDP at PPP exchange rate	3.45	14.67	3.86	17.71
GDP at PPP "multiplier"	*2.37*	*3.02*	*1.76*	*2.80*
Consumption PPP exchange rate	3.46	13.58	3.87	11.25
Consumption PPP "multiplier"	*2.37*	*3.26*	*1.75*	*4.40*
Equipment PPP exchange rate	8.79	36.84	9.84	44.46
Equipment PPP "multiplier"	*0.93*	*1.20*	*0.69*	*1.11*
Military PPP exchange rate (a composite unique to this study)	5.22	21.26	5.84	25.66
Military PPP "multiplier"	*1.57*	*2.08*	*1.16*	*1.93*

Source: Except for "Military PPP," all 2005 data are from *2005 International Comparison Program: Preliminary Results* (Washington, DC: World Bank, December 2007). Year 2010 market exchange rates and GDP at PPP exchange rates are from International Monetary Fund, *World Economic Outlook Database*, October 2010.

For the year 2005 we use PPP exchange rates published by the World Bank in late 2007, both for the broad GDP at PPP exchange rate and for individual sector PPP exchange rates. The World Bank and the IMF published a broad estimate of GDP at PPP exchange rates for 2010 but did not publish sector-level PPP exchange rates for 2010. We estimate these 2010 sector-level prices based on the change in GDP at PPP exchange rates between 2005 and 2010. Strictly speaking, our method for estimating 2010 sector-level PPP exchange rates is not as accurate as an estimate based on actual prices collected for 2010. However, given that no such data is available, we believe our estimate is reasonable, and superior to continuing to use 2005 data to estimate 2010 exchange rates.

In addition to the sector-level PPP exchange rates from the World Bank, we have created a "military PPP" exchange rate estimate. Military PPP is a composite unique to this study. We have constructed this estimate to reflect both military operations and personnel costs, based on World Bank PPP exchange rates for consumption, equipment, and fuels.

For convenience, we also provide an "implied PPP multiplier" in Table A.2, derived from the relationship between the market exchange rate and the sector PPP exchange rate in this table. We provide this because some students and analysts are more accustomed to viewing this figure

Table A.3. *India 2005: Estimated full defense spending at appropriate PPP U.S. dollars*

Nuclear weapons, space, and intelligence programs not included	Billion 2005 Rupees	Appropriate PPP exchange rate		Billion 2005 PPP USD	Billion 2005 MER USD
A. PUBLISHED DEFENSE SPENDING					
1. Official Defense Budget					
Army	307	"Military"	21.26	14	7
Navy	63	"Military"	21.26	3	1
Air Force	91	"Military"	21.26	4	2
Defense Ordnance Factories	–3	"Equipment"	36.84	–0.1	–0.1
Capital Outlay on Defense Services (includes weapons imports)	331	"Equipment"	36.84	9	7
Defense R&D	28	MER	44.26	1	1
Subtotal Official Defense Budget	**817**			**31.2**	**18.5**
2. Published Defense-Related Spending (not in official budget)					
Defense Pensions	127	"Consumption"	13.58	9	3
Ministry of Defense Administration	15	"Military"	21.26	1	0.3
Paramilitaries and Internal Security	76	"Military"	21.26	3.6	1.7
Subtotal Other Published Defense-Related Spending	**219**			**13.7**	**4.9**
Subtotal A. Total Published Defense Spending	**1,036**			**44.9**	**23.4**
B. ADDITIONAL OFF-BUDGET ITEMS					
Government R&D with potential dual-use applications (est.)	19.3	MER	44.26	0.4	0.4
Subsidies to potential dual-use industries (est.)	2.8	MER	44.26	0.1	0.1
Subtotal B. Additional Off-Budget Items	**22**			**0.5**	**0.5**
Baseline Estimate Full Defense Spending	**1,058**			**45.4**	**23.9**

Table A.4. *China 2005: Estimated full defense spending at appropriate PPP U.S. dollars*

Nuclear weapons, space, and intelligence programs not included	Billion 2005 Yuan	Appropriate PPP exchange rate		Billion 2005 PPP USD	Billion 2005 MER USD
A. PUBLISHED DEFENSE SPENDING					
1. Official Defense Budget					
PLA all services personnel	83	"Consumption"	3.46	24.0	10.2
PLA all services operations and training	81	"Military"	5.22	15.5	9.9
PLA all services equipment (imports not included)	84	"Equipment"	8.79	9.5	10.2
Total Official Defense Budget	**247**			**49.0**	**30.2**
2. Published Defense-Related Spending (not in official budget)					
Additional Military Family Compensation and Pensions	21.7	"Consumption"	3.46	6.3	2.6
Paramilitaries and Internal Security	32.7	"Military"	5.22	6.3	4.0
Subtotal Other Published Defense Expenditure	**54**			**12.5**	**6.6**
Subtotal A. Published Defense Spending	**301**			**61.5**	**36.8**
B. ADDITIONAL OFF-BUDGET ITEMS					
Government R&D with potential dual-use application	49	MER	8.19	6.0	6.0
Subsidies to defense-related industry	1.3	MER	8.19	0.2	0.2
Arms imports	11.5	MER	8.19	1.4	1.4
Arms sales profits	2	MER	8.19	0.2	0.2
Subtotal B. Additional Off-Budget Items	**63.8**			**7.8**	**7.8**
Baseline Estimate Full Defense Spending	**365**			**69.3**	**44.6**

Table A.5. *India 2010: Estimated full defense spending at appropriate PPP U.S. dollars*

Nuclear weapons, space, and intelligence programs not included	Billion 2010 Rupees	Appropriate PPP exchange rate		Billion 2010 PPP USD	Billion 2010 MER USD
A. PUBLISHED DEFENSE SPENDING					
1. Official Defense Budget					
Army	605	"Military"	25.66	23.6	12.2
Navy	98	"Military"	25.66	3.8	2.0
Air Force	150	"Military"	25.66	5.8	3.0
Defense Ordnance Factories	2	"Equipment"	44.46	0.03	0.03
Capital Outlay on Defense Services (includes weapons imports)	608	"Equipment"	44.46	13.7	12.3
Defense R&D	52	MER	49.50	1.1	1.1
Subtotal Official Defense Budget	**1,516**			**48.0**	**30.6**
2. Published Defense-Related Spending (not in official budget)					
Defense Pensions	340	"Consumption"	11.25	30.2	6.9
Ministry of Defense Administration	42	"Military"	25.66	1.6	0.8
Paramilitaries and Internal Security	193	"Military"	25.66	7.5	3.9
Subtotal Other Published Defense-Related Spending	**574**			**39.3**	**11.6**
Subtotal A. Published Defense Spending	**2,090**			**87.4**	**42.2**
B. ADDITIONAL OFF-BUDGET ITEMS					
Government R&D with potential dual-use applications (est.)	45.3	MER	49.50	0.9	0.9
Subsidies to potential dual-use industries (est.)	4	MER	49.50	0.1	0.1
Subtotal B. Additional Off-Budget Items	**50**			**1**	**1**
Baseline Estimate Full Defense Spending	**2,140**			**88.4**	**43.2**

Table A.6. *China 2010: Estimated full defense spending at appropriate PPP U.S. dollars*

Nuclear weapons, space, and intelligence programs not included	Billion 2010 Yuan	Appropriate PPP exchange rate		Billion 2010 PPP USD	Billion 2010 MER USD
A. PUBLISHED DEFENSE SPENDING					
1. Official Defense Budget					
PLA all services personnel	181	"Consumption"	3.87	46.8	26.7
PLA all services operations and training	179	"Military"	5.84	30.7	26.5
PLA all services equipment (imports not included)	172	"Equipment"	9.84	17.4	25.3
Total Official Defense Budget	**532**			**94.9**	**78.5**
2. Published Defense-Related Spending (not in official budget)					
Additional Military Family Compensation and Pensions	56.4	"Consumption"	3.87	14.6	8.3
Paramilitaries and Internal Security	93.5	"Military"	5.84	16.0	13.8
Subtotal Other Published Defense Expenditure	**149.9**			**30.6**	**22.1**
Subtotal A. Published Defense Spending	**682**			**125.5**	**100.6**
B. ADDITIONAL OFF-BUDGET ITEMS					
Government R&D with potential dual-use application	72	MER	6.78	10.6	10.6
Subsidies to defense-related industry	–	MER	6.78	–	–
Arms imports	10.2	MER	6.78	1.5	1.5
Arms sales profits	4	MER	6.78	0.6	0.6
Subtotal B. Additional Off-Budget Items	**86**			**12.7**	**12.7**
Baseline Estimate Full Defense Spending	**768**			**138.2**	**113.3**

308 Appendix

Table A.7. *Gross domestic product, selected years*

GDP in local currency, current year, billion	2005	2010 (e)
China	18,494	38,946
India	35,708	70,842

Source: International Monetary Fund, World Economic Outlook Database, October 2010. Data for 2010 are IMF estimates.

rather than an exchange rate number.[1] In the cases where it is appropriate to use PPP to measure defense-related spending, we encourage the direct use of the PPP exchange rate for the appropriate sector and the appropriate year to convert local currency prices into PPP prices.

The tables above show detailed calculations for appropriate PPP-adjusted full defense spending used to generate the PPP adjusted estimates in Chapter 4. The appropriate sector PPP exchange rate to use for conversion is listed in each table under the column heading "Appropriate PPP Exchange Rate."

Where we have provided a calculation of defense spending as a percentage of GDP in Chapter 4, we used GDP data from the International Monetary Fund World Economic Outlook Database. These data are presented in Table A.7.

[1] Those familiar with the "PPP multiplier" terminology will recall that in the December 2007 revision to its PPP price series for China, the World Bank reduced its GDP at PPP prices estimate of China's 2005 economy by about 40%. So, the "multiplier" that could be used to inflate local GDP to generate an estimated PPP U.S. dollar figure fell to about 2.37, from about 3.93 (note that the "multiplier" itself already accounts for a conversion to a U.S. dollar figure). Using the PPP exchange rate directly in sector-by-sector calculation is more accurate and less susceptible to methodological mistakes.

Bibliography

Acharya, Amitav, "Theoretical Perspectives on International Relations in Asia," in David Shambaugh and Michael Yahuda, eds., *International Relations of Asia*. Lanham: Rowman & Littlefield Publishers, 2008, 57–84.

Agnihotri, K. K., and Sunil Kumar Agarwala, "Legal Aspects of Marine Scientific Research in Exclusive Economic Zones: Implications of the Impeccable Incident." *Maritime Affairs: Journal of the National Maritime Foundation of India*, 5:2 (December 2009): 135–150.

Alagappa, Muthiah, ed., *Asian Security Order: Instrumental and Normative Features*. Stanford: Stanford University Press, 2002.

Alagappa, Muthiah, ed., *Asian Security Practice: Material and Ideational Influences*. Stanford: Stanford University Press, 1998.

Allen, Kenneth and Maryanne Kivlehan-Wise, "Implementing PLA Second Artillery Doctrinal Reforms," in Finkelstein and Mulvenon, eds., *The Revolution in Doctrinal Affairs*, 159–219.

Allen, Kenneth W., "PLA Air Force Operation and Modernization." Paper presented at Conference on the People's Liberation Army, Carlisle, Pennsylvania, September 10–12, 1999.

Allen, Kenneth W., Glenn Krumel, and Jonathan D. Pollack, *China's Air Force Enters the 21st Century*. Santa Monica: RAND Corporation, 1995.

Anand, Vinod, "Evolution of a Joint Doctrine for the Indian Armed Forces." *Strategic Analysis*, 24:4 (July 2000).

Armitage, Richard L., Nicholas Burns, and Richard Fontaine, *Natural Allies: A Blueprint for the Future of U.S.-India Relations*. Washington, DC: Center for a New American Security, 2010.

Ashraf, Tariq, "Doctrinal Reawakening of the Indian Armed Forces." *Military Review*, 84:6 (November 1, 2004), 53–62.

Bajpai, K. Shankar, "Engaging with the World," in Sinha and Mohta, eds., *Indian Foreign Policy*, 75–90.

Bajpai, Kanti P. and Amitabh Mattoo, eds., *Securing India, Strategic Thought and Practice: Essays by George K. Tanham with Commentaries*. New Delhi: Manohar Publishers, 1996.

Bajpai, Kanti, "Indian Strategic Culture," in Chambers, ed., *South Asia in 2020: Future Strategic Balances and Alliances*, 245–303.

"Nuclear Policy, Grand Strategy, and Political Values in India." Seventeenth P.C. Lal Memorial Lecture, New Delhi, February 18, 2000.

Bajpai, Kanti, P. R. Chari, Pervaiz Iqbal Cheema, Stephen P. Cohen, and Sumit Ganguly, *Brasstacks and Beyond: Perception and the Management of Crisis in South Asia*. New Delhi: Manohar Press, 1995.

Bakshi, G. D., *The Indian Art of War: The Mahabharata Paradigm (Quest for an Indian Strategic Culture)*. New Delhi: Sharada Press, 2002.

Bardhan, Pranab, "Crouching Tiger, Lumbering Elephant? The Rise of China and India in a Comparative Perspective." *Brown Journal of World Affairs*, 13:1 (Fall/Winter 2006), 49–62.

Awakening Giants: Feet of Clay. Princeton: Princeton University Press, 2010.

Barnett, A. Doak, *China and the Major Powers in East Asia*. Washington, DC: Brookings Institution, 1977.

Bartholomew, Carolyn, and Daniel Blumenthal, "Letter to the Honorable Robert Byrd, President Pro Tempore of the Senate, and the Honorable Nancy Pelosi, Speaker of the House of Representatives," in United States-China Economic and Security *Review Commission, China's Military Modernization and Its Impact on the United States and the Asia-Pacific, Hearing Before the U.S.-China Economic and Security Review Commission, One Hundred Tenth Congress, First Session, March 29–30 2007*. Washington, DC: United States-China Economic and Security Review Commission, May 2007.

Behera, Laxman Kumar, "The Indian Defence Budget 2007–2008." Institute for Defence Studies and Analyses (IDSA) Strategic Comment, March 9, 2007.

Bergsten, C. Fred, "Correcting the Chinese Exchange Rate: An Action Plan." Testimony before the Committee on Ways and Means, U.S. House of Representatives, March 24, 2010.

Berlin, Donald L., "India in the Indian Ocean." *Naval War College Review*, 59:2 (Spring 2006): 80.

Bidwai, Praful, "Military Overdrive." *Frontline*, 25:7 (March 29–April 11, 2008).

Bitzinger, Richard A., "Analyzing Chinese Military Expenditures," in Stephen J. Flanagan and Michael E. Marti, eds., *The People's Liberation Army and China in Transition*. Honolulu: University Press of the Pacific, 2004, 177–193.

"India's Once and Future Defence Industry." *RSIS Commentaries*, Nanyang Technological University, Singapore, October 8, 2007.

"Just the Facts, Ma'am: The Challenge of Analysing and Assessing Chinese Military Expenditures." *The China Quarterly* 173 (2003): 164–175.

Blank, Stephen, "India and Central Asia: Part of the New Great Game," in Pant, ed., *Indian Foreign Policy in a Unipolar World*, 277–304.

Blasko, Dennis J., "PLA Ground Force Modernization and Mission Diversification: Underway in All Military Regions," in Kamphausen and Scobell eds., *Right-Sizing the People's Liberation Army*, 281–373.

Blasko, Dennis J., Chas W. Freeman, Jr., Stanley A. Horowitz, Evan S. Medeiros, and James C. Mulvenon, "Defense-Related Spending in China: A Preliminary Analysis and Comparison with American Equivalents," United States-China Policy Foundation, 2007.

Blasko, Dennis J., *The Chinese Army Today: Tradition and Transformation for the 21st Century*. New York: Routledge Press, 2006.

Blumenthal, Daniel, "Obama's Asia Trip: A Series of Unfortunate Events." *Foreign Policy, Shadow Government*, November 18, 2009.

Boesche, Roger, "Kautilya's Arthasastra on War and Diplomacy in Ancient India." *The Journal of Military History*, 67:1 (January 2003): 9–37.

Bolkcom, Christopher et al., "Combat Aircraft Sales to South Asia: Potential Implications." Congressional Research Service Report to Congress, Order Code RS22148, May 19, 2005.

Bose, Sumantra, *Kashmir: Roots of Conflict, Paths to Peace*. Cambridge, MA: Harvard University Press, 2003.

Bottome, Edgar M., *The Missile Gap: A Study in the Formulation of Military and Political Policy*. Rutherford: Fairleigh Dickinson University Press, 1971.

Brahm, Laurence J., *China's Century: The Awakening of the Next Economic Powerhouse*. New York: Wiley Press, 2001.

Brown, Harold et al., *Chinese Military Power: Report of an Independent Task Force*. New York: Council on Foreign Relations, 2003.

Brown, Michael E., Sean M. Lynn-Jones, and Steven E. Miller, eds., *Debating the Democratic Peace*. Cambridge, MA: MIT Press, 1996.

Burles, Mark, and Abram N. Shulsky, *Patterns in China's Use of Force: Evidence from History and Doctrinal Writings*. Santa Monica: RAND Corporation, 2000.

Bush, Richard C., *Untying the Knot: Making Peace in the Taiwan Strait*. Washington, DC: Brookings Institution, 2005.

Bush, Richard C., and Michael E. O'Hanlon, *A War Like No Other: The Truth about China's Challenge to America*. New York: Wiley Press, 2007.

Bussert, James C., and Bruce A. Elleman, *People's Liberation Army Navy: Combat Systems Technology, 1949–2010*. Annapolis: Naval Institute Press, 2011.

Buzan, Barry, "New Patterns of Global Security in the Twenty-First Century." *International Affairs*, 67:3 (1991): 431–451.

Buzan, Barry, and Ole Wæver, *Regions and Powers: The Structure of International Security*. New York: Cambridge University Press, 2003.

Campbell, Kurt M., and Michael E. O'Hanlon, *Hard Power: The New Politics of National Security*. New York: Basic Books, 2006.

Carr, E. H., *The Twenty Years' Crisis: An Introduction to the Study of International Relations*. New York: Macmillan Press, 1939.

Chambers, Michael R., ed., *South Asia in 2020: Future Strategic Balances and Alliances*. Carlisle: U.S. Army War College, 2002.

Chari, P.R., Pervaiz Iqbal Cheema, and Stephen P. Cohen, *Four Crises and a Peace Process: American Engagement in South Asia*. Washington, D.C.: Brookings Institution, 2007.

Charlton, Sue Ellen M., *Comparing Asian Politics: India, China, and Japan*. 2nd ed. Boulder: Westview Press, 2004.

Chase, Michael S., and Evan Medeiros, "China's Evolving Nuclear Calculus: Modernization and Doctrinal Debate," in Finkelstein and Mulvenon eds., *The Revolution in Doctrinal Affairs*, 119–154.

Chaudhuri, Shubham, and Martin Ravallian, "Partially Awakened Giants: Uneven Growth in China and India," in Winters and Yusuf, eds., *Dancing with Giants*, 175–210.

Chen Jian, *Mao's China and the Cold War*. Chapel Hill: University of North Carolina Press, 2001.

Chen Xikang et al., "Domestic Value Added and Employment Generated by Chinese Exports: A Quantitative Estimation." MPRA Paper No. 15663, June 11, 2009.

Cheung, Tai-Ming, *Fortifying China: The Struggle to Build a Modern Defense Economy*. Ithaca: Cornell University Press, 2009.

Cho, Young Nam, *Local People's Congresses in China: Development and Transition.* New York: Cambridge University Press, 2009.

Christensen, Per Bigum, "Task Force 150 Anti-Piracy Operations." MARLO Conference Report, January 25, 2009.

Christensen, Thomas J., "China, the US-Japan Alliance, and the Security Dilemma in East Asia." *International Security*, 23:4 (Spring 1999): 49–80.

"Shaping the Choices of a Rising China: Recent Lessons for the Obama Administration." *The Washington Quarterly*, 32:3 (July 2009), 89–104.

Useful Adversaries: Grand Strategy, Domestic Mobilization, and Sino-American Conflict, 1947–1958. Princeton: Princeton University Press, 1996.

Clausewitz, Carl Von, *On War*, translated and edited by Michael Howard and Peter Paret. Princeton: Princeton University Press, 1989.

Cliff, Roger, Mark Burles, Michael S. Chase, Derek Eaton, and Kevin L. Pollpeter, *Entering the Dragon's Lair: Chinese Antiaccess Strategies and Their Implications for the United States.* Santa Monica: RAND Corporation, 2007.

Cliff, Roger, John Fei, Jeff Hagen, Elizabeth Hague, Eric Heginbotham, and John Stillion, *Shaking the Heavens and Splitting the Earth: Chinese Air Force Employment Concepts in the 21st Century.* Santa Monica: RAND Corporation, 2011.

Cohen, Craig, and Derek Chollet, "When $10 Billion Is Not Enough: Rethinking U.S. Strategy Towards Pakistan." *The Washington Quarterly*, 30:2 (Spring 2007): 7–19.

Cohen, Jerome, "Law in Political Transitions: Lessons from East Asia and the Road Ahead for China." Written statement before the United States Congressional Executive Commission on China, July 26, 2005.

Cohen, Stephen P., *Emerging Power: India.* Washington, DC: Brookings Institute Press, 2001.

Cohen, Stephen P., and Sunil Dasgupta, *Arming without Aiming: India's Military Modernization.* Washington, DC: Brookings Institution Press, 2010.

Cohen, Stephen S., and John Zysman, *Manufacturing Matters: The Myth of the Post-Industrial Economy.* New York: Basic Books, 1987.

Cole, Bernard D., "China's Maritime Strategy," in Erickson, Goldstein, Murray, and Wilson, eds., *China's Future Nuclear Submarine Force*, 22–42.

The Great Wall at Sea: China's Navy Enters the Twenty-First Century. Annapolis: Naval Institute Press, 2001.

Cook, Malcolm et al., *Power and Choice: Asian Security Futures.* Sydney: Lowy Institute for International Policy, 2010.

Cooper, Cortez A., III, "'Preserving the State:' Modernizing and Task-orienting a 'Hybrid' PLA Ground Force," in Kamphausen and Scobell eds., *Right-Sizing the People's Liberation Army*, 237–280.

Cordesman, Anthony H., *Iran's Developing Military Capabilities.* Washington, DC: Center for Strategic and International Studies, 2004.

Cordesman, Anthony H., and Martin Klieber, *Chinese Military Modernization: Force Development and Strategic Capabilities.* Washington, DC: Center for Strategic and International Studies, 2007.

Crane, Keith, Roger Cliff, Evan Medeiros, James Mulvenon, and William Overholt, *Modernizing China's Military: Opportunities and Constraints.* Santa Monica: RAND Corporation, 2005.

D'Amato, C. Richard, "Statement on 'National Security Dimensions of the Possible Acquisition of UNOCAL by CNOOC and the Role of CFIUS.'" Washington, DC: House Committee on Armed Services, July 13, 2005.

Dahlman, Carl, and Anuja Utz, *India and the Knowledge Economy Leveraging Strengths and Opportunities*. Washington, DC: World Bank, 2005.

Damodaran, A. K., "Non-Aligned Movement and Its Future," in Sinha and Mohta, eds., *Indian Foreign Policy*, 125–138.

Dasgupta, Chandrashekar, "India and the Changing Balance of Power," in Sinha and Mohta, eds., *Indian Foreign Policy*, 91–112.

deLisle, Jacques, "Legalization without Democratization in China under Hu Jintao," in Cheng Li, ed., *China's Changing Political Landscape: Prospects for Democracy*. Washington, DC: Brookings Institution Press, 2008, 185–211.

Denoon, David B. H., *The Economic and Strategic Rise of China and India: Asian Realignments after the 1997 Financial Crisis*. New York: Palgrave Macmillan 2007.

Devotta, Neil, "When Individuals, States, and Systems Collide: India's Foreign Policy towards Sri Lanka," in Sumit Ganguly ed., *India's Foreign Policy: Retrospect and Prospect*, 32–61.

Diamond, Andrew F., "Dying With Eyes Open or Closed: The Debate over a Chinese Aircraft Carrier." *Korean Journal of Defense Analysis*, 18:1 (Spring 2006): 35–58.

Dittmer, Lowell, "Conclusion," in Hao, Wei, and Dittmer, eds., *Challenges to Chinese Foreign Policy*, 335–348.

Dougherty, Sean M. et al., "India's Growth Pattern and Obstacles to Higher Growth." OECD Economics Department Working Paper No. 63, Paris: Organization for Economic Cooperation and Development, August 11, 2008.

Doyle, Michael W., "Kant, Liberal Legacies, and Foreign Affairs, Part 1," *Philosophy and Public Affairs*, 12:3 (1983): 205–235.

"Liberalism and World Politics," *American Political Science Review*, 80:4 (December 1986): 1151–1169.

Drezner, Daniel, "The New New World Order." *Foreign Affairs*, 86:2 (March/April 2007), 93–106.

Dutz, Mark A., ed., *Unleashing India's Innovation: Toward Sustainable and Inclusive Growth*. Washington, DC: World Bank, 2007.

Earle, Edward Mead, "Introduction," in Edward Mead Earle, ed., *The Makers of Modern Strategy*. Princeton: Princeton University Press, 1943, 3–25.

Easton, Ian, *The Assassin under the Radar: China's DH-10 Cruise Missile Program*. Arlington: Project 2049 Institute, September 2009.

Economy, Elizabeth, "Asia's Water Security Crisis: China, India, and the United States," in Ashley J. Tellis, Mercy Kuo, and Andrew Marble, eds., *Strategic Asia 2008–2009: Challenges and Choices*. Seattle: National Bureau of Asian Research, 2008, 365–390.

Economy, Elizabeth C., *The River Runs Black: The Environmental Challenge to China's Future*. Ithaca: Cornell University Press, 2004.

Economy, Elizabeth C., and Adam Segal, "The G2 Mirage," *Foreign Affairs*, 88:3 (May/June 2009), 14–23.

Eisenman, Joshua, Eric Heginbotham, and Derek Mitchell, eds., *China and the Developing World: Beijing's Strategy for the Twenty-First Century*. Armonk: M.E. Sharpe, 2007.

Ellis, R. Evan, *China in Latin America: The Whats and Wherefores*. Boulder: Lynne Rienner Publishers, 2009.

Encarnation, Dennis J., *Rivals beyond Trade: America versus Japan in Global Competition.* Ithaca: Cornell University Press, 1993.

Engardio, Pete, ed., *Chindia: How China and India Are Revolutionizing Global Business.* New York: McGraw Hill, 2007.

Erickson, Andrew, and Lyle Goldstein, "Gunboats for China's New 'Grand Canals'? Probing the Intersection of Beijing's Naval and Oil Security Policies." *Naval War College Review,* 62:2 (Spring 2009), 43–76.

Erickson, Andrew, and David Yang, "On the Verge of a Game Changer." *U.S. Naval Institute Proceedings,* 135:3 (May 2009): 26–32.

Erickson, Andrew S., Lyle J. Goldstein, William S. Murray, and Andrew R. Wilson, eds., *China's Future Nuclear Submarine Force.* Annapolis: Naval Institute Press, 2007.

Erickson, Andrew S., and Justin D. Mikolay, "Welcome China to the Fight against Pirates," *U.S. Naval Institute Proceedings,* 135:3 (March 2009): 34–41.

Erickson, Andrew S., and David D. Yang, "Using the Land to Control the Sea? Chinese Analysts Consider the Antiship Ballistic Missile." *Naval War College Review,* 62:4 (Autumn 2009): 53–86.

Fair, C. Christine, "India and Iran: New Delhi's Balancing Act," *Washington Quarterly,* 30:3 (Summer 2007): 145–159.

Fairbank, John K., ed., *The Chinese World Order: Traditional China's Foreign Relations.* Cambridge, MA: Harvard University Press, 1968.

Fairbank, John King, *The United States and China.* 4th ed. Cambridge, MA: Harvard University Press, 1983.

Farber, Henry S., and Joanne Gowa, "Polities and Peace." *International Security,* 20:2 (Fall 1995): 123–146.

Feickert, Andrew, "Missile Survey: Ballistic and Cruise Missiles of Selected Foreign Countries." Congressional Research Service Report to Congress, Order Code RL30427, July 26, 2005.

Feickert, Andrew, and K. Alan Kronstadt, "Missile Proliferation and the Strategic Balance in South Asia." Congressional Research Service Report to Congress, Order Code RL32115, October 17, 2003.

Fewsmith, Joseph, "Staying in Power: What Does the Chinese Communist Party Have to Do?" in Cheng Li, ed., *China's Changing Political Landscape: Prospects for Democracy.* Washington, DC: Brookings Institution Press, 2008, 212–226.

Fingleton, Eamonn, *In Praise of Hard Industries: Why Manufacturing, Not the Information Economy, Is the Key to Future Prosperity.* New York: Houghton Mifflin, 1999.

Finkelstein, David M., *China's National Military Strategy.* Alexandria: CNA Corporation, 2000.

"China's National Military Strategy Revisited: An Overview of the Military Strategic Guidelines," in Kamphausen and Scobell, eds., *Right-Sizing the People's Liberation Army,* 69–140.

"Thinking about the PLA's 'Revolution in Doctrinal Affairs,'" in Finkelstein and Mulvenon eds., *The Revolution in Doctrinal Affairs,* 1–27.

Finkelstein, David M., and James Mulvenon, eds., *The Revolution in Doctrinal Affairs: Emerging Trends in the Operational Art of the Chinese People's Liberation Army.* Alexandria: Center for Naval Analyses, 2005.

Fisher, Richard D., *China's Military Modernization: Building for Regional and Global Reach.* London: Praeger Security Press, 2008.

Flournoy, Michèle, and Shawn Brimley, eds., *Finding Our Way: Debating America's Grand Strategy*. Washington, DC: Center for a New American Security, 2008.

Fogel, Robert, "$123,000,000,000,000: China's estimated economy by the year 2040. Be warned." *Foreign Policy*, 177 (January/February 2010).

Forney, Matt, and Arthur Kroeber, "Focus: The Real Reason Why Google Quit China." GaveKal Economics *DragonWeek*, March 29, 2010.

Frankel, Francine, *India's Political Economy 1947–2004*. 2nd ed. New York: Oxford University Press, 2005.

Frankel, Francine R., and Harry Harding, *The India-China Relationship: What the U.S. Needs to Know*. Washington, DC: Woodrow Wilson Center Press, 2004.

Fravel, M. Taylor, "China's Search for Military Power." *The Washington Quarterly*, 31:3 (Summer 2008): 125–141.

"Power Shifts and Escalation: Explaining China's Use of Force in Territorial Disputes." *International Security*, 32:3 (Winter 2007/2008): 44–83.

"Regime Insecurity and International Cooperation: Explaining China's Compromises in Territorial Disputes." *International Security*, 30:2 (Fall 2005): 46–83.

"Securing Borders: China's Doctrine and Force Structure for Frontier Defense." *Journal of Strategic Studies*, 30:4–5 (2007): 705–737.

Strong Borders, Secure Nation: Cooperation and Conflict in China's Territorial Disputes. Princeton: Princeton University Press, 2008.

Friedberg, Aaron L., "The Future of U.S.-China Relations: Is Conflict Inevitable?" *International Security* 30 (Fall 2005): 7–45.

Friedman, Barry, Estelle James, Cheikh Kane, and Monika Queisser, "How Can China Provide Income Security for Its Rapidly Aging Population? Volume 1." World Bank Policy Research Working Paper No. WPS 1674, October 10, 1996.

Friedman, Edward, and Bruce Gilley, eds., *Asia's Giants: Comparing China and India*. New York: Palgrave Macmillan, 2005.

Fuchs, Andreas, and Nils-Hendrik Klann, "Paying a Visit: The Dalai Lama Effect on International Trade." Center for European Governance and Economic Development Research Paper No. 113, University of Goettingen, Department of Economics, October 19, 2010.

Ganguly, Sumit, "The Genesis of Nonalignment," in Sumit Ganguly ed., *India's Foreign Policy: Retrospect and Prospect*. New Delhi: Oxford University Press, 2010., 1–10.

Ganguly, Sumit ed., *India's Foreign Policy: Retrospect and Prospect*. New Delhi: Oxford University Press, 2010.

Ganguly, Sumit, "India's Alliances 2020," in Chambers, ed., *South Asia in 2020: Future Strategic Balances and Alliances*, 363–384.

"India's Foreign Policy Grows Up." *World Policy Journal*, 20:4 (Winter 2003/2004), 41–47.

Ganguly, Sumit, and Andrew Scobell, "India and the United States: Forging a Security Partnership?" *World Policy Journal*, 22:2 (Summer 2005), 37–44.

Ganguly, Sumit, and Devin T. Hagerty, *Fearful Symmetry: India-Pakistan Relations in the Shadow of Nuclear Weapons*. Seattle: University of Washington Press, 2005.

Garthoff, Raymond, "CIA Estimates of Soviet Defense Spending: A Review." *Post-Soviet Geography and Economics*, 39:9 (1998), 549–533.

Garver, John, *Foreign Relations of the People's Republic of China*. Englewood Cliffs: Prentice Hall, 1993.

Garver, John W., *China & Iran: Ancient Partners in a Post-Imperial World*. Seattle: University of Washington Press, 2006.

Protracted Contest: Sino-Indian Rivalry in the Twentieth Century. Seattle: University of Washington Press, 2001.

Gharekhan, Chinmaya R., "India and the United Nations," in Sinha and Mohta, eds., *Indian Foreign Policy*, 193–215.

Ghosn, Faten, Glenn Palmer, and Stuart Bremer, "The MID3 Data Set, 1993–2001: Procedures, Coding Rules, and Description." *Conflict Management and Peace Science*, 21 (2004): 133–154.

Gilboy, George J., and Eric Heginbotham, "Getting Realism: U.S. Asia (and China) Policy Reconceived." *The National Interest*, 69 (Fall 2002): 99–109.

Giles, Lionel, *Sun Tzu on The Art of War: The Oldest Military Treatise in the World*. Toronto: Global Language Press, 2007.

Gill, Bates, *Rising Star: China's New Security Diplomacy*. Washington, DC: Brookings Institution, 2007.

Gill, Bates, and Yanzhong Huang, "Sources and Limits of Chinese Soft Power." *Survival*, 48:2 (Summer 2006): 17–36.

Gilpin, Robert, "The Theory of Hegemonic War." *Journal of Interdisciplinary History*, 18 (Spring 1988): 591–614.

War and Change in World Politics. New York: Cambridge University Press, 1981.

Glaser, Bonnie S., and Evan S. Medeiros, "The Changing Ecology of Foreign Policy-Making in China: The Ascension and Demise of the Theory of "Peaceful Rise." *The China Quarterly*, 190 (2007): 291–310.

Glosny, Michael A., "Stabilizing the Backyard: Recent Developments in China's Policy Toward Southeast Asia," in Eisenman, Heginbotham, and Mitchell, eds., *China and the Developing World*, 150–188.

Godwin, Paul, "From Continent to Periphery: PLA Doctrine, Strategy, and Capabilities Toward 2000." *China Quarterly*, 146 (June 1996): 464–487.

Godwin, Paul H. B., "China's Emerging Military Doctrine: A Role for Nuclear Submarines?" in Erickson, Goldstein, Murray, and Wilson, eds., *China's Future Nuclear Submarine Force*, 43–58.

"Force Projection and China's National Military Strategy," in C. Dennision Lane, Mark Weisenbloom, and Dimon Liu, eds., *Chinese Military Modernization*. New York: Kegan Paul International, 1996, 69–99.

Goldstein, Avery, "Great Expectations: Interpreting China's Arrival." *International Security*, 22:3 (Winter 1997/1998): 36–73.

"Parsing China's Rise: International Circumstances and National Attributes," in Ross and Feng, eds., *China's Ascent*, 55–86.

Rising to the Challenge: China's Grand Strategy and International Security. Stanford: Stanford University Press, 2005.

Goldstein, Morris, and Nicholas R. Lardy, "The Future of China's Exchange Rate Policy." Peterson Institute for International Economics, Policy Analyses in International Economics 87, July 2009.

Goldstein, Steven M., "China and Taiwan: Signs of Change in Cross-Strait Relations." *China Security*, 5:1 (Winter 2009): 65–70.

Gordon, Sandy, "Indian Defense Spending: Treading Water in the Fiscal Deep." *Asian Survey*, 32:10 (October 1992): 934–950.

Government of India, Indian Army, *Indian Army Doctrine Part 1*. Simla: Headquarters Army Training Command, October 2004.

Graff, David, and Robin Higham, eds., *A Military History of China*. Boulder: Westview Press, 2002.

Green, Michael J., "Obama's Self-Defeating 'Realism' in Asia," *Foreign Policy, Shadow Government*, October 6, 2009.

Grimmett, Richard F., "Conventional Arms Transfers to Developing Nations 2001–2008," Congressional Research Service Report for Congress, Order Number R40796, September 4, 2009.

Guha, Ramachandra, *India after Gandhi: The History of the World's Largest Democracy*. New York: Harper Collins, 2007.

Guiney, Jessica, "India's Space Ambitions: Headed Toward Space War?" Center for Defense Information Policy Brief, May 2008.

Gulati, Ashok, and Shenggen Fan, *The Dragon and the Elephant: Agricultural and Rural Reforms in China and India*. Washington, DC: International Food Policy Research Institute, 2007.

Gundu, Raja Karthikeya, and Teresita C. Schaffer, "India and Pakistan in Afghanistan: Hostile Sports," *South Asia Monitor*, Number 117, Center for Strategic and International Studies, April 3, 2008.

Gupta, Amit, *The U.S. India Relationship: Strategic Partnership or Complementary Interests?* Carlisle: U.S. Army War College, 2005.

Gupta, Ranjit, "India's Look East Policy," in Atish Sinha and Madhup Mohta, eds., *Indian Foreign Policy: Challenges and Opportunities*. New Delhi: Foreign Service Institute, 2007, 351–382.

Hagt, Eric, and Matthew Durnin, "China's Antiship Ballistic Missile: Developments and Missing Links." *Naval War College Review*, 62:4 (Autumn 2009): 87–117.

Hao Yufan, C. X. George Wei, and Lowell Dittmer, eds., *Challenges to Chinese Foreign Policy: Diplomacy, Globalization, and the Next World Power*. Lexington: University of Kentucky Press, 2009.

Harrison, Selig S., ed., *Seabed Petroleum in Northeast Asia: Conflict or Cooperation*. Washington, DC: Woodrow Wilson International Center for Scholars, 2005.

Hathaway, Robert M. et al., *The "Strategic Partnership" between India and Iran*. Asia Program Special Report, Washington, DC: Woodrow Wilson Center, April 2004.

Heginbotham, Eric, "The Fall and Rise of Navies in East Asia: Military Organizations, Domestic Politics, and Grand Strategy." *International Security*, 27:2 (Fall 2002): 86–125.

Hilali, A. Z., "India's Strategic Thinking and Its National Security Policy." *Asian Survey*, 41:5 (October 2001): 737–764.

Holbrooke, Richard et al., *A Roadmap for U.S. China Cooperation on Energy and Climate Change*. Washington, DC: Asia Society, 2008.

Holmes, James R., and Toshi Yoshihara, *Asia Looks Seaward: Power and Maritime Strategy*. New York: Routledge Press, 2008.

Chinese Naval Strategy in the 21st Century: The Turn to Mahan. New York: Routledge Press, 2008.

Houser, Trevor, and Roy Levy, "Energy Security and China's UN Diplomacy." *China Security* 4:3 (Summer 2008): 63–73.

Howarth, Peter, *China's Rising Sea Power: The PLA Navy's Submarine Challenge*. New York: Routledge Press, 2006.

Hu Jintao, "Build Towards a Harmonious World of Lasting Peace and Common Prosperity." Statement at the United Nations Summit, New York, September 15, 2005.

Huang, Yasheng, and Tarun Khanna, "Can India Overtake China?" *Foreign Policy*, 82:4 (July–August 2003):74–81.

Huntington, Samuel P., *The Clash of Civilizations and the Remaking of World Order*. New York: Touchstone, 1996.

Ikenberry, G. John, and Michael Mastanduno, "Images of Order in the Asia Pacific and the Role of the United States," in Ikenberry and Mastanduno, eds., *International Relations Theory and the Asia-Pacific*, 421–439.

Ikenberry, G. John, and Michael Mastanduno, eds., *International Relations Theory and the Asia-Pacific*. New York: Columbia University Press, 2003.

International Centre for Trade and Sustainable Development, "China Relaxes Innovation Standard." International Centre for Trade and Sustainable Development, China Programme, 14:3 (September 16, 2010).

International Institute for Strategic Studies, *The Military Balance 2008*. London: Routledge Press, 2008.

The Military Balance 2009. London: Routledge Press, 2009.

International Intellectual Property Alliance (IIPA), "IIPA 2008 'Special 301' Recommendations: 2006 and 2007 Estimated Trade Losses Due to Copyright Piracy and 2006–2007 Estimated Levels of Copyright Piracy." Washington, DC: International Intellectual Property Alliance, November 5, 2008.

"India: 2009 Special 301 Report on Copyright Protection and Enforcement." Washington, DC: International Intellectual Property Alliance, February 17, 2009.

Jacques, Martin, *When China Rules the World: The End of the Western World and the Birth of a New Global Order*. New York: The Penguin Press, 2009.

Jain, B. M., *Global Power: India's Foreign Policy 1947–2006*. Lanham: Lexington Books, 2008.

Jervis, Robert, "Cooperation under the Security Dilemma." *World Politics*, 30:2 (January 1978): 167–214.

Ji Guoxing, "The Legality of the 'Impeccable Incident,'" *China Security*, 5:2 (Spring 2009), 16–21.

Johnston, Alastair Iain, *Cultural Realism: Strategic Culture and Grand Strategy in Chinese History*. Princeton: Princeton University Press, 1995.

"Is China a Status Quo Power?" *International Security*, 27:4 (Spring 2003): 5–56.

Social States: China and International Institutions 1980–2000. Princeton: Princeton University Press, 2007.

Johnston, Alastair Iain, and Robert S. Ross, eds., *New Directions in the Study of China's Foreign Policy*. Stanford: Stanford University Press, 2006.

Jones, Rodney W., "Indian Strategic Culture." Science Applications International Corporation, October 31, 2006.

Kadian, Rajesh, "Nuclear Weapons and the Indian Armed Forces," in SarDesai and Thomas eds., *Nuclear India in the Twenty-First Century*, 211–227.

Kamphausen, Roy, and Andrew Scobell, eds., *Right-Sizing the People's Liberation Army: Exploring the Contours of China's Military*. Carlisle: U.S. Army War College, 2007.

Kan, Shirley A., "U.S.-China Counterterrorism Cooperation: Issues for U.S. Policy," Congressional Research Service Report to Congress, Order Code RL33001, October 2007.

Kaplan, Robert, "How We Would Fight China," *Atlantic Monthly* (June 2005).

Kaplan, Robert D., "Behind the Indian Embassy Bombing," *The Atlantic Monthly*, August 1, 2008.

"Center Stage for the 21st Century." *Foreign Affairs*, 88:2 (March/April 2009), 16–32.

Kapur, Ashok, *India – From Regional to World Power*. New York: Routledge Press, 2006.

Karnad, Bharat, "India's Force Planning Imperative: The Thermonuclear Option," in SarDesai and Thomas, eds., *Nuclear India in the Twenty-First Century*, 105–138.

Nuclear Weapons and Indian Security. New Delhi: MacMillan India Limited, 2002.

Kasturi, Bhashyam, "The State of War with Pakistan," in Marston and Sundaram, eds., *A Military History of India and South Asia*, 139–156.

"The State of War with Pakistan," in Marston and Sundaram, eds., *A Military History of India and South Asia*, 146–149.

Katzman, Kenneth, "Afghanistan: Post-Taliban Governance, Security and U.S. Policy." Congressional Research Service Report to Congress, Order Code RL30588, February 9, 2009.

Kautilya, *Arthashastra*, translated by L. N. Rangarajan. New Delhi: Penguin Books, 1987.

Keay, John, *India: A History*. New York: Grove Press, 2000.

Kelly, Joseph E. et al., *National Security: Impact of China's Military Modernization in the Pacific Region*. Washington, DC: United States General Accounting Office, GAO/NSIAD-95-84, June 1995.

Kennedy, Paul, "Mahan vs. Mackinder," in Paul Kennedy, *The Rise and Fall of British Naval Mastery*, 3rd ed. Amherst: Humanity Books, 2006., 177–202.

Kennedy, Scott, ed., *Beyond the Middle Kingdom: Comparative Perspectives on China's Capitalist Transformation*. Stanford: Stanford University Press, 2011.

Kennedy, Scott, "The Political Economy of Standards Coalitions: Explaining China's Involvement in High-Tech Standards Wars," *Asia Policy*, 2 (July 2006): 41–62.

Kennedy, Scott, Richard P. Suttmeier, and Jun Su, "Standards, Stakeholders, and Innovation: China's Evolving Role in the Global Knowledge Economy." National Bureau of Asian Research, *NBR Special Report*, September 2008.

Keohane, Robert O., *After Hegemony: Cooperation and Discord in the World Political Economy*. Princeton: Princeton University Press, 1984.

Kerr, Paul K., "U.S. Nuclear Cooperation with India: Issues for Congress." Congressional Research Service Report for Congress, Order Code RL 33016, November 3, 2008.

Khanna, Tarun, *Billions of Entrepreneurs: How China and India Are Reshaping Their Futures and Yours*. Cambridge, MA: Harvard Business School Press, 2008.

Kim, Samuel S., "Chinese Foreign Policy Faces Globalization Challenges," in Alastair Iain Johnston and Robert S. Ross, eds., *New Directions in the Study of China's Foreign Policy*. Stanford: Stanford University Press, 2006, 276–306.

Korukonda, Appa Rao, Giovanna Carrillo, Chenchuramaiah Bathala, and Mainuddin Afza, "The Dragon and the Elephant: A Comparative Study of Financial Systems, Commerce, and Commonwealth in India and China." *The Icfai Journal of International Business*, 2:3 (August 2007): 7–20.

Kristensen, Hans M., Robert S. Norris, and Matthew G. McKinzie, *Chinese Nuclear Forces and U.S. Nuclear War Planning*. Washington, DC: Federation of American Scientists, November 2006.

Kroeber, Arthur, "China & India: Friends, Rivals, or Just Two Different Countries?" Dragonomics Research & Advisory, Presentation to British Chamber of Commerce Beijing, April 2, 2008.

"Developmental Dreams: Policy and Reality in China's Economic Reforms," in Scott Kennedy, ed., *Beyond the Middle Kingdom: Comparative Perspectives on China's Capitalist Transformation*. Stanford: Stanford University Press, 2011, 44–65.

"Rising Inflation and a Possible Currency Surprise." GavKalDragonomics China Insight, December 18, 2009.

Kronstadt, K. Alan, *Major U.S. Arms Sales and Grants to Pakistan Since 2001*, Congressional Research Service Report to Congress, Order Code RS22757, April 23, 2008.

"U.S.-India Bilateral Agreements and Global Partnership." Congressional Research Service Report for Congress, Order Code RL 33072, March 10, 2006.

Kronstadt, K. Alan, and Kenneth Katzman, "India-Iran Relations and U.S. Interests." Congressional Research Service Report for Congress, Order Code RS22486, August 2, 2006.

Kumar, Y. P., "India's International Cooperation in Science and Technology." Speech to Federation of Indian Chambers of Commerce and Industry, IC Department, Science & Technology Ministry, December 4, 2006.

Kundu, Apurba, *Militarism in India: The Army and Civil Society Consensus*. New York: Tauris Academic Studies, 1998.

Kwei, Elaine, "China, India, and Energy Security: Implications for the United States." Presentation delivered at RAND Corporation, Santa Monica, August 9, 2006.

Ladwig, Walter C., "A Cold Start for Hot Wars? The Indian Army's New Limited War Doctrine." *International Security* 32:3 (2008): 182–184.

Lal, Rollie, *Understanding India and China: Security Implications for the United States and the World*. Westport: Praeger Security International, 2006.

Lampton, David M., "China's Rise in Asia Need Not Be at America's Expense," in Shambaugh, ed., *Power Shift: China and Asia's New Dynamics*, 306–326.

ed., *The Making of Chinese Foreign and Security Policy in the Era of Reform*. Stanford: Stanford University Press, 2001.

Same Bed, Different Dreams: Managing U.S.-China Relations, 1989-2000. Berkeley: University of California Press, 2001.

The Three Faces of Chinese Power: Might, Money, and Minds. Berkeley: University of California Press, 2008.

Lane, C. Dennison, Mark Weisenbloom, and Dimon Liu, eds., *Chinese Military Modernization*. New York: Kegan Paul International, 1996.

Lanteigne, Marc, *China and International Institutions: Alternate Paths to Global Power*. New York: Routledge, 2005.

Chinese Foreign Policy: An Introduction. New York: Routledge, 2009.

Lardy, Nicholas R., "China: Towards a Consumption-Driven Growth Path." Peterson Institute for International Economics, Policy Brief Number PB06-6, October 2006.

Lau, Lawrence J. et al., "Estimates of U.S.-China Trade Balances in Terms of Domestic Value-Added." Working Paper no 295, Stanford Center for International Development, Stanford University, 2006.

Lavoy, Peter R., *Asymmetric Warfare in South Asia: The Causes and Consequences of the Kargil Conflict.* New York: Cambridge University Press, 2009 .

"Introduction: The Importance of the Kargil Conflict," in Peter R. Lavoy, ed., *Asymmetric Warfare in South Asia: The Causes and Consequences of the Kargil Conflict.* New York: Cambridge University Press, 2009, 1–38.

Levi, Michael A., and Charles D. Ferguson, "U.S.-India Nuclear Cooperation: A Strategy for Moving Forward." Council on Foreign Relations, CSR No. 16, June 2006.

Levy, Jack S., "Power Transition Theory and the Rise of China," in Ross and Feng, eds., *China's Ascent*, 11–33.

Lewis, John, and Xue Litai, *Imagined Enemies: China Prepares for Uncertain War.* Stanford: Stanford University Press, 2006.

Lewis, John Wilson, and Xue Litai, *China Builds the Bomb.* Stanford: Stanford University Press, 1988.

China's Strategic Seapower: The Politics of Force Modernization in the Nuclear Age. Stanford: Stanford University Press, 1994.

Lieberthal, Kenneth, "The U.S.-China Agenda Goes Global." *Current History*, 108:719 (September 2009): 243–249.

U.S. China Clean Energy Cooperation: The Road Ahead. Washington, DC: Brookings Institution, 2009.

The U.S. Intelligence Community and Foreign Policy: Getting Analysis Right. Washington, DC: Brookings Institution, 2009.

Lieberthal, Kenneth, and David Sandalow, *Overcoming Obstacles to U.S.-China Cooperation on Climate Change.* Washington, DC: Brookings Institution, 2008.

Lin-Greenberg, Erik, "Offensive Airpower with Chinese Characteristics: Development, Capabilities, and Intentions." *Air & Space Power Journal*, 21:3 (Fall 2007).

Logan, Jeffrey, "China's Space Program: Options for U.S.-China Cooperation." Congressional Research Service Report for Congress, Order Code RS22777, May 21, 2008.

Lum, Thomas, and Dick K. Nanto, "China's Trade with the United States and the World." Congressional Research Service Report to Congress, Order Code RL31403, January 4, 2007.

Mabbett, I. W., "The Date of the Arthasastra." *Journal of the American Oriental Society*, 84:2, (April 1965): 162–169.

MacDonald, Bruce W., "China, Space Weapons, and U.S. Security." Special Report No. 38, Council on Foreign Relations, September 2008.

Malone, David M., *Does the Elephant Dance? Contemporary Indian Foreign Policy.* New York: Oxford University Press, 2011.

Mansfield, Edward D., and Jack Snyder, "Democratization and the Dangers of War." *International Security*, 20:1 (Summer 1995): 5–38.

Electing to Fight: Why Emerging Democracies Go To War. Cambridge, MA: MIT Press, 2005.

Mansingh, Surjit, *In Search of Power: Indira Gandhi's Foreign Policy 1966–1982.* New Delhi: Sage Publications, 1984.

Maoz, Zeev, and Bruce M. Russett, "Normative and Structural Causes of Democratic Peace, 1946–1986." *American Political Science Review*, 87:3 (September 1993): 624–638.

Marston, Daniel P., and Chandar S. Sundaram, eds., *A Military History of India and South Asia: From the East India Company to the Nuclear Era*. Westport: Praeger Security International, 2007.

Martin, Michael F., and K. Alan Kronstadt, "Pakistan's Capital Crisis: Implications for U.S. Policy." Congressional Research Service Report for Congress, Order Code RS22983, November 7, 2008.

Mason, Mark, and Dennis Encarnation, eds., *Does Ownership Matter? Japanese Multinationals in Europe*. New York: Oxford University Press, 1995.

Maxwell, Neville, *India's China War*. New York: Random House, 1970.

McCain, John, "An Enduring Peace Built on Freedom: Securing America's Future." *Foreign Affairs*, 86:6 (November/December 2007), 19–35.

McDevitt, Michael, "The Strategic and Operational Context Driving PLA Navy Building," in Kamphausen and Scobell, eds., *Right-Sizing the People's Liberation Army*, 481–522.

Mearsheimer, John, *The Tragedy of Great Power Politics*. New York: W.W. Norton, 2001.

Medeiros, Evan S., "Beijing, the Ambivalent Power." *Current History*, 108:719 (September 2009): 250–256.

Medeiros, Evan S., and M. Taylor Fravel, "China's New Diplomacy." *Foreign Affairs*, 82:6 (November/December 2003), 22–35.

Medeiros, Evan S. et al., *A New Direction for China's Defense Industry*. Santa Monica: RAND Corporation, 2005.

Meredith, Robyn, *The Elephant and the Dragon: The Rise of India and China and What It Means for All of Us*. New York: W.W. Norton & Co., 2008.

Ministry of Defence [Navy], Republic of India, *Freedom to Use the Seas: India's Maritime Military Strategy*. New Delhi: Integrated Headquarters, Ministry of Defence [Navy], May 2007.

Ministry of Defence, Republic of India, *Classification Hand Book of Defence Services*. New Delhi: Controller General of Defence Accounts, 2009.

Mitra, Subrata, "Engaging the World: The Ambiguity of India's Power," in Subrata Mitra and Bernd Rill, eds., *India's New Dynamics of Foreign Policy, India's New Dynamics of Foreign Policy*. Munich: Hanns Seidel Foundation, 2006, 7–35.

Mohan, C. Raja, "How Obama Can Get South Asia Right," *The Washington Quarterly*, 32:2 (April 2009): 173–189.

Mohanty, Deba R., *Changing Times? India's Defence Industry in the 21st Century*. Bonn: Bonn International Center for Conversion, 2004.

Morgan, T. Clifton, and Sally Howard Campbell, "Domestic Structure, Decisional Constraints, and War: So Why Kant Democracies Fight?" *Journal of Conflict Resolution*, 35:2 (June 1991): 187–211.

Mott, William H., IV, and Jae Chang Kim, *The Philosophy of Chinese Military Culture: Shih vs. Li*. New York: Palgrave MacMillan, 2006.

Mukherjee, Pranab, "Speech of H.E. Mr. Pranab Mukherjee, Minister of External Affairs." Remarks at Seminar on India and Iran: Ancient Civilizations and Modern Nations, Teheran, November 2, 2008.

Muni, S. D., and Girijesh Pant, *India's Energy Security: Prospects for Cooperation with Extended Neighbourhood*. New Delhi: Rupa & Company Publishers, 2005.

Nair, Pavan, "Defence Budget Leaves Out Rs 26,000 Crores." *India Together*, May 18, 2005.

Nath, Kamal, *India's Century: The Age of Entrepreneurship in the World's Biggest Democracy*. New York: McGraw-Hill, 2007.

Nathan, Andrew, and Robert S. Ross, *The Great Wall and the Empty Fortress: China's Search for Security*. New York: W.W. Norton & Co., 1997.

National Intelligence Council, *Mapping the Global Future: Report of the National Intelligence Council's 2020 Project*. Washington, DC: U.S. Government Printing Office, December 2004.

Nayar, Baldev Raj, and T.V. Paul, *India in the World Order: Search for Major Power Status*. New York: Cambridge University Press, 2003.

Norris, Robert S., and Hans Kristensen, *Pakistani Nuclear Forces 2009*. Bulletin of the Atomic Scientists, September/October 2009.

Novick, David, "The Federal Budget as an Indicator of Government Intentions and the Implications of Intentions." Santa Monica: RAND Corporation, 1959.

Nye, Joseph S., *Soft Power: The Means to Success in World Politics*. New York: Public Affairs Press, 2004.

O'Hanlon, Michael, *Defense Planning for the Late 1990s: Beyond the Desert Storm Framework*. Washington, DC: Brookings Institution, 1995.

Defense Policy Choices for the Bush Administration 2001–2005. Washington, DC: Brookings Institution, 2001.

O'Neill, Jim et al., *BRICs and Beyond*. New York: Goldman Sachs Group, 2007.

O'Rourke, Ronald, "China Naval Modernization: Implications for U.S. Navy Capabilities – Background and Issues for Congress." Congressional Research Service Report for Congress, Order Code RL33153, October 8, 2008.

Olson, Stephen, and Clyde Prestowitz, "The Evolving Role of China in International Institutions," The Economic Strategy Institute, January 2011.

Organization for Economic Cooperation and Development, *Science, Technology and Industry Outlook 2006*. Paris: Organization for Economic Cooperation and Development, 2006.

Organski, Abramo F. K., *World Politics*. New York: Knopf, 1958.

Oye, Kenneth A., *Economic Discrimination and Political Exchange: World Political Economy in the 1930s and 1980s*. Princeton: Princeton University Press, 1993.

Panagariya, Arvind, *India: Emerging Giant*. New York, Oxford University Press, 2008.

Pang, Zhongying, "The Dragon and the Elephant." *The National Interest*, May 1, 2007.

Pant, Harsh V., "India's Relations with Iran: Much Ado about Nothing," *The Washington Quarterly*, 34:1 (Summer 2007): 61–74.

Contemporary Debates in Indian Foreign and Security Policy: India Negotiates Its Rise in the International System. New York: Palgrave MacMillan, 2008.

"India's Search for a Foreign Policy." *Yale Global*, June 26, 2008.

ed., *Indian Foreign Policy in a Unipolar World*. New York: Routledge, 2009.

Pardesi, Manjeet Singh, "Deducing Indian's Grand Strategy of Regional Hegemony from Historical and Conceptual Perspectives." Institute of Strategic and Defense Studies, Singapore, April 2005.

Paul, T. V., "India, the International System, and Nuclear Weapons," in SarDesai and Thomas, eds., *Nuclear India in the Twenty-First Century*, 85–104.

Perkovich, George, *India's Nuclear Bomb: The Impact on Global Proliferation*. 2nd ed. Berkeley: University of California Press, 2001.

"What Makes the Indian Bomb Tick?" in SarDesai and Thomas, eds., *Nuclear India in the Twenty-First Century*, 25–60.

Pollpeter, Kevin, "The Chinese Vision of Space Military Operations," in Finkelstein and Mulvenon, eds., *The Revolution in Doctrinal Affairs*, 329–369.

Posen, Barry, "A Grand Strategy of Restraint," in Flournoy and Brimley, eds., *Finding Our Way: Debating America's Grand Strategy*, 83–102.

The Sources of Military Doctrine: France, Britain, and Germany Between the World Wars. Ithaca: Cornell University Press, 1984.

Prabhakar, Lawrence W., Joshua H. Ho, and W. S. G. Bateman, eds., *The Evolving Maritime Balance of Power in the Asia-Pacific: Maritime Doctrines And Nuclear Weapons at Sea*. Singapore: World Scientific Publishing Company, 2006.

Prados, John, *The Soviet Estimate: US Intelligence and Russian Military Strength*. New York: Dial Press, 1982.

Prasad, Eswar S., "The U.S.-China Economic Relationship: Shifts and Twists in the Balance of Power." Testimony to the U.S. China Economic and Security Commission, Revised March 10, 2010.

Preeg, Ernest H., *India and China: An Advanced Technology Race and How the United States Should Respond*. Arlington: Manufacturer's Alliance/MAPI, 2008.

Radhakrishnan, Sarvepalli, and Charles A. Moore, eds., *A Sourcebook in Indian Philosophy*. Princeton: Princeton University Press, 1957.

Raghavan, Srinath, "A Bad Knock: The War with China, 1962," in Marston and Sundaram, eds., *A Military History of India and South Asia*, 157–174.

Raman, B., *The Kaoboys of R&AW: Down Memory Lane*. New Delhi: Lancer Press, 2007.

Ramesh, Jairam, *Making Sense of Chindia: Reflections on China and India*. New Delhi: India Research Press, 2005.

Rice, Condoleezza, "Rethinking the National Interest: American Realism for a New World," *Foreign Affairs*, 87:4 (July/August 2008): 2–26.

Robert, J. Art, "The United States and the Rise of China: Implications for the Long Haul," in Ross and Feng, eds., *China's Ascent*, 260–290.

Robinson, Thomas W., and David Shambaugh, eds., *Chinese Foreign Policy: Theory and Practice*. New York: Oxford University Press, 1994.

Romberg, Alan D., "Cross-Strait Relations: 'Ascend the Heights and Take a Long-Term Perspective." *China Leadership Monitor*, 27 (Winter 2009).

"Cross-Strait Relations: In Search of Peace," *China Leadership Monitor*, 23 (Winter 2008).

Rosecrance, Richard, and Gu Guoliang, eds., *Power and Restraint: A Shared Vision for The U.S.-China Relationship*. New York: Public Affairs Press, 2009.

Rosen, Daniel H., and Trevor Houser, *China Energy: A Guide for the Perplexed*. Washington, DC: Center for Strategic and International Studies and Peterson Institute for International Economics, May 2007.

Rosen, Stephen P., *Societies and Military Power: India and Its Armies*. Ithaca: Cornell University Press, 1996.

Ross, Robert, "The Geography of the Peace: East Asia in the Twenty-first Century." *International Security*, 23:4 (Spring 1999), 81–118.

Ross, Robert S., and Zhu Feng, eds., *China's Ascent: Power, Security, and the Future of International Politics*. Ithaca: Cornell University Press, 2008.

Rotberg, Robert I., ed., *China into Africa: Trade, Aid, and Influence*. Washington, DC: Brookings Institution, 2008.

Rubin, Barnett R., "Saving Afghanistan." *Foreign Affairs*, 86:1 (January/February 2007): 57–78.

Rubin, Barnett R., and Abubakar Siddique, "Resolving the Pakistan-Afghanistan Stalemate." U.S. Institute of Peace, Special Report No. 176, October 2006.

Rumsfeld, Donald, "Secretary Rumsfeld's Remarks to the International Institute for Strategic Studies." International Institute for Strategic Studies, Singapore, June 4, 2005.

Russett, Bruce, "The Democratic Peace – And Yet It Moves." *International Security*, 19:4 (Spring 1995): 164–175.

Sabathier, Vincent G., and G. Ryan Faith, "India's Space Program." Center for Strategic and International Studies, January 25, 2008.

Sakhuja, Vijay, "Indian Navy: Keeping Pace with Emerging Challenges," in Prabhakar, Ho, and Bateman, eds., *The Evolving Maritime Balance of Power in the Asia-Pacific*, 95–116.

"Iran Stirs India-US Waters." Institute for Peace and Conflict Studies, Article No. 1986, New Delhi, April 10, 2006.

Samuels, Richard J., *"Rich Nation, Strong Army": National Security and the Technological Transformation of Japan*. Ithaca: Cornell University Press, 1994.

SarDesai, D. R., and Raju G. C. Thomas, eds., *Nuclear India in the Twenty-First Century*. New York: Palgrave-MacMillan, 2002.

Saunders, Phillip C., and Charles D. Lutes, "China's ASAT Test: Motivations and Implications." Institute for National Strategic Studies Special Report, National Defense University, June 2007.

Saunders, Philip C., and Erik R. Quam, "China's Air Force Modernization," *Joint Forces Quarterly*, 47 (2007), 28–33.

Sawyer, Ralph, *The Tao of Deception: Unorthodox Warfare in Historic and Modern China*. New York: Basic Books, 2007.

Sawyer, Ralph D., "Military Writings," in Graff and Higham, eds., *A Military History of China*, 97–114.

Schaffer, Teresita C., and Suzanne Fawzi, "India and Iran: Limited Partnership, High Stakes." *South Asia Monitor*, No. 114, Center for Strategic and International Studies, December 20, 2007.

Scheuer, Michael, "India's Strategic Challenge in Pakistan's Afghan Hinterland," Jamestown Foundation Global Terrorism Analysis, 5:30, August 12, 2008.

Scobell, Andrew, *China's Use of Military Force: Beyond the Great Wall and the Long March*. New York: Cambridge University Press, 2003.

"'Cult of Defense' and 'Great Power Dreams': The Influence of Strategic Culture on China's Relationship with India," in Chambers, ed., *South Asia in 2020: Future Strategic Balances and Alliances*, 329–384.

"Soldiers, Statesmen, Strategic Culture, and China's 1950 Intervention in Korea," in Zhao, ed., *Chinese Foreign Policy: Pragmatism and Strategic Behavior*, 107–127.

Segal, Adam, *Advantage: How American Innovation Can Overcome the Asian Challenge.* New York: W.W. Norton, 2011.

Shahi, R.V., "India's Strategy Towards Energy Development and Security." Indian Ministry of Power paper presented at the International Energy Agency Seminar on "Energy Insights from Asia Pacific," Sydney, December 12, 2006.

Shambaugh, David, *Beautiful Imperialist: China Perceives America 1972–1990.* Princeton: Princeton University Press, 1991.

"China Engages Asia: Reshaping the Regional Order." *International Security,* 29:3 (Winter 2004/2005): 64–99.

Modernizing China's Military: Progress, Problems, and Prospects. Berkeley: University of California Press, 2003.

"Patterns of Interaction in Sino-American Relations," in Robinson and Shambaugh, eds., *Chinese Foreign Policy: Theory and Practice,* 197–223.

Shambaugh, David, ed., *Power Shift: China and Asia's New Dynamics.* Berkeley: University of California Press, 2005.

Shambaugh, David, and Michael Yahuda, eds., *International Relations of Asia.* New York: Rowman and Littlefield, 2008.

Shankar, Vinay, "Defence Industry." *Indian Defence Review,* 23:1 (September 11, 2008).

Shi Jingxia, "China's Indigenous Innovation and Government Procurement," International Centre for Trade and Sustainable Development, China Programme, 14:3 (September 2010).

Shirk, Susan L., *China: Fragile Superpower.* New York: Oxford University Press, 2007.

Shuja, Sharif, "The Realignment of India-US Relations: Strategic Dimensions," *Contemporary Review,* 287 (October 2005): 203–209.

Sidhu, Waheguru Pal Singh, and Jing-Dong Yuan, eds., *China and India: Cooperation or Conflict?* Boulder: Lynne Rienner Press, 2003.

Singh, Madhvendra, "The Indian Navy in 2020." *Security Research Review,* June 21, 2006.

Sinha, Atish, and Madhup Mohta, eds., *Indian Foreign Policy: Challenges and Opportunities.* New Delhi: Foreign Service Institute, 2007.

Smith, Alan B., "Costing Nuclear Programs." Central Intelligence Agency, September 18, 1995.

Smith, David, *The Dragon and the Elephant: China, India and the New World Order.* London: Profile Books, 2007.

Snyder, Jack, "Civil-Military Relations and the Cult of the Offensive, 1914 and 1984." *International Security,* 9:1 (Summer 1984), 108–146.

The Ideology of the Offensive: Military Decision Making and the Disasters of 1914. Ithaca: Cornell University Press, 1984.

Spiro, David E., "The Insignificance of the Liberal Peace." *International Security,* 19:2 (Autumn 1994): 50–86.

Squassoni, Sharon, "India and Iran: WMD Proliferation Activities." Congressional Research Service Report for Congress, Order Code RS2253, November 8, 2006.

Stålenheim, P., C. Perdomo, and E. Sköns, "Military expenditure," in Stockholm International Peace Research Institute, *SIPRI Yearbook 2008,* 175–206.

Steinfeld, Edward S., *Playing Our Game: Why China's Rise Doesn't Threaten the West.* New York: Oxford University Press, 2010.

Stephen Van Evera, *Causes of War: Power and the Roots of Conflict.* Ithaca: Cornell University Press, 1999.

"The Cult of the Offensive and the Origins of the First World War." *International Security*, 9:1 (Summer 1984): 58–107.

Steury, Donald P., ed., *Intentions and Capabilities: Estimates on Soviet Strategic Forces, 1950-1983*. Washington, DC: Central Intelligence Agency, 1996.

Stockholm International Peace Research Institute, *SIPRI Yearbook 2006: Armaments, Disarmament, and International Security*. New York: Oxford University Press, 2006.

SIPRI Yearbook 2008. New York: Oxford University Press, 2008.

Stokes, Bruce, "The U.S. and India: Friendship, Warily." *The National Journal*, February 13, 2010.

Stokes, Mark A., *China's Evolving Conventional Strategic Strike Capability: The Antiship Ballistic Missile Challenge to U.S. Maritime Operations in the Western Pacific and Beyond*. Arlington: Project 2049 Institute, September 2009.

"The Chinese Joint Aerospace Campaign: Strategy, Doctrine, and Force Modernization," in Finkelstein and Mulvenon, eds., *The Revolution in Doctrinal Affairs*, 221–304.

Strassler, Robert B., ed., *The Landmark Thucydides: A Comprehensive Guide to The Peloponnesian War*. New York: Simon and Schuster, 1998.

Strauss, Leo, "Niccolo Machiavelli," in Strauss and Cropsey, eds., *History of Political Philosophy*, 296–317.

Thoughts on Machiavelli. Chicago: University of Chicago Press, 1958.

Strauss, Leo, and Joseph Cropsey, eds., *History of Political Philosophy*. 3rd ed. Chicago: University of Chicago Press, 1987.

Subrahmanyam, K., "India and the International Nuclear Order," in SarDesai and Thomas, eds., *Nuclear India in the Twenty-First Century*, 63–84.

Suettinger, Robert L., "The Rise and Descent of 'Peaceful Rise.'" *China Leadership Monitor*, 12 (Fall 2004).

Sun Tzu, *The Art of War*, translated by Roger Ames. New York: Ballantine Books, 1993.

The Art of War, translated by Ralph Sawyer. New York: Basic Books, 1994.

Sutter, Robert G., "China's Regional Strategy and Why It May Not be Good for America," in Shambaugh, ed., *Power Shift: China and Asia's New Dynamics*, 289–305.

Chinese Foreign Relations: Power and Policy Since the Cold War. New York: Rowman & Littlefield, 2008.

Swaine, Michael D., *America's Challenge: Engaging a Rising China in the Twenty-First Century*. Washington, DC: Carnegie Endowment for International Peace, 2011.

"China's Assertive Behavior, Part One: On 'Core Interests,'" *China Leadership Monitor*, 34 (Fall 2010).

Swaine, Michael D., and Oriana Skylar Mastro, "Assessing the Threat," in Swaine, Yang, and Medeiros, eds., *Assessing the Threat: The Chinese Military and Taiwan's Security*, 337–366.

Swaine, Michael D., and Ashley J. Tellis, *Interpreting China's Grand Strategy: Past, Present, and Future*. Santa Monica: RAND Corporation, 2000.

Swaine, Michael D., Andrew N. D. Yang, and Evan S. Medeiros, eds., *Assessing the Threat: The Chinese Military and Taiwan's Security*. Washington, DC: Carnegie Endowment for International Peace, 2007.

Talbott, Strobe, *Engaging India: Diplomacy, Democracy and the Bomb*. Washington, DC: Brookings Institution, 2004.

Tammen, Ronald L. et al., *Power Transitions: Strategies for the 21st Century*. New York: Chatham House, 2000.

Tang Shiping, "From Offensive to Defensive Realism: A Social Evolutionary Interpretation of China's Security Strategy," in Ross and Feng, eds., *China's Ascent*, 152–156.

Tanham, George K., *Indian Strategic Thought: An Interpretive Essay*. Santa Monica: RAND Corporation, 1992.

Tellis, Ashley J., "China's Military Space Strategy." *Survival*, 49:3 (September 2007): 41–72.

"The Merits of Dehyphenation: Explaining U.S. Success in Engaging India and Pakistan." *The Washington Quarterly*, 31:4 (Autumn 2008), 21–42.

"Punching the U.S. Military's 'Soft Ribs': China's Antisatellite Weapon Test in Strategic Perspective." Carnegie Endowment, June 2007.

Tellis, Ashley J., and Michael Wills, eds., *Strategic Asia 2005–2006: Military Modernization in an Era of Uncertainty*. Washington, DC: National Bureau of Asian Research, 2005.

The White House, "White Paper of the Interagency Policy Group's Report on U.S. Policy toward Afghanistan and Pakistan," Washington, DC: The White House, March 27, 2009.

The National Security Strategy of the United States. Washington, DC: The White House, 2006.

Thomas, Raju G. C., "The Armed Services and the Indian Defense Budget." *Asian Survey*, 20:3 (March 1980): 280–297.

"Wither Nuclear India?" in SarDesai and Thomas, eds., *Nuclear India in the Twenty-First Century*, 3–24.

Thucydides, *History of the Peloponnesian War*, translated by C.F. Smith. Cambridge, MA: Loeb Classical Library, Harvard University Press, 2003.

Tilly, Charles, *Coercion, Capital, and European States: 990–1992*. Oxford: Blackwell Publishers Ltd., 1990.

Tkacik, John, "China's Superpower Economy." Heritage Foundation Webmemo No. 1762, December 28, 2007.

Twomey, Christopher P., "Dangerous Differences: Crisis Management & Sino-American Naval Doctrines in the Taiwan Strait." Paper prepared for the International Studies Association Annual Meeting, March 18, 2008.

The Military Lens: Doctrinal Difference and Deterrence Failure in Sino-American Relations. Ithaca: Cornell University Press, 2010.

United Nations Conference on Trade and Development, *Information Economy Report, 2007–2008: Science and Technology for Development, the New Paradigm of ICT*. New York: United Nations, 2007.

United Nations, United Nations-Habitat, *State of the World's Cities 2008/2009 – Harmonious Cities*. New York: United Nations, October 2008.

United States Department of Defense, *The Military Power of the People's Republic of China*. Washington, DC: Office of the Secretary of Defense, 2006.

The Military Power of the People's Republic of China. Washington, DC: Office of the Secretary of Defense, 2007.

Military Power of the People's Republic of China. Washington, DC: Office of the Secretary of Defense, 2008.

Military Power of the People's Republic of China: Annual Report to Congress. Washington, DC: Office of the Secretary of Defense, 2009.

Military Power of the People's Republic of China. Washington, DC: Office of the Secretary of Defense, 2010.

National Defense Strategy 2008. Washington, DC: Office of the Secretary of Defense, June 2008.

Quadrennial Defense Review Report. Washington, DC: United States Department of Defense, February 2006.

Quadrennial Defense Review Report. Washington, DC: Office of the Secretary of Defense, February 2010.

United States Economic and Security Review Commission, *Annual Report to Congress 2005.* Washington, DC: United States Economic and Security Review Commission, 2005.

United States International Trade Commission, *Competitive Conditions for U.S. Foreign Direct Investment in India*, Publication Number 3931. Washington DC: United States International Trade Commission, July 2007.

"Very High Tariff Barriers Impede U.S. Agricultural Exports to India, Says USITC." News release No. 09-104, Washington DC: United States International Trade Commission, December 11, 2009.

United States Navy Office of Naval Intelligence, *The People's Liberation Army Navy: A Modern Navy with Chinese Characteristics.* Suitland: Office of Naval Intelligence, July 2009.

United States-China Economic and Security Review Commission, *2008 Report to Congress of the U.S.-China Economic Security Review Commission*, Washington, DC: U.S.-China Economic and Security Review Commission, November 2008.

Valencia, Mark, "The Impeccable Incident: Truth and Consequences," *China Security*, 14 (2009), 22–28.

Van Dyke, Jon M., "Military Ships and Planes Operating in the Exclusive Economic Zone of Another Country." *Marine Policy*, 28:1 (January 2004): 29–39.

Verma, B. K., "Cooperative Maritime Engagement – Exercise Aman 2009: Facilitating US Chinese Interaction." National Maritime Foundation (India), May 1, 2009.

Wang, Jisi, "China's Search for Stability with America," *Foreign Affairs* 395 (September/October 2005): 39–48.

Whiting, Allen S., "China's Use of Force 1950–1996, and Taiwan." *International Security*, 26:2 (Fall 2001): 103–131.

The Chinese Calculus of Deterrence: India and Vietnam. Ann Arbor: University of Michigan Press, 1975.

Winner, Andrew C., "India as a Maritime Power?" in Yoshihara and Holmes, eds., *Asia Looks Seaward: Power and Maritime Strategy*, 125–145.

Winters, L. Alan, and Shahid Yusuf, eds., *Dancing with Giants: China, India, and the Global Economy.* Washington, DC: World Bank, 2007.

World Bank, *2005 International Comparison Program: Preliminary Results.* Washington, DC: World Bank, December 2007.

2008 World Development Indicators. Washington, DC: World Bank, 2008.

China Quarterly Update. Beijing: World Bank, February 2008.

"Introduction to the International Comparison Program," in World Bank, *ICP 2003–2006 Handbook.* Washington DC., World Bank, April 2006.

Wortzel, Larry M., "China's Foreign Conflicts Since 1949," in Graff and Higham, eds., *A Military History of China*, 267–284.

The Chinese People's Liberation Army and Space Warfare: Emerging United States-China Military Competition. American Enterprise Institute, October 2007.

Wyatt, Philip, "India: A Sea Change for Trade?" UBS Investment Research South Asia Focus, April 26, 2011.

Yang, Andrew N. D., "Taiwan's Defense Preparation Against the Chinese Military Threat," in Swaine, Yang, and Medeiros, eds., *Assessing the Threat: The Chinese Military and Taiwan's Security*, 265–284.

Yildirim, Julide, and Nadir Ocal, "Arms Race and Economic Growth: The Case of India and Pakistan," *Defence and Peace Economics*, 17:1 (February 2006): 37–45.

Yoshihara, Toshi, and James R. Holmes, eds., *Asia Looks Seaward: Power and Maritime Strategy*. Westport: Praeger Security International, 2008.

You Ji, "China's Naval Strategy and Transformation," in Prabhakar, Ho, and Bateman, eds., *The Evolving Maritime Balance of Power in the Asia-Pacific*, 71–94.

Younger, Stephen M., *The Bomb: A New History*. New York: Harper Collins, 2009.

Yuan Jing Dong, "The Dragon and the Elephant: Chinese-Indian Relations in the 21st Century." *The Washington Quarterly*, 30:3 (Summer 2007), 131–144.

Zhang Baijia, "The Evolution of China's Diplomacy and Foreign Relations in the Era of Reform, 1976–2005," in Hao, Wei, and Dittmer, eds., *Challenges to Chinese Foreign Policy*, 15–33.

Zhang Junbo, and Yao Yunzhu, "Traditional Chinese Military Thinking: A Comparative Perspective," in Zhao, ed., *Chinese Foreign Policy: Pragmatism and Strategic Behavior*, 128–139.

Zhao Suisheng, ed., *Chinese Foreign Policy: Pragmatism and Strategic Behavior*. Armonk: M.E. Sharpe, 2004.

Zheng Bijian, "China's 'Peaceful Rise' to Great-Power Status," *Foreign Affairs*, 84:5 (September/October 2005), 18–24.

Zoellick, Robert, "Whither China: From Membership to Responsibility?" Speech at the National Committee on U.S.-China Relations, New York City, September 21, 2005.

中共中央文献编辑委员会 [Chinese Communist Party Central Literature Editorial Committee], 《江泽民文选》 [Selected Works of Jiang Zemin]. Beijing: The People's Press, 2006.

中华人民共和国国务院 [The State Council of the People's Republic of China], "2008年中国的国防" [China's National Defense in 2008]. Beijing: State Council Information Office of the People's Republic of China, 2009.

[The State Council of the People's Republic of China], "2010年中国的国防" [China's National Defense in 2010]. Beijing: State Council Information Office of the People's Republic of China, 2011.

中华人民共和国民政部[Ministry of Civil Affairs of the People's Republic of China], 《2009年民政事业发展统计报告》 [2009 Civil Administration Affairs Development Statistical Report], February 3, 2010.

中国人民解放军第二炮兵部队 [PLA Second Artillery], 《第二炮兵战役学》 [Science of Second Artillery Campaigns]. Beijing: People's Liberation Army Press, 2004.

中国空军百科全书编审委员会[Editorial Committee of the People's Liberation Army Air Force Encyclopedia], 《中国空军百科全书》 [China Air Force Encyclopedia]. Beijing: Aviation Industry Press, 2005.

刘华清 [Liu Huaqing], 《刘华清回忆录》 [Memoirs of Admiral Liu Huaqing]. Beijing: People's Liberation Army Press, 2004.

卢利华[Lu Lihua], 《军队指挥理论学习指南》 [Military Command Theory Study Guide]. Beijing: National Defense University Press, 2005.

孙艳玲[Sun Yanling], "中国外交政策的调整与中苏关系正常化" [The Adjustment of Chinese Foreign Policy and the Normalization of Sino-Soviet Relations], 《中共党史研究》 2009第二期, [Research in Chinese Communist Party History], 2, 2009.

张玉良 [Zhang Yuliang], 《战役学》 [The Science of Military Campaigns]. Beijing: National Defense University Press, second edition 2006.

彭光谦 [Peng Guangqian], 《中国军事战略问题研究》 [Research on Chinese Military Strategy]. Beijing: People's Liberation Army Press, 2006.

李承红 [Li Chenghong], "当代中国外交的根本转型与分期问题——一个外交政策分析理论的视角" [The Question of the Fundamental Reorientation and Periodization of China's Contemporary Diplomacy: A Point of View on Foreign Policy Theory], 《外交评论》 [*Foreign Affairs Review*], 107, December 2008.

杨奎松 [Yang Kuisong], "'反帝反修'的历史困惑——1960年代中国对外政策的历史考察" [The Historical Puzzle of 'Anti-Imperialist and Anti-Revisionist': A Review of the History of 1960s Foreign Policy], 《领导者》 [Leaders], 26, February 2009.

杨学军, 张望新主编 [Yang Xuejun and Zhang Wangxin, eds.], 《优势来自空间--论空间战场与空间作战》 [Advantage Comes From Space: The Space Battlefield and Space Operations]. Beijing: National Defense Industry Press, 2006.

林立民[Lin Limin], "航母:不敢说爱你"[Aircraft Carrier: I Don't Dare Say I Treasure You], 《北京世界知识》 [Beijing World Affairs], Volume 18, 2005.

王厚卿, 张兴业 主编 [Wang Houqing, and Zhang Xingye, eds.] 《战役学》 [The Science of Military Campaigns]. Beijing: National Defense University Press, 2000.

王明武, 常永志, 徐戈, 章楠 [Wang Mingwu, Chang Yongzhi, Xu Ge, Zhang Nan], 《非战争军事行动》 [Non-War Military Activities]. Beijing: National Defense University Press, 2006.

盛大泉, 罗贞裁, 周燕红, 罗晶晶, 杨学娟, 胡琳 [Sheng Daquan, Luo Zhencai, Zhou Yanhong, Luo Jingjing, Yang Xuejuan, and Hu Lin], "2001–2010 自主择业十年报告, 转业军官编辑部" [Report on Self-job selection system 2001-2011: the demobilized army cadres editorial department," 《中国人才》 2011年02期 [China Talent], Volume 2, 2011.

科技部 国家发展改革委 财政部关于开展2009年国家自主创新产品认定工作的通知 (国科发计[2009]]618号), [Notice Regarding National Indigenous Innovation Product Accreditation System (Circular 618) issued by The Ministry of Science and Technology, National Development and Reform Commission, and Ministry of Finance], October 30, 2009.

章百家 [Zhang Baijia], "从'一边倒'到'全方位': 对50年来中国外交格局演进的思考," [From 'Lean to One Side' to 'All Directions': Reflections on The Evolving Pattern of Chinese Foreign Policy Over the Last 50 Years], 《中共党史研究》 [Research in Chinese Communist Party History], Issue No. 1, 2000, 21–28.

肖天亮[Xiao Tianliang], 《军事力量的非战争运用》 [The Non-War Use of Military Force]. Beijing: National Defense University Press, 2009.

舒建国 [Shu Jianguo], 毛泽东"反帝反修"外交战略的内涵及其实践效应 [The Meaning and Practical Effects of Mao Zedong's 'Anti-Imperialist and

Anti-Revisionist' Diplomacy], 《南昌大学学报》, [Journal of Nanchang University], 39:3, May 2008.

蔡风震, 田安平, 主编 [Cai Fengzhen and Tian Anping eds.],《空天一体作战学》 [Study of Integrated Air-Space Operations]. Beijing: People's Liberation Army Press, 2009.

薛兴林主编 [Xue Xinglin, chief editor], 《战役理论学习指南》 [Campaign Theory Study Guide]. Beijing: National Defense University Press, 2002.

解放军总政治部[PLA General Political Department], 《江泽民国防和军队建设思想*Neighbourhood*学习纲要》 [Outline for Studying Jiang Zemin Thought on National Defense and Army Building]. Beijing: Military Science Press, 2003.

迟浩田[Chi Haotian], "关于中华人民共和国的国防法（草案）的说明" [An Explanation of the PRC National Defense Law (Draft)], in 《中华人民共和国第八届全国人民代表大会第五次会议文件汇编》 [Documents on the PRC Fifth Session of the Eighth National People's Congress] (Beijing: Zhejiang People's Press, 1997).

Index